A SHORT DICTIONARY OF FURNITURE

A Short Dictionary of Furniture

BY

JOHN GLOAG
F.S.A., Hon. A.R.I.B.A.

Containing 1767 Terms Used
in Britain and America

*

*With 630 illustrations
in the text*

BONANZA BOOKS · NEW YORK

*Dedicated to Robert Wemyss Symonds,
in admiration of his scholarship,
and in gratitude for his kindness, advice and help
in the making of this book*

*

CONTENTS

*

ACKNOWLEDGMENTS

FOR their advice about many of the entries in Section III of this book, I am indebted to Sir Ambrose Heal, R. W. Symonds, Hamilton Temple Smith, and H. P. Shapland, and to Grace Lovat Fraser for her help and comments on many of the entries concerned with textiles and upholstery. I have had valuable suggestions from Mr L. John Mayes, the Librarian of the Central Library at High Wycombe, and much assistance from the Librarians of the Royal Institute of British Architects and the Royal Society of Arts. My thanks are also due to the Director of the Fitzwilliam Museum at Cambridge, for allowing me to have drawings made by Mr Escott of several specimens of furniture in the Museum; to Robert Harling for permission to reproduce an illustration from his book, *Home: a Victorian Vignette*; to Heal & Son, Ltd., for letting me examine and make notes from their early catalogues; and to Waring & Gillow, Ltd., and particularly to Mr B. Barber, the manager of their Lancaster branch, for allowing me to see the early Gillow records, and for the time and trouble they have taken in helping me to verify and supplement the notes, sketches, and extracts I made therefrom. Finally, I must express my gratitude to Mr Ronald Escott for his excellent drawings in Section III, and to Dora Ware for her help in assembling the material, and for bringing to that work her practical knowledge of planning and making dictionaries, and for giving permission for several illustrations from her own *Short Dictionary of Architecture* to be included.

JOHN GLOAG

PLAN AND PURPOSE OF THE BOOK

THIS is a short dictionary of furniture and various accessories of furnishing, made and used in England since A.D. 1100 and in North America since the mid-17th century. It is neither a concise glossary nor a comprehensive encyclopaedia. I have tried to make a book of reference that is more than a barren list of terms, old, new, authentic, or doubtful; and, inevitably, there are omissions. Like architecture, furniture is a visible record of social history, and it is a rewarding study. An exhaustive and authoritative survey of the subject is supplied by Ralph Edwards and the late Percy Macquoid in the three superbly illustrated volumes of *The Dictionary of English Furniture*, published between 1924 and 1927 by Country Life, Ltd.

In my short dictionary I have confined the entries to 1764 names and terms, and have included those of European or Asiatic origin only when they have influenced the design, materials, or use of English or American furniture. In attempting to define and, where necessary or possible, to trace the age and derivation of the names and terms in Section III, which constitutes the principal part of this book, I have sought to identify the contemporary word for an article of furniture, a structural or decorative part, a material, or a method of construction. This third main section is preceded by two others that deal briefly with: I, the *description*, and II, the *design* of furniture. Interest in the age and terminology of furniture without a corresponding interest in design may easily degenerate into a sterile obsession; an affliction that has transformed many otherwise normal men and women into human magpies. Only when a lively and general interest in design has informed the people of a country has there been a period of great and satisfying accomplishment in the making of furniture.

Following Section III are three supplementary sections, giving: IV, a short list of furniture makers in Britain and America; V, notes on relevant books and periodicals; and, finally, in the form of a series of tables, VI, an outline of the types of furniture, the materials and craftsmen employed, and the influences that have affected design and promoted styles and fashions during the last eight and a half centuries.

SECTION I

The Description of Furniture

*

MANY of the names now used for various articles of furniture are of mediaeval origin; many of them have acquired fresh or additional meanings, so that the length of the entries in Section III varies considerably, because certain names, now familiar and obvious, have demanded more than a concise definition of their present meaning. Therefore, the definition is often supplemented by a condensed history of the social and structural changes which have affected an article; and when it has developed specialised functions, or some peculiarity of form, it is entered and described under the appropriate heading. Some account, too, is given of the classical prototypes of an article or a feature; for these have occasionally been resuscitated at some much later period; as exemplified by the use of the sabre leg on chairs during the Greek revival at the end of the 18th and the beginning of the 19th century.

During the last hundred years, the nomenclature of furniture has been greatly enlarged and obscured as a result of the romanticism of undiscerning collectors (who reverence age and ignore, or fail to appreciate, merit in design) and the ingenuity of the dealers who serve them; though the use of fancy names for familiar articles is a very old practice. The inventive powers of those who make and sell furniture are usually activated by new fashions that reflect some movement in design. Fresh labels based on old names followed the classical revival of the mid-18th century, which was stimulated by the excavation of the buried Roman cities of Herculaneum and Pompeii; others were suggested by the Greek revival; and recurrent waves of taste for Oriental things have, since the mid-17th century, introduced and established names which are now commonplace, though once they were modish innovations. Of these, china cabinet and tea table are obvious survivals; while japanning and lacquering are still current as technical terms for various surface finishes.

It was during the mid-17th century that the distinction between antique and modern design began to be consciously recorded. John Evelyn writes of a couch and seats being 'carv'd *à l'antique*' (*Diary*,

May 8th, 1654), and a house 'built *à la moderne*' (*Diary*, June 9th, 1654). By antique, Evelyn meant the work of classical antiquity, the forms and ornamentation derived from the Graeco-Roman world; he also used the word ancient in that sense; and throughout the 18th century, the word antique was applied exclusively to Greek and Roman remains; retaining that meaning until late in the Victorian period.

Within a hundred years of these entries in Evelyn's *Diary*, an intermittent interest in Gothic architecture and ornamentation encouraged architects and designers of furniture to flirt with forms which would have horrified that 17th century connoisseur of design; for during a visit to Rome, Evelyn had described the Palazzo Farnese as 'a magnificent square structure, built by Michael Angelo of the 3 orders of columns after the ancient manner, and when Architecture was but newly recovered from the Gotic barbarity' (*Diary*, November 4th, 1644). The taste for Gothic forms fluctuated during the mid-18th century, and though it had merely a superficial effect upon the design of furniture and was recognised as an ephemeral but recurrent influence, it encouraged a respect for age, as such, which began to give new significance to the word ancient. The use of the label Gothic excused many extravagances and stupidities, which were recognised as transient modes of ornamentation by cultivated people in the 18th century; even Horace Walpole drew a distinction between 'charming and venerable Gothic and pure architecture' when he was describing Gosfield House in a letter to George Montagu (July 25th, 1748); but the romantic appeal of age began to diminish appreciation of the principles of design. Popular interest in Gothic prepared the soil for a crop of archaic terms for various articles, from which a rich harvest of confusion has been reaped in the late 19th and the present century. Such terms were occasionally suggested by some borrowed feature, as exemplified by the 'embattled' bookcase, included in the second edition of *Genteel Household Furniture in the Present Taste* (which was undated, but probably published in 1765); though the supposed ancient use of an article was a more potent source of inspiration for names.

The word ancient was variously used in the early 19th century to denote the works of remote antiquity and of Graeco-Roman civilisation, also the furniture and architecture of the Middle Ages and much later periods. A book entitled *Specimens of Ancient Furniture* was published in 1836, with drawings by Henry Shaw and descriptions by Sir Samuel Rush Meyrick, which included examples ranging from the 13th to the late 17th century: a state bed of the time of James II having apparently qualified as a piece of 'ancient' furniture.[1] There were occasional attempts to re-

[1] London: William Pickering, 1836.

establish the meanings of ancient and antique, and in 1838 John Britton tried to sort out their relative significance in *A Dictionary of the Architecture and Archaeology of the Middle Ages*.[1] He defined *Antique* as 'A term used by classical and other writers on the fine arts to imply such works of sculpture and architecture as belong to the best times of the Greeks; hence it "is synonymous with 'beautiful', 'most excellent', 'perfect'," etc. It is contradistinguished from old, or ancient, being applied only to that period in which the best masters produced their most eminent works, particularly in architecture and sculpture. The buildings of the Egyptians, although of much higher antiquity than even those of the Greeks, are called *ancient*, not *antique*.' But under *Antiquities*, he admitted that 'The words *antique* and *antiquity*, are not clearly defined, or applied with precision'. They were not; but the word antique in the middle years of the 19th century was still used as Evelyn had used it two hundred years before. In an *Encyclopaedia of Architecture*, issued in 1852, which was described as 'A New and Improved edition of Nicholson's Dictionary of the Science and Practice of Architecture, Building, etc.',[2] there is the following definition: 'Antique, in a general sense, denotes something ancient; but the term is chiefly employed by architects, sculptors, and painters, and applied to works, in their respective professions, executed by the Romans, or others anterior to their time. . . .'

In the previous century Isaac Ware had defined Antique as 'a term at large expressing any thing antient, but appropriated to signify a building, part of a building, or other work, that has been executed by Greeks or Romans, when the arts were in their greatest purity and perfection among those people'. (*A Complete Body of Architecture*, published in 1767.)

An edition of George Smith's *Cabinet Maker and Upholsterer's Guide* that was published in 1836, includes a plate (No. CXLVI), dated November 10th, 1827, when it was first issued by Jones & Co., which illustrates two chairs under the title of Antique Chairs. One, described as a French chair, has cabriole legs and an upholstered seat, and a back elaborately carved with scroll work: the other, labelled Indian, has turned legs and an upholstered seat, and is highly ornamented with unrelated and ill-chosen motifs. These designs have no relation to ancient 'Gothic' or pre-Georgian furniture or to` a classical antique prototype. The use of the word antique on this plate appears to be purely fortuitous; an accidental and inappropriate label; but it is the earliest use of the word antique in connection with furniture that I have been able to trace.

The word *antique* had not replaced *ancient* in relation to furniture either at the Great Exhibition of 1851 or at the International

[1] London: Longman, Orme, Brown, Green and Longmans, 1838.
[2] Edited by Edward Lomax, C.E., and Thomas Gunyon, Architect and C.E., and published in two volumes by Peter Jackson, London, 1852.

Exhibition of 1862; but in 1869, in the second edition of Charles L. Eastlake's *Hints on Household Taste*, there was a reference to "antique" as a Wardour Street label, though he still used the word ancient for the examples of old furniture that he illustrated. Robert W. Edis delivered a series of Cantor lectures before the Society of Arts in 1880, later amplified in book form under the title of *Decoration and Furniture of Town Houses*,[1] and in referring to the revived interest in mid-18th century styles of furniture, he said: 'It is to be regretted, however, that the craze for all this kind of work should practically not only give the dealers the chance of charging exorbitant prices for old examples, but, to a certain extent, encourage a somewhat extravagant idea of the worth of modern imitations'.[2] He uses the word *old*; and perhaps in the 'eighties the word *ancient* was beginning to sound a little mannered in connection with the fashionable pastime of collecting old furniture.

A book of drawings by William Sharp Ogden, an architect, that was published in 1888, was entitled *Sketches of Antique Furniture*,[3] with a sub-title explaining that they were 'Taken from eighty examples, not hitherto illustrated, of chiefly 17th-century English carved oak furniture'. The book had a morally instructive purpose, and was intended to be both a protest against what was apparently the already widespread practice of faking old furniture and a guide to those who wished to detect the difference between the genuine and the spurious article; but the drawings were neither helpful nor accomplished examples of draughtsmanship. In the introduction, the author said:

The Fabrication of antique furniture, generally richly and sometimes tastefully carved, is an outrage of very old standing, and one the wary collector is well acquainted with. With reference to this, it is curious to note how, in deference to the more intelligent appreciation that has grown up of late years, there is practised a skilful but most mischievous falsification of really old furniture, by covering the plain faces with new carving, often well executed; this, copied from old examples and carefully manipulated, is too frequently passed off by the dealer as genuine old work and will serve as effectually to put the judicious collector on his mettle as that other species of forgery, the framing up into attractive pieces of furniture of carvings gathered from widely different sources.

It is hoped that this little series of unpretentious sketches will be found of interest and service to the Student and Collector, they are taken from genuine and hitherto unpublished examples of the old middle-class furniture, such as rejoiced the heart of the citizen, the well-to-do yeoman, and the squire of yore, and similar to many which still remain the cherished heir-looms of old families—or buildings that have undergone no change for centuries.

[1] London: C. Kegan Paul & Co., 1881. [2] Lecture III, p. 102.
[3] Published by B. T. Batsford.

Those paragraphs suggest that during the eighteen-eighties the antique furniture trade was enjoying the patronage both of 'the judicious collector' and of the undiscriminating innocent who amplified a lavish enthusiasm for old things by adopting a word that seemed to be suffused with romance.

It is difficult to say at what date a term becomes popular; and the description 'antique furniture' was probably current among dealers and amateur collectors long before it was printed anywhere; but its adoption during the present century as a generic term for furniture that is over one hundred years old has made us forget how misleading and inappropriate it would have seemed to anybody with a classical education during the Victorian period.

Many other misleading and inappropriate terms have gained popularity; often because of the appeal of some particular word, which may evoke a vision of 'the good old times', or because some article, made perhaps three hundred years ago, is assumed to serve some modern purpose. Post-dating the function of some old design does not offer such romantic possibilities as ante-dating it; and examples of this are afforded by monk's bench, or monk's seat, which are modern names for what was originally called a chair-table, or a table-chairewise in the 17th century; and by refectory table, which is dealers' English for the four- or six-legged dining table of the late 16th and 17th centuries, described in contemporary inventories as a 'long table'. R. W. Symonds selects monk's bench and refectory table as characteristic examples of invented terms, suggesting that the latter was used 'in order to conjure up a picture of jovial monks dining . . .' [1] These inaccurate terms have become 'dealers' aids', to borrow the technical jargon of commercial advertising, though they do not always originate in the old furniture trade. Some of them embalm the happy illusions of 'Merrie Englanders', who have been captivated by the vision of mediaeval felicities, first revealed by William Cobbett in 1824 in his *History of the 'Protestant' Reformation*, subsequently dramatised by William Morris and the practitioners of the handicraft revival, and kept bright in the opening decades of the present century by the writings of Belloc and Chesterton. Monk's bench and refectory table may well have emanated from this school of thought.

Many spurious terms are accepted today; many seem to have such an authentic ring about them; they sound like 'genuine antiques', but they are only picturesque fakes. Other modern terms, which are usually assumed to be of ancient origin, are the result of some quite accidental application of popular sentiment, of which grandfather clock and its offspring, grandfather chair, are perhaps the best examples.

[1] 'The Renaming of Old English Furniture', by R. W. Symonds, *The Antique Collector*, vol. 19, No. 4, August 1948, p. 127.

A court cupboard illustrated in the first English book on old furniture: Henry Shaw's *Specimens of Ancient Furniture*, which was published in 1836, by William Pickering. There are some unfortunate additions to this piece: for example, the top with the heavily carved frieze has obviously been added; a back piece has also been added to the lower part, with some regrettable scratch carving on it, and the pot board has been elevated above another piece of spurious carved work. It is odd that Shaw should have included such a doubtful example. In the text of that book, Sir Samuel Meyrick stated that it was not in its original condition, and admitted that it was 'of recent composition.' (*See* page 17.) It was described as an 'Oak Cabinet'.

`Post-dating the function of an article may establish an error which stubbornly resists all attempts to refute it, particularly when the initial mistake has been unequivocally accepted by two or more generations of authoritative writers, or by several generations of craftsmen. An example of this is the confusion of the court cupboard with the press cupboard. The former is usually described as a buffet, its open tiers of shelves having perhaps suggested the adoption of that term, and, as I shall presently show, the use of buffet for court cupboard may date from the mid-18th century. There are some contemporary references to court cupboards, of which the best known is the line from *Romeo and Juliet*, Act I, Scene 5:

Away with the joint-stools; remove the court-cupboard; look to the plate.

In Shaw's *Specimens of Ancient Furniture*, Plate XXVI shows an oak court cupboard, to which various clumsy additions have been made, and this mutilated and grotesque muddle is certainly of late 16th or early 17th century origin, though hardly recognisable as a result of its treatment at some subsequent date. Describing it in the text, Sir Samuel Meyrick says: 'This article of furniture is undoubtedly of the time of Elizabeth; and, if in its original form, instead of recent composition, may have belonged to the class of sideboards. If this be the case, we may have before us the representation of a court-cupboard, mentioned in the play of *Romeo and Juliet....*' Buffets are shown on a separate plate in that work, and are late 15th century examples taken from illuminated manuscripts: there is no suggestion that the court cupboard should be identified either with them or with the press cupboard. (*See* illustrations on page 16 *and under* Plate Cupboard on pages 366 and 367.) In an edition of Shakespeare edited by A. J. Valpy, and published in 1870, there is an explanatory footnote which describes a court cupboard as 'A sideboard, on which the plate was placed'.[1] This suggests that in the mid-Victorian period the court cupboard had not yet become confused with the press cupboard, and that its original function was understood.

The origin and meaning of the word cupboard 'comprises in itself, a difficult study of no inconsiderable magnitude', as Mr Pickwick said about the word politics. Contemporary records indicate that the word meant exactly what it sounded like—a board for cups. In mediaeval times board and table were synonymous terms, with any specialised function denoted by a prefix. In the second half of the 16th century, William Harrison's use of the word garnish in his *Description of England*, implies that cupboards were open shelves upon which plate was displayed. If such shelves

---

[1] London: Bell & Daldy. In fifteen volumes.

had been enclosed by doors, the word garnish would have been meaningless. The displaying of plate in a room, upon a cupboard, was a practice common alike to the nobility and gentry, yeomen, and artisans. The relevant passage from Harrison has two references to the furnishing and garnishing of cupboards with silver vessels and other plate, which specify the function and suggest the open character of the cupboard.

Certes, in noble mens houses it is not rare to see abundance of Arras, rich hangings of tapistrie, silver vessell, and so much other plate, as may furnish sundrie cupbords, to the summe oftentimes of a thousand or two thousand pounds at the least: whereby the value of this and the rest of their stuffe dooth grow to be [almost] inestimable. Likewise in the houses of knights, gentlemen, merchantmen, and some other wealthie citizens, it is not geson to behold generallie their great provision of tapistrie, Turkie worke, pewter, brasse, fine linen, and thereto costlie cupbords of plate, worth five or six hundred [or a thousand] pounds, to be deemed by estimation. But as herein all these sorts doo far exceed their elders and predecessors, [and in neatness and curiositie the merchant all other;] so in time past, the costlie furniture staied there, whereas now it is descended yet lower, even unto the inferiour artificers and manie farmers, who [by vertue of their old and not of their new leases] have [for the most part] learned also to garnish their cupbords with plate, their [joined] beds with tapistrie and silke hangings, and their tables with [carpets &] fine naperie, whereby the wealth of our countrie [God be praised therefore, and give us grace to imploie it well] dooth infinitelie appeare.[1]

In tracing the development of the cupboard from mediaeval times to the 17th century, R. W. Symonds states that the original form of the cupboard was a table or board upon which vessels containing drink and gifts could be set down and household plate displayed, and that it was a piece of furniture used in the hall, when that apartment was the general dining-room of the household. In an article in the *Connoisseur* entitled 'The Evolution of the Cupboard',[2] he quotes a 14th century inventory in which reference is made to a board for cups, called a cup board.

These open shelves for the display of plate and the accommodation of cups and drinking vessels were called court cupboards in the latter half of the 16th century. This term, court cupboard, which properly applies only to those open for the accommodation of plate, is frequently used to describe press cupboards, which are cupboards with doors in the lower part, and a smaller cupboard in the upper part, usually recessed to form a narrow shelf in front of the top cupboard. R. W. Symonds, in another article in the *Connoisseur*,[3] called 'The Dyning Parlour and its Furniture',

[1] *Description of England in Shakespeare's Youth*, by William Harrison, edited from the first two editions of Holinshed's *Chronicle*, A.D. 1577–87, by Frederick J. Furnivall. Published for the New Shakspere Society by N. Trübner & Co., London, 1877. Pp. 238-9.   [2] December 1943.   [3] January 1944.

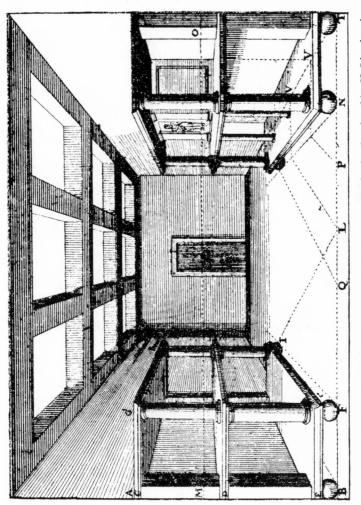

'Court cup-boards.' This forms subject 99 in *Perspective Practical*, a book printed by H. Lloyd and sold by Robert Pricke, in London, 1672. A copy of the first edition, from which this is reproduced, is in the library of Mr R. W. Symonds.

provides pictorial proof that the term court cupboard was a contemporary description of the open cupboard for the display of plate. He illustrates two pieces of furniture from a book entitled *Perspective Practical*, which was a translation of a French work on drawing in perspective, published in London in 1672, and printed by H. Lloyd and sold by Robert Pricke. These two pieces of furniture are described in the text as court cupboards, and they are reproduced on the previous page, from a copy of the original edition which is in the possession of Mr Symonds.

Later editions of *Perspective Practical* were issued, and the third edition, published in 1749, shows that by the middle of the 18th century the term court cupboard had been dropped. The plates in this third edition are identical with those used in the first English translation, but the text has been changed and the court cupboards are described as buffets.

It is possible that the renaming of court cupboards as buffets was popularised by the later editions of this book on perspective, which would certainly be seen and studied by innumerable draughtsmen in cabinet-makers' shops and architects' offices. The original English translation issued in 1672, indisputably supports Mr R. W. Symonds' contention that court cupboard is a contemporary name for the piece of furniture with two open shelves above a pot board, which has for so long been called a buffet, while the press cupboard, upon which it would be difficult to display plate, has been called a court cupboard.

Mr F. Gordon Roe, in discussing Mr Symonds' conclusions on this subject, in Section 8 of his admirable book, *English Cottage Furniture*, quotes contemporary evidence that indicates a structural affinity, if not an identity, between the court cupboard with its open shelves and the livery cupboard. (*See* the entry for Livery Cupboard on page 318.) From this he suggests that the use of the term court cupboard for pieces with their tiers of shelves enclosed above and below by doors may have had a contemporary origin, and though he is not prepared to discard this description, he accepts Mr Symonds' use of the term press cupboard as being appropriate for many examples.[1] That the term buffet, which appears to have been introduced during the 16th century, was in general use at the end of the 17th and the beginning of the 18th centuries, is recorded in *The Journeys of Celia Fiennes*, who describes 'a neat booffett furnish'd with glasses and china for the table', which may mean that the glasses and china were displayed on open shelves.[2] In the second edition of Bailey's *Dictionarium Britannicum*, which he described as 'a more compleat universal etymological English

[1] *English Cottage Furniture*, by F. Gordon Roe, F.S.A. (London: Phoenix House Ltd., 1949). Pp. 74-5.

[2] *The Journeys of Celia Fiennes*, edited by Christopher Morris (London: The Cresset Press, 1947). Part IV (*circa* 1701-3), section 10, p. 345.

dictionary than any extant', which was published in 1736, a buffet is defined as follows: 'A repository or sort of cupboard for plate, glasses, china-ware, etc., also a large table in a dining room, called a side-board, for the plates, glasses, bottles, etc.' [1]

The original name of an article of furniture is often based upon its function, and is nearly always agreeably descriptive; though occasionally some later term is more convenient. For instance, bureau bookcase is more compact than desk and bookcase, which was the name used by cabinet makers in the mid-18th century; though bureau bookcase may well have been a contemporary term. In the *Memoirs of William Hickey* there is a brief description of one of the cabins of the *Plassey*, an East Indiaman, which includes 'a beautiful bureau and bookcase . . .' and the text suggests that Hickey was referring to a single article, and not to separate pieces of furniture. [2]

There is a later reference by Hickey to 'a large bureau with a book-case top'. [3] Sheraton uses the term for a small bureau surmounted by a couple of open bookshelves, which is an entirely different article from the tall bureau bookcases with glazed doors in the upper part, for which designs are shown both in Chippendale's *Director* and Hepplewhite's *Guide*, where they are called desk and bookcase, and also—in the *Guide*—secretary and bookcase. Sheraton describes his version of a bureau bookcase under the entry Bureau in *The Cabinet Dictionary* (1803), on p. 111, and on Plate 25 illustrates an example. John Claudius Loudon uses the description for the tall type with glazed doors, in his *Encyclopaedia of Cottage, Farm and Villa Architecture and Furniture*, which was published in 1833, proving that the term was current in the 19th century, though not in the sense in which Sheraton used it.

Some names have changed their meaning completely in the course of a century. The word toilet, for example, was a common abbreviation for toilet table in the 18th century; and toilet table was an alternative term for dressing table, occasionally masquerading as toiletta. (*See* illustrations on pages 478 and 479.) William Hickey uses the abbreviation when he says 'her own woman delivered a letter which she had just found upon Mrs Horneck's toilet'. [4] Janet Schaw, describing her visit to Antigua and St. Christopher, in 1774, recorded that 'We have seen every body of fashion in the Island, and our toilet is loaded with cards of Invitation. . . .' [5] At some time during the following century,

[1] Printed in London for T. Cox at the Lamb under the Royal-Exchange.
[2] London: Hurst & Blackett, Ltd. (10th edition, 1948). Vol. I (1749–75). Chapter x, p. 121. [3] *Ibid.* Vol. III (1782–90). Chapter ii, p. 21.
[4] Ibid. Vol. I (1749–75). Chapter xxiv, p. 307.
[5] *Journal of a Lady of Quality: being the Narrative of a Journey from Scotland to the West Indies, North Carolina, and Portugal, in the years 1774 to 1776* (Yale University Press, 1921). Chapter ii, p. 93.

probably in the late 'sixties or 'seventies—the exact date is unknown —the word toilet was adopted in America as a polite name for a water closet, and is used throughout the United States in that sense today; while the term dressing table has supplemented toilet table, save when it is used as a descriptive label for some antique example, made in the 18th century, or for a copy of an old model. The term survived far into the Victorian period in Britain, and in the popular series of handbooks, *Art at Home*, by Lady Barker, published in the 'seventies, the volume on *The Bedroom and Boudoir* devotes Chapter VI to 'The Toilet'.[1] The author opens that chapter by asserting that 'There is no prettier object in either bedroom or boudoir than the spot where "the toilet stands displayed"'. There is no reference to dressing tables; only to toilet tables. The term dressing table was current in the 18th century, and three specifications are included under that name in *The Prices of Cabinet Work*, 1797 edition.[2] Loudon uses it in his *Encyclopaedia*, both in the first edition of 1833 and in the supplement to the 1846 edition compiled by his widow; but Eastlake's *Hints on Household Taste*, published during the third quarter of the 19th century, reverts to toilet table. In America, the sanitary significance of the word toilet checked the fluctuations of taste in description which occurred in Britain, where they could be freely indulged because lavatory was accepted as the genteel and (for foreign visitors) hopelessly misleading euphemism for water closet.

Names and types of furniture increased and multiplied during the 18th century, particularly when makers like Chippendale, Ince and Mayhew, and Hepplewhite, issued books of their designs, which were really trade catalogues, intended to secure orders by stimulating the ideas of customers. The first edition of Thomas Chippendale's book was published in 1754, and was called *The Gentleman and Cabinet Maker's Director*. It was an obvious catalogue, not only of his works, but of designs which he was prepared to execute, and succeeding editions were more ambitious. The third edition, published in 1762, fully justified the sub-title which described it as 'a large collection of the most elegant and useful designs of household furniture in the most fashionable taste'. It included many newly named articles, of which some remained and some disappeared; others, like the term 'commode table', represented a tradesman's catalogue label, for a commode table could equally well be a kneehole table, or a combination of chest and cupboard. What Chippendale was pleased to call a 'French commode table' was a chest of drawers, shaped in imitation of contemporary French design.

These books prepared by makers probably recorded many current trade terms, such as the saddle check, which is the description

[1] London: Macmillan and Co., 1878.   [2] Occupying pp. 153 to 158 inclusive.

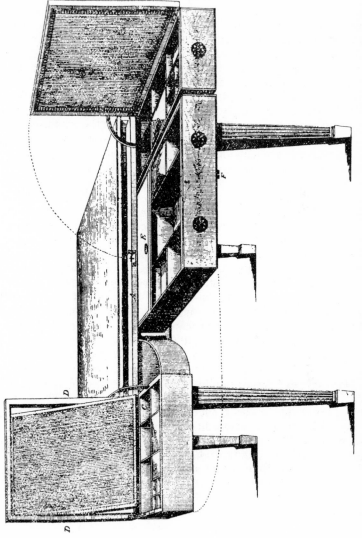

Rudd's table or reflecting dressing table. (From Hepplewhite's *Cabinet-Maker and Upholsterer's Guide*, 1788.)

Hepplewhite uses for an easy chair with a high back and wings, that somewhat resembled the form of a saddle. A few terms have preserved the names either of their original designers or the customers for whom they were designed. In Hepplewhite's *Guide*, which was published in 1788, there is a plate and a detailed specification of a fitted dressing table, called 'Rudd's table or reflecting dressing table'. (The plate is reproduced on the preceding page.) It was described as 'the most complete dressing table made, possessing every convenience which can be wanted, or mechanism and ingenuity supply. It derives its name from a once popular character, for whom it is reported it was first invented.' No other hint is given about the 'once popular character', but the implication is that Rudd was a man—no more fussy and finicky than most 18th century gentlemen who took an interest in their appearance—who had originally commissioned the design. Hepplewhite's text is so vague about the identity of Rudd, and is obviously recording something that somebody has heard at second-hand, that Rudd might easily be the name of the designer of the table. We know nothing of Rudd, the 'once popular character', but we do know that there was an English cabinet maker of that name, who lived in the 18th century, though the dates of his birth and death are unknown. Indeed, all we can learn about Rudd the cabinet maker is derived from an entry in the *Dictionary of Architecture* (Vol. VII), which records the existence of one Jean Baptiste Rudd, who was born in 1792 at Bruges, and is described as the son of an English cabinet maker who had settled there. The younger Rudd ultimately became the city architect of Bruges. His father may have been the inventor of Rudd's table; it is not an uncommon name.

Two types of Rudd's table are recorded in the 1797 edition of *The Prices of Cabinet Work*, which was compiled and published by 'a committee of masters, cabinet-makers', one being described and illustrated as 'a Rudd, or lady's dressing table'—which is a simplified drawing of a design by Thomas Shearer, and is reproduced on page 401, and the other as 'a Rudd dressing chest'. Sixteen years after Hepplewhite had published Rudd's table in his *Guide*, Sheraton mentioned it in *The Cabinet Dictionary*, as 'a kind of dressing table for ladies, not much in present use'. He then proceeded to describe it in a manner that was effectually calculated to prevent anybody from wanting one, for he makes it sound more complicated than it really was, and does not trouble to include an illustration. But Thomas Sheraton had a habit of making the simplest matter seem complex, although *The Cabinet Dictionary*, from which I have made many quotations in Section III, is an illuminating and indispensable work, to which I shall presently return.

There are several other pieces of furniture that are supposed to have derived their names either from the original maker or some famous person who ordered the first model or habitually used that particular article. Some attributions of this kind are wholly fanciful, and an example of casual fancifulness is what may be called 'The Case of the Hogarth Chair'. At some time, most probably during the Victorian period, Hogarth's name became associated with a type of chair that was made in the opening decades of the 18th century, and is called a bended back chair. Hogarth probably owned one or more of these chairs, and his self-portrait shows him sitting in a bended back chair with arms. He uses chairs of this type in various drawings and paintings, and a good example is a single bended back chair in his famous caricature of John Wilkes. Hogarth made the sketch for this caricature in the Court of Common Pleas when Wilkes appeared there; but finishing it off in his studio, he seated his victim in a bended back chair—a type which had then been out of fashion for some forty years, for the caricature of Wilkes was published in 1763. This Victorian label for the bended back chair implies that it was either designed by or was made for Hogarth; and although there may be some substance in the belief that Hogarth liked this type of chair, used it himself, and occasionally introduced it in his interiors, there was certainly no contemporary association of this design with his name.

Some articles named after their makers have left no trace of their form or function. Rudd's table survives only in histories of furniture; but nobody knows what Cobb's table was really like, though we have a description of its purpose. We know that John Cobb was an upholsterer and a cabinet maker, who was in partnership with William Vile, and from 1751 occupied the corner house in Long Acre, which became No. 72, during the latter part of the 18th century. The firm of Vile and Cobb ran a large and successful business, whose clients included the Royal Household and many members of the nobility. Cobb continued in business as a cabinet maker and upholsterer on his own account after Vile's retirement. He died in 1778. That most readable collector of gossip and anecdotes, John Thomas Smith (1766–1833), has some paragraphs about him in the second volume of his best known work, *Nollekens and his Times*.[1] He describes Cobb as an exceptionally haughty character, who was, perhaps, one of the proudest men in England. He used to dress in the most superb and costly fashion, and would strut through his workshops in his elaborate clothes, issuing orders to his workmen.

'He was the person', says Smith, 'who brought that very convenient table into fashion that draws out in front, with upper and

---

[1] *Nollekens and his Times*, by John Thomas Smith (John Lane, 1920. Reprint of the 2nd edition). Edited and annotated by Wilfrid Whitten.

inward rising desks, so healthy for those who stand to write, read or draw.' Unfortunately, we know far less about Cobb's table than we know about the man himself; and thanks to Smith's irrepressible garrulity, we know far more about Cobb than we do about Thomas Chippendale or George Hepplewhite. The depth and breadth of Cobb's pomposity is disclosed by Smith's account of an occasion when it was neatly punctured by George III. 'One day, when Mr Cobb was in his Majesty's library at Buckinghamhouse, giving orders to a workman, whose ladder was placed before a book which the King wanted, his Majesty desired Cobb to hand him the work, which instead of obeying, he called to his man, "Fellow, give me that book!" The King, with his usual condescension, arose, and asked Cobb, what his man's name was. "Jenkins," answered the astonished Upholsterer. "Then," observed the King, "Jenkins, you shall hand me the book." ' [1]

Smith states that he had the information about Cobb from 'Banks, the cellaret maker'.

There were hundreds of individual cabinet makers and upholsterers in London and other cities during the 18th and early 19th centuries, but few have left records of their work and designs. Thomas Sheraton made a list 'Of most of the Master Cabinetmakers, Upholsterers and Chair Makers, in and about London', in 1803, and published it at the end of *The Cabinet Dictionary*. It contained 253 names, and included that of Thomas Chippendale, who is described as an upholsterer, at the address 60 St. Martin's Lane.

Furniture made between the middle of the 18th and the early years of the 19th century is overshadowed by the names of Chippendale, Hepplewhite, and Sheraton; and the popular survival of those names may be attributed to the influence of their published books. *The Gentleman and Cabinet Maker's Director*, by Thomas Chippendale, was a best-seller in its day, the first edition appearing in 1754, with 160 plates, the second edition in 1755, with the same contents; and a third and enlarged edition in 1762. J. T. Smith, in *Nollekens and his Times*, includes a paragraph about Chippendale in the second volume of his book under the section called 'Recollections of Public Characters'. He lists the houses in St. Martin's Lane, and comes to No. 60, which had been known formerly by its sign, 'The Chair'; but at the time Smith was writing, the premises were occupied by Martin Stuteley, a builder. Describing them as extensive premises, Smith says they 'were formerly held by Chippendale, the most famous Upholsterer and Cabinetmaker of his day, to whose folio work on householdfurniture the trade formerly made constant reference. It contains, in many instances, specimens of the style of furniture so much in

[1] *Nollekens and his Times.* Vol. II, p. 178.   [contd. on page 30.

Self-portrait of William Hogarth, introducing the bended back chair,
which suggests that it was part of the furniture of his own studio—
hence its recurrence in his work.

Hogarth's caricature of John Wilkes, published on May 16th, 1763. The chair is the same type of bended back chair which appears in Hogarth's self-portrait. (*See* previous page.)

JOHN WILKES Esqr.

Another portrait of John Wilkes, published in 1763, in which he is seated on a simple chair of the period, with straight legs and a vase-shaped splat in the back.

vogue in France in the reign of Louis XIV but which for many years past has been discontinued in England. However, as most fashions come round again, I should not wonder, notwithstanding the beautifully classic change brought in by Thomas Hope, Esq., if we were to see the unmeaning scroll and shell-work, with which the furniture of Louis's reign was so profusely incumbered, revive; when Chippendale's book will again be sought after with redoubled avidity, and, as many of the copies must have been sold as waste paper, the few remaining will probably bear rather a high price.' [1]

He was right. Chippendale's published designs, particularly those which he had styled 'French', had a noticeable effect upon the form of furniture during the mid-19th century; and by the end of that century, respect for the magic of his name was far more potent than the example of his work. To the late Victorians and Edwardians he had ceased to be a man—he had become a label. Chippendale's own brood of terms for various articles were forgotten, though some of his fanciful ideas supplied descriptive prefixes; thus collectors and dealers spoke of 'Chinese Chippendale', and 'Gothic Chippendale', and as more and more people thought of him, not as a great chair maker and cabinet maker, but as a style, his name was arbitrarily attached to most of the furniture that was made in the middle decades of the 18th century: even the heavy, elaborately carved furniture made in Ireland during that period acquired the purely romantic label of 'Irish Chippendale'. (The persistent influence exerted by Chippendale's *Director* upon furniture, and in particular upon chair design, is examined in Section II.)

The other two makers whose names have secured this kind of immortality by becoming associated with a recognisable style, are George Hepplewhite and Thomas Sheraton. Hepplewhite, who had been apprenticed to Gillow of Lancaster, died in 1786, and two years after his death *The Cabinet Maker and Upholsterer's Guide* was published by the firm of A. Hepplewhite and Co., Cabinet Makers, under which title his widow, Alice, had carried on his business. Many of the designs included in the *Guide* were probably originated by Richard Gillow, but it is Hepplewhite's name that, like Chippendale's, has become the label for much of the furniture that was characteristic of the seventh, eighth, and ninth decades of the 18th century. Through the courtesy of Waring and Gillow, Ltd., I have enjoyed the opportunity of looking through some of the Gillow records at Lancaster, and have seen in them many of the designs that are usually attributed to Hepplewhite or Shearer. It seems to me highly probable that the shield back chair, with which the name of Hepplewhite is nearly always associated, was first designed by the firm of Gillow.

[1] *Nollekens and his Times.* Vol. II, p. 175.

Sheraton also has given his name to the styles that prevailed in the last decade of the 18th and the opening years of the 19th centuries; though most of his designs were on paper, and unlike Chippendale and Hepplewhite, he was not a maker publishing an illustrated catalogue. Born at Stockton-on-Tees in 1751, he had worked as a journeyman cabinet maker; but after settling in London about 1790, he devoted his time to drawing and authorship. He was far from resembling such prosperous and fashionable master makers as John Cobb, and with inappropriate pathos he disclosed his modest circumstances, under the entry of Cabinet, in *The Cabinet Dictionary*, when he wrote: 'I can assure the reader though I am thus employed in racking my invention to design fine and pleasing cabinet work, I can be well content to sit on a wooden bottom chair myself, provided I can but have common food and raiment wherewith to pass through life in peace' (p. 118). Some of the work attributed to him is either borrowed from or based upon that of Robert Adam and other contemporary designers and makers; but though much of it was original, the label Sheraton is as loose and inexact as the labels Chippendale and Hepplewhite.

Sheraton published *The Cabinet Maker and Upholsterer's Drawing Book*, in parts between 1791 and 1793, a second edition appearing in 1794, and a third in 1802. He published *The Cabinet Dictionary* in 1803, and his last work, *The Cabinet Maker and Artist's Encyclopaedia*, was to have been issued in one hundred and twenty-five parts, but Sheraton died in 1806 when only a few parts had been printed.

As a record of terms current in the cabinet- and chair-making trade at the beginning of the 19th century, *The Cabinet Dictionary* is invaluable. The entries in it show clearly that furniture design was still dependent upon classical architecture, and that a working knowledge of the orders and their various members and characteristic embellishments was an essential part of a cabinet maker's technical education. Many entries are devoted to materials and such processes as varnishing, polishing, and gilding, and there is a long entry for furnishing, from which some quotations are made in Section II. Sheraton occasionally invented names for special designs, such as curricle, for a type of armchair, and explained his reasons for doing so; but *The Cabinet Dictionary* is disappointing when he attempts to explain the derivation of some name that was in general use. He does little to clear up the mystery of the name Canterbury, though his statement that it had 'of late years been applied to some pieces of cabinet work, because the bishop of that see first gave orders for these pieces', implies that the term was then old enough for its origin to be conjectural. Sheraton does not say whether the original canterbury was for serving food or for storing music. He illustrates both types, and has a separate entry for supper-canterbury. Again, he dismisses the word cabriole, which was used in the late 18th century for a type of easy chair with a semi-circular back, as 'a French easy chair—from the name of the person who invented or introduced them'.

Many of the illustrations in *The Cabinet Dictionary* had been previously published in *The Drawing Book*; some were subsequently incorporated in *The Cabinet Maker and Artist's Encyclopaedia*. The numbering of the plates in *The Cabinet Dictionary* does not always correspond with the references in the various entries. Sheraton's engraver and printer were often out of step, and although he includes nearly five pages of corrections (335 to 339), he misses a good many errors. Where subjects from the plates have been reproduced in Section III, the correct number of the plate and not the number of Sheraton's reference is given: for example, the sideboard table shown on page 430 is from Plate 71, but in the text of his entry under that heading Sheraton refers to this design as appearing on Plate 73. Though this makes *The Cabinet Dictionary* exasperating as a work of reference, its interest and value for the student are not impaired.

Some of the trade terms used in the latter part of the 18th century are ignored by Sheraton; he may have regarded them as commonplace technicalities unworthy of mention or explanation, but it would have been interesting to have had a contemporary view of the origin of the term Marlboro' leg and the exact nature of a toad back moulding. Both are mentioned in the 1797 edition of *The Prices of Cabinet Work*, *with Tables and Designs*, as revised and corrected by a Committee of Masters Cabinet Makers.

The Marlboro' leg was a trade name for a tapered leg of square section. A faint clue to its possible origin is supplied by the wording of the dedication in Ince and Mayhew's *Universal System of Household Furniture*, which is addressed to George Spencer, the fourth Duke of Marlborough. In the dedication the authors suggest that the Duke had a close interest in design. This is what they wrote:

. . . Being sensible of Your Grace's extensive Knowledge, in the Arts and Sciences, but more particularly in Drawing and your being ever willing to promote, and encourage Industry and Ingenuity, will justly account for our presumption in claiming the protection of so worthy a Patron to this work, which if so fortunate as to merit your Grace's approbation will be esteem'd as the greatest Honour—ever conferred on your Graces most Respectful, most Obedient and very faithful servants, Mayhew and Ince.

Ince and Mayhew's book was published in 1760, and the Marlboro' leg may have been so called as a compliment to the Duke's artistic sensibilities.

Sometimes the name of a famous person was deliberately attached to a piece of furniture, and perhaps the most unfortunate example of this is provided by some of Sheraton's worst work—his Nelson chairs. Designed to celebrate the Battle of Trafalgar, they were sometimes called Trafalgar chairs, a name given after 1805 to a variety of chair types. Professor Ernest Weekley has suggested that many names, such as Canterbury and Chesterfield, have been popularised by imaginative tradesmen; but (as Sheraton frequently asserts without adducing a particle of evidence) an article has often been named after the customer who placed the order. This was the origin of the term Davenport for a small writing desk that became popular in the early 19th century. The original design was made to the order of a Captain Davenport, by the firm of Gillow, probably towards the end of the 18th century, and thereafter repeat orders for this type of writing desk, under the name of the original customer, were executed by Gillow at Lancaster.

An inspection of the Gillow records at Lancaster is instructive. The firm kept what were called 'waste books'. A waste book is not an order book or a ledger, and it is not used in auditing, but it contains notes of a variety of transactions and special orders. In one of the waste books the original entry, 'Captain Davenport, a desk', made at some time in the late 18th century (the exact date unfortunately cannot be traced), was observed by Mr B. Barber, the manager of the Lancaster branch of Waring & Gillow, Ltd. In addition to the waste books there are the E. and S. books—that is books containing an estimate and a rough sketch. It was in these books that repeat orders for Davenport desks were entered.

By 1833 Loudon was listing two varieties of what he called a devonport in his *Encyclopaedia of Cottage, Farm and Villa Architecture*. He said (entry 2114, p. 1065) that they were 'so-called from the inventor's name', and he described them as 'drawing room writing cabinets used by ladies'. In the United States the word davenport also meant a small writing desk, but at some later time in the 19th century the word was used for an upholstered sofa, and davenport bed meant a couch which could be extended to form a bed, while a davenport table was a long, narrow table, though this was an inexact term.

The East has contributed many names and terms to furniture and furnishing, apart from those that were adopted because of habits implanted by some of the earlier waves of Oriental taste, such as tea drinking and china collecting. Sometimes articles of established design and use were introduced, which, when transported to England, became the progenitors of a large family of recognisably related pieces of furniture, rather confusingly described under one all-embracing term. An example of this is the ottoman. Introduced during the early part of the 19th century, its exotic character, suggestive of wicked Eastern luxury, was modified by giving it a variety of forms. Instead of remaining a long, low, backless seat with an air of lascivious abandon, it was briskly buttoned up in the most respectable upholstery of that name, its level was raised, castors sprouted from its feet, it became circular, and, presently, with a low back, it was fitted snugly into a corner, thus becoming the ancestor of what is always presumed to be a typical English invention of late Victorian times, the cosy corner.

Throughout the 19th century, in all its various forms, it was still called the ottoman. How general the term became for any fairly low, stuffed seat that was dumped down in a room, may be judged from the illustration on page 35, of a drawing by du Maurier, published on May 24th, 1879, in *Punch*. That circular ottoman is a simplified version of the circular French sofa called a *borne*. A *jardinière* or a lamp sometimes uprose from the circular back of a *borne*, and du Maurier has shown a palm ascending gracefully from the centre of his ottoman.

Our close association with India was responsible for several names, such as cot, which is derived from the Hindu word *Khāt*, and was adapted by Anglo-Indians and introduced at some time during the 18th century. Another article of furniture once fairly common, but now comparatively rare, is the teapoy, which comes from the Hindu word *Tīpāi*. Professor Weekley points out that the teapoy has been altered 'under the influence of *tea*, from an original which is ultimately identical with "tripod" while a *charpoy*, or light bedstead, is etymologically a "quadruped" '.[1]

Apart from imported and adopted terms, and those that are derived from the names of famous or obscure people, or based upon the original uses of articles, are those suggested by some obvious affinity with the animal kingdom or the insect world; and whether contemporary or modern, such terms are usually apposite. Perhaps the butterfly table, the eagle table, the giraffe piano, and the kangaroo sofa are the most striking. Of these, the eagle table only reproduces the natural form: the butterfly, the giraffe, and the kangaroo are suggested merely by contours. An eagle table should be classified as belonging to what may be called the fauna of furniture, evolved during the long history of ornamentation, in which would be included not only birds and beasts, but such mythological creatures as the chimera, griffin, and sphinx. Some names for shapes are suggested by avian, reptilian, or animal characteristics, like the swan-neck pediment, the bird's beak lock and bird's beak moulding, and the serpentine front. These, and similar terms, are in a class apart from those that arise from the

---

[1] *Something about Words*, by Ernest Weekley (John Murray, 1935). Chapter X, p. 187.

Circumstantial Evidence.

"Who's that frizzly black-haired woman talking to my husband on the Ottoman?"—"She's a Mrs Cadogan Smythe."—"Indeed! She's good at flattering people, I should say; and knows how to lay it on pretty thick!"—"Ah! you infer that, no doubt, from her attitude and expression?"—"Oh dear no! From my husband's!"

(Reproduced by permission of the Proprietors of *Punch* from the issue of May 24th, 1879.)

direct borrowing and careful reproduction of some animal feature, such as the claw or the hoof. Then there are what may be called anatomical terms, like the kidney table.

In quite a different class from the names given to specific pieces or parts of furniture are the innumerable terms used in woodworking, both for materials and their condition, for tools, and for various forms of craftsmanship. That some of these terms have been suggested originally by shapes and colours and the nature of some operation in carpentry or cabinet making is obvious; but others are strangely baffling. Perhaps one of the strangest is the term 'bodger', which occurs in Buckinghamshire as a description of the turners of chair legs and stretchers who work in the beech woods and bring their turned stuff to the chair manufacturers of High Wycombe. It is a regional term, apparently of recent origin, and is not elsewhere associated with the work of turners. Boger or Bodger is an English surname, both variations representing 'an archaic spelling of Bowyer', according to Professor Weekley.[1] This surname is found in the northern counties of England, and it is possible that some members of the Bodger family moved south to Buckinghamshire during the late 18th or early 19th centuries; though it seems unlikely that they should have given their name to the practitioners of an established craft, even if they became engaged in it. The oldest industry in High Wycombe was paper making, which had been carried on in several mills there since the late 17th century. It was during the first thirty years of the 19th century that chair making was developed on an increasingly large scale. According to the returns made to Parliament under the Population Act of 1801, the total number of inhabitants in the town and parish was 4248, and of these 724 only were employed in trade, manufacture, and handicraft. This is recorded in Lysons' *Magna Britannia*, Volume I, page 675 (published in 1806). There is no reference to chair making or turnery. But in 1831 Samuel Lewis, in *A Topographical Dictionary of England*, states that chairs 'in great quantities' were made at High Wycombe. It seems likely that at some time during the early 19th century the term bodger came into use in the locality; and I am indebted to Mr L. John Mayes, the Borough Librarian of High Wycombe, for an interesting suggestion regarding a possible origin of its use in that district. In conversation with an old paper maker, in High Wycombe, he mentioned the term 'bodger', and the reply was that paper makers, who were the really skilled craftsmen, had first applied this term to the wood turners, the phrase used being 'bodging about in the woods and their poky little sheds in the town'. As paper making in High Wycombe is older by a century or more than chair making,

---

[1] *The Romance of Names*, by Ernest Weekley (London: John Murray, 1914). Chapter XV, p. 149.

this explanation, which was quite new to Mr Mayes, does sound plausible. Incidentally, the old man's final words were to the effect that paper making was a clean trade, and paper makers 'allus did look down on they bodgers, dirty folk all on 'em, allus'.

Bodger is an old English word, and has sometimes been used to describe a pedlar; and in this sense it may first have been applied to the Buckinghamshire turners, who peddled their wares to the chair makers who assembled them; then, in their turn, loaded them on to farm carts and peddled them as 'White Wycombes' through the countryside and the Midland counties. Halliwell, in *A Dictionary of Archaic and Provincial Words*, under the word Bodge, gives as one of its meanings, 'To begin a task and not complete it'. This specifically describes what the bodger does: he begins the task of chair making, by turning the legs, stretchers, and sticks, on his pole lathe, but his work is completed by the chair maker, who assembles these turned members. This is the most complimentary explanation of a term which, upon the face of it, appears derogatory. (Halliwell compiled his *Dictionary* over a century ago, and he dated the Preface to the first edition February 1st, 1847.)

Some words relating to the nature and quality of materials have probably survived from mediaeval days. In George Sturt's book, *The Wheelwright's Shop* (Cambridge University Press, 1923), there is a reference to the word 'crips', that was used by a very old craftsman named Cook, whom the author describes. 'When a new plane or chisel proved over-brittle, so that a nick chinked out of it and needed grinding wholly away, Cook used to look disapprovingly at the broken edge and mutter "Crips". What was that word? I never asked. Besides, Cook was too deaf. But after some years it dawned upon me that he had meant crisp.'[1]

Now, the word 'crips' occurs in Chaucer's poem, *The House of Fame*, and is used in these lines (1386–87):

> Hir heer, that oundy was and crips,
> As burned gold hit shoon to see.

In Skeat's edition of Chaucer, 'crips' is defined in the glossary as 'crisp'; but Chaucer uses the word 'crisp' as well, in line 824 of *The Romaunt of the Rose*: 'Crisp was his heer. . . .' The transposition of the final letters of a word often occurs, and it would perhaps be too facile to suggest that old Cook in George Sturt's book was using 14th-century English. But many old building terms and names for woods, and, indeed, the uses for woods, have persisted from mediaeval times. Chaucer writes of 'corbets', and the reference is obviously to corbels.

> Ne how they hatte in masoneries,
> As, corbets fulle of imageries.
> *(The House of Fame*, line 1304.)

[1] Section XI, p. 56.

In *The Parlement of Foules*, Chaucer gives this list of woods and their uses (lines 176-80):

> The bilder ook, and eek the hardy asshe;
> The piler elm, the cofre unto careyne;
> The boxtree piper; holm to whippes lasshe;
> The sayling firr; the cipres, deth to pleyne;
> The sheter ew, the asp for shaftes pleyne;
> The olyve of pees, and eek the drunken vyne,
> The victor palm, the laurer to devyne.

This almost constitutes a mediaeval woodworker's guide. The names of many trees have remained unchanged since Chaucer recorded them, and in *The Canterbury Tales* ('The Knightes Tale', lines 2921-23), he gives 'ook, firre, birch, asp, alder, holm, popler, wilow, elm, plane, ash, box, chasteyn [chestnut], lind [lime], laurer, mapul, thorn, beech, hasel, ew, whippeltree [the cornelian cherry or dogwood]'. In *The House of Fame* 'a table of sicamour' is mentioned (line 1278); but although Chaucer refers occasionally to chests, tables, chairs—in the sense of thrones—stools, and benches (incidentally using the last term both for a seat and, in 'The Shipmannes Tale', line 1548, for a table), it is apparent that the richness and variety of mediaeval furnishing depended upon a lavish use of fabrics, and through the names of many of these, and of the basic articles of furniture, continuity with the Middle Ages is still preserved in our homes.

SECTION II

The Design of Furniture

*

FOR over eight hundred years, from before the Norman Conquest until the middle of the 20th century, the history of furniture design in England has been a record of fluctuating independence for craftsmen, alternating with periods of direct or remote control by architects or fashionable, non-executant designers. The periods of independence, when craftsmen ordered their own affairs, regulated their working conditions, and established standards of workmanship, were won by the cumulative skill of many generations of workers in wood. The periods of control have usually followed some great social or economic change, and the first began during the 16th century, when the structure of society was altered and a new mercantile class came into power. That class discovered in the Italian Renaissance and its various manifestations in Europe a stimulant of remarkable potency. It went to the heads of the new, well-travelled English aristocrats; and their 'Italianate' taste, imposed upon their houses and furniture, was satisfied by variously malformed versions of the external features of classical architecture.

Craftsmen may have struggled against those fashions in ornament; the furniture of the second half of the 16th century frequently suggests a conflict of purpose; for a sturdy form is often bedizened with applied decoration that is ill chosen, ill placed, and executed without sympathy or understanding. The furniture is structurally as robust as the society that it served; but the profusion and meretricious character of the ornamentation disclose an intemperate appetite for foreign ideas accompanied by an incapacity to digest them. Elizabethan and Jacobean furniture resembles that of the Victorian period, which was also robust, overburdened with applied ornament, and made to satisfy the taste of a rich and undiscriminating class. The Victorian appetite was for romantic Gothic ideas, derived from the mediaeval civilisation that had ended with the Tudors and whose artistic accomplishments the Elizabethans had rejected.

During the middle decades of the 17th century, craftsmen regained some of their independence, for fashionable taste was in eclipse; the Puritans would have none of it, as they believed in austerity for its own sake, and the sturdy simplicity of furniture reflected their beliefs. By the end of the 17th century, fashion was again in charge of furniture design; the introduction of the highly skilled craft of veneering had established a new specialist craftsman, the cabinet maker; and the architect was gradually assuming a comprehensive responsibility for design.

To architects practising in the 18th century, it seemed eminently right and obvious that they should be the guardians of taste and dictators of design. Their fitness for these offices was sanctioned by a classical precedent; and classical precedents were highly respected in the Augustan age. So they were prepared to apply literally to all aspects of their contemporary environment their belief that architecture was the mistress art; and they would have accepted as a basic truth the views H. G. Wells once condensed into a memorable sentence, when he wrote: 'Painting, sculpture, all furnishing and decoration, are the escaped subsidiaries of architecture, and may return, very largely, to their old dependence'.[1]

During the Graeco-Roman civilisation, the relationship between furniture and architecture was established and maintained in terms of design, and the dependence of the former was aesthetic rather than structural. Greek and Roman furniture was shaped and ornamented in accordance with a set of conventions that employed a variety of formalised natural objects. From the earliest times men have copied the shapes of plants and animals; in a static civilisation such functionalised shapes become first petrified and dully repetitive, and finally debased; in a lively, growing, intellectually and artistically alert civilisation they are fluent, expressing with an infinity of subtle inflections the vitality of the men who carved or painted them and the people who used and appreciated the articles they adorned. Both the fauna and flora of furniture began their evolution in the old kingdom of Egypt, certainly as early as 3000 B.C., perhaps much earlier. Centuries later, in the service of the classic orders of architecture, they developed an apparently inexhaustible decorative quality, of a kind that the frustrating rigidity of Egyptian design had never permitted. The original Greek orders, Doric, Ionic, and Corinthian, were adapted by the Romans, who added two others: the Tuscan and the Composite, the last allowing abundant scope for the exuberant vulgarity that occasionally disfigured Roman architecture. Nearly all the ornamentation associated with the five orders was derived from organic sources: the labyrinth, or Greek fret, and the bead and reel being among the few devices that were independently conceived, without reference to any natural prototype.

[1] *The Work, Wealth and Happiness of Mankind*, by H. G. Wells (London: William Heinemann, Ltd., 1932). Chapter xiv, p. 711.

Of all the forms adopted and employed with various refinements, that of the acanthus leaf became ubiquitous: it has, since its use in the Greek Corinthian order, spread to all parts of the habitable globe, and may indeed be regarded as symbolic of the formalism and discipline of classic architecture. In the fourth of his ten books on Architecture, Marcus Vitruvius Pollio records a legend about the origin of the Corinthian capital. According to this story, the elegant form incorporating the feathery acanthus leaves was suggested to one Callimachus, whom the Athenians called Catatechnos, when he was passing the tomb of a young Corinthian girl, whose

Legendary origin of the Corinthian capital. (From Lomax and Gunyon's *Encyclopaedia of Architecture*.)

nurse had collected in a basket a number of small articles of which the dead girl had been fond, and had put them on her tomb, with a tile on the top of the basket to preserve the contents. The basket had been placed accidentally on a root of an acanthus plant, which, in the spring time, put forth its stems and foliage, and in the course of its growth reached the corners of the tile, and formed volutes at the extremities. Callimachus was so impressed by the sight of this basket surrounded by delicate foliage, that he was prompted to invent the Corinthian order. It is obvious from the context, that Vitruvius liked this story, even though he might not have taken it seriously.

Anthemion ornament from the Erechtheion, Athens. (After Wornum.) Compare this with the variation shown on page 114 and with the use of the basic motif in a chair back on page 115.

While a picturesque fable may have stimulated conjecture about the origin of familiar forms, there are many obvious models in nature to encourage such speculation: for instance, it has been suggested that the shape of the nautilus shell is imitated by the scroll or spiral ornaments that form the volutes on the Ionic and Corinthian capitals. The volute is an ancient device, which appears on the capitals of some Egyptian columns. In Egypt the buds and flowers of the lotus and papyrus were as popular as the acanthus ultimately became in Greece and the Roman Empire; and the tendrils and grapes of the vine have since the earliest times provided a motif for the carver and decorator.

The honeysuckle or palmette inspired a type of Greek ornament, which supplied to the Doric order the motif for those ornamental blocks called antefixae, that were set upright at regular intervals along the lower edge of a roof to hide the ends of the tiles, and was used to decorate the necking on the Ionic capital, appearing also on the upper part of some Corinthian capitals, and on entablatures and elsewhere in Greek and Roman architecture.

Many ornamental and structural forms that were ultimately carved in stone were probably tried out first in other materials; but sometimes a shape may have been brought to its final perfection in stone. In Greece the chair form may have evolved from a stone prototype. The elegant concave curve below some of the solid stone seats in the Theatre of Dionysos at Athens is reproduced in the legs of the chairs that are shown in detail on many Greek vases. The free standing chair in ancient Greece may have developed from the marble seat, set against a wall, or carved complete from one solid block of stone. Although some of the later refinements

The Greek prototype of the sabre leg. These subjects, taken from the Hamilton vases, are illustrated in Fosbroke's *Encyclopaedia of Antiquities*, 1825, Vol. II.

of form were probably derived from stone models, as early as the 6th and 5th centuries B.C., stools and chairs with turned legs are depicted on the reliefs of the Parthenon and on some Athenian tombs.

Examples of Roman furniture have survived, in marble and metal. They are recognisably a part of the architectural background, for the Roman architect, like the Georgian architect in England, was the master designer, exerting control over the form and colour and ornamentation of houses and their contents. The Roman patrician would have found himself very much at home, visually, in an 18th century English town or country house. Though he might have been rather surprised by open fireplaces—for Roman houses were centrally heated—and have found the custom of sitting on chairs at meal times awkward—for, like the Greeks, the Romans reclined upon cushioned couches when they ate—he would have been agreeably impressed by the various appointments and the proportions and decoration of the furniture. Both Roman patrician and Georgian gentleman would have regarded mediaeval furnishing, and the mediaeval interior, as barbarous.

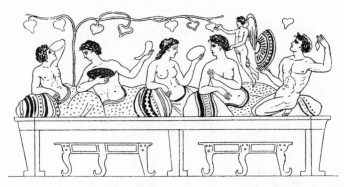

A Greek festival, showing a dining couch with cushions, and small tables below which have a rudimentary form of the cabriole leg. Taken from the Hamilton vases, and illustrated in Fosbroke's *Encyclopaedia of Antiquities*, 1825, Vol. II.

After the collapse of western Roman civilisation, the refinements of life disappeared. In Saxon England, architecture reverted to primitive woodwork, to wattle and daub walls, and once again furniture began to evolve from the simplest beginnings, as it had evolved hundreds of years earlier in Egypt and Asia Minor and Greece.

At first, furniture was structurally dependent upon building, because it was an extension of or closely associated with the wall. Receptacles were put against the walls of a room, or were hollowed out of them, and covered by a crude wooden door. Beds were built as a series of cabins against a wall, and closed with curtains or doors; forms and benches stood along a wall. From the days of the Anglo-Saxon states, and throughout the Middle Ages, furniture and building remained in this close relationship, from which furniture only escaped during the 15th century. For luxury, and the alleviation of discomfort, fabrics were used. For example, the bench placed against the wall was provided with a dorcer, a piece of fabric hung on the wall against which people could lean back. Recesses were furnished with seats; and by the early 16th century the bay window was provided with a fixed wooden seat that was supported and backed by a continuation of the panelling with which the walls of a room were clothed. After the beginning of the 16th century, furniture was structurally separated from the wall, and became free standing, although certain pieces still stood against a wall. (Now, midway in the 20th century, furniture is returning to its mediaeval dependence upon the wall, for the reduced size of rooms in the smaller houses and flats of today has increased the use of fitted furniture, and the architect has again taken control of furniture design as a matter, not of fashion, but of plain utility.)

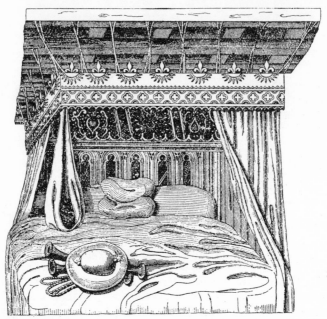

A 15th century bed, with the canopy suspended from the ceiling beams. (From a French MS., *des Miracles de Saint Louis*, reproduced in Shaw's *Specimens of Ancient Furniture*.)

The evolution of the bedstead and the bed from pre-Norman times to the 19th century provides an instructive study. Bedsteads in the 9th century were mere elevated platforms, upon which cushions and bedding were heaped. (*See* illustration on page 134.) The bed relied for its comfort almost wholly upon its feather mattress and for luxury upon the use of various fabrics, while the old dependence upon the wall was still suggested by the form of beds with canopies. Sometimes those canopies were suspended from the rafters of the ceiling, like the example of a 15th century bed from a French MS. of the period, shown above, and the bed illustrated on page 119.

The richness of mediaeval bedroom furnishing is described in a late 15th century document entitled: 'The Co'minge into Englande of the Lorde Grautehuse from the Right high' and myghty Prince Charles Duke of Burgoine'.

This French nobleman was entertained by Edward IV in 1472, and was created Earl of Winchester. The account of the apartments prepared for him reads as follows:

Then, aboute ix of the clocke, the Kinge and quene, w^t her ladies and gentlewomen, brought the sayde Lorde Grautehuse to iij chaumbres of Pleasance, alt hanged w^t whyte Sylke and lynnen clothe, and alt the

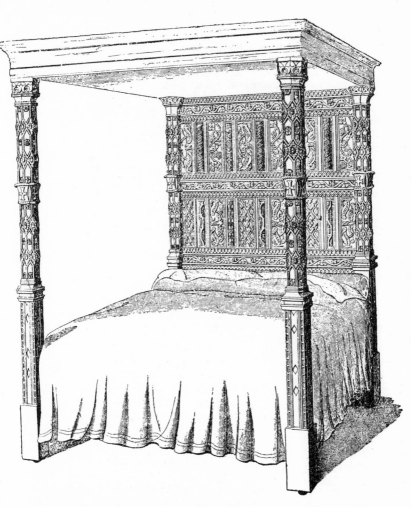

Early 16th century bedstead, showing the elaborately carved head and posts. The original tester is missing. This example shows the bed as a free standing piece of furniture: independent of wall and ceiling, and structurally self-contained. (Reproduced from Shaw's *Specimens of Ancient Furniture*.)

Floures couered w^t carpettes. There was ordeined a Bedde for hym selue, of as good doune as coulde be gotten, the Sheies of Raynys, also fyne Fustyans; the Counterpoynte clothe of golde, furred w^t armyn, the Tester and the Celer also shyninge clothe of golde, the Curteyns of whyte Sarsenette; as for his hedde Sute and Pillowes, [they] were of the quenes owen Ordonnance. Itm̄, [in] the ij^{de} chambre was a other of astate, the whiche was alte whyte. Also in the same chambre was made a couche w^t Fether beddes, hanged w^t a Tente, knytt lyke a nette, and there was a Cuppborde. Itm̄, in the iij^{de} chambre was ordeined a Bayne or ij, which were couered w^t Tentes of white clothe. And when the Kinge and the quene, w^t alt her ladyes and gentlewemen, had shewed him these chambres, they turned againe to theire owen chambres, and lefte the sayde lorde Grautehuse there, accompanied w^t my lorde chamberlein, whiche dispoyled hym, and wente both together to the Bayne [bath].[1]

Chaucer includes 'clothe of Reynes' in a description of a luxurious bed in *The Book of the Duchesse*, and the relevant lines are given under the entry for Satin in Section III on page 409. Chaucer's descriptions of beds and bedding, the account just quoted, and the evidence of contemporary illustrations, indicate the masking of all framework by richly decorative materials. The couch with feather beds 'hanged w^t a Tente, knytt lyke a nette', suggests detachment from the wall, though the 'Tente' may, like the canopy of the bed on page 44, have hung from the ceiling rafters.

During the late 15th and early 16th centuries, the bed, in common with other articles of furniture, became free standing: it could be placed in the middle of a room, and the wooden framework of the bedstead became visible, and was no longer masked by fabrics. Thereafter, from the 16th century to the end of the 19th, the posted bed with the tester was structurally self-contained, its external appearance being varied chiefly by the prominence given to the decorative wooden framework or to the draperies. In the first decades of the 16th century, the four-post bed, in common with other furniture, exemplified the native English style. As yet there was no hint of the 'Italianate' confusions that afflicted furniture later in that century. The loss of good proportions in shape and congruity in ornamentation is apparent when the early 16th century bed illustrated on page 45 is compared with the great bed of Ware on page 47. Both illustrations show the wooden framework of the bedstead without the draperies; but when curtains hung from the tester and were drawn at night, the bed became a room within a room, completely enclosed. Although the great bed of Ware was exceptionally large, its solidity and amplitude were characteristic, for beds did become gigantic in size during the

---

[1] *Archaeologia*, Vol. XXVI, section ix, pp. 279-80, 'Narratives of the arrival of Louis de Bruges, Seigneur de la Gruthuyse, in England, and of his creation as Earl of Winchester, in 1472'. This includes a copy of a document MS. Add. 6113, f. 103, in which this description of the bedroom furnishing occurs.

The great bed of Ware, Hertfordshire. (From the illustration in Shaw's *Specimens of Ancient Furniture*.) The cornice is not original. The bed is of oak, carved, inlaid and painted in colour. It is now in the Victoria and Albert Museum, and was bought in 1931. It was once owned by Charles Dickens, who bought it in 1864 for 100 guineas. The earliest reference to the bed is in the Poetical Itinerary of Prince Ludwig, of Anhalt-Köhten, who visited England in 1596, and wrote some lines about it, which were translated by William Brenchley Rye as follows:

> At Ware was a bed of dimensions so wide,
> Four couples might cosily lie side by side,
> And thus without touching each other abide.

(From *England as Seen by Foreigners in the days of Elizabeth and James the First*. London: John Russel Smith, 1865. Note 53, p. 212.) Shakespeare refers to it in *Twelfth Night*, Act III, Scene 2, when Sir Toby Belch says: 'And as many lies as will lie in thy sheet of paper, although the sheet were big enough for the bed of Ware in England, set 'em down. . . .'

47

An early 19th century tent bed. This design, dated 1827, is from George Smith's *Cabinet Maker and Upholsterer's Guide*, 1836 edition.

Elizabethan period, their testers being upheld by various malformations of classical columns, and the headboards crammed with elaborately carved decoration.

These big wooden four-post, or posted, beds, which formed ornate frames for curtains, continued in use throughout the 17th century; and the great state beds were far more elaborate, for they were immensely tall, and the whole framework—posts, tester, cornice, and headboard—was covered in fabric, the posts being hidden by the curtains which hung from both ends of the tester. Graceful and decorative four-post beds were made during the 18th century, with slender columns and testers with delicately moulded cornices; there were domed beds and Chinese designs with testers that borrowed their form from the pagoda; and the mediaeval idea of the tent bed was revived in an elaborate manner, and again the framework disappeared beneath draperies. Tent beds and field beds persisted into the 19th century—the curtains of a tent bed shielded Mr Pickwick when he first discovered that he was in the wrong bedroom at the Great White Horse at Ipswich—and they were characterised by the lavish use of fabrics. The idea of a bed as a room within a room survived in a modified form until the end of the Victorian period; but it could never be satisfactorily expressed with a metal bedstead, and the compromise of the half-

48

tester, which had been used in mediaeval times and became popular during the 19th century, merely provided curtains that shielded the head of the bed. The heavily curtained, completely enclosed bed was incompatible with the fresh air, open window cult that was favoured by the young Edwardians; also, its dimensions were an embarrassment in the new houses with small rooms and low ceilings that were replacing the big Victorian houses with lofty and spacious apartments.

So the bed, after centuries of association with the wall, and a much shorter period of structural independence in which it was virtually an apartment with fabric walls, to be opened or closed at will, has again become a raised platform for bedding as it was in pre-Norman England. This outline sketch of the evolution of the bed from the 9th century to the 20th has been deliberately

An early 19th century field bed. This design, dated 1827, is from George Smith's *Cabinet Maker and Upholsterer's Guide*, 1836 edition.

simplified; for there were many variations and elaborations of design, and some of them are recorded under their appropriate entries in the next Section, but it is intended to show that the influence of fashion, while considerable, is not always decisive. Fashions in furniture design and the sparing or lavish use of fabrics in furnishing were often determined by the architect and builder. The rooms of 17th and 18th century houses where the great curtained beds stood were icily cold in winter; and the improved heating appliances of the 19th century made the creation of a cosy, stuffy cabin within a bedroom unnecessary.

The bed is one of the basic articles of furnishing: the others are seats, receptacles, and tables. All were used in their most elementary forms during the early Middle Ages, acquiring in the late mediaeval period numerous refinements, as the skill of woodworkers increased and fresh techniques were either invented or re-discovered. For a hundred and fifty years, from the end of the 15th to the middle of the 17th century, those basic articles were dominated by new fashions, and when the Puritan period provided a respite from modish ideas, the joiners and turners and leather workers, who were the makers of furniture, provided a simple and vigorous style, recognisably English in character and obviously related to the pre-Italianate native style of the early 16th century. This resumption of a natural development, that had been temporarily diverted by the imperious taste of the Elizabethan and Jacobean aristocracy, disclosed great advances in skill, and an ingenious and sympathetic mastery of materials.

During the 17th century, many specialised forms of furniture were introduced; and their novel and sometimes exacting needs could always command the appropriate forms of skill, for though English craftsmen might resist foreign fashions, they were quick to learn and adopt new methods. This was demonstrated when the craft of veneering was introduced, for it created and established the cabinet maker as a new form of craftsman in England. An example of the exacting work that was occasionally demanded from furniture makers is supplied by a detailed specification for a billiard table, which was included in a book published in 1684 in London. It was entitled: *The School of Recreation: or the Gentlemans Tutor, to those most Ingenious Exercises of Hunting, Racing, Hawking, Riding, Cock-fighting, Fowling, Fishing, Shooting, Bowling, Tennis, Ringing, Billiards*, by R. H. (The author was Robert Howlett.) This first edition has a frontispiece, divided into six separate illustrations, and the last shows a billiard table, with a player on each side. (This is reproduced in Section III, on page 143.) The author describes this billiard table as follows:

First then, he that would rightly understand this excellent Pastime, must be very careful of the Form and Make of the table, and the right ordering, framing, and fitting it for the Game, which is known by these ensuing Marks:

1. The Form of a Billiard Table ought to be Oblong, that is to say, somewhat longer than it is broad; Both the length and breadth being left to your Discretion to make; proportionable to the Room you design it for; It ought to be railed round, and this Rail or Ledge a little swelled or stufft with fine Flox or Cotton, that may yield to the Ball when struck against it, and expedites rather than deads the Flight of the Ball; though that happens according to the violence of the Stroke or Push: the Superficies of the Table ought to be covered with Green fine Cloath, clean and free from knots; the Board must be levelled as exactly as is possible for the Eye and Hand of the most curious Joyner to Level, to the end your Ball may run true upon any part of the table, without leaning or declining to any side of it: I must confess I do believe there are few have been so careful in this last thing, as they ought, because they have not timely foreseen, if the Boards, whereof the Table is made, be well-seasoned, and not subject to Warp, and that the Floor whereon it stands be even and level; so that through the Ill-seasonedness of the one or Unevenness of the other, as likewise in time by the weight of the Table, and the Gamesters yielding and giving way, there are very few found true. . . .

2. The four Corners of the Table must be furnished with four Holes, and exactly in the middle of each side one Hole, and these Holes must be hung at the bottoms with Nets; which Holes are named Hazards . . . the Nets are made to receive the Ball, and keep them from falling to the Ground when hazarded; and indeed it is a very commendable way, far better than wooden Boxes which some use, these being apt to let a Ball to fly out again. . . . (Pages 186-190.) [1]

The making of such an elaborate piece of furniture required far more skill than the joiners of the early 16th century could have commanded; the skill of craftsmen had broadened and deepened in the interval; and it was upon this accomplished body of skill that the fashionable cabinet makers and chair makers and the architects of the golden age of English design relied. That golden age of design began to flourish after the restoration of Charles II, and declined during the first half of the 19th century; but for over a hundred and seventy years it was constantly refreshed by the genius of English architects.

In the first half of the 17th century, Inigo Jones brought order out of the architectural chaos of the early English Renaissance, and by the example of his work, implanted in the minds of his countrymen a proper understanding of the principles of design represented by the classic orders of architecture. Since then, architects, working in the English tradition, have exercised a profound influence upon the form and embellishment of furniture. At first their influence was barely perceptible, becoming apparent only

[1] Two editions of *The School of Recreation* were published in 1710, without a frontispiece or illustrations, but an edition in 1732 includes the frontispiece of the 1684 edition. A later edition, published in 1736, has a completely different frontispiece, showing an outdoor scene.

when furniture makers in the latter part of the 17th century used some architectural features appositely, such as correctly proportioned Tuscan columns for the legs of a table, or the elegant profile of an Ionic cornice for the moulded detail of a cabinet. The direction of the carver and the cabinet maker by the architect became an accepted practice, which developed into a mutually stimulative form of partnership during the 18th century; and this practice had its beginnings even before Sir Christopher Wren had provided, in St. Paul's Cathedral and elsewhere, a majestic framework within whose limits the genius of Grinling Gibbons discovered such a happy exuberance of expression.

Early in the 18th century, architect and craftsman were united in the person of William Kent, the coach-painter's apprentice who became a master architect and a master decorator. He designed complete interiors; and his furniture fitted into, and was part of, an ornate background: when separated from that background—taken out of the context, as it were—individual pieces seem ornamentally overpowering, such as the marble-topped side table shown on page 329. Because Kent's furniture is as conspicuously decorative as the clothes of a gentleman of the period it has often been misjudged by critics who forget that it was once harmoniously adjusted to a nobly proportioned room. William Hogarth has depicted the splendour of one of these rooms by Kent, in his painting of the Assembly at Wanstead House, executed about 1740, and now in the John Howard McFadden Collection in the Philadelphia Museum of Art. Wanstead House, demolished in 1824, was designed by Colin Campbell. Hogarth's work reveals many aspects of contemporary furnishing, in such humble examples as the room shown in 'The Sleeping Housewife', which is ascribed to him, and the more elaborate interiors of the familiar series of prints like 'Marriage à la Mode' and 'The Industrious 'Prentice'. It is disappointing that one of the projected subjects of the latter series, showing the industrious 'prentice married and furnishing his house, was not engraved: it remained in the pen-and-ink stage, and the various articles of furniture are only sketchily indicated.[1]

The second plate of 'Marriage à la Mode' shows how completely the character of the mid-18th century interior was controlled by the architect, whose taste influenced the design of everything that went into those spacious rooms. The Georgian architects excelled in the selection and use of ornament: the discipline of correct proportion, exercised by the rules for harmonising horizontal and vertical elements, conferred upon their buildings, inside and out-

[1] This sketch, the property of the Marquess of Exeter, is reproduced in Paul Oppé's excellent monograph on *The Drawings of William Hogarth* (London: Phaidon Press Ltd., 1948).

side, a bland serenity: and as cabinet makers and chair makers drew upon the same classical treasury for the ornamentation of their work, and revered and thoroughly understood the rules which governed the practice of architecture, the relationship between architecture and furniture design was everywhere happily apparent.

Cabinet makers may occasionally have enjoyed the advantages of an architectural training; and it seems likely that Richard Gillow, one of the three sons of Robert Gillow who founded the great Lancaster firm of cabinet makers, had such training, for he was an accomplished architect, and designed the Customs House at Lancaster. It is an elegant little building, with a fine portico in the Roman Ionic order, with angular capitals on the columns.

Occasionally architects recorded their ideas about furniture design, and in beautifully engraved plates showed their interest in cabinet making; but that interest was usually conditioned by their approach to the problem, which they thought of in terms of architectural design. The contribution that could be made by the cabinet maker was apt to be disregarded: not that his skill was ignored, but he was thought of as a clever interpreter and seldom as a collaborator. This attitude of mind is apparent in the series of designs by Batty Langley, engraved on copper plates and dated 1739, which included interior architecture and furniture—bookcases, chests, and the like. These designs have a slightly monumental air; no cabinet maker could have conceived them; and they are typical products of the drawing board. Possibly Langley's ideas were influenced by Kent's more massive types of furniture; for even Kent often seemed to forget that what he was designing was to be executed in wood and not in stone, while on paper Langley's larger pieces suggest masonry rather than cabinet making, as shown by the illustrations on pages 58 and 59. Four hundred of Langley's designs, occupying one hundred and eighty-six plates, were published in book form in 1750, with the title of: *The Builder's and Workman's Treasury of Designs: or the Art of Drawing and Working the Ornamental Parts of Architecture.*

Another architect, William Jones, published and sold at his London house in 1739 a collection of copper-plate engravings in book form, entitled: *The Gentlemens or Builders Companion, Containing Variety of Useful Designs for Doors, Gateways, Peers, Pavilions, Temples, Chimney-pieces, Slab Tables, Pier Glasses, or Tabernacle Frames, Ceiling Pieces, etc.* The designs are very sketchy, and appear to be the architect's rough notes, casually jotted down, for the guidance of joiners and cabinet makers. The furniture includes a table with hoof feet surmounted by strange, bearded masks; and the ornamentation of this and of the five other marble topped slab tables given in the plates suggests Roman prototypes.

 [contd. on page 56.

Many of Hogarth's prints showed contemporary furnishing, and the second Plate in his series, 'Marriage à la Mode', is rich in examples. Above, is the chimneypiece with its crowd of ornaments and the antique marble bust, and to the left is a complicated girandole (*see* detail on page 56), which includes a clock. A fire screen, a stool, and a pillar-and-claw table also appear. The date is 1745, and the chairs that appear in the print still have cabriole legs, although they are clumsy in form. The continuation of the scene is shown on the opposite page. (From Plate II of 'Marriage à la Mode', printed and published by William Hogarth, and engraved by B. Baron, April 1st, 1745.)

This gives a close-up view of one of the chairs, and in the background there are card tables with rather corpulent cabriole legs. On the pages that follow, details are given of the girandole and the chandelier. (From Plate II of 'Marriage à la Mode', printed and published by William Hogarth, and engraved by B. Baron, April 1st, 1745.)

Detail of ornate girandole with clock, shown on the left of the chimneypiece in Plate II of 'Marriage à la Mode'. (*See* page 54.)

Incidentally, the fragments of Romano-British table legs preserved
in the Dorset County Museum at Dorchester, with their claw feet
and cabriole form, and the heads of animals carved above the knee,
could easily be mistaken for parts of some table designed by an
English architect in the mid-18th century.[1]

In 1744 John Vardy published in book form *Some Designs by
Mr Inigo Jones and Mr Wm. Kent*, and the plates included some
of Kent's lavishly decorated furniture. (Some illustrations from
this book are reproduced in Section III under the entries Lion
Mahogany and Marble Table, pages 318 and 328.) As copybooks
multiplied, the influence of the architect extended, for all these
early works on furniture and architectural design came from architects. Thomas Chippendale, the first English cabinet maker to
publish a book, did not issue *The Gentleman and Cabinet Maker's
Director* until 1754. Even in remote country districts, builders and

[*contd. on p. 58.*

[1] A detailed description with illustrations of these table legs is given by Joan
Liversage in a well-documented article on 'Tables in Roman Britain', published in
Antiquity, Vol. XXIV, No. 93, pp. 25-9.

Detail of chandelier, from Plate II of 'Marriage à la Mode'.
(*See* page 55.)

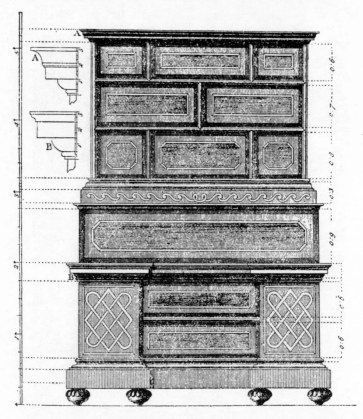

Chest of drawers designed by Batty Langley. Like the Tuscan bookcase on page 59, this shows a fundamental disregard of the properties of wood. (From one of the plates in Batty Langley's book, *The City and Country Builder's and Workman's Treasury of Designs*, 1739.)

makers of furniture shared the prevailing respect for the classic orders and their proportions and ornamentation; though obviously there was a time-lag in taste, and no refurnishing for the sake of fashion except on the part of the nobility and gentry who could well afford it: the interior of the farmhouse, the cottage, and the country tavern would be much the same in the mid-18th century as it had been a hundred years earlier.

The gratifying tyranny of fashion was never questioned by the modish, and one of the great assets of the architect's control over design was the establishment of universal understanding of good proportions, as well as respect for them. Because of this, not only architects, but cabinet makers, joiners, carvers, and other craftsmen, were able to accommodate the innumerable eccentricities

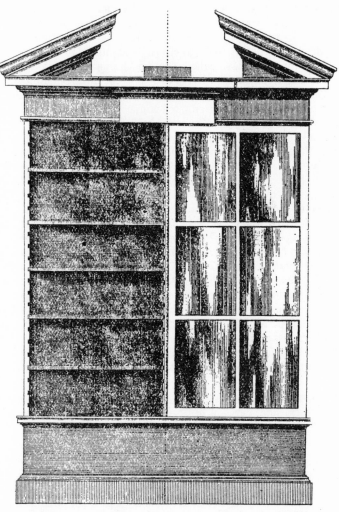

A Tuscan bookcase designed by Batty Langley. Monumental in conception, this seems to be designed for execution in stone rather than wood. (From one of the plates in Batty Langley's book, *The City and Country Builder's and Workman's Treasury of Designs*, 1739.)

of fashionable taste without malforming the shapes of furniture, as the Elizabethan craftsmen, unenlightened by rules and merely copying alien patterns of ornament, had malformed them. Thus, the recurrent waves of taste for Oriental ideas and the genteel interest in romantic Gothic forms, displayed in the middle years of the 18th century, were graciously accommodated.

The interest in so-called Gothic design began long before Horace Walpole had started to embellish his 'little plaything house' at Strawberry Hill. The growth of the taste for Gothic architecture and ornament, and its attenuated connection with mediaeval work, have been traced by Sir Kenneth Clark in his comprehensive study of the subject, *The Gothic Revival*.[1] These waves of taste washed over the fashionable world periodically. Sometimes architects supplied a few exiguous directions for keeping their extravagance in hand; for example, Batty Langley attempted to formalise the taste for Gothic by inventing some unfortunate orders, which he published in 1747 in a book ponderously entitled: *Gothic Architecture, Improved by Rules and Proportions, In many Grand Designs of Columns, Doors, Windows, Chimney-pieces, Arcades, Colonades, Porticos, Umbrellos, Temples and Pavillions, etc., with Plans, Elevations and Profiles, Geometrically Expressed.* The last twenty-five plates of *The Builder's Director or Bench-Mate*, which he published in 1751, were devoted to Gothic details, including six designs for chimneypieces which suggested a pre-view of the Victorian period. The transitory nature of these fashions is indicated by a contribution to *The World* on the subject of 'Taste', which appeared on March 22nd, 1753, and is attributed to William Whitehead, who was appointed the poet-laureate in 1757.

A few years ago everything was Gothic; our houses, our beds, our bookcases, and our couches, were all copied from some parts or other of our old cathedrals. The Grecian architecture, where, as Dryden says,

> Firm Doric pillars found the lower base,
> The gay Corinthian holds the higher space,
> And all below is strength, and all above is grace,[2]

that architecture, which was taught by nature and polished by the graces, was totally neglected. Tricks and conceits got possession every where. Clumsy buttresses were to shock you with disproportion; or little pillars were to support vast weights; while ignorant people, who knew nothing of centers of gravity, were to tremble at their entrance into every building, lest the roofs should fall upon their heads. This, however odd

[*contd. on page 63.*

[1] Constable & Co., 1928.
[2] In Dryden's 'Epistle to Congreve', this is rendered:

> Firm Doric pillars found your solid base,
> The fair Corinthian crowns the higher space,
> Thus all below is strength, and all above is grace.

Interior of a mid-18th century tavern. This shows the crude odds and ends that were used for furnishing the public rooms of a low-grade inn. The table with its baluster legs and clumsy stretcher is a design that belongs to the previous century; though such patterns continued to be made by country craftsmen long after they had been discarded in towns, where fashions were followed with greater attention. (From the frontispiece of the 10th edition of *The Adventures of Roderick Random*, Vol. II, 1778.)

The characteristic designs of Chippendale and his contemporaries appear in this interior, which is the setting of Scene I, Act V, of Benjamin Hoadly's comedy, *The Suspicious Husband*, with Mrs Baddeley taking the part of Mrs Strictland. (From a contemporary engraving, published July 6th, 1776.)

it might seem, and unworthy of the name of Taste, was cultivated, was admired, and still has its professors in different parts of England. There is something, they say, in it congenial to our old Gothic constitution; I should rather think to our modern idea of liberty, which allows every one the privilege of playing the fool, and of making himself ridiculous in whatever way he pleases.

According to the present prevailing whim, every thing is Chinese, or in the Chinese taste: or, as it is sometimes more modestly expressed, 'partly after the Chinese manner'. Chairs, tables, chimney-pieces, frames for looking-glasses, and even our most vulgar utensils, are all reduced to this new-fangled standard. . . .[1]

In one of his frivolous assessments of the abilities of his fore-runners and contemporaries, Horace Walpole wrote (in a letter to Sir Horace Mann, April 22nd, 1775): 'As Vanbrugh dealt in quarries and Kent in lumber, Adam, our most admired, is all gingerbread, filigraine and fan painting'. This was grossly unfair to designers of the calibre of Robert and James Adam, whose firm-ness of touch gave an incisive significance to the delicate ornament which they employed. This was apparent in the carved decoration they used on mahogany furniture; apparent too, in their control over the decorative situation, so to speak, even in the most pro-fusely ornamental examples of their work. Ornament was chosen to give point to the proportions, subtly to emphasise lines and masses; and, as usual, the approach to the problem was essentially an architectural approach. It would have been impossible for people of fashion, apart altogether from architects or craftsmen, to have tolerated in the middle years of the 18th century the casual lavishness that occasionally marred the ornamentation of furniture in the closing years of the previous century. They would never have given house room to many of the things that were made or im-ported in the reigns of William and Mary and Queen Anne. For example, they would have rejected the clumsy roundabout chairs —the so-called burgomaster chairs—made in the East Indies by the Dutch, and sold in England and Europe in large numbers during the late 17th and early 18th centuries. Compare the illus-tration of one of these chairs on the following page with the most extravagant of Chippendale's designs, which appear on pages 84 to 107, or his ribband back chair shown on page 393, and observe the difference between trained imagination, that has embellish-ment under control, and the almost primitive enthusiasm which carves for the sake of carving. Differences in nationality or struc-ture do not account for the missing sense of fitness in the use and placing of ornament on the roundabout chair.

In the half century between the Queen Anne period and the publication of Chippendale's book, chair making and cabinet making had been progressively refined, as architectural design had

[1] Edition of 1794, Vol. I, p. 52.

Roundabout or Burgomaster chair: *circa* 1690–1710. Chairs of this type were imported from the Dutch East Indies and sold in Holland and other parts of Europe, and in England. (*See* entry on page 398.) Compare the design and ornamentation of this chair with the designs reproduced from Chippendale's *Director* on pages 84 to 107, and on 393. (This illustration is from Shaw's *Specimens of Ancient Furniture*.)

been refined in the previous century; and this was because the will of the architect-designer was increasingly imposed upon the chair maker and cabinet maker, without ever flouting the canons of good craftsmanship. No Georgian architect made the craftsman wholly subservient to the drawing board; nor were the materials he used expected to perform the impossible at the expense of their capacity for endurance.

Throughout the 18th century the recognisable effect of the architect's influence on furniture design was a sureness of touch in embellishment; for behind the choice, form, and placing of all ornament was the knowledge of good proportion, of work conceived and executed in what Sir Christopher Wren had called a 'good Roman manner'. In America, Samuel McIntire, the Salem architect, gave to his clients that same sureness of touch that distinguished the work of the brothers Adam. McIntire, like every architect whose imagination was disciplined by study of the classic orders, knew his proportions; and knew exactly how to begin and where to stop. Following his own characteristic forms of decoration, he used delicate, floral motifs, with such discretion that even a critic as fastidious as Horace Walpole would have abjured the finicking complaint that it was 'all gingerbread, filigraine and fan painting'. Some of the refinements of form associated with the Greek revival are apparent in Samuel McIntire's work, notably in his choice of carved ornament for sofas and couches, although he did not use Greek motifs. McIntire in America, like the brothers Adam in England, and Batty Langley and William Kent before them, all demonstrated how well an architectural training endows the mind of an imaginative designer with fine conceptions for furniture.

Remove the discipline of an architectural training based upon the study of the classic orders, and replace it with enthusiasms generated by the spurious romanticism of the 19th century Gothic revival, and you get monumental furniture indeed—furniture that reflects a basic inability to observe, to compare, or to absorb anything with predictable results. Just over a century after the publication of Batty Langley's book of heavy but orderly designs, a young Victorian architect committed to paper a bureau bookcase, or, as it was described, a bookcase with writing table. It was made of oak, and was shown at the International Exhibition held in 1862. (See illustration on page 66.) Its designer was the future architect of London's Police Headquarters at New Scotland Yard, and his name was Norman Shaw. Architects at that time in the 19th century had their minds filled with a rag-bag of ideas: tattered bits of Gothic ornament were jumbled against scraps from Byzantine and Saracenic buildings; and as architectural training and taste had sunk back into a period of chaos far worse than that

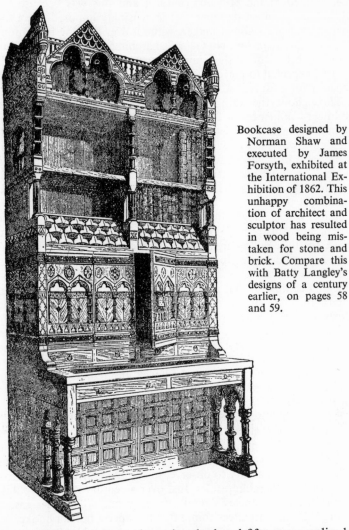

Bookcase designed by Norman Shaw and executed by James Forsyth, exhibited at the International Exhibition of 1862. This unhappy combination of architect and sculptor has resulted in wood being mistaken for stone and brick. Compare this with Batty Langley's designs of a century earlier, on pages 58 and 59.

from which it was rescued two hundred and fifty years earlier by Inigo Jones, it was hardly surprising that furniture should display an infinite complexity of form and that good proportions should be wholly abandoned. After all, Ruskin was praising chaos in splendid words and calling it a new revelation; and William Morris was beginning to weave his way back to the Middle Ages. The classic orders of architecture and all that they implied were denigrated by the pundits of good taste. Architects had lost their respect for the orders; many of them had either forgotten or were unaware that those orders represented a great and comprehensive system of design; and as manufacturers and craftsmen had lost their respect for the architectural profession, the form and character of the things that were made for the furnishing and equipment of houses were no longer regulated and seldom affected in any way by the judgment and taste of men with trained imaginations who had formerly been the master designers. It became impossible to give fashionable taste any harmonious relationship with the form of furniture, particularly as the predominating fashion was determined by a moral outlook rather than a modish whim. The Gothic revival, that gathered strength and became all powerful during the first half of the 19th century, was preached as a crusade against the pagan order and beauty of classical architecture by such men as Pugin, whose ardour as a crusader was almost pathological. Gothic revivalists of the Pugin and Ruskin type were morbidly earnest; and because they identified design with religious emotion, they succeeded in giving emotional instability to contemporary taste in place of the standards that previously had guided the judgment of designers and their patrons. It took time to break down the disciplined sense of order which governed design; for there had been a resurgence of interest in classical architecture in the second half of the 18th century, encouraged by the work and influence of the brothers Adam, and this affected both the form and decoration of furniture. In the middle of the seventeen-nineties, the Greek and neo-Greek revivals began, and developed during the opening decades of the 19th century. The writings and designs of Thomas Hope (1770–1831) nourished this fresh interest in classical prototypes; and in 1807 he published a volume entitled *Household Furniture and Interior Decoration*, illustrated with his own drawings, in which he used Roman and Egyptian motifs in his schemes for furnishing. Hope was a wealthy and gifted amateur of architecture; and had travelled extensively in Europe, Asia, and Africa in order to study ancient buildings. His travels supplied him with materials for a novel called *Anastasius*, which was published anonymously in 1819 and caused a great sensation. Of this work Sydney Smith wrote: 'Is this Mr Thomas Hope?—Is this the man of chairs and tables? —the gentleman of the sphinxes—the Œdipus of coalboxes— he who has meditated on muffineers and planned pokers,—Where has he hidden all this eloquence and poetry up to this hour?' He was nicknamed 'Anastasius' Hope, though his influence on contemporary taste makes 'the gentleman of the sphinxes' a far better label. 'From an infant, architecture was always my favourite amusement', he wrote; and his devotion to the subject had a marked effect upon the design and character of furnishing in England during the Regency period.

A few years before Hope's book appeared, Sheraton had given detailed directions for the contents of various types of rooms in *The Cabinet Dictionary* (1803), under the entry for Furnishing. These he set forth with the confidence of Vitruvius, who, two thousand years earlier, had specified in the sixth book of his work on architecture, the forms of houses suited to different ranks of people, and the character and function of the rooms, with their appropriate arrangement and furnishing.[1] Both Sheraton and Vitruvius were writing for a settled and orderly society; their thoughts and ideas were regulated by the acknowledged supremacy of architectural design, and both the Roman architect and the English furniture designer revered the same prototypes. Sheraton, in the opening paragraph of his entry for Furnishing, hinted at the existence of pretentious and vulgar taste, and suggested how it could be discreetly circumvented. He said that 'when any gentleman is so vain and ambitious as to order the furnishing of his house in a style superior to his fortune and rank, it will be prudent in an upholsterer, by some gentle hints, to direct his choice to a more moderate plan'.[2]

Over forty years earlier Ince and Mayhew had concluded their preface to *The Universal System of Household Furniture* by saying: 'In Furnishing all should be with Propriety—Elegance should always be joined with a peculiar Neatness through the whole House, or otherwise an immense Expense may be thrown away to no Purpose, either in Use or Appearance; and with the same Regard any Gentleman may furnish as neat at a small Expense, as he can elegant and superb at a great one'.

Such warnings against excessive lavishness were apparently necessary; and in the 18th and early 19th centuries they were taken to heart. In his directions for furnishing a house, Sheraton advocates fitness and moderation, though his published designs often belied this advice. He wrote with the confidence of a designer who was serving a society that was accustomed to formal behaviour, and was not ashamed or in any way apologetic about the time it gave to the pursuit of pleasure. After dealing with the kitchen, the library, the gallery, the music room, and entrance hall, he described the principal living rooms.

The dining parlour must be furnished with nothing trifling, or which may seem unnecessary, it being appropriated for the chief repast, and should not be encumbered with any article that would seem to intrude on the accommodation of the guests.

The large sideboard, inclosed or surrounded with Ionic pillars: the handsome and extensive dining-table; the respectable and substantial looking chairs; the large face glass; the family portraits; the marble fire-places; and the Wilton carpet; are the furniture that should supply the dining-room.

[1] Chapters viii, ix, and x.   [2] *The Cabinet Dictionary*, pp. 215-16.

The mid-Victorian bedroom was filled with an incoherent assembly of flimsy furniture, and a few reproductions of the less attractive examples of 18th century French designs. (From *The Young Ladies' Treasure Book*.)

The drawing-room is to concentrate the elegance of the whole house, and is the highest display of richness of furniture. It being appropriated to the formal visits of the highest in rank, and nothing of a scientific nature should be introduced to take up the attention of any individual, from the general conversation that takes place on such occasions. Hence, the walls should be free of pictures, the tables not lined with books, nor the angles of the room filled with globes; as the design of such meetings are not that each visitant should turn to his favourite study, but to contribute his part towards the amusement of the whole company. The grandeur then introduced into the drawing-room is not to be considered, as the ostentatious parade of its proprietor, but the respect he pays to the rank of his visitants.

The anti-room, is an introduction to the drawing-room, and partakes of the elegance of the apartment to which it leads, serving as a place of repose before the general intercourse be effected in the whole company. Here may be placed a number of sofas of a second order with a piano-forte or harp, and other matters of amusement till the whole of the company be collected.

The tea-room or breakfast-room, may abound with beaufets, painted chairs, flower-pot stands, hanging book shelves or moving libraries, and the walls may be adorned with landscapes, and pieces of drawings, etc. and all the little things which are engaging to the juvenile mind.[1]

The transition from orderly furnishing with well made articles of good design, to incoherent assemblies of ill designed and often flimsy pieces of furniture of the kind shown in the bedroom interior on the preceding page, occurred within fifty years of the publication of *The Cabinet Dictionary*. The Gothic revival had helped to destroy good standards of design; and the great increase in the use of machinery had debilitated standards of workmanship; but an enormous reserve of skill remained among woodworkers, and an enterprising, experimental spirit existed among those much-abused but able and courageous manufacturers in the Midlands, who were always seeking fresh uses for the comparatively new industrial materials. In some branches of the woodworking industry mass production had long been established, and was conducted with great ability in such a furniture-making locality as High Wycombe, in Buckinghamshire, where thousands of Windsor chairs were made. The entries in Section III for Windsor Chair and White Wycombe record the ramifications of this traditional craft, and show how the use of turned and bentwood members antici-pated the technique of mass production.

Although it was not appreciated at the time, the mid-19th century was a period of experimental design in furniture, both in England and America. The history of the rocking chair, of which some details are given under that entry in Section III, reveals the influence of new materials upon design. The use of metal, and then of bentwood, changed the characteristic appearance of the

[1] *The Cabinet Dictionary*, pp. 218-19.

Bentwood table in rosewood and walnut, designed and shown by Michael Thonet at the Great Exhibition of 1851. (From *The Art Journal Illustrated Catalogue.*)

rocking chair, which began as an ordinary ladder back chair, mounted like a cradle on rockers; and this original type has retained its popularity in the United States to this day. In England, rocking chairs with flat bent strips of iron or brass were made during the eighteen-forties and -fifties; and a few years later the bentwood rocking chair was introduced by a Viennese designer, Michael Thonet, who had made bentwood chairs and underframes for tables, and whose work was shown at the Great Exhibition of 1851. A bentwood table by Thonet, which is illustrated on this page, was included in the catalogue of the Exhibition published by *The Art Journal*. The top, which was elaborately inlaid with woods of various colours, covered a receptacle 'of a semispherical form' which had 'some peculiarities of construction'. The table was described as follows: 'It is formed of rosewood, so bent that the grain of the wood invariably follows the line of the curve and shape required, by which means lightness and elasticity is gained with the least possible material. The legs are similarly bent from the solid piece. . . .' [1]

[1] *The Art Journal Illustrated Catalogue*, p. 296.

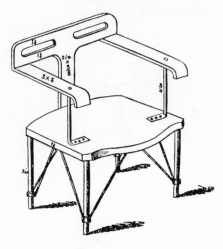

An elbow chair for a kitchen, in cast iron, with a wooden seat. Designed by Robert Mallet, and illustrated in Loudon's *Encyclopaedia* (published in 1833). Compare this with the chair with tubular iron legs, by the same designer, shown on page 333.

The unsuspected progenitors of designs that seem to belong to the mid-20th century are occasionally to be found in the illustrated records of the 1851 Exhibition; but earlier still, in the pages of Loudon's *Encyclopaedia of Cottage, Farm and Villa Architecture and Furniture*, which was published in 1833, there are some experimental suggestions for chairs in wood and cast iron which show a modern approach to the use of materials and an unusual independence of prototypes. Of these, two designs for chairs by Robert Mallet (1810–81), a young Dublin engineer, display an innovating audacity, for the form is unrelated to any traditional model, and represents a fresh solution to a problem, achieved with a new combination of materials, and an objective regard for function and economy of means. Both chairs have wooden seats supported by legs of cast iron; and amid the pseudo-Gothic chairs which throng the pages of Loudon's *Encyclopaedia*, they are as startling as Marcel Breuer's cantilever chairs of steel tubing seemed at the end of the nineteen-twenties. The accompanying illustration shows what Mallet called an elbow kitchen chair, and which he described as follows: 'The back and elbows are cast in one piece; the supports for the elbows and also the legs are of gas tubing, screwed into a cross frame of iron, which proceeds from the back of the chair under the wooden seat.' [1] Mallet's second design was a round-seated chair, with three tubular legs of cast iron. (*See* illus-

[1] *The Encyclopaedia of Cottage, Farm and Villa Architecture and Furniture*, by J. C. Loudon (London: Longman, Rees, Orme, Brown, Green & Longman, 1833). P. 320, description of Fig. 650. The designer, Robert Mallet, was the son of John Mallet, a Devonshire man who had settled in Dublin as an iron, brass, and copper founder. In 1831 Robert was made a partner in his father's business, and subsequently became a famous engineer. He was made a Fellow of the Royal Society in 1854.

tration in Section III under the entry Metal Furniture, on page 333.) It is significant that the designer of these chairs was an engineer; and although the term was then unknown, he was really an industrial designer.

Inventions and new uses for materials seldom came from within the furniture manufacturing industry that had grown up during the first half of the 19th century. The manufacturers had inherited from the cabinet makers and chair makers of the Georgian age a traditional loyalty to timber; their technique of production was based upon the use of that abundant and convenient material; and all their machinery was woodworking machinery. Experiments in metal furniture were made chiefly by Birmingham manufacturers; and during the eighteen-thirties, as a result of improved methods of joining metal parts, the metal bedstead industry was established in that city, and it rapidly expanded.[1] Vast quantities of metal bedsteads were made in innumerable patterns; and this branch of the furniture industry remained separate from the rest of the trade, which depended primarily on the use of wood.

By the middle of the 19th century, the furniture industry was producing cheap cabinet work and upholstery; and machine-made bedroom and dining-room suites and parlour furniture went into the new, cheap, jerry-built houses that were pushed out in rows along the roads of new suburbs. The better class cabinet makers and chair makers continued to invent variations on Gothic and what were called 'Old English' patterns and French designs. The variety of sources from which they drew their ideas is shown in the copybooks which were in use; and the interest in 'Old English' furniture, and particularly in so-called 'Elizabethan' furniture, was greatly enlarged by the publication in 1836 of the first modern book on old furniture, Henry Shaw's *Specimens of Ancient Furniture*. Other books on old furniture began to appear, and one that soon followed Shaw's was a conglomeration of designs for furniture based on old models, and a few carefully recorded drawings of authentic examples. It was published in London by William Pickering in 1838, and was entitled *Furniture with Candelabra and Interior Decoration*, the subjects being 'designed' by R. Bridgens. Twenty-five of the plates were in 'the Grecian Style', twenty-five in 'the Elizabethan Style', and seven in 'the Gothic Style'. (A Gothic sideboard from this book is shown on page 272.) For example, Plate 37 included detailed drawings of a table in the Great Hall at Penshurst Place, and a table in the Chapter Room of Christ Church Cathedral, Oxford: both authentic late 16th century

[1] The swiftness of its growth is described in *The Industrial Development of Birmingham and the Black Country*, by G. C. Allen (London: George Allen & Unwin Ltd. 1929). Chapter I, p. 60. According to Loudon's *Encyclopaedia* (p. 331, sect. 656) thousands of iron half-tester bedsteads were made in Dublin by William Mallet (Robert Mallet's uncle) as early as 1833.

examples. Such accurate representations of old furniture were followed and preceded by plates devoted to fantastic, hybrid abominations, masquerading as 'Elizabethan' designs. Books such as these provided the furniture trade with a lot of confusing material; and they also gave the collector of old furniture an assortment of misinformation, which helped the dealer in old furniture to sell plausible rubbish that had a venerable look—even Shaw's book contained some doctored examples, of which one is reproduced in the previous Section, on page 16.

The French models that were used by the furniture trade were either copied from contemporary designs or from the fashions of the pre-Revolutionary period, thus qualifying for the equivocal label of 'the Louis style'. Not only French influence survived from the 18th century: many of the English books of designs remained in use, and in particular *The Prices of Cabinet Work*, which had first appeared in 1788 as *The Cabinet-Makers' London Book of Prices*, and had included designs by Hepplewhite and Shearer. This went through various editions, and many of the original designs or modifications of them were retained, and the book stayed in print during the 19th century. In cabinet work, but principally in chair making, the influence of Thomas Chippendale's published designs persisted, and the ghosts of his chairs haunted the whole of the Victorian period. The third edition of *The Gentleman and Cabinet Maker's Director*, and its various reprints and adaptations, became one of the indispensable copybooks of the furniture trade. (At the end of this Section, twenty-four pages are occupied by examples of Chippendale's chair designs, which appeared in the third edition of the *Director*.)

Furniture making became associated with certain well-defined localities: in London, the trade was concentrated in and around Shoreditch, though when Sheraton made his list of cabinet makers, upholsterers, and chair makers in 1803, only a few names appear with addresses in that district—the majority being then settled in Soho, and in the neighbourhood of Golden Square, St. Martin's Lane, Long Acre, and further west in Mayfair and north along Oxford Street. Many of the firms listed by Sheraton were both makers and retailers; and one of the few for whom he gives a Shoreditch address, J. Cockerill's japanned-chair manufactory in Curtain Road, also had a west end branch at 203 Oxford Street. The separation of manufacturing from selling became a characteristic of the furniture trade after the opening decades of the 19th century; for with the new methods of mechanical production, it was no longer economical to make furniture on a large scale and sell it on the same premises; though the retailer generally maintained a small cabinet and upholstery shop, where a few special articles were made and repairs carried out for his customers. This

change in the commercial structure of the trade led to the development of big factories, grouped in a few areas, so that the manufacturers gradually lost touch with the public, and the professional
buyers who acted for the retail houses eventually became the
arbiters of design.

Outside London, High Wycombe was the chief chair-making
centre, and furniture manufacturing was well established in Manchester and in many adjacent Lancashire towns, and in the west
country at Bath and Bristol, while the principal Scottish centre was
Beith, in Ayrshire. Throughout the countryside, small makers and
rural craftsmen maintained a precarious independence, and prolonged the life of the old wood-working traditions; but they
worked without guidance or example in design, and their independence diminished as large scale production was organised with
ever increasing efficiency.

Comparable changes occurred in the United States during the
first half of the 19th century; making and retailing became recognised as separate functions; and a great manufacturing centre
grew up at Grand Rapids, in Kent County, Michigan. This was
originally an Indian village, and its industrial history began in
1833 with the building of a sawmill.

The first effect of machine production on furniture was to debase
its quality: its design had already been debased, partly by the
Gothic revival, but more thoroughly by the general decay of taste.
Certainly there were many experiments, but they seldom led to
anything except increases in a rather wallowing kind of comfort.
The elimination of elegance was typical of this pursuit of comfort,
which was eagerly led by the upholsterers of the Victorian period,
and the results were aptly described at the very end of that period
in Rosamund Marriott Watson's book, *The Art of the House*. Of
that typical Victorian invention, the Chesterfield, she wrote: 'An
indirect descendant of the Empire sofa, with the comfort kept, but
all the grace left out, is the obese, kindly-natured couch known to
modern upholsterers as the Chesterfield. It is about as comely as a
gigantic pin-cushion, and as little convenient in a room of moderate
dimensions as an elephant; plethoric and protuberant with springs
and stuffings, it is at best a tiresome piece of goods, decoratively
worse than useless, and not so very easeful after all.' [1]

The possibilities of using materials in new ways that were suggested by the tentative designs of inventive people like Robert
Mallet lay dormant: they were hardly ever explored by English
makers of domestic furniture. A new movement in design was beginning, and in architecture it found its most spectacular expression
in Joseph Paxton's use of prefabricated cast iron units and glass

[1] *The Art of the House*, by Rosamund Marriott Watson (London: George Bell
and Sons, 1897). Chapter v, p. 75.

in the Crystal Palace; but this new technique of architectural design was largely ignored. Architects and furniture designers were preoccupied with the past, and Pugin's Mediaeval Court at the Great Exhibition encouraged a fresh enthusiasm for Gothic forms and ornament.

Even when William Morris attempted to arrest the decay of English handicrafts, and to re-establish good standards of craftsmanship, the movement he started was a revival, inspired by the work of the Middle Ages; and even if he was conscious of the stirrings of a new movement in design, he disregarded it, and rejected the new materials and industrial techniques that were seldom used imaginatively in architecture and the allied arts. His splendid and quite stupendous personal creative powers did not respond to the challenge and promise of contemporary industry; and his handicraft revival seriously retarded the development of industrial design in England by confusing the whole subject. In the making of furniture, he inspired a few artist-craftsmen, like Ernest Gimson and Sidney Barnsley, whose work ultimately affected the furniture industry; for the artist-craftsman has done and still does research work in design, though its scope is limited to the use of traditional materials, for Gimson, like Morris, repudiated contemporary materials and industrial methods.

Gimson was outspokenly frank about the intentional segregation of the handicraft revival from contemporary commercial and industrial life. His belief that industrial technique was incompatible with the arts and crafts was recorded in the essay contributed by A. H. Powell to the memorial volume, published in 1924 under the title of *Ernest Gimson: his Life and Work*.[1] 'He desired commercialism might leave handiwork and the arts alone and make use of its own wits and its own machinery', Powell wrote. 'Let machinery be honest, he said, and make its own machine-buildings and its own machine-furniture; let it make its chairs and tables of stamped aluminium if it likes: why not?'

Only the trained imagination of the industrial designer could give such honesty of purpose to machinery in the production of furniture; and the handicraft revival, apart from allowing a small number of gifted artist-craftsmen to express their personal preference for economic and aesthetic isolation, delayed the advent of the industrial designer and implanted doubts and prejudices in the minds of manufacturers about his proper function. That revival, by putting an emphasis on the personal skill of the craftsman, caused 'hand-made' things to become fashionable in the second half of the 19th century, so that woodwork was left with rough and unfinished surfaces, and metal was speckled with hammer marks, mechanically impressed: and as the thoughts of

[1] London: Ernest Benn, Ltd. Oxford: Basil Blackwell.

the artistically modish turned back with romantic relish to 'the good old times' and the 'good old craftsmen', singing away as they carved and wove and painted this and that, the already prosperous branch of the furniture trade which dealt in antiques, genuine and otherwise, received an additional fillip, for it was so exciting to buy and so wonderful to live with furniture that was made centuries ago by such joyful workmen. What such furniture looked like was not so important; so long as it was old, and preferably of oak, it passed.

To acknowledge these unintentional results of the idealism and genius of William Morris is not to discount the excellence of his own work or that of the artist-craftsmen who followed his example. Both Ernest Gimson and Sidney Barnsley, who were for many years in partnership, had been trained as architects, and they resumed the tradition of English furniture design where it had been interrupted after the mid-17th century. Gimson's work in wood and metal always attained that ideal balance between structure and ornamentation which Morris had described as a characteristic of Popular Art when he said: 'The craftsman, as he fashioned the thing he had under his hand, ornamented it so naturally and so entirely without conscious effort, that it is often difficult to distinguish where the mere utilitarian part of his work ended and the ornamental began'.[1]

That sentence suggests how ably Morris might have practised the unification of form, function, and decorative character which is the conspicuous achievement of the modern industrial designer; but Morris and his disciples deliberately limited their power and medium of expression. Within those self-imposed limitations they originated a fresh and vigorous style of furniture, which continued an old English tradition of wood-working, mediaeval in inspiration, though far more accomplished in woodworking technique than anything made by craftsmen in the 15th, 16th, or early 17th centuries.

Artist-craftsmen of the Gimson and Barnsley school were uninfluenced by the cabinet making of the 18th century: they ignored the long golden age of design achieved under the direction of architects; and they were unsympathetic with the idea of such orderly control. Among the artist-craftsmen who worked in the late Victorian period and the opening decades of the present century, few approached the stature of Gimson; and their work frequently suffered from lack of contact with life, for many of them retired to country districts where they successfully insulated themselves from contemporary ideas. The things they made were very expensive; for a well-made thing slowly produced by hand with loving care obviously costs far more than a well-designed

[1] From the essay, 'Useful Work versus Useless Toil'.

thing rapidly produced by mechanical methods with the object of selling it in large quantities at a reasonable price. Only rich people could afford the work of the artist-craftsmen; so their influence was small in their own country, though in Europe their work was taken seriously and widely imitated, to such an extent that it has since been assumed by many people that all modern furniture design originated in France, Germany, Austria, or Scandinavia. Many of the pioneers of modern furniture design were architects: and apart from Gimson, who was also an executant craftsman, there were C. F. A. Voysey, C. R. Mackintosh, and George Walton. Their designs appear in the early volumes of *The Studio*, which was founded by Charles Holme in 1893, and several of them in a book published in 1901, on *Modern British Domestic Architecture and Decoration*, which Holme edited. This book includes designs by Charles Spooner, M. H. Baillie Scott, William James Neatby, Frances and Herbert McNair, G. M. Ellwood, Edgar Wood, and some of the early work of Sir Ambrose Heal, as well as furniture by Voysey, Walton, Charles Rennie Mackintosh, and Margaret Macdonald Mackintosh. (There is nothing by Gimson.) All the examples illustrated are influenced by Morris; many are affected by the characteristic motifs of *l'Art nouveau*, though the anarchical naturalistic forms of that florid Continental fashion have been used soberly and sparingly.

Of all the original designers who were at work at the beginning of this century, Ambrose Heal was the only one in the furniture trade. Designing, making, and selling furniture, and becoming the head of a large, long-established retailing business in London, his position and opportunities in the trade were unique; and his work gave coherence to the taste for simple, well-made furniture that the handicraft revival and the growing interest in the arts and crafts had fostered. The only original style in furniture that appeared in the first two decades of the 20th century was largely derived from Heal's work.

After the first war the work of a new artist-craftsman, Gordon Russell, brought fresh and vigorous character to furniture made in that English tradition of design which Gimson had resuscitated. It is always difficult to assess the effect of contemporary work; but Gordon Russell and his brother, Richard Drew Russell, have exerted an indisputable influence on the use not only of traditional but of modern materials during the second quarter of this century. Both are industrial designers, and Gordon Russell is himself an executant craftsman of a high order.

Among the leading designers of furniture who are also architects is R. W. Symonds, whose work has affinities with the 18th century makers. His furniture continues an English tradition, but not from the mid-17th century, where Gimson had resumed it:

Symonds recaptures the spirit that still activated designers at the beginning of the 19th century, before the period of decadence. Like the artist-craftsmen, he conceives designs which are to be executed in traditional materials; and although his work is original, its scope though not its originality is circumscribed, like Gimson's and the early designs of Gordon Russell, by the nature and variety of wood.

Many architects and industrial designers have experimented with furniture made from materials other than wood, or from combinations of materials. The mastery of the multitude of new materials, and the development of a coherent system of design, represent an almost intimidating array of problems for architects and designers, far exceeding in complexity those that confronted their forerunners in the mid-16th century. The solution was found then; and the 20th century, with its course half run, still awaits an Inigo Jones who will resolve the discords of functionalism and copyism by creating a new harmony of form and colour.

The study of furniture design should today include far more than the historic periods and styles which have been made familiar by so many books that have appeared since the beginning of the century. Some indication of the nature and extent of existing literature on the subject is given in Section V, but here two books should be mentioned which assess the nature and extent of the impact made by mechanical techniques and industrial materials upon the character of furniture design. Both have been published since the second war, and the first to appear was *Furniture from Machines*,[1] by Gordon Logie, an architect, who has re-examined the whole subject of furniture production and design, and based his objective survey upon careful and detailed research, personally conducted in various branches of the furniture industry. In the preface he states that the purpose of the book is 'to explore the possibilities of the machine production of furniture', and into that preface he condenses much common sense about the use and abuse of machinery; and he describes the present structure of the British furniture industry in one short paragraph, as follows: 'The furniture industry is very sharply divided into groups. There are the makers of wooden domestic furniture; the chair makers; the steel tube furniture makers; the hospital furniture specialists; the office furniture makers; the woven cane furniture makers, and so on, each intent on their own processes and difficulties. Some are bound to traditional ways and are resistant to change. Others, generally the newer branches such as the steel tube makers, are much more enterprising and are trying to extend their activities to new fields.

[1] *Furniture from Machines*, by Gordon Logie, A.R.I.B.A. (London: George Allen & Unwin, Ltd., 1947).

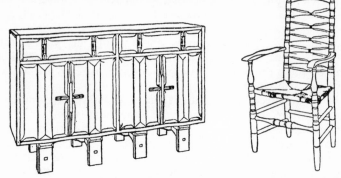

The English tradition in furniture design during the nineteen-twenties. A side-board in brown oak, and a ladder back, rush-seated chair in yew. (From designs by Gordon Russell, R.D.I.)

Intruding into all groups are the new moulded plywood and light alloy industries. . . .'

The fifteen chapters and excellent illustrations of Logie's book show that all branches of the furniture industry are remarkably well equipped with materials and mechanical techniques.

The other book is Dr Siegfried Giedion's *Mechanization takes Command*, published just over a year after *Furniture from Machines*.[1] The author describes his work as 'a contribution to anonymous history'. The humble objects that are examined in its sections have collectively 'shaken our mode of living to its very roots'; and the cumulative effect of the changes caused by the mechanisation of many forms of activity is certainly not fully apprehended by those who derive benefit, danger, or irritation from them. Dr Giedion brings into focus many diverse views and theories that have been expressed and accepted about the manifestations of mechanised industry; much in the same way that Darwin in the mid-19th century brought into focus many views and theories about natural history that had previously gained only fragmentary acceptance. Using the technique of Lewis Mumford, without resorting to that sociologist's ponderous phraseology, Dr Giedion can examine a matter exhaustively, without ever exhausting the reader. His book consists of seven sections, and in Section V the growth and changing conceptions of comfort are described, from mediaeval times to the 19th century. By tracing the evolution of various types of furniture, and the transition from handicraft to mechanical production, Dr Giedion has in this fifth section written a history of furniture with new vision. His book is erected upon a plinth of research and scholarship, and it may make some

[1] *Mechanization takes Command*, by Siegfried Giedion (Geoffrey Cumberlege, Oxford University Press, 1948).

enthusiasts for modern design feel humble, for many of the designs that have, during the last twenty-five years or so, been reverently saluted for their proud independence of tradition, are based upon some early or mid-Victorian prototype, invented in America or England. Continuity in design appears to be inescapable: and this is demonstrated by the recent history of furniture, and particularly by the development of patent and convertible furniture, which Dr Giedion deals with in a most comprehensive and illuminating manner.

These two books bring the history of furniture manufacture and the account of materials available to the manufacturer up to date.

Meanwhile, the architect is slowly regaining his control over furniture design; not only directly by designing furniture, like Wells Coates and Brian O'Rorke in Britain and Walter Dorwin Teague in America, but indirectly through the character he is giving to contemporary domestic architecture. The architect who designs housing schemes is slowly but inexorably determining the future of the furniture trade. The furniture manufacturer may think he controls his own destiny: the professional retail buyer, confident that he 'knows what the public wants', may imagine that he is the overlord of the manufacturer; and the architect is apparently quite unconscious of the ultimate effect of his work on a trade about which he knows very little. But the economic and structural tendencies in contemporary domestic building may, before long, begin to confine the activities of the furniture manufacturer to chair making and upholstery. Before the end of the century, he may be left only with control over seating, for all other forms of free-standing furniture, all receptacles, and even beds, may by then have returned to an almost mediaeval dependence upon and structural partnership with the walls of rooms.

One of the most socially significant characteristics of domestic architecture in the first half of this century is the loss of spaciousness within houses. This loss is most apparent in the vernacular architecture of the speculative builder, who has drawn his variously picturesque models from the now forgotten pattern books of the early 19th century—of which J. C. Loudon's *Encyclopaedia of Cottage, Farm and Village Architecture and Furniture* was the most comprehensive—and also from the attempts by the disciples of William Morris to re-create a native English architecture. Rooms have become mean in size, and everywhere minimum standards have gradually been imposed. Even in houses designed by architects for private individuals before 1914 and between the wars, the old Victorian and Georgian spaciousness was missing: rooms might be large, but ceilings were low.

Life within doors has consequently become narrower and more

congested than it was for our grandparents; though it was a long time before the furniture industry realised that because of this tendency the day of the monumental bedroom suite and the vast dining-room sideboard was over. At present another stage in the development of domestic architecture is being ignored by that industry, for although the size of rooms in houses has not been increased, the architect has, before and since the second war, released more floor space by filling all the odd corners and recesses that were formerly left to take care of themselves, and in those once wasted spaces he has put fitted furniture—book shelves, cupboards, wardrobes, drawers, folding tables, and even bunk beds.

The increasing use of the factory-made house, assembled from standardised, prefabricated units, must inevitably accelerate the tendency to design in advance all receptacles, fittings, and storage equipment, so that houses may perhaps be more than half furnished by the builder as they are erected. Within a couple of generations the building industry may accept as common practice the supply of all furniture other than chairs and possibly one or two tables, as it now accepts the supply of baths, lavatory basins, water closets, and sinks. This may make life a lot less troublesome for most people; although it does represent another step in the control and limitation of personal taste.

The personal taste of large numbers of people has led them to furnish their homes with assorted loot from the past, with genuine antiques or conscientious copies if they can afford them, or if they cannot, with the mechanically produced parodies of period designs hitherto offered by the furniture trade. Noel Carrington, in his essay on *Life in an English Village*,[1] has suggested that the country cottage style of furnishing, developed by the middle class settlers in villages throughout England and 'bred by the magazines of taste', is the nearest approach to a contemporary style that we possess. He considers that it is 'a very dim descendant of Petit Trianon rustic. . . .' True; but such a style is only a makeshift; a sort of camping out with odds and ends, while we await the emergence of a style that is neither a revival of something old and tried (and obsolete), nor an aridly functional assembly of materials, unadventurously disposed in minatory or repellent shapes. It may well be on the way: its lineaments may already be discernible, though as yet unrecognised. Fortunately, there is good cause for optimism. Once again the architect, through his own profession and as a practitioner of industrial design, seems likely to be restored to the position of master-designer which he enjoyed a century and a half ago, and which everybody else enjoyed too.

[1] King Penguin Books, 1949.

THE CHAIR DESIGNS OF THOMAS CHIPPENDALE

The designs on the twenty-four pages that follow are included in the third edition of *The Gentleman and Cabinet Maker's Director*, which was published in 1762. The ribband back chair shown under that entry on page 393 in the next Section, is reproduced from the first edition of the *Director*, published in 1754. Chippendale's designs eventually became ancestral types, for many of the chairs made during and after the mid-19th century were derived from the plates in the third edition of the *Director*. The models selected here for illustration include what Chippendale called 'French' chairs, also a range of chairs in the Chinese taste. (*See* page 187.)

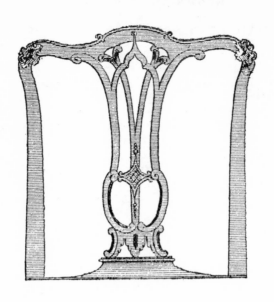

Chair backs from **Plate XVI** of Chippendale's *Director*.

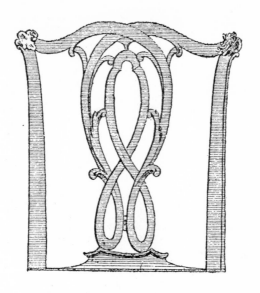

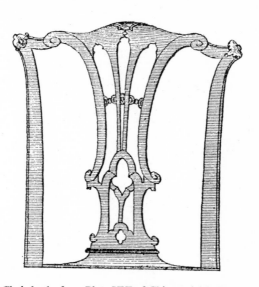

Chair backs from Plate XVI of Chippendale's *Director*.
A simplified version of the lower design appears in the scene from
The Suspicious Husband on page 62.

85

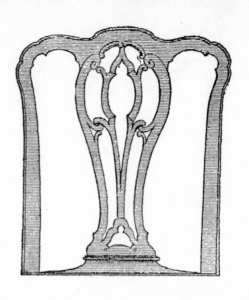

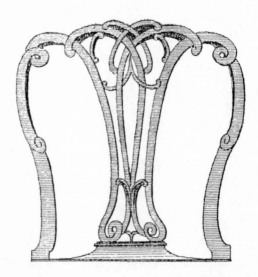

Chair backs from Plate XVI of Chippendale's *Director*.

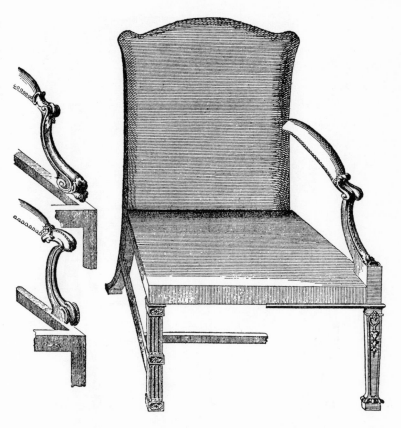

French chair from Plate XIX of Chippendale's *Director*.

French chair from Plate XIX of Chippendale's *Director*.

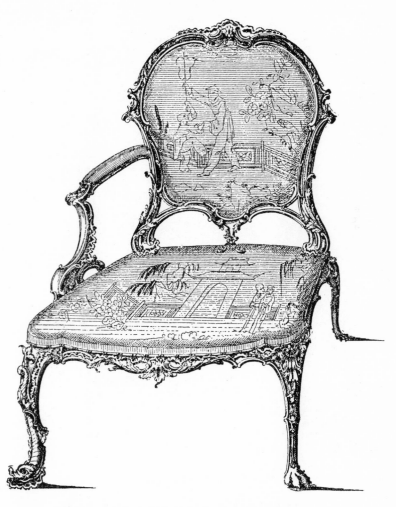

French chair from Plate XXI of Chippendale's *Director*.

French chair from Plate XXII of Chippendale's *Director*.

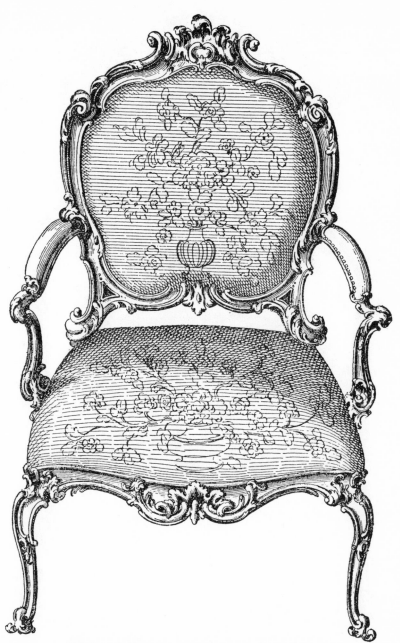

French chair from Plate XXII of Chippendale's *Director*.

French chair from Plate XXIII of Chippendale's *Director*.

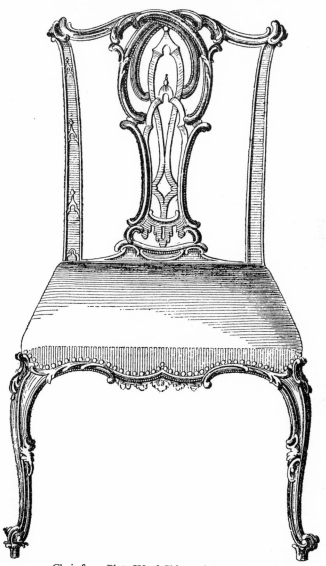

Chair from Plate IX of Chippendale's *Director*.

Chair from Plate XI of Chippendale's *Director*.

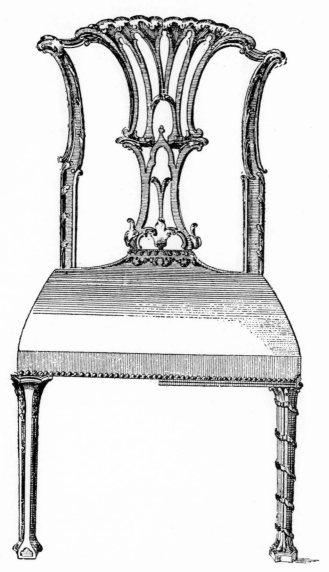

Chair from Plate XII of Chippendale's *Director*.

Chair from Plate XII of Chippendale's *Director*.

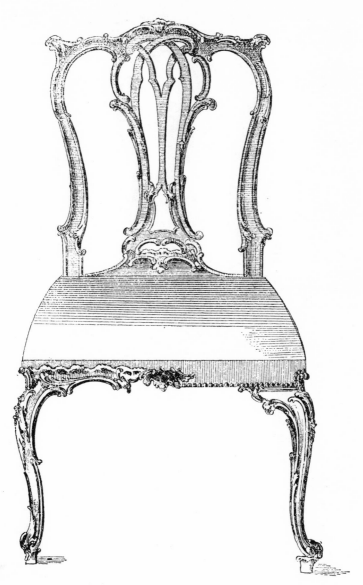

Chair from Plate XII of Chippendale's *Director*.

Chair from Plate XIII of Chippendale's *Director*.

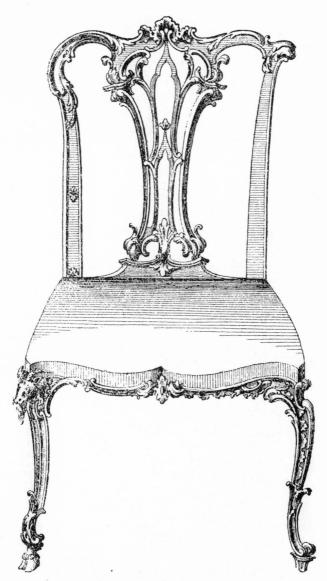

Chair from Plate XIV of Chippendale's *Director*.

Chair from Plate XIV of Chippendale's *Director*.

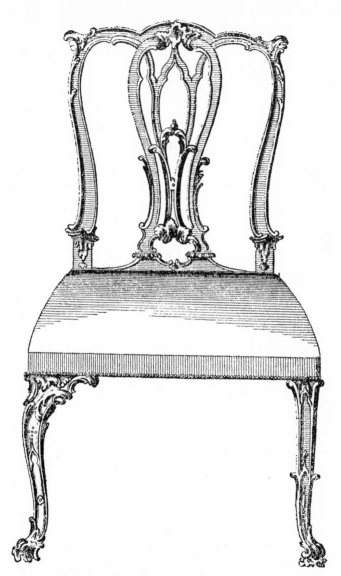

Chair from Plate XIV of Chippendale's *Director*.

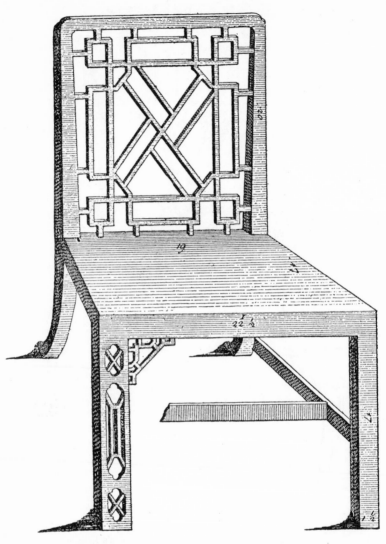

Chinese chair from Plate XXVI of Chippendale's *Director*.

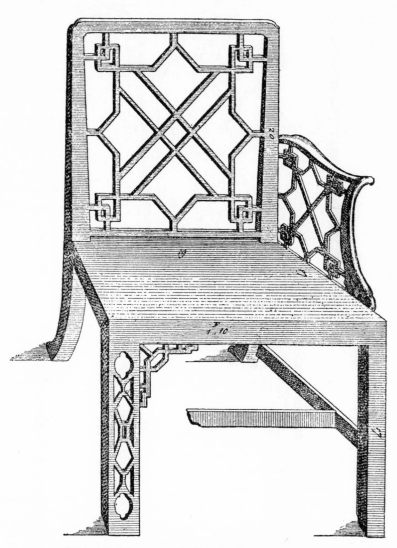

Chinese chair from Plate XXVI of Chippendale's *Director*.

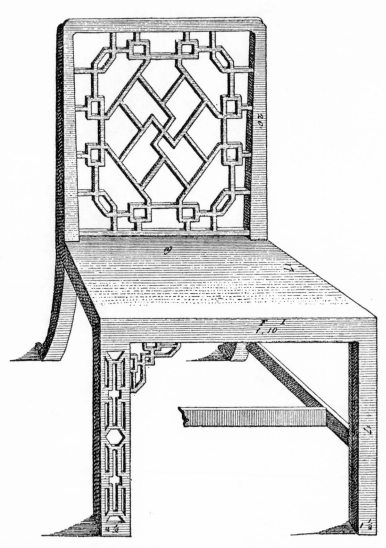

Chinese chair from Plate XXVI of Chippendale's *Director*.

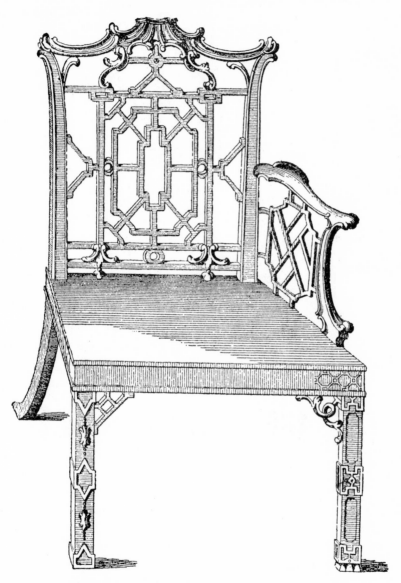

Chinese chair from Plate XXVII of Chippendale's *Director*.

Chinese chair from Plate XXVII of Chippendale's *Director*.

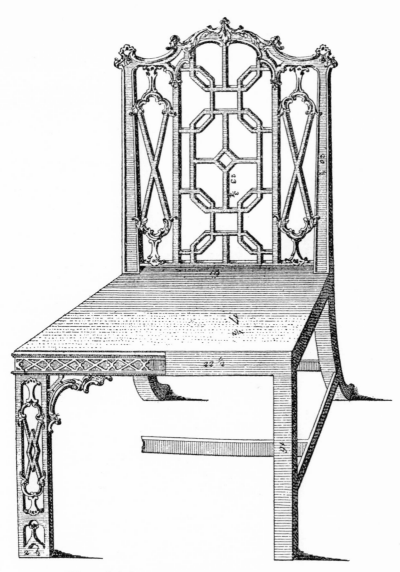

Chinese chair from Plate XXVIII of Chippendale's *Director*.

SECTION III

SECTION III

Dictionary of Names
and Terms

*

AUTHORITIES. Unless otherwise indicated, quotations from
authorities are from the following editions:

BOOKS OF GENERAL REFERENCE

*A Concise Glossary of Terms used in Grecian, Roman, Italian
and Gothic Architecture*, by J. H. Parker (London: James
Parker & Co., 1875, 4th edition revised).

*Dictionarium Britannicum: or a more compleat Universal Etymo-
logical English Dictionary*, by N. Bailey (London: 1736).

A Dictionary of Archaic and Provincial Words, by James Orchard
Halliwell, in 2 volumes (London: John Russell Smith, 1874,
8th edition).

*A Dictionary of the Architecture and Archaeology of the Middle
Ages*, by John Britton (London: Longman, Orme, Brown,
Green and Longmans, 1838).

An Universal Etymological English Dictionary, by N. Bailey
(London, 1775).

The Complete Works of Geoffrey Chaucer, edited by the Rev.
Walter Skeat (Oxford: The Clarendon Press, 1925).

Costume in England, by F. W. Fairholt (London: Chapman and
Hall, 1860).

Description of England in Shakespeare's Youth, by William
Harrison. (Edited from the first two editions of Holinshed's
Chronicle, A.D. 1577–87, by Frederick J. Furnivall. Published
for the New Shakespere Society by N. Trübner & Co., London, 1877.)

The Diary of John Evelyn (edited by William Bray).

The Diary of Samuel Pepys (edited by Lord Braybroke).

The Elizabethan Home: discovered in two dialogues by Claudius
Hollyband and Peter Erondel. (Edited by M. St. Clare Byrne.
London: Cobden-Sanderson, 1930.)

The Homes of Other Days, by Thomas Wright (London: Trübner
& Co., 1871).

The Journeys of Celia Fiennes. (Edited by Christopher Morris.
London: The Cresset Press, 1947.)

Nollekens and His Times, by John Thomas Smith. The reprint
of the 2nd edition, in 2 volumes, was issued in 1920 by John
Lane: it was edited and annotated by Wilfrid Whitten, and

contained all the original voluminous footnotes, and 85 illustrations. The edition issued in 1949 by the Turnstile Press omits the footnotes, and compresses the biography into one volume, making it much more readable, but unfortunately omitting a great deal of extremely interesting contemporary information about artists, tradesmen, and the topography of London in the late 18th and early 19th centuries.

Nomenclature of Commercial Timbers, British Standard Specifications—881: Hardwoods, and 589: Softwoods (London: British Standards Institution, 1946).

The Paston Letters. (Edited by James Gairdner, in 4 volumes. Edinburgh: John Grant, 1910.)

Society in the Elizabethan Age, by Hubert Hall (London: Swan Sonnenschein & Co., 1901, 4th edition).

Sports and Pastimes of the People of England, by Joseph Strutt. (Edited by William Hone. London: 1831.)

BOOKS ON FURNITURE AND RELATED SUBJECTS

An Encyclopaedia of Cottage, Farm and Villa Architecture and Furniture, by J. C. Loudon (London: Longman, Rees, Orme, Brown, Green and Longman, 1833).

Analysis of Ornament, by Ralph N. Wornum (London: Chapman and Hall, 1879).

The Architecture of Country Houses; including Designs for Cottages, Farm Houses, and Villas, With Remarks on Interiors, Furniture, and the Best Modes of Warming and Ventilating, by A. J. Downing. (New York: D. Appleton & Co., 1850.)

The Cabinet Dictionary, by Thomas Sheraton (London: 1803).

The Cabinet Maker's and Upholsterer's Drawing Book, by Thomas Sheraton (published in parts between 1791 and 1794).

The Cabinet Maker and Upholsterer's Guide: or Repository of Designs for every article of Household Furniture, by A. Hepplewhite & Co. (London, 1788).

The Cabinet-Maker and Upholsterer's Guide, by George Smith (London: Jones & Co., 1836).

The City and Country Builder's and Workman's Treasury of Designs: Or the Art of Drawing and Working the Ornamental Parts of Architecture, by Batty Langley (London: 1750).

Decoration and Furniture of Town Houses, by Robert W. Edis (London: Kegan Paul, 1881).

English Furniture, from Charles II to George II, by R. W. Symonds (London: The Connoisseur, Ltd., 1929).

Furniture with Candelabra and Interior Decoration, designed by R. Bridgens (London: William Pickering, 1838).

The Gentleman and Cabinet Maker's Director, by Thomas Chippendale (London, 1762, 3rd edition).

The Gillow Records. These records, which are at the Lancaster branch of Waring and Gillow, Ltd., include the Estimate and Sketch Books (abbreviated as E. & S. Books) since 1784, and the Waste Books. The Waste Books were not order books or ledgers, and were not used in auditing, but they recorded various transactions.

Hand-Woven Carpets, Oriental and European, by A. F. Kendrick and C. E. Tattershall, in 2 volumes. (Benn Brothers Limited, 1922.)

High Wycombe Furniture, by Sir Lawrence Weaver (London: The Fanfare Press, 1929).

Hints on Household Taste, by Charles L. Eastlake (London: Longmans, Green & Co., 1878, 4th edition).

Masterpieces of English Furniture and Clocks, by R. W. Symonds (London: Batsford, 1940).

Mechanization takes Command, by Siegfried Giedion (New York: Oxford University Press, 1948).

Metropolitan Museum of Art, New York: Handbook of the American Wing opening exhibition, by R. T. H. Halsey and Charles O. Cornelius (New York, 1925, 2nd edition).

Mr Samuel McIntire, Carver, the Architect of Salem (published by the Southworth-Anthoensen Press, Portland, Maine, U.S.A., for the Essex Institute, 1940).

Old Clocks and Watches, and their Makers, by F. J. Britten (London: Batsford, 1904).

The Practical Cabinet Maker, Upholsterer and Complete Decorator, by Peter and Michael Angelo Nicholson (London: H. Fisher, Son & Co., 1826).

The Practical Decoration of Furniture, by H. P. Shapland (London: Ernest Benn, 1926, in 3 volumes).

The Prices of Cabinet Work, by a Committee of Masters Cabinet Makers (London: S. Low, 1797).

Specimens of Ancient Furniture, by Henry Shaw (London: William Pickering, 1836).

Sylva, or a Discourse of Forest-Trees, by John Evelyn (1679, 3rd edition).

The Universal System of Household Furniture, by Ince and Mayhew (London, 1760).

ILLUSTRATIONS. This Section is illustrated partly by reproductions from contemporary sources, such as the published works of Chippendale, Ince and Mayhew, Hepplewhite, and the drawings based on designs by Hepplewhite and Shearer included in *The Prices of Cabinet Work* (1797 edition), also Sheraton's works, and Loudon's *Encyclopaedia.* Mr Ronald Escott has drawn 144 subjects specially for this Dictionary, and a few of the small black-and-white illustrations are from drawings by A. B. Read, R.D.I., the late E. J. Warne, and the author.

* A *

Acacia (*Robinia pseudoacacia*)

A white, hard wood, used in the 17th century for inlaying. This use is mentioned by John Evelyn in *Sylva* (2nd edition, 1670). It is a durable wood, and has sometimes been used for chair frames. The name acacia has been discontinued upon the recommendation of the British Standards Institution, and the standard name is now Robinia, *q.v.*

Acanthus

A form of ornament, based on the leaves of the acanthus plant, conventionally treated, and used on the capitals of the Corinthian and Composite orders of architecture. In furniture it is used for the enrichment of mouldings and surfaces, and on the knees of chairs and tables, also on the arms and cresting of chairs.

Acanthus leaf.

Accordion Pleat

A machine-made pleat formed by the application of heat and pressure, resulting in a series of knife pleats, each one completely overlapping the next. This type of pleating is used only on light materials in furnishing.

Acorn Turning

Ornaments turned in the form of an acorn and used as a decorative *motif* on furniture in the late 16th century and throughout the 17th and 18th centuries.

Act of Parliament Clock, *see* **Coaching Inn Clock**

Adam Style

The classical revival in architecture, interior decoration, and furnishing that took place in the second half of the 18th century, and was associated with the name of its most fashionable and conspicuous interpreters, the brothers Robert and James Adam. It is characterised

Acorn turning. From a finial on an early 17th century chair.

by extreme delicacy of ornament, based on Greek and Roman *motifs*. The brothers Adam designed schemes of furnishing and decoration, complete in every detail, including the patterns of carpets and furnishing fabrics.

Adriatic Oak, *see* **Austrian Oak**

Adze

A type of axe with the cutting edge at right angles to the haft. For trimming concave surfaces, such as the seats of Windsor chairs, the cutting edge is crescent-shaped. When chair makers are cutting a seat—which is usually of elm—they put it on the ground, with one foot on each side to hold it down, and use the long-handled adze to hollow out the shape, using the adze much as a pickaxe is used, with horizontal rather than vertical strokes. (*See* **White Wycombe**, *also* **Windsor Chair.**)

African Mahogany (*Khaya ivorensis*)

This comes from the west coast of Africa and is sometimes known as Gambia or Lagos. The wood is inclined to be pale red, almost pink in colour, though it darkens to a deeper, reddish brown upon exposure. It is sometimes well figured, and is used for cabinet making, turned work, mouldings, and also for veneers.

African Walnut (*Lovoa klaineana*)

Sometimes known as Benin or Nigerian walnut. A wood of golden-brown colour, shading into dark brown; used for cabinet making and chair making.

African Whitewood, *see* Obeche

Alarm Clock

Also known as an alarum, or alarum clock. A clock with special bell-ringing mechanism which may be set to arouse a sleeper at a specific time. An early reference in an inventory taken at the 'Palloice at Westminster, 34th Year, Henry VIII', mentions: 'Item oone clocke of Iron with a larum to the same with the Kinges Armes crownyd'.

Albany Couch, *see* Reading Seat

Alcove

A recess specially designed for a seat or a bed. Both the device and the word are of Spanish origin. Alcoves were used occasionally in the furnishing and decoration of large rooms in the 18th century.

Alder (*Alnus glutinosa*)

A tree native to Europe and the British Isles, which supplies a durable wood that is strongly resistant to decay. It is sometimes used for the turned members of Windsor chairs.

Almery, *see* Aumbry

Almirah

A movable cupboard or wardrobe. An Anglo-Indian term often applied to all types of cupboards.

Amaranth, *see* Purpleheart

Amboyna (*Pterocarpus indicus*)

A decorative wood, hard and durable, resembling bird's-eye maple in figure, but of a deeper brown colour. From the islands of Amboyna and Ceram in the Dutch East Indies.

Ambry, *see* Aumbry

American Black Walnut (*Juglans nigra*)

A richly figured wood of a golden-brown colour, streaked with dark brown. It takes a very high polish, and is also used for carved and turned work. American cabinet makers in the early 19th century used this wood so extensively that the furniture made in the U.S.A. during the eighteen-twenties and eighteen-thirties, including some of the later work of Duncan Phyfe, is often labelled as 'the black walnut period'. (*See also* **Virginia Walnut**.)

American Empire Style

A modern term for the furniture and furnishing fashions prevalent in the United States during the early part of the 19th century. American designers were directly influenced by French fashions during the period of the French Empire, for the United States had continuous and friendly contact with France while Britain was engaged in the Napoleonic wars; French taste had therefore a marked effect upon the form of American furniture. Large and rather ponderous designs in mahogany, incorporating a variety of classical motifs, characterise this period. Rosewood was also used, and during and after the eighteen-twenties, American black walnut, *q.v.*, was very popular. Late American Empire is a term sometimes used to describe the last phase of this style, when furniture became heavier and often clumsy, and ornamentation began to get out of control.

American Federal Style

This term refers to the use of certain decorative *motifs* on American furniture during the opening decades of the 19th century, indicative of patriotic emotion rather than genuine national taste. Of these, the spread eagle was the most popular; and it appeared chiefly on frames for convex mirrors. Crossed cannons were also used occasionally.

American Lime, *see* **Basswood**

American Plane, *see* **Buttonwood**

American Red Gum (*Liquidambar styraciflua*)

This wood, sometimes known as satin walnut, comes from the south-eastern states of North America. It is reddish brown, veined with streaks of darker brown, and has a satiny surface when it is finished. It is not a satisfactory wood to work, and is only used for cheap furniture.

Amercian Red Oak (*Quercus rubra*)

A pale, reddish-brown wood, the lightest shades being almost pink: it is coarse-grained, but takes a good polish after filling.

American White Oak (*Quercus alba*)

A pale-brown wood, yellowish in its lighter shades, coarse-grained, that has to be filled before polishing.

American Whitewood, *see* **Canary Wood**

Amorini

An Italian word, describing the carved or painted cupids used in the decoration of furniture.

Andaman Marblewood, *see* **Coromandel Wood**

Andaman Padauk (*Pterocarpus dalbergioides*)

Sometimes known as Andaman redwood. A richly coloured wood, varying from dark crimson to brown and red. Used for decorative woodwork, cabinet making, and turnery.

Andirons or **Firedogs**

A pair of iron bars standing independently on a hearth to support the ends of logs in a wood fire. An early form of the word was

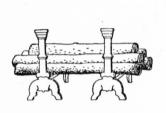 

Pair of andirons supporting logs, and detail of early 17th century example.

awndierns: they were also known as cob-irons, and creepers. (*See* illustration.) In the western counties of England they are sometimes known as andogs. (Halliwell.)

Angle Chair, *see* **Writing Chair**

Angular Capital

An Ionic capital, *q.v.*, formed alike on all four faces.

Anobium Punctatum, *see* **Furniture Beetle**

Angular capital.

Anodising

A finish used on metalwork, particularly aluminium, consisting of a hard, protective oxide film, formed by an electro-chemical process.

Anthemion or **Honeysuckle Ornament**

A form of ornament derived from Greek and Roman architecture, and based on the honey-

Anthemion ornament. (*See also* page 41.).

114

suckle flower and leaves, conventionally treated. It was very popular during the Greek revival. (*See* illustration, *also* page 41.)

Anthemion Back or Honeysuckle Chair

A modern term for a type of chair made in the late 18th century, with an oval back framing a pierced splat and curved bars which formed an outline of the anthemion ornament. This device was used by Hepplewhite and his contemporaries.

Antimacassar

A detachable covering for the backs of armchairs, settees, and sofas, to protect them from the stains made by the use of macassar oil for hairdressing. Introduced originally as a protective device, it became, during the latter part of the 19th century, purely ornamental.

Antique

Chair with anthemion back.

A term formerly used for Greek and Roman remains, but since late Victorian times in current use as a label for furniture over a century old. (*See* Section I, pages 12-15.)

Antique Bevel, *see* Vauxhall Bevel

Applewood (*Malus pumila*)

An English fruit wood of a rich, reddish-brown colour. It is very hard, and is used for turned work: furniture made in the countryside during the late 17th and early 18th centuries often had legs and spindles of turned applewood. Occasionally, when large boards were available, it was used for flat surfaces.

Applied Facets

Faceted pieces of wood, usually in the form of lozenges or triangles, applied to the surface of the panels or framework of a chest or cupboard, the headboard of a bed, or the woodwork of a chimneypiece. A form of ornamentation used in the late 16th and early 17th centuries.

Applied Mouldings

Mouldings applied to the surfaces of cabinets and chests for decorative effect. Some of the furniture designed by William Kent in the early Georgian period had carved mouldings applied on doors and other surfaces to form panels. In the 19th century the practice of applying mouldings was often used to give an air of spurious richness to cheap and ill-made furniture.

Applied Turning

Turned ornament, split and applied to the surface of furniture. (*See also* Split Turning.)

Appliqué

A type of surface decoration on fabrics, consisting of shaped pieces of material applied to form a pattern on the ground material. Each separate piece to be applied is cut out, its edges turned in and stitched down before it is laid in its place in the design: it is finally secured to the ground by an embroidery stitch, or by couching a braid or cord round the edges. Appliqué is often enriched by embroidery between the applied parts of the design, or by couched scrolls of cord or braid.

Apron

The shaped piece below the seat rail of a chair or the frieze rail of a table or cabinet stand, extending between the legs, and usually treated ornamentally, being shaped, carved, or pierced. (*See also* **Skirting Piece** *and* **Valance**.)

Arabesque

The word means Arabian, but it is used to describe forms of decoration based on the intricate interweaving of flowing lines against a background, either in painted or carved ornamentation. Such forms of decoration are classical in origin; and when they were revived during the Renaissance they were sometimes known as grotesque, though generally they were described as arabesque, a term used previously to designate the Saracenic forms of intricate ornament that had been introduced from the Near East during the Middle Ages. Thereafter, decorative forms of Saracenic or Arabian origin were frequently known as Moresque.

Arcaded panels on a late 16th century chest.

Arcading

The ornamental use of arches applied on panels, either singly or in series. Used particularly during the late 16th and 17th centuries on chests, presses, panelled bed backs, and overmantels of chimneypieces. (*See* illustration.)

Arched Stretcher

The upward-curving hooped stretcher between the front legs of a late 17th century chair.

Architectural Frames, *see* Tabernacle Frames

Architectural Furniture

A modern term used by some writers to describe furniture made during the Queen Anne and early Georgian periods, either from

Arched stretcher.

the designs of architects or under their direction. It applies particularly to the work of William Kent, when he employed architectural features on such large-scale pieces of furniture as library bookcases and cabinets. (*See* Section II, pages 58 to 60, *and* illustrations on pages 270 and 311.)

Architrave

The lowest member of an entablature in an order of architecture, *q.v.*; the term also denotes the moulded frame surrounding a door or window. (*See* illustration on page 248.)

Ark

A north country term, used originally in mediaeval times for a meal bin or receptacle, of the type made of planks of oak that were split, not sawn, wedged together, and pegged. Sometimes called a meale-arke or bolting ark—the word bolting meaning to sift—and in eastern and southern England, known as a whiche. The word ark was in use as late as the 19th century as a name for flour or meal chests. Ark was once the term used for the cupboard in the vestry of a church where the clergy hung their vestments.

Arkwright

A north country name for the craftsman who made receptacles of split wood boards that were wedged and pegged.

Armada Chest

An iron strong-box with a lock which was fitted in the under side of the lid and secured it to the four sides of the chest by a system of bolts, of which there were sometimes as many as sixteen. A dummy keyhole appeared on the front of the box. These chests, which were unconnected with the Armada, were imported into England from Flanders, Germany, and Austria, where they were made in the 16th and 17th centuries. (*See The Parish Chest*, by W. E. Tate: Cambridge University Press, 1946, p. 39.)

Arm Rail

The curved horizontal member on some types of Windsor chair, which forms the arms and continues across the back, being pierced to allow the back spindles to pass through it.

Armchair

A chair with arms, called an 'arming chair', thus named to distinguish it from the single or side chair. Up to the late 16th century, all chairs were armchairs, and a single chair without arms was called a back stool; so the term armchair was at first adopted to differentiate between the chair and the back stool. (*See also* **Back Stool, Carver Chair, Curricle, Easy Chair,** *and* **Elbow Chair.**)

Armoire

A large press or wardrobe. (French.)

117

Arras

Originating from the tapestries manufactured at Arras, in northern France, in the 14th and 15th centuries, this became a generic term in England for woven wall hangings.

Arrow Back

A name used in America to describe a type of Windsor chair or Windsor rocker, *q.v.*, in which three or more arrow-shaped spindles are used in the back. Arrow-back chairs were made in large quantities in the United States during the second quarter of the 19th century.

Art Pot Stand

A three- or four-legged stand, usually of mahogany or oak, designed to accommodate a brass or copper pot for flowers or plants, introduced about 1900. A form of *jardinière, q.v.* The alternative name is palm stand.

Ash (*Fraxinus excelsior*)

A tree native to Britain, which supplies a tough, light-brown wood that has great elasticity. Ash burrs are used for decorative veneers in cabinet making. John Evelyn, in his *Sylva* (3rd edition, 1679), records that 'Some *Ash* is curiously *camleted* and vein'd, I say, so differently from other *Timber*, that our skilful *Cabinet-makers* prize it equal with *Ebony*, and give it the name of *green Ebony*, which the *Customer* pays well for; and when our *Woodmen* light upon it, they may make what mony they will of it: But to bring it to that curious lustre, so as 'tis hardly to be distinguished from the most curiously diaper'd *Olive*, they *Varnish* their *Work* . . .' (chapter vi, p. 42).

Astragal, *see* Bead

Aspidistra Stand

An open framework, consisting usually of three short bamboo poles, 3 to 4 ft. in length, which form a tripod, secured below by stretchers. The poles cross each other a few inches from the top to provide a forked support for a pot containing an aspidistra or other plant. In some designs three smaller fern pots are suspended by light chains from the top of each pole. Introduced during the late 19th century, primarily for the popular pot plant, *Aspidistra lurida*.

Aubusson

A French tapestry, named after the town of Aubusson in the department of Creuse. Furniture coverings, carpets, and rugs have been manufactured there since the early 16th century.

Aumbry, Ambry, or Almery

The aumbry and the press were the earliest cupboards, and the aumbry, with doors pierced for ventilation, was the food cupboard

Mediaeval cup-board with an aumbry below. It stands by a bed of the type that has a canopy hanging from the ceiling. 15th century. (Reproduced from Shaw's *Specimens of Ancient Furniture*.)

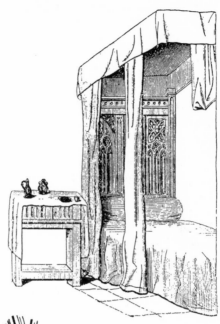

Almery in Lincoln cathedral. *Circa* 1200. (After Parker.)

of the Middle Ages. (*See* illustrations on pages 119, 366, and 367.) Its use as a storage place for food survived until the 16th century, for in *Five hundreth points of good husbandry united to as many of good huswiferie*, by Thomas Tusser (1573), the following couplet occurs, on page 5, fol. 2:

> Some slovens from sleeping, no sooner be up,
> but hand is in aumbrie, and nose in the cup.

In mediaeval times the aumbry was often formed in the thickness of a stone wall, and enclosed by wooden doors. A wall aumbry of this type, fixed near the altar in a church, was used for the sacramental vessels, and was sometimes called an almery. (*See* illustration on previous page, *also* **Livery Cupboard**.)

Australian Blackwood (*Acacia melanoxylon*)

A reddish brown wood, deepening to black, with streaks of yellow, brown, and red; occasionally it is elaborately figured. It may be carved and turned easily, and takes a high polish.

Australian Walnut, *see* **Queensland Walnut**

Austrian or **Adriatic Oak** (*Quercus robur*)

Oak that was formerly supplied by the forests of the pre-1914 Austrian Empire. Light in colour and with a small figure, occasionally resembling the marking of English oak.

Axminster

Hand-woven carpets, named after the town of Axminster in Devonshire, where a carpet-manufacturing industry was established in 1755. (*See also* **Wilton**.)

Bachelor's Chest

A small, low chest of drawers, with a folding top which converts it into a table. Such chests were made during the first half of the 18th century, but the term is not contemporary.

Back Board

A term for the wooden boards at the back of a piece of furniture or the back of a looking glass frame. Sheraton uses the alternative term, blind frame, for the back board of a looking glass. (*The Cabinet Dictionary*, 1803, p. 25.) For furniture of good quality, made in the late 18th and early 19th centuries, back boards were usually panelled. In modern furniture plywood is often used. This term is sometimes used to describe the headboard of a fourpost bed. (*See* **Headboard**.)

Back Stool

A stool with a back fitted to it, to increase its comfort. It then became a single chair. Although referred to in Elizabethan inventories, back stools were not in common use until the middle years of the 17th century, and the name survived during the 18th century. As late as 1762, Ince and Mayhew described single chairs with stuffed backs as back stools, in Plates LV and LVI of *The Universal System of Household Furniture*. (*See also* **Low Back Chair**.)

Backgammon Table

The mediaeval game called tables has been identified with backgammon; and the folding or double backgammon board may have originally brought the word table into general use to describe a flat horizontal supported surface. (*See* **Table**.)

Back Rest

The back of a chair: this term, which is still in use, may have originated during the 16th century when side chairs, or single chairs, were called back stools, *q.v.*

Bahia Rosewood, *see* **Rosewood**

Baize

Formerly known as bayes. The name is derived from the colour, bay. It is an open, woollen material with a long nap. It may have been introduced into England in Elizabeth's reign by refugees from France and the Netherlands. The manufacture was certainly practised in England by Huguenot refugees in the late 17th century.

Ball Foot

A turned foot of spherical form, used in the late 17th and early 18th centuries for supporting heavy pieces of furniture, such as a scrutoire or a chest of drawers.

Ball Fringe

A decorative fringe used in upholstery, with little balls covered with the same material used for the fringe, hanging at evenly spaced intervals among the threads or loops of the fringe.

Balloon Chair

A term sometimes used for a hoop back chair, *q.v.*, with a pronounced waist, also for the Victorian round back, *q.v. (See also* **Bended Back Chair.)**

Balloon Clock

A term which describes the design of a case for a spring-driven clock, dating from the last quarter of the 18th century. The case below the dial curves inwards to form a waist between it and the base. A clock in a balloon case designed to stand on a pedestal was sometimes a weight clock, the pedestal accommodating the weights and pendulum. (*See* illustration.)

Baluster

A small turned column: a unit in a balustrade.

Baluster Back

A Windsor chair with the back splat in the form of a plain or pierced baluster. (*See* illustrations *under* **Windsor Chair.)**

Balloon clock.

Baluster Leg

A name sometimes used for the turned leg of a table, when it closely follows the form of a baluster of the Tuscan or other classical order. Baluster legs were used on long tables from the late 16th to the end of the 17th century. (*See* illustration of tavern interior in Section II, page 61.) An elongated form was also used on the legs of joined stools.

Baluster Turning

A characteristic form of late 16th and early 17th century ornament, derived originally from the vertical members of a balustrade, but varying greatly in section and profile.

Baluster-and-Spindle, *see* **Spindle-and-Baluster**

Bamboo Furniture

Originally made in the East, from lengths of the slender, woody stems of bamboo, the popular name for the giant Indian reed, *Bambusa arundinacea.* Such furniture was imported into England, and extensively copied in the late 18th and early 19th centuries. Turned beech, painted the colour of cane, and chairs and settles of this imitation bamboo, were popular in the late 18th and early

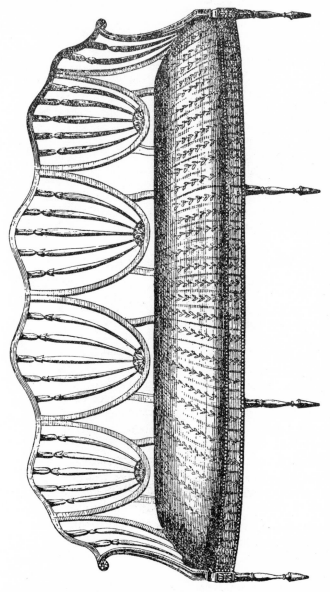

Bar back sofa. (From Hepplewhite's *Guide*, 1788.)

19th centuries. Light tables, bookcases, and whatnots were also made in this fashion.

Band or **Fillet**

A flat moulding. The term is common to architecture and cabinet making. Bandelet is the name sometimes used to describe 'any very narrow flat moulding'. Isaac Ware includes it in his 'Explanation of the Terms of Art' in *A Complete Body of Architecture*. (*See* illustration, *also* **Listel**.)

Band or fillet.

Bandelet, *see* **Band**

Banding

A strip or band of veneer, usually edging a panel or the front of a drawer. When a band of veneer is cut with the grain of the wood it is called straight banding: when across the grain, it is cross banding, and when cut at an angle between the two, it is known as feather banding.

Bandy Leg, *see* **Cabriole Leg**

Banisters

The upright members in a chair back or a staircase balustrade. A corrupt form of the word baluster.

Banister Back

A chair back formed of vertical banisters between the seat and the top rail. (*See* **Spindle Back Chair**.)

Banjo Clock

A form of mural clock made in the early 19th century in the United States. The term banjo is not contemporary. Below the circular dial the case curved inwards slightly throughout its length, giving the effect of an elongated waist, and terminating in a rectangular base. (*See* illustration.)

Banker

A mediaeval term for a loose cloth placed over a bench or the back of a seat.

Banjo clock.

Banner Screen, *see* **Fire Screen**

Bar Back

A shield-shaped open back on a chair or settee, with ornamental bars, curving upwards from the base of the shield to the top rail. (*See* illustration on previous page.)

Barber's Chair

In its simplest form, this is an armchair with an adjustable head rest rising above the top rail of the back, and was an early 19th century development of the 18th century shaving chair, which was a corner chair with a fixed head rest. (*See* **Shaving Chair**.) The elaborate type of barber's chair, with a swivel seat and mechanism which allowed seat and back to be tilted to any convenient angle, was, according to Giedion, a simplified form of the adjustable railroad car seat, which had been developed on American railroads during the eighteen-fifties. (*Mechanization Takes Command,* p. 446.)

Barefaced Tenon

A term used in joinery and cabinet making, for a tenon shouldered on one side only. (*See* illustration.)

Barefaced Tongue

A term used in joinery and cabinet making, for a tongue that is flush on one side of a board. (*See* illustration.)

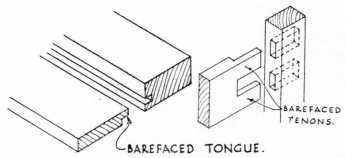

BAREFACED TENONS.

BAREFACED TONGUE.

(From *A Short Dictionary of Architecture.* Ware and Beatty.)

Barley Sugar Twist

A form of decorative turning, sometimes termed double rope or double twist, resembling a stick of barley sugar, introduced during the reign of Charles II, and used on the framework of chairs, tables, and the stands of cabinets, and occasionally for the columns supporting the cornice on the hood of a clock. (*See* illustration, *also* **Gate Leg Table.**)

Barley sugar twist.

Baroque

The term used to describe the elaborate styles of classical architecture, interior decoration, and furnishing, which developed in Europe, with characteristic national variations, during the 17th and early 18th centuries.

Bas-Relief or Bass-Relief

Decorative subjects or ornamental patterns, carved in low relief on wood or cast in plaster or composition. Sometimes known as low relief. The Italian term, *basso-rilievo,* is occasionally used.

Base

An architectural term for the lowest member of a column or a pilaster. In cabinet making it denotes the lowest horizontal member of a carcass. (*See also* **Plinth**.)

Basin and Ewer

These utensils were usually mentioned together in inventories, their functions being complementary. In mediaeval times, and later, they were used for washing the hands before dining, and in bedrooms and closets. Originally of simple form, and made of pewter or latten, *q.v.*, they became more elaborate during the 16th century, in imitation of European examples. (*See* illustration.)

16th century basin and ewer. (From Thomas Wright's *Homes of Other Days*.)

Basin Stand

A small mahogany stand, introduced during the 18th century, with a circular hole in the top to hold a wash basin. Often made to fit into a corner, three-sided in plan, with three legs and a slightly bowed front. (*See* illustrations, *also* **Wash Hand Stand**, **Washing Stand**, *and* **Wig Stand**.)

Basket Chair

An armchair made of basket work or wicker work, plaited twigs or rushes, or, in the present century, chemically treated woven strands of coarse grass. The term wanded chair, found in 15th and 16th century inventories, may refer to chairs of woven wands or twigs. (Halliwell gives wanded as meaning: 'covered with boughs or twigs'.) Basket work was used for chairs in Romano-British times, and evidence of their existence is furnished by sepulchral monuments. (*See* illustration on page 129.) An early reference to a basket chair occurs in Elegie I, on Jealosie, by John Donne, which was composed in the last decade of the 16th century:

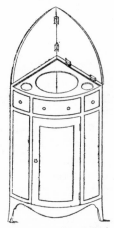

A corner enclosed basin stand. (From *The Prices of Cabinet Work*, 1797 edition.)

Nor when he swolne, and pamper'd with great fare
Sits downe, and snorts, cag'd in his basket chaire . . .

126

[contd. on page 129.

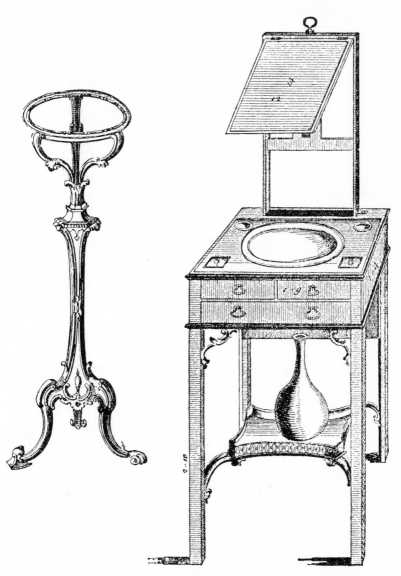

Designs for Basin stands. (From the 3rd edition of Chippendale's *Gentleman and Cabinet Maker's Director*.) *Left:* A tripod 'bason stand' included on Plate LV. *Right:* A 'bason stand' with a glass 'to rise out with a Spring-Catch'—a device used by Chippendale in a design for a shaving table which is shown with this basin stand on Plate LIV. (*See* page 128.)

Three designs for basin stands. (From Sheraton's *Cabinet Dictionary*, 1803.) *Above, left:* Corner basin stand 'with three legs, having the two front ones to spring forward, to keep them from tumbling over'. *Above, right:* This 'circular Tripod Bason-stand' is described by Sheraton as 'entirely novel, and is designed for a young lady to wash at. The back, to which the curtains are fixed, is made separate, and turned over in a scroll, where the lights are fixed.' He explains that the curtains 'are intended not merely for ornament, but to cover the bason, by being brought forward. . . .' The design to the right has the top enclosed by a tambour. (From Plate 10.)

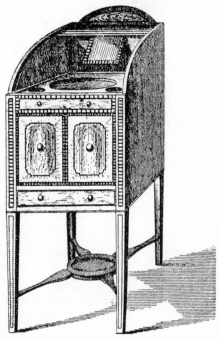

There is a reference to 'one wicker chayer' in an inventory of the goods and chattels of William Carding of Roxwell in Essex, dated November 27th, 1637. (*Farm and Cottage Inventories of Mid-Essex*, 1635–1749. Essex Record Office Publications, No. 8, 1950, p. 73.) In *The History of Tom Jones*, Henry Fielding writes of 'a great chair made with rushes'. (Book VII, chapter x.) Basket-work chairs, being easy to make and cheap, were very popular during the 19th century, when the population of Britain was rapidly increasing. A loose cushion in the seat transformed the basket chair into a comfortable armchair. (*See* illustrations on next page.) Special types of basket chairs with retractable leg rests were designed for invalids. (*See also* **Croquet Chair**, **Straw Chair**, *and* **Twiggen Chair**.)

EARLY EXAMPLES OF BASKET WORK FOR CHAIRS

Left: Part of a Romano-British sepulchral monument. Late 2nd or early 3rd century. Erected to Julia Velva. The figure shown is seated on what is obviously a basket-work chair. This was rough, crude provincial sculpture; but the texture and character of the chair are unmistakable. The monument is preserved at York in the Yorkshire Museum.

A group of 14th century people, showing a king seated on a chair, the back and sides of which appear to be made of wicker. (Reproduced from a contemporary MS. and included in F. W. Fairholt's *Costume in England*.)

Progress of basket chair design. The illustrations on this page are separated only by thirty years, and they show how the rather crude 'wicker' chair, with its obvious affinity with the straw beehive chair (*see* page 456) was supplanted by a more luxurious article, with wide arms and an inclined back. The illustration above is from *The Adventures of Mr Verdant Green*, by Cuthbert Bede (Edward Bradley), which was published in 1853–56: that below appeared in *Punch* on March 18th, 1882.

(Reproduced by permission of the Proprietors of *Punch*.)

Basket Stand

A form of work table consisting of a column on claws or a base with feet, and two circular tiers, surrounded by galleries. The design was probably derived from the dumb waiter, *q.v.*, and was a much simplified form of the circular-topped supper canterbury, designed by Sheraton. (*See* **Canterbury.**) Two types of basket stand are illustrated and described by A. J. Downing in *The Architecture of Country Houses* (New York; D. Appleton & Co., 1850). He describes them as 'suitable to the parlour', and states that they could be made 'very tastefully and fancifully of rosewood or mahogany, curiously carved for the villa; or of rustic work, varnished,

Mid - 19th century basket stands. (From Downing's *The Architecture of Country Houses*.)

in the Swiss manner, or of bamboo after the Chinese fashion, for the cottage'. (Page 422, referring to Figs. 207 and 208.)

Basket Weave

A coarsely woven furnishing cloth which resembles basket work.

Basket Work, *see* Basket Chair

Bass-Relief, *see* Bas-Relief

Basset Table

Probably a small card table, designed for the card game called basset or bassette. The game was introduced into France, probably from Italy, in the latter part of the 17th century, and became popular in England during the early 18th century.

Bassinet

A hooded basket used as a cradle for infants. Also denotes a perambulator with a hooded, basket body.

Basso-Rilievo, *see* Bas-Relief

Basswood (*Tilia americana*)

A soft, straight-grained wood of fine texture, varying in colour from pale brown almost to white. Supplied from Canada and the eastern U.S.A. Used for cabinet making, furniture, and wood carving. Sometimes known as American lime.

Bath

A wooden, marble, or japanned metal receptacle, large enough to hold sufficient water for bathing. Wooden, cask-like baths were used in mediaeval times. (*See* illustration.) Japanned tin and cast-iron baths were introduced during the early 19th century. (*See also* **Hip Bath** *and* **Slipper Bath**.)

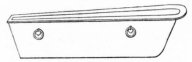

Bronze Roman bath. This was 5 ft. in length, with four handles to allow it to be lifted and moved. It is the prototype of the 19th century bath of cast iron. (From Edward Trollope's *Illustrations of Ancient Art*.)

Bath Stool, *see* **Bathroom Furniture**

Bath Tray, *see* **Bathroom Furniture**

Bathroom Furniture

A comprehensive term of late 19th century origin, used generally to cover furniture made of enamelled wood or metal, used in bath-rooms; such as stools, usually cork-seated, small hanging cabinets, and open trays that span the bath.

Mediaeval bath tub. This drawing is copied from the MS. of the St. Graal (13th century) and is included in Thomas Wright's *Homes of Other Days*.

Batten

A thin strip of wood.

Batten and Button

A method of jointing boards to guard against warping.

Baywood, *see* **Honduras Mahogany**

Bead or Astragal

A small moulding, semi-circular in section. Sometimes called a roundel.

Bead or astragal.

Bead and Butt

A term used in connection with flush panels in framed work, when the sides of the panels are separated from the stiles, or vertical members, with a bead, and the ends of the panels abut directly against the rails, or horizontal members. (*See* opposite page, *also* **Rail** *and* **Stile**.)

Bead and Flush

When a bead is worked on all four sides of a flush panel, the term bead and flush is used. (*See* illustration on opposite page.)

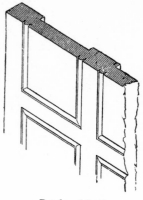

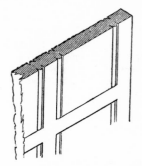

Bead and butt.   Bead and flush.

Bead and Quirk, *see* **Quirked Bead**

Bead and Reel

A form of enrichment with alternating beads and reels.

Bead Curtain

A curtain formed from a number of individual threads with beads of glass and wood of different lengths and sizes; introduced during the mid-19th century, and popularly associated with Indian decoration.

Bearer

This is a term in joinery for almost any type of horizontal member whose function is to carry something else. (For a specific use of a bearer, *see* **Drawer Runner.**)

Beau Brummell Table

A name sometimes used in the United States for a gentleman's fitted toilet table, of a type used during the second half of the 18th century. It was a variation of the dressing stand, *q.v.*, with Marlboro' legs, a small rising glass and compartments in the top for cosmetics, and drawers in the front for various toilet accessories. The top had side leaves, hinged to fold over and close the table. The term is not contemporary, and such tables were in use before 1788, when George Bryan Brummell was born.

Beauvais Tapestry

Tapestry made at the works established by Colbert in 1604, at Beauvais in northern France. Beauvais tapestry is used extensively for furniture coverings.

Bed

Originally, the term may have referred only to the materials upon which people slept. It appears to be used in this sense by

Beds and bedding of the 9th century. (These drawings, copied from a 9th century MS., are included in *The Homes of Other Days*, by Thomas Wright.)

Mediaeval bed with a canopy. Curtain rings are shown, threaded on rods. A chest stands at the foot of the bed. Like the bed shown below, the canopy is of the type that, four hundred years later, was called a half tester. (The illustration is copied from a 15th century MS. Latin Bible in the National Library in Paris, and is included in *The Homes of Other Days*, by Thomas Wright.)

A 15th century bed with a canopy. (The drawing, included in *The Homes of Other Days*, is copied from a MS. of the *Romance of the Comte d'Artois*.) Compare these mediaeval beds with the examples on pages 44 and 119, which have complete canopies.

Chaucer in *The Canterbury Tales,* when in 'The Reves Tale' the making of a temporary bed for some guests is described:

> And in his owne chambre hem made a bed
> With shetes and with chalons faire y-spred . . .

Since the 16th century the term bed has included the bedstead as well as the bedding. Sheraton, in *The Cabinet Dictionary* (1803), says that 'it includes the bedstead, and other necessary articles incident to those most useful of all pieces of furniture'. The various types of bed are entered under their respective names as follows:

Box Bedstead	Low Post Bed
Bureau Bedstead	Marlboro' Bedstead
Camp Bedstead	Posted Bed
Chair Bed	Press Bedstead
Charpoy	Sleigh Bed
Cot	Sofa Bed
Couch Bed	State Bed
Dome Bed	Stump Bedstead
Feather Bed	Stump End Bedstead
Field Bed	Summer Bed
Fourpost Bedstead	Table Bedstead
Half-headed Bedstead	Tent Bed
Half-tester Bedstead	Truckle Bed

Bed Joiner

The craftsman employed by upholsterers, who made the frames of beds, easy chairs and couches. This division of the joiner's craft occurred during the 18th century, and there was some overlapping between the trade of bed joiner and chair maker. The former made all the joinery work for bedsteads, such as the wooden frames that held the mattresses; also the frames of couches and chairs that were covered with upholstery, like the wing armchair, the frame of which, excepting the legs, is entirely covered. It is a contemporary term that passed out of use during the 19th century.

Bed Steps

A set of two or three steps to stand beside a high bed. Occasionally, two of the steps were enclosed to form cupboards, with a space for a bidet or chamber pot. Bed steps were in use during the 18th century, and were probably introduced much earlier. (*See* illustration.)

Bed steps. From Loudon's *Encyclopaedia of Cottage, Farm and Villa Architecture,* 1833, where this article is described as follows: 'The tread of the top step is hinged and lifts up; the middle step pulls forward; and when drawn out, its lid lifts up and shows a space for a bidet or other convenience'.

135

Bed Table

A tray with folding legs, designed to fit like a bridge across a bed, and providing a steady surface. Bed tables are described in *The Prices of Cabinet Work* (1797) as being 2 ft. 5 ins. long, 1 ft. 8 ins. wide, with 'a hollow in the middle of the front', 6 ins. deep, a rim grooved in all round, the edge of the top rounded, two clamps under the top, and four turned, tapered legs, which could be screwed into the top. Another type was introduced during the early 19th century, consisting of a pillar supported upon a base which rested on feet. It is illustrated and described as an adjustable bed table in Loudon's *Encyclopaedia of Cottage, Farm and Villa Architecture* (1833). 'The top of this table is made to rise and fall at pleasure, by raising or lowering the upper part of the pillar. . . .' The top was secured at the desired level by a pin attached by a chain to the pillar, and inserted in one of the slots made for that purpose in the upper part of the pillar. It was designed primarily for invalids. (*See* accompanying illustration.)

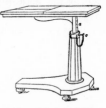

Adjustable bed table.
(After Loudon.)

Bed Wagon

An open wooden frame consisting of four hoops joined by six lateral slats and braced by four wooden spindles, the space between the inner hoops being partly enclosed to form a platform with a canopy over it, for a small charcoal-burning pan. The bed wagon may have been a clumsy alternative to the warming pan, *q.v.*, but E. H. Pinto suggests that it was more likely to have been used for airing beds that had been disused, rather than as a bed warmer. (*Treen, or Small Woodware Throughout the Ages*, by Edward H. Pinto. London: B. T. Batsford Ltd., 1949. Part XI, p. 72.)

Bedpost or Bedpillar

The posts, usually of a decorative nature, which support both the bed and the tester above it. (*See also* **Fourpost Bedstead** *and* **Low Post Bed**.)

Bedpost Clock, *see* Lantern Clock

Bedroom Chair

In the late 18th century light-framed bedroom chairs were made of japanned beech, often with rush seats. Chairs specially designed for the bedroom are illustrated in Sheraton's *Cabinet Dictionary* (1803), but they differ little in character from the side chairs or single chairs used in other rooms. (*See* illustrations on page 137.) A light type of single chair, designed as part of a bedroom suite, was used in the late 18th century; and such chairs were

Bedroom chairs. (From Plate 30 of Thomas Sheraton's *Cabinet Dictionary*, 1803.)

usually of rather flimsy build. Stools for use at dressing tables, and what were called dressing chairs, were produced in the 18th century; and a dressing chair is mentioned as early as 1740. No chair shown in any of the editions of Chippendale's *Director* is specifically labelled for bedroom use. The term chamber chair was used in the late 18th century.

Bedside Cupboard

A small cupboard standing at table height, to accommodate a chamber pot. Often there is a close stool (or night commode) below. The name used in the 18th century was pot cupboard.

Bedside Table

A small table, for use beside a bed, with one or more shelves below the top.

Bedspread, *see* **Counterpane**

Bedstead

The framework, of wood or metal, which supports the mattress and bedding. (*See* **Bed**.)

Bedstead Bolt

The iron bolt and nut, used for linking the side rails of wooden bedsteads to the bedposts.

Bed-Steddle

An obsolete term for a bedstead, formerly used in Essex. (*See* Halliwell's *Dictionary of Archaic and Provincial Words*.) In the inventory of the goods of William Coleman of Writtle in Essex, dated April 20th, 1635, 'one halfeheaded bedstedle' is included. (*Farm and Cottage Inventories of Mid-Essex*, 1635–1749. Essex Record Office Publications, No. 8, 1950, p. 71.)

Bedstock

The head and bottom of a bed, into which the rails are fixed, are known as a pair of bedstocks. The term is obsolete.

Beech (*Fagus sylvatica*)

A native British wood, ranging from pale brown to light reddish brown in colour. It is easily worked, and often used for the turned members of stick furniture, such as Windsor chairs. It was used extensively by chair makers from the 17th to the 19th centuries, and in the reign of Charles II many beech chairs were made, owing to a scarcity of English walnut.

Beehive Chair, *see* **Straw Chair**

Bench

A long, backless seat; either a free standing piece of furniture like a form, or fixed to a wall. The term is also used by cabinet makers to describe the strong, wooden tables at which they do their work, and now extends to many kinds of work tables in factories.

Bench Board

A term that occurs in the first half of the 17th century, and refers presumably to a type of bench or form, the back of which was hinged so that it could act as a table top. This is only a conjectural interpretation of the term, which appears in *Farm and Cottage Inventories of Mid-Essex* (Essex Record Office Publications, No. 8, 1950), the earliest reference being dated November 27th, 1637, in the inventory of William Carding of Roxwell. This inventory has the term, '2 bench boards, 3s. 4d.' (p. 71).

Bench End

The upright end of a pew, squared off, or terminating in a finial or some form of carved decoration. (*See* illustration, *also* **Box-end**, **Pew End**, **Poppy-head**, *and* **Standard**.)

Bench end of pew at Steeple Aston. *Circa* 1500. (After Parker.)

Bench Table

A bench with arms and a hinged back, that rests horizontally upon the arms when lowered. It is similar to the settle table, *q.v.*, and is the term generally used in the United States. Like the settle table and the chair table, it is of mid-17th century origin. In the colony of Pennsylvania it was known as the dischbank.

Bended Back Chair

An early 18th century chair, with or without arms, having a vase-shaped splat in the back, which was curved to give comfortable support to the back. Incorrectly described as a Hogarth chair. (*See* accompanying illustration, and pages 25, 27, and 28, *also* **Fiddle Back Chair** *and* **Spoon Back**.)

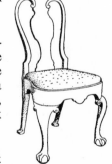

Bended back chair.

Bends

The pair of curved members which connect the front and back feet of a rocking chair, *q.v.*

Bentwood Furniture

Furniture made from wood which has been bent, by heat or moisture, and pressure, so that its shape is permanently changed.

139

Bentwood underframing on sleighs shown in the Canadian Court of the Great Exhibition of 1851. Compare these characteristic bentwood forms with the mid-Victorian rocking chair on page 396.

During the eighteen-sixties the bentwood chair was accepted as an article of household furniture. This drawing was published on February 18th, 1865, and is reproduced by courtesy of the proprietors of *Punch*.

The bowed back of a Windsor chair represents one of the earliest forms of bentwood chair. The common type of mass-produced bentwood chair with a cane or plywood seat was introduced in the mid-19th century, and was used extensively in shops for seating customers. A cane-seated bentwood chair by Michael Thonet (1796–1871), who perfected the design, was exhibited in London in 1851, also a bentwood table. (*See* Section II, page 71.) By the eighteen-sixties, the bentwood chair was accepted as an article of household furniture. (*See* accompanying illustration, *also* opposite page.)

Bentwood chair with plywood seat.

Bergère

An armchair with canework sides, back, and seat, with a loose cushion on the seat, or an upholstered seat. A French name, used originally to describe upholstered armchairs. Such chairs are illustrated on Plate LX of *The Universal System of Household Furniture* (1760–62), by Ince and Mayhew, where they are called burjairs. (*See* page 142.) Gillows made what was described as 'a large and handsome mahogany bergier, stuffed back in green morocco'. (Entry: 1784–87, E. & S. Book, No. 153.) Sheraton in *The Cabinet Dictionary* (1803) describes a *bergère* as 'having a caned back and arms. Sometimes the seats are caned, having loose cushions.' Sheraton's description indicates the prototype of the modern *bergère* chair. (*See* accompanying illustration.)

A modern *bergère* chair. Cane work is used on the back and sides only

Betty Lamp

A crusie, *q.v.*, lamp used in America during the 18th century, consisting of a flat iron vessel with a floating wick, sometimes taking the form of a portable lamp, suspended from a hook, so it could be hung upon a nail or suspended from an adjustable stand. When separate wick hold-

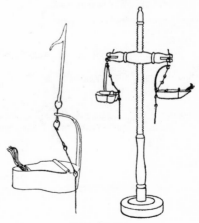

Betty lamps.

Burjairs. Illustrated on Plate LX of *The Universal System of Household Furniture*, by Ince and Mayhew, published in 1760.

ers were introduced, crusies were called 'better lamps,' a name transformed to 'Betty Lamps' by American Collectors.

Bevel

A term used to describe the sloping edge of a flat metal or glass surface. (*See also* **Chamfer** *and* **Vauxhall Bevel**.)

Bezel

The metal ring that encircles and frames the glass over a clock face. It is usually hinged.

Bible Box

A term, probably of Victorian origin, that is wrongly applied to 17th century joined boxes. Theoretically, the receptacle below the lid was supposed to contain the family Bible.

Bidet

A small stool with four legs and a pierced seat, containing a pan made of metal or earthenware. In use during the last half of the 18th century, and probably before in Europe. Sheraton, in *The Cabinet Dictionary* (1803), describes seat bidets and travelling bidets; the former having a seat that conceals the pan, the latter being made in the form of a chest with a removable top.

Biedermeir

A style of furnishing and interior decoration that originated in Germany. Biedermeir was the name of a Philistine character who figured in the journal *Fliegende Blätter*. Between 1815 and the middle of the 19th century Biedermeir became a debased variation of the French Empire style, with extravagantly carved furniture, enriched by embossed metal decoration, and frequently upholstered in black horsehair.

Billiard Table

A table designed and made for the game of billiards. Originally, billiard tables were square with a single pocket under a hole in the centre of the table. An early 17th century example at Knole, is rectangular. A detailed description of the construction of the billiard table is given in Robert Howlett's book, published in London

Billiard table. (From Howlett's *The School of Recreation*, published in 1684.)

in 1684, called *The School of Recreation*. (*See* accompanying illustration.) The author states that 'the form of the billiard table ought to be oblong, that is to say, somewhat larger than it is broad'. (This description is quoted in full in Section II, pages 50-51.) The present rectangular form, in the proportion of a double square, was in use in the early 18th century, and this form was much improved by the Lancaster firm of Gillow, which for many years had a monopoly of the manufacture. By the end of the 18th century the making of billiard tables was a special branch of joinery, owing to the highly skilled work needed in framing the tops to prevent the playing surface from warping.

Binding

A term used in upholstery to describe the various types of narrow laces which are used to strengthen and embellish the edges of draperies, such as bed curtains.

Birch (*Betula alba*)

A tree native to England. Used in cheaper types of furniture, but chiefly for the veneers employed in the making of plywood, *q.v.*

Birdcage

A term for a device which allows the top of a tripod table to be movable, and to be tipped up when not in use. It consists of two squares of wood, connected by small, turned pillars, the lower square pierced by a hole, through which the pillar of the stand is fixed by means of a wedge. The upper part is hinged to the table top by means of two long bearers, screwed to the underside. Birdcages were used on tripod tables during the 18th century. (*See* illustration.) Birdcage tables often revolve: when the top is horizontal it may be spun round.

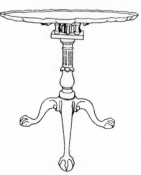

Table with birdcage.

Birdcage Clock

A modern term sometimes used to describe the iron or brass weight-driven wall clocks which were made in large numbers during the 17th century, and continued to be used in the first half of the 18th century, when, through the dial increasing in size, the design changed. (*See also* **Lantern Clock.**)

Birdsbeak

A moulding which, in section, resembles the outward curve of a bird's beak.

Birdsbeak Lock

A lock which is used on cylinder tables, piano falls, and tambours, so called because the bolt resembles a bird's beak in appearance.

Bird's-Eye Maple, *see* Maple

Black Bean (*Castanospermum australe*)

An Australian wood, dark brown, hard and straight-grained, not unlike walnut in colour. Used for cabinet work.

Black Oak, *see* **Bog Oak**

Black Sea Walnut, *see* **Circassian Walnut**

Black Virginia, *see* **Virginia Walnut**

Black Walnut Period, *See* **American Black Walnut**

Blanket Chest

A development of the mule chest. In the American colonies during the late 17th and early 18th centuries it took the outward form of a chest with four drawers. The two top drawers were false

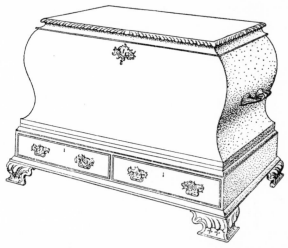

English blanket chest. Mahogany. *Circa* 1750. Compare the design with that of the clothes chest from Chippendale's *Director* on page 191. (From a drawing by Ronald Escott of the original chest in the Fitzwilliam Museum, Cambridge.)

and formed the front of a receptacle for blankets in the upper part of the chest, which had a hinged lid. A different type was made in England, with the chest unconcealed and mounted upon a base with two drawers in it. A mid-18th century specimen of an English blanket chest in mahogany is in the Fitzwilliam Museum, Cambridge. (*See* illustration.)

Blind Frame, *see* **Back Board**

Blind Tracery

The characteristic forms of Gothic tracery, *q.v.*, carved upon a solid wooden surface. (*See* illustration of bench end on page 139.)

Block Front

When the front of a chest, cabinet, or bookcase is made in different planes, so that either the centre section projects beyond the side sections, or is recessed, while the side sections project, the term block front is used. (*See also* **Broken Front, Recessed Front,** *and* **Tub Front.**)

Board

In mediaeval times the terms board and table were synonymous, and the former was used in relation to specific functions: hence oyster board, dressing board, meat board, moulding board, cheese board, cup board, which were all used for preparing or serving various kinds of food or drink. Folding or double boards for the game of backgammon were called tables. (*See* **Cupboard, Sideboard,** *and* **Table.**)

Boarded Bedstead, *see* Wainscot Bedstead

Boasting or Boosting

The rough preliminary outline of any carved work. Sheraton describes it as 'the massy and rude formation of any general outline'.

Bobbin Turning

A form of ornamental turning used in the 17th century on the legs and stretchers of chairs and tables, representing a succession of small bulbs or bobbins.

Bodger

A local name for the chair-leg turners who work in the beech woods of Buckinghamshire. The derivation of the word is not known. (*See* Section I, page 36, for some views regarding its possible origin.)

Bodying-in

This is one of the processes of French polishing, and describes the filling of the grain of wood before polishing.

Bobbin turning.

Bog Oak or Black Oak

Oak of a very dark colour, almost resembling ebony, obtained from timber that has been buried in a peat bog.

Bokhara

The name given to most of the carpets and rugs that are made in western Turkestan. They are made almost wholly of good quality wool. Deep and dark colourings are used, bright colours only occurring in very small amounts. Kendrick and Tattersall state that 'most of the rugs made in Western Turkestan are called Bokhara though very few are made there'.

Bolection

A bolection moulding covers the joints between two members with surfaces at different levels, and projects beyond both surfaces.

146

Bolster

A long, round pillow, probably introduced during the 16th century.

Bolster Arm

A term used in the 19th century when the arm rests of an upholstered easy chair were cylindrical in form and resembled miniature bolsters.

Bolting Ark, *see* **Ark**

Bombay Blackwood, *see* **Indian Rosewood**

Bombé

The outward curving front or sides of cabinets and commodes: a fashion originating in France during the reign of Louis XIV. (*See also* **Kettle Front**.)

Bolster arm.

Bonnet Top

A term sometimes used in America for a curved or hooded pediment on the top of a tallboy, bookcase, or cabinet: sometimes called a hooded top. The English term is dome or hood.

Bookcase

Originally, bookshelves in libraries were fixtures; some of the most valuable books were chained to the shelves. The free standing bookcase, or press, as it was then called, only developed in the 17th century. By the 18th century the free standing library bookcase had assumed architectural proportions, with large glazed doors. The term bookcase is today generally applied when glazed doors are used. (*See* illustration on page 153, *also* **Bookshelves, Bookstand, Bureau Bookcase, Library Case, Revolving Bookcase,** *and* **Wing Bookcase**.)

Bookcase Table

A table with one or two sets of shelves below the top, to accommodate books.

Bookshelves

This term today applies to open shelves for books.

Bookstand

Tiers of four or more shelves held by corner posts, and open on all sides. Known in the late 18th century as a moving bookstand. (*See* illustration, *also* **Chiffonier**.)

Moving bookstand. (From *The Prices of Cabinet Work*, 1797 edition.)

Boosting, *see* **Boasting,**

Boot Rack

A rack consisting of horizontal bars on which boots and shoes may be placed at an angle.

Boss

In architecture this is an ornament covering the intersection of ribs in a roof; and bosses are occasionally used at the intersection of angles in mouldings in cabinet work.

Boston Rocker, *see* Rocking Chair

Bottle-end Glazing

An incorrect term applied to the use of bullions or bulls' eyes, sometimes used for the glazing of cupboard doors. (*See* **Bullion**.)

Bottle Turning

A form of turning introduced in the late 17th century, which resembled a bottle in form. Probably of Dutch origin.

Boulle Work, *see* Buhl

Bow Back

The curved outer frame of a stick back or Windsor chair is known as a bow. Such chairs are sometimes called bow-backed.

Bow Front or Swell Front

The front of a chest of drawers, commode, cabinet, table, or sideboard, with a convex curve like a bow, is called a bow front. (*See* illustrations on page 361.)

Bow Top

When the top rail of a chair has a convex curve, it is sometimes known as a bow top.

Box Bedstead

A box bedstead is enclosed by wooden panels on three sides, with curtains which may be drawn across the open side.

Box bedstead. (From Loudon's *Encyclopaedia*, 1846 supplement.)

Box Chair

A modern term for an unusual type of 16th century armchair with a high panelled back, panelled sides which support flat arms, a solid seat, and a receptacle below the seat, fitted with a panelled door. There is a specimen in the Victoria and Albert Museum, London, that is dated 'about 1550'. (Illustrated and described in the V. & A. *Catalogue of English Furniture and Woodwork*, Vol. II, No. 513, p. 4 and Plate 3.)

Box End

The rectangular end of a pew in a church is sometimes called a box end. (*See* illustration on page 139.)

Box Iron

An early form of hollow smoothing iron, consisting of a metal

receptacle with a handle, resembling in shape an ordinary flat iron,
A heated iron was put inside the box iron, so that linen was not
touched by any metal that had
been directly in contact with a
flame.

Box Ottoman

A couch or divan without back
or arms, with a hinged upholstered lid which forms a seat, with
a receptacle below. Introduced
during the 19th century. (*See also*
Ottoman.)

Box Pleat

This requires greater width than
an ordinary pleat. The fabric is
creased at regular intervals, the
fold made forming a pleat of the

Box iron. A 16th century example
of French origin. (From Thomas
Wright's *Homes of Other Days*.)

required width: the material is then stitched down the length of the
crease and opened out flat. The pleat is creased again on each side,
forming a box shape, and stitched. Where several box pleats are
made, their edges may meet, or a space may be left between each
edge.

Box Settle

The name given to a settle that has a box seat with a hinged lid.
Not a contemporary name.

Box Stool

A low joint stool with a box in the upper part for which the seat
acts as a lid. These miniature stools were made during the 17th
century, and were probably designed for children.

Box Toilet Glass, *see* Toilet Glass

Box Wood or Boxwood (*Buxus sempervirens*)

Box grows in Britain, Europe, Asia Minor, and western Asia,
and supplies a hard, smooth, pale yellow wood, generally used for
decorative inlays.

Boxed Heart

A piece of square sawn timber, cut so that the pith or heart,
which is the central core, is enclosed throughout its whole length
within the four surfaces.

Brace

A term sometimes applied to the ties or stretchers of the legs of
chairs and tables. (*See* **Stays**, *also* **Stretcher**.)

Brace Back Chair, *see* Stays

149

Two designs by Thomas Chippendale of 'Brackets for Bustos'. Selected from six which occupy Plate CLXI of the 3rd edition of *The Gentleman and Cabinet Maker's Director*, 1762.)

Bracket

A projection from a vertical surface, which forms a support. (*See* illustrations, *also* **Console** and **Corbel**.)

Bracket Clock

A modern term commonly applied to a spring-driven clock, which in the late 17th and 18th centuries was called a table clock because it usually stood on a table. Such clocks seldom stood on brackets, so the term is misleading.

Bracket Foot

A foot shaped like a bracket, used on chests of drawers and cabinets, and extending a short way in both directions from the corner of the base. (*See* illustration, also page 459).

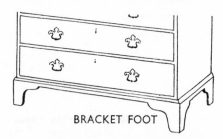

BRACKET FOOT

Braid

A narrow woven band used to decorate upholstered furniture and curtains, made in all kinds of fanciful weaves, and in varying widths. (*See* **Laces**.)

Brasswork

This is used extensively for ornamental and practical purposes in furniture making, and the term covers such articles as locks, hinges, handles, decorative mounts, and inlaid brass lines. (*See* **Ormolu.**)

Brattishing

A form of cresting which is sometimes known as Tudor flower, and is used occasionally as an embellishment at the top of early 16th century screens or panelling.

Brazilian Rosewood, *see* **Rosewood**

Brazilian Tulip Wood, *see* **Tulip Wood**

Bread Trough, *see* **Kneading Trough**

Break

That portion of the carcase, plinth, or cornice of a piece of furniture which projects forwards, and breaks the continuity of line and surface. (*See* illustration of Broken Front on page 153.)

Break Front, *see* **Broken Front**

Breakfast Table

Small, four-legged tables, with two hinged flaps to allow the top to be extended. Such tables were made from the mid-18th century onwards; but they are specifically labelled as breakfast tables by Chippendale in the *Director* (1762), where he shows two designs on Plate LIII (*see* illustrations on next page). He describes them thus: 'One hath a Stretching-Rail, and the Feet are canted and sunk in. The other hath a Shelf, inclosed with Fretwork. Sometimes they are inclosed with Brass Wirework. In the Front is a Recess for the Knees, &c.'

Brilliant-cutting

A form of incised decoration used on glass, made with a wheel which cuts various sections in the surface, which are subsequently smoothed or polished.

Britannia Metal

A white metal, with a bluish tint, based on an alloy of tin and antimony, to which copper, lead, zinc, or bismuth are added in small quantities. Used in the making of spoons, and such domestic articles as teapots.

Brocade

A finely woven silk fabric, to which one or more colours have been added, so that the additional colour appears on the face of the material. The term today applies to any finely woven multicoloured fabric which suggests the character of the original material.

Brocatelle

A cloth with a raised design in the warp, with a plain weft background. Today, the term is often used to describe any cloth with a plain background and a raised woven design.

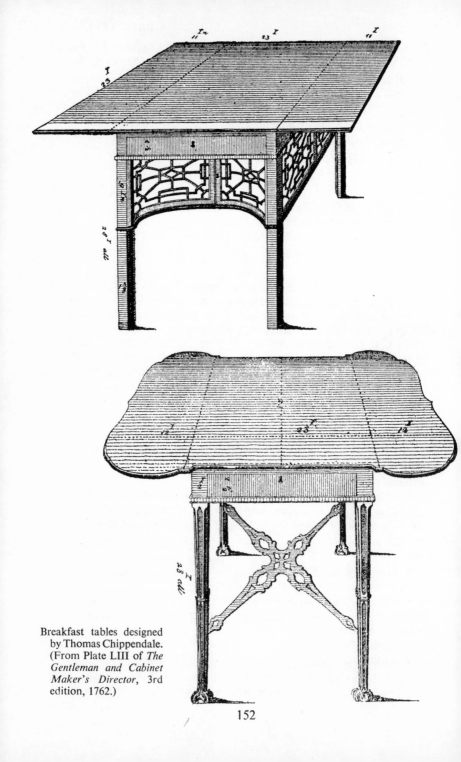

Breakfast tables designed
by Thomas Chippendale.
(From Plate LIII of *The
Gentleman and Cabinet
Maker's Director*, 3rd
edition, 1762.)

152

Broken Cabriole, *see* **Hock Leg**

Broken Front or **Break Front**

The term used for a piece of furniture when the front is made in different planes. Large bookcases made in the 18th and 19th centuries often had a central section that projected beyond the flank-

BROKEN PEDIMENT

BROKEN FRONT

ing sections. The 19th century winged wardrobe is an elaborate example of the use of a broken front. (*See* accompanying illustration of mid-18th century bookcase, also that on page 509.)

Broken Pediment

A pediment, broken in the centre, occasionally used to accommodate a pedestal for a bust or urn, or some such decorative object. (*See* illustration above, *also* page 59 and **Desk and Bookcase** on page 156.)

Brown Oak

A variety of English oak, of a rich, warm brown hue, taken from a tree that has suffered from the form of decay called foxiness.

Buffet

A form of side or serving table. The term appears to have come into use during the 16th century, and is sometimes applied to a court cupboard, *q.v.* (*See* Section I, pages 20 to 21, *also* illustrations on page 215.) The Gillow records include a buffet in the form of a corner cupboard, with doors enclosing shelves in the upper part, and two doors below. (Dated 1798, E. & S. Book, No. 1450.) Sheraton made an attempt to resurrect the buffet in an elaborate form. (*See* illustration opposite.)

Buffet Stool

A term that often occurs in inventories of the late 16th and early 17th centuries, and which may refer to a joined stool. R. W. Symonds contends that the frequency of its use 'suggests that it cannot be otherwise than a joined stool, for no other type has survived in sufficient numbers, which would account for its so frequent mention'. ('The Renaming of English Furniture', *The Antique Collector*, Vol. 19, No. 4, August 1948, p. 128.)

Buhl

Sometimes known as boulle work. An elaborate form of surface decoration consisting of inlays of tortoiseshell, ivory, and metals such as brass and silver. Invented by the French cabinet maker, André Charles Boulle (1642–1732).

Built-in Furniture, *see* Fitted Furniture

Bulb

An ornamental device introduced in the late 16th century, and used on table legs, bedposts, and the columns on the upper part of press cupboards. It consisted of a melon-shaped swelling in the leg or post. (*See* **Melon Bulb**.)

Bulbous

A term sometimes used to describe turned work in which considerable use is made of spherical forms and knobs.

Bull's Eye

The circular or oval glazed aperture in the trunk door of a long case clock.

Bullion or Bull's Eye

The circular scar in the centre of a disc of crown glass, caused by the blowing process that was formerly used in its manufacture.

Bun Foot

A foot in the form of a bun-like, flattened sphere, used on chairs, tables, stands, and chests, which came into general use during the latter part of the 17th century.

Bunk

The term generally used to describe a fixed sleeping berth on board ship.

Bureau

A piece of furniture with the writing space or flap hinged, so that it rests at an angle of 45° when closed. The space behind this flap has pigeon-holes with small drawers below them and usually a

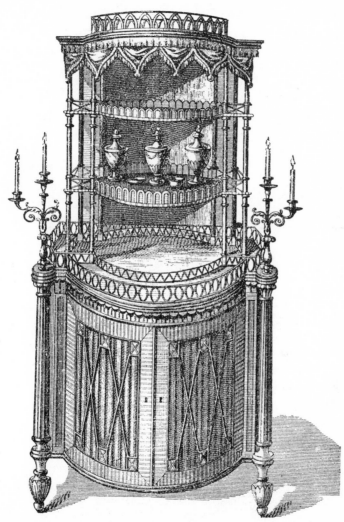

Buffet designed by Thomas Sheraton, and reproduced from Plate 24 of *The Cabinet Dictionary*. (The publication date of this plate is given as December 15th, 1802: many of the plates in the *Dictionary* were published separately before the book was issued in 1803.) Sheraton observed that 'a buffet may, with some propriety, be restored to modern use, and prove ornamental to a breakfast room, answering as the repository of a tea equipage.'

Desk and bookcase. (From Plate CVII of *The Gentleman and Cabinet Maker's Director*, by Thomas Chippendale, 3rd edition, 1762.)

156

central cupboard. When open, the hinged flap rests on lopers, *q.v.* There may be either a flat top or a superstructure with cupboards or bookshelves. (*See* illustration, *also* **Bureau Bookcase** *and* **Scrutoire**.) Introduced during the late 17th century, bureaux developed a great variety of forms throughout the 18th and early 19th centuries.

Bureau Bedstead

A bed that could be folded up and concealed in a carcase which outwardly resembled a bureau. The device did not come into general use. One was designed and made by the firm of Gillow in 1788, and was described in their records as a 'Desk Buro Bedstead'. (E. & S. Book, No. 311.) The accompanying illustration is based on a sketch in the Gillow records. When closed, the front had five dummy drawers. Bureau bedsteads were advertised among other types by John Taylor, in the *New York Gazette* of March 31st, 1769. A bureau bedstead is included and costed in *The Prices of Cabinet Work* (1797), where it is described as: 'Three feet six inches long, to shew four drawers in front, cock beaded, on plinth or common brackets' (p. 40).

Early 18th century bureau.

Bureau Bookcase

A bureau surmounted by a bookcase, with glazed or panelled doors. The term probably originated in the mid-18th century, though a contemporary description, which was used both by

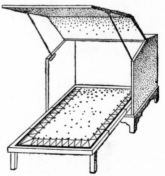

Bureau bedstead.

Chippendale and Hepplewhite, was desk and bookcase. Hepplewhite's *Guide* gives three plates to these articles (Nos. 40, 41, and 42). Sheraton in *The Cabinet Dictionary* (1803) describes as a bureau bookcase a small bureau, open below and with three open bookshelves above. (Page 111, and Plate 25.) But his use of the term was exceptional. By the second quarter of the 19th century it was established as a description of the desk and bookcase, and in 1833 Loudon uses it in this sense on p. 302 of his *Encyclopaedia*. (*See* illustrations on pages 156 and 272, *also* Section I, page 21.)

Bureau bookcase, mid-18th century. (From a drawing by E. J. Warne.)

Bureau Cabinet

A bureau surmounted by shelves designed for the display of china.

Bureau Dressing Table

A dual purpose piece of furniture, first made in the early 18th century, consisting of a bureau supported upon cabriole legs, with two or three shallow drawers below the writing space, and the top surmounted by a toilet glass. A combined writing and dressing table came into use in the mid-18th century, and was described and illustrated by Chippendale under the name of Buroe dressing table. Two of these designs, from the 3rd edition of the *Director*, are shown on the opposite page.

Bureau Table

A form of kneehole writing table, *q.v.*, with a drawer below the top, and drawers on either side of the kneehole space. The term is misleading, for it is a flat-topped table, and not a true bureau with the writing space hinged.

Burgomaster Chair, *see* **Roundabout Chair**

Burjair, *see* **Bergère**

Burr

A growth on the trunk or root of a tree, which often provides elaborately marked wood which may be used for decorative purposes, such as burr elm and burr yew.

Butt Hinge

A type of hinge used for hanging doors, so that only a thin line of metal is visible externally.

Early 18th century bureau dressing table.

Butt Joint

A butt or square joint is formed by two pieces of timber meeting end to end.

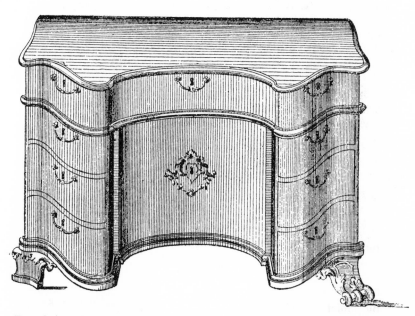

Two designs for 'buroe dressing tables' by Thomas Chippendale. (From Plate LXII of *The Gentleman and Cabinet Maker's Director*. 3rd edition, 1762.)

Butterfly Table

A drop-leaf table used chiefly in inns, and made in the American colonies during the late 17th and early 18th centuries. The name arises from the shape of the table when both supporting wings are extended. (*See* illustration.) The wing supports are sometimes called rudders, *q.v.*

Butterfly table.

Buttoning

A decorative method of attaching the upholstery material to the back of a chair or sofa. The back is first well padded and covered with light canvas; the material is then stretched into place rather more loosely than for ordinary upholstery, and attached to the outer frame. Strong thread is stitched through both the padding and the outer cover, and is taken right through to the back of the chair or sofa. The stitches are pulled in tightly, thus drawing the padding and its cover into a form of quilting, and are then hidden beneath a covered button, which may be of the same material and colour as the upholstery, or in contrast to it. The back is then covered in the ordinary way to hide the stitching which has been taken through from the front. Buttoning is always done in a neat and regular pattern, generally in the form of elongated diamonds, though squares and even straight lines are used. It was popular in Victorian and Edwardian furniture, and was used extensively in the upholstery of seat backs in railway coaches. Its use for small occasional chairs persists. (*See* illustration.)

Buttoning on the seat of a round back chair. (From a mid-19th century trade catalogue).

Buttonwood

A commercial name for the wood of the American plane tree (*Platanus occidentalis*), which is reddish brown in colour, hard, and cross-grained. Occasionally used for chair making.

* C *

C-Scroll

An ornamental scroll, in the form of the letter C, used in carved enrichment, and introduced in the early 18th century.

Cabin Trunk, *see* **Wardrobe Trunk**

Cabinet

A piece of furniture with shelves and drawers, designed primarily as a decorative article which also served as a receptacle wherein objects of value could be kept in safety. Cabinets veneered with ebony were the first to be made. They were used in Italy and France before they were introduced in England during the second half of the 17th century. The French name for a cabinet maker, *ébéniste*, was derived from the characteristic decorative veneer employed. During and after the Carolean period, cabinets became elaborately decorative in character, and were often designed for the display of rare ornaments. (*See also* **Bureau Cabinet, China Cabinet, Filing Cabinet, Kitchen Cabinet,** *and* **Print Cabinet.**)

Cabinet Maker

A highly skilled and specialised maker of furniture, whose craft was created and developed by the technique of veneering, which was introduced into England during the second half of the 17th century. (*See* **Veneering.**) The cabinet maker and cabinet making became identified with fine furniture throughout the Queen Anne and Georgian periods, and cabinet making has since become a generic term for the manufacture of furniture generally. (*The Cabinet Maker* is the name of the oldest weekly furniture trade paper circulating in Britain, and was founded in 1880, by Sir John Williams Benn.)

Cable Moulding

A form of enrichment representing twisted ropes, on a convex moulding.

Cabochon

A spherical or oval ornamental *motif*, either convex or concave, surmounted by carved ornament, generally based on the conventionalised leaf of the acanthus. Of French origin, and used in England during the middle years of the 18th century.

Cabriole Bracket

A bracket foot with a convex knee curving outwards, like a dwarf cabriole leg, terminating in a plain or a claw-and-ball foot. (*See* illustration on p. 145, *also* **Bracket Foot** *and* **Cabriole Leg.**)

Cabriole Chair

Described by Sheraton in *The Cabinet Dictionary* (1803) as an 'arm-chair stuffed all over. The legs are mahogany' (p. 19, *under* the general entry of Arm-chair). He also describes it under a special entry as 'a French easy chair' (p. 120). The cabriole chair Sheraton illustrates has sabre legs, *q.v.*, back and front, mounted on castors; a seat that is almost semi-circular in plan, with a bow front; and a semi-circular back. This type of chair was known and the term for it was current during the last quarter of the 18th century. (*See* Section I, page 32.) An advertisement published in the *Bristol Journal*, April 16th, 1783, reads as follows: 'For sale. Mrs Gordon, Abbots Leigh Court, Somerset. Sophas and Cabriole Chairs to match, in great perfection. . . .' Another advertisement in the same paper in that year appeared on February 22nd, notifying a sale at St. James's in London, which included the items 'Drawing room Cabriole Chairs and Soffa, cover'd with blue Morine. . . .'

Cabriole Leg or Bandy Leg

A leg consisting of two well-defined curves, with the upper part—the shoulder or knee—convex, and the lower part, above the shaped foot, concave. These legs were introduced during the William and Mary period, and came into general use in the early 18th century for chairs, stools, tables, bureaux, and the stands of cabinets. The form is ancient, having originated from the conventionalised representations of animals' legs used in Greek and Roman furniture. (*See* pages 43, 238, and 306, *also* accompanying illustrations.) The term does not appear to be contemporary; and in the late 18th and early 19th centuries, cabriole meant

Cabriole leg on mid-18th century card table.

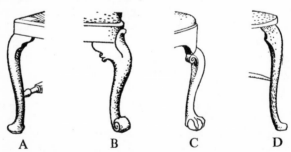

Four types of cabriole leg. A: leg from early 18th century chair with a club foot and side stretchers. (The chair from which this detail is taken is shown on page 445.) B: hipped leg with carved knee and whorl or French scroll foot; mid-18th century. C: Early Georgian type, with claw-and-ball foot. D: from a Windsor chair: second half of 18th century.

a type of armchair (*see* previous entry); but at some time at the end of the Victorian period or in the opening years of the present century the word began to be used to describe legs with a double curve. Arthur Hayden uses the term in the first edition of his *Chats on Old Furniture*, published in 1905 (T. Fisher Unwin).

Cabriole Period

A term used by some writers for the period between the last decade of the 17th and the middle of the 18th centuries. During those sixty years, the cabriole leg, *q.v.*, was used extensively on chairs, tables, and the stands of cabinets.

Caddy, *see* **Tea Caddy**

Cadenas, *see* **Nef**

Calamander Wood, *see* **Coromandel Wood**

Calico

A plain weave cotton cloth.

Camel Back Chair, *see* **Shield Back Chair**

Camp Bedstead

A portable bedstead consisting of a light framework with legs which fold up below the frame. Sheraton, in *The Cabinet Dictionary* (1803), refers to camp or field bedsteads, and states that 'they all have folding tester lathes, either hexagonal or elliptical shaped, and hinged so as to fold close together'. But Sheraton had in mind something more elaborate than the small, easily packed appliance which was actually used during military campaigns. (*See* illustrations on next page, *also* **Field Bed.**)

Camp Stool

A small, folding stool with a detachable seat of canvas or leather.

Canadian Birch (*Betula lutea*)

Also known as yellow birch, Quebec birch, and, when curly grained and highly figured, as Canadian silky wood. It comes from Canada, Newfoundland, and the eastern states of North America. In colour it varies from pale to dark reddish brown, and the grain is curly or wavy. It is used for furniture making and veneers, and takes a high polish.

Canadian Silky Wood, *see* **Canadian Birch**

Canary Wood (*Liriodendron tulipifera*)

Although this is known in Britain as canary wood, or, incorrectly, as canary whitewood, it is really American whitewood, and is classified as such by the British Standards Institution. It comes from Canada and the eastern states of North America. In colour it is light yellow or brown with a tinge of green. It is a straight-grained wood, easy to work, and lacks decorative character. It is used in cabinet work, chiefly for the backs and sides of drawers.

Candelabrum

A term variously used to describe branched candlesticks, chandeliers, or lampstands. In *The Practical Cabinet Maker, Upholsterer*

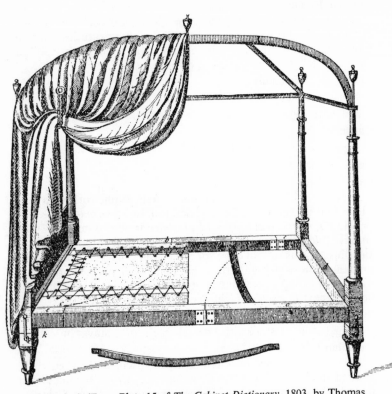

Camp bed. (From Plate 15 of *The Cabinet Dictionary*, 1803, by Thomas Sheraton.)

Folding camp bed. Designed for use in cottages. (From Loudon's *Encyclopaedia of Cottage, Farm and Villa Architecture*, 1833.)

and Complete Decorator (1836), under Candelabra, the following description is given: 'A candlestick supported from the floor, and used in various situations. Sometimes one is placed at each end of a sideboard.' (*See also* **Tripod Light.**)

Candle Beam

An early form of chandelier. Thomas Wright quotes the will of Agnes Ridges of Bury, made in 1492, which mentions 'my candylbeme that hangyth in my hall. . . .' The candle beam had four or six arms, and the candles were stuck on spikes which were surrounded by shallow metal cups to catch the melting tallow or wax.

Candle Board

A small shelf or ledge fitted below a table top to accommodate a candlestick.

Candle Box

A rectangular wooden box, with a shaped back, designed for hanging upon a wall, and occasionally fitted with a lid. Used for storing candles.

Candle Chest

Probably a form of candle box. Thomas Wright quotes an inventory, dated 1567, of the contents of the principal chamber in the house of Mrs Elizabeth Hutton, at Hunwick, which includes: 'a little chest bound with iron, a candle-chest, and another old chest. . . .'

Candle Screen

Really a miniature sliding screen on a pole, used in the 18th century on a writing table to shield the face from the glare of a candle. Gillows record one 27 ins. high, with a base $6\frac{7}{8}$ ins., the dimensions of the screen being 1 ft. by 10 ins. (E. & S. Book, No. 681.)

Candle Slide

A narrow pull-out tray, sometimes fitted on either side of a bureau bookcase, designed as a stand for candles.

Candle Stand

A small stand, usually a tripod, designed to carry not only candles and lamps, but various ornaments. Introduced during the early part of the 18th century. (*See* illustration on next page, from the 3rd edition of Chippendale's *Director*.) A candle stand is sometimes called a *torchère*.

Candlestick

The earliest form of mediaeval candlestick was an iron spike on which the candle was stuck. (*See* **Pricket**.) Candlesticks with sockets did not come into general use until the 16th century, though this form was probably known much earlier. They were usually made of iron, brass, copper, or latten, *q.v.*, sometimes of pewter. Elegant designs in silver, with two or more branches, were made during the 18th century. (*See* **Candelabrum**.) The bedroom candlestick, with a dish-shaped base, a handle for carrying, and an extinguisher fitting into a socket in the handle, is sometimes called a flat candlestick. (*See also* **Save-all**.)

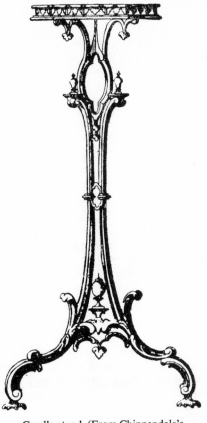

Candle stand. (From Chippendale's *Director*.)

Canework

Woven cane was introduced for chair seats and backs during the second half of the 17th century. The material is provided by the class of palms known as rattans (usually of the grass *Calamus*) and the canes are split into thin strips and interwoven to form an openwork, resilient surface. (*See* illustration of Day Bed, which shows canework in the seat and back, on page 226.) A large mesh was used originally, but a smaller, closer mesh was adopted before the end of the 17th century. A revival of taste for canework furniture occurred during the 19th century, and it was used extensively for chair seats, and on other forms of furniture. (*See* **Bamboo** *and* **Bentwood Furniture**.)

Canopy, *see* Tester

Cant

A form of chamfer or bevel.

Canted

When the legs or feet of a piece of furniture are inclined outwards at an angle they are known as canted legs or canted feet, though for the latter the term splayed, *q.v.*, is generally used. Another use of the word canted refers to a projecting chamfered member.

Canteen

A chest or small cabinet designed to accommodate cutlery or cooking utensils.

Canterbury

A term for a small stand with divisions, designed to hold books or music. According to Sheraton in *The Cabinet Dictionary* (1803), it is also 'A supper tray, made to stand by a table at supper, with a

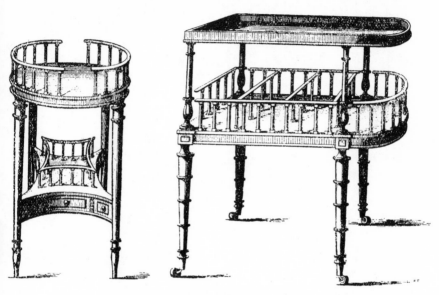

Supper canterburies. (From Plate 28 of *The Cabinet Dictionary*, by Thomas Sheraton.)

circular end, and three partitions cross-wise, to hold knives, forks and plates. . . .' It was really a forerunner of the modern trolley table. Sheraton conjectures that this type of cabinet work was thus named because an Archbishop of Canterbury 'first gave orders for these pieces'. At some time after the middle of the 19th century the word canterbury was also used to describe a music stool, with a hinged lid and a receptacle below for music. (*See* illustrations above and on next page.)

Canvas

A plain open-weave cloth, made with hard, twisted yarns. Used extensively in upholstery, particularly on the underside of chairs, and for strong seats such as those used on camp stools, tubular metal furniture, and deck chairs.

Cape Boxwood, *see* **Kamassi**

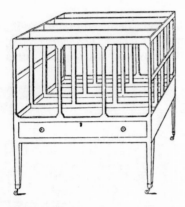

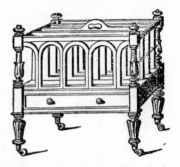

A canterbury or music box. (From *The Prices of Cabinet Work*, 1797 edition.)

Music canterbury. (From Loudon's *Encyclopaedia*, 1833.)

Upright canterbury. Mid-19th century. (Reproduced from *The Young Ladies' Treasure Book* in Robert Harling's *Home: a Victorian Vignette*, 1938.)

Capital

The head of a column or a pilaster, variously moulded and sculptured. (*See* accompanying illustration, *also* page 114.)

Carcase

The basic, box-like body of a piece of furniture, without doors, drawers, or fittings.

Carcase Work

Work connected with carcases, as distinct from table work.

Card Table

Tables for card games were introduced towards the end of the 17th century, and were usually of the folding type, with small depressions at the corners to take candlesticks, and deeper depressions or holes, for money. The playing surface, when opened out, was generally covered with green baize. (*See* **Ombre Table**.) Tables were used for card playing as early as the 14th century; and there is some evidence that special types of circular topped tables were used for cards in the following century. (*See* illustrations on page 170.) There is a reference in a record dated the twentieth year of Henry VIII's reign (1529), which reads: '. . . for avoydinge of dyce and carde tables and all other unlawful gamys which were then by comandement

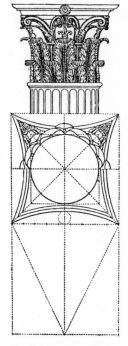

Capital (Roman Corinthian order).

prohybett. . . .' But this probably means the game of tables (*see* **Table**) and not a specific piece of furniture. (Quoted from 'The Case of William Waryng' included in the Appendix to chapter viii of *Society in the Elizabethan Age*, by Hubert Hall, F.S.A. London: Swan Sonnenschein and Co., Ltd., 4th edition, 1901.)

Carlton Table or Carlton House Table

The name given to a form of writing table with the writing space backed and flanked by a superstructure containing small drawers and cupboards. The name, derived from an original design for the Prince of Wales whose residence was Carlton House, was first used by the firm of Gillow, who made this table in 1796. (E. & S. book. No. 1245.) (*See* illustrations on page 171.)

Carolean

A term frequently used to describe the period of Charles II's reign, 1660–85.

Card table, 14th century. The drawing is copied from a MS. of *Meliadus*, and is included by Thomas Wright in *The Homes of Other Days*. Wright suggests that the MS. was written in the south of France at some time between the years 1330 and 1350. From the drawing it is difficult to see how the table is supported: the sloping member at the bottom left-hand corner might be either a leg or part of a trestle.

Circular card table, 15th century. This is draped with a cloth and supported by a central pillar rising from a circular base. The drawing, copied from an early 15th-century MS., is included in *The Homes of Other Days*, by Thomas Wright, who suggests that the MS. was of Flemish origin.

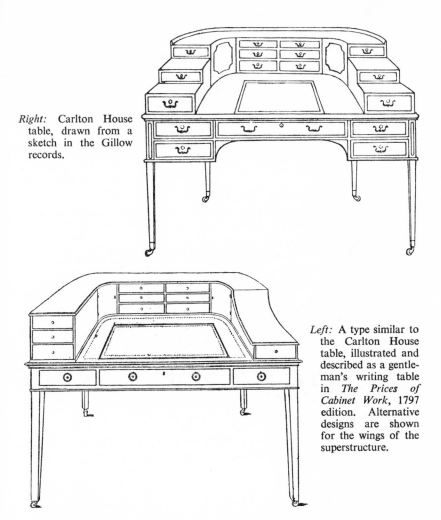

Right: Carlton House table, drawn from a sketch in the Gillow records.

Left: A type similar to the Carlton House table, illustrated and described as a gentleman's writing table in *The Prices of Cabinet Work*, 1797 edition. Alternative designs are shown for the wings of the superstructure.

Carpenter

In mediaeval times the carpenter was concerned chiefly with structural woodwork in building, such as timber-framed roofs. It was from his craft that the joiner's craft was evolved; but woodwork that was directly concerned with building construction, whether on a large or small scale, remained in the carpenter's hands.

Carpet

Today, a generic term for any woven or felted covering for floors or stairs; originally the term described any rich material that was either hung on walls or used on tables, and occasionally on chests and seats.

Cartouche

An ornamental feature resembling a tablet or scroll.

Cartridge Pleat or Organ Pipe Pleat

This is narrower than a box pleat, and is made in the same way, but after stitching the main crease the box-shaped pleat is omitted. The fold formed by the crease is tightly wadded to make a round pleat, shaped like an organ pipe, with the stuffing invisibly secured to the material. These pleats are used chiefly as a finish at the tops of curtains.

Carver

Since mediaeval times the wood carver has generally been in partnership with furniture makers or joiners, or other craftsmen, like coachmakers, who were responsible for making a complete object. The carver supplied the skill for embellishing furniture, and during the late 17th century and throughout the 18th as a *carver* and *gilder* he acquired greater independence, and became responsible for the carving and gilding of such ornate articles as looking-glass frames, console tables, candelabra and girandoles.

Carver Chair

An American name for a rush-seated chair with turned legs that rise vertically above the seat as framing posts for the back, terminating in ornamental finials above the top rail, the front legs rising also as posts to support the arm spindles. The back usually consists of three vertical spindles. Such chairs, made in the 17th century, are supposed to have derived their name from John Carver, an Englishman, born in Nottinghamshire about 1575, who became one of the 'Pilgrim Fathers' and the first governor of the Plymouth Colony in America, which he founded in 1620. He died in 1621, and is alleged to have owned the prototype of the Carver chair. Another use of the term is to distinguish the arm chair or elbow chair in a set of dining-room chairs, used at the head of the table by the carver. This does not appear to be a contemporary term.

Caryatid

A sculptured female figure occasionally used in place of a column, and supporting an entablature.

Carvers' Wood

A name sometimes given to lime wood, *q.v.*, because of its extensive use by wood-carvers.

Cascade

Sometimes known as Old English Tail, the term describes a long, narrow, and evenly folded piece of drapery that is used to finish the ends of swag drapery. The material is cut with a straight top edge and one straight side edge; the bottom and the other side edge are cut at an acute angle. This shaped piece of material, when evenly folded, produces a drapery which shows the reverse side of the material at intervals. For this reason, a lining in a contrasting colour is often used.

Case Furniture

A term generally applied to bookcases, escritoires, or bureau bookcases.

Casement Cloth

A furnishing material of plain weave cotton. It is made in plain self colours, and also with printed designs on coloured grounds.

Casket

A box or small chest, originally made as a receptacle for documents and small articles of value, such as jewellery.

Cassone

An Italian dower chest, elaborately carved, and often painted or gilded.

Cast Iron Furniture

Garden furniture, hall stands, umbrella stands, and hall chairs were made from cast iron during the middle and later years of the 19th century. Very elaborate castings were used, and although some of the early examples were based upon classical prototypes, after 1830 the character of design degenerated, and the great technical skill of ironfounders was misdirected. (*See* L. N. Cottingham's *Smith and Founders Director*, published in 1823 for early designs in cast iron; also Loudon's *Encyclopaedia of Cottage, Farm and Villa Architecture and Furniture*, 1833; and *A History of Cast Iron in Architecture*, by John Gloag and Derek Bridgwater, 1948. *See also* **Flower Stand** *and* **Metal Furniture**.)

Hall chair of cast iron. (From the *Art Journal*, 1862.)

Castellated

A term sometimes used to describe the ornamental coping moulding that separates the panelling from the frieze in 15th and 16th century interior woodwork. The moulding forms a continuous pattern of miniature battlements.

Castors or **Casters**

Small, pivoted wheels screwed on to the ends of legs and furniture. Used in the second half of the 17th century, when they were made of wood or leather. They were probably introduced earlier. Metal wheels were used during and after the 18th century.

Cat

A small, six-legged stand for plates, in the form of a double-tripod, with the six legs or spokes radiating from a central sphere, so that, however placed, the stand rests always upon three legs, the other three pointing upwards as a firm support for a plate. Cats were usually made of mahogany, sometimes of ebony, and stood in front of a fire to keep food warm. The term appears to date from the early 19th century, a fanciful explanation of its origin being that, like a cat, this type of stand always landed on its feet.

Cavetto

A hollow moulding, used chiefly on cornices, and containing a quarter of a circle.

Cavetto.

Caxton Chair

The simplest form of cheap wooden chair, with a flat seat, slightly tapered legs, and three straight splats or bars in the back. These chairs have for over a century been the staple product of the English furniture-making centre of High Wycombe in Buckinghamshire, and are to be found in parish halls, concert halls, and schools throughout the country. The origin of the name is not known.

Cedarwood

The cedar of Lebanon (*Cedrus libanotica*) was introduced into England in the reign of Charles II, and it was with this species that the name cedar was originally associated. It supplied an aromatic wood which was occasionally used for cabinet making, though employed chiefly for panelling, caskets, and other small receptacles. Cedar now stands for various types of aromatic hard and soft woods, such as Virginian pencil cedar (*see* **Pencil Cedar**), which is sometimes used for the lining of wardrobes and the sides of drawers.

Cele, *see* Celure

Cellar, *see* Celure

Cellaret

A deep drawer or tray in a sideboard to accommodate bottles. The term is also used for wine coolers or wine cisterns. (*See also* **Garde du Vin** and **Sarcophagus**.)

Celluloid

The earliest plastic, patented in 1855 by Alexander Parkes, of Birmingham, England. It is a transparent, chemically produced material, made in various colours. Today, celluloid is the American trade name for cellulose nitrate. (*See* **Plastics**.)

Celure

One of the parts that formed the more elaborate type of mediaeval bed. Also known as cele and cellar, or celler (Halliwell), and often as selour, under which entry it is fully described.

Chair

A seat with a back, with or without arms, designed for one person. Chairs are of ancient origin, and were used in the old kingdom of Egypt (3rd to 6th dynasties, 2980–2475 B.C.), also in the Assyrian, Greek, and Roman civilisations. Greek and Roman designs furnished the prototypes for many of the chairs made during the classical revivals of the late 18th and early 19th centuries. (*See* illustrations on pages 42, 286, and 404.) The various types of chairs are entered under their names, as follows:

Anthemion Back Chair	Flanders Chair
Armchair	Forest Chair
Back Stool	French Chair
Barber's Chair	French Corner Chair
Basket Chair	Glastonbury Chair
Bedroom Chair	Gouty Chair
Bended Back Chair	Grandfather Chair
Bergère	Hall Chair
Cabriole Chair	Hogarth Chair
Carver Chair	Hunting Chair
Caxton Chair	India Back Chair
Chair Bed	Indian Chair
Chair Table	Knitting Chair
Child's Chair	Ladder Back Chair
Close Chair	Ladies' Easy Chair
Cock-fighting Chair	Lath Back Chair
Coffer Maker's Chair	Lattice Back Chair
Companion Chair	Lounge Chair
Conversation Chair	Love Seat
Courting Chair	Low Back Chair
Cromwellian Chair	Lug Chair
Croquet Chair	Lyre Back Chair
Curricle	Marquise Chair
Darby and Joan Chair	Matted Chair
Deck Chair	Mendlesham Chair
Derbyshire Chair	Mortuary Chair
Double Chair	Nelson Chair
Draught Chair	Pan Back Chair
Drawing-room Chair	Panel Back Chair
Drunkard's Chair	Parlour Chair
Easy Chair	Porter's Chair
Elbow Chair	Reading Chair
Fan Back Chair	Restoration Chair
Farthingale Chair	Revolving Chair
Fauteuil	Ribband Back Chair
Fiddle Back Chair	Rocking Chair

Round Back Chair	Steamer Chair
Rout Chair	Straw Chair
Saddle Back	Tablet Chair
Saddle Check	Trafalgar Chair
Shaving Chair	Tub Chair
Shield Back Chair	Turned Chair
Side Chair	Twiggen Chair
Slat Back Chair	Wainscot Chair
Sleeping Chair	Wheatsheaf Back Chair
Sleepy Hollow Chair	Wheel Back Chair
Small Chair	White Wycombe
Smoker's Bow	Windsor Chair
Spindle Back Chair	Wing Chair
Spoon Back	

Chair Back

The back part of a chair above the seat level. In the early 17th century this was designed separately and applied to a stool (*see* **Back Stool**), though earlier and later chairs had been designed as complete entities.

Chair-Back Settee

A settee with the back formed by two or three conjoined chair backs. When two chair backs only are used, the settee is sometimes called a double chair. (*See* illustrations of Bar Back Settee *and* Double Chair, on pp. 123 and 230.)

Chair Bed

A chair with a back that may be lowered, and an extension to the seat which may be drawn out, so that the whole forms a bed. The original prototype may have been the sleeping chair, *q.v.*, introduced in the second half of the 17th century. Sheraton describes a 'bed-chair for sick persons' in *The Cabinet Dictionary* (1803) with an adjustable back that had 'side wings at top as a fence to the head, projecting out about 5 inches, and two stump elbows' (p. 336). Sheraton's hunting chair, *q.v.*, had a slide out frame which extended the seat in front, and was a form of chair bed. The term came into general use during the 19th century.

Chair Maker

Chairs were made both by joiners and turners from mediaeval times; by the former up to the 17th century, and by the latter to the present day. Coffer makers developed a specialised chair-making craft in the 15th century. (*See* **Coffer Maker's Chair**.) During the 17th century, the joiner who made chairs began to specialise in this work, and a partnership between joiner and turner came about, though cheap chairs made in the countryside were often wholly the work of the turner. The joiner, who had concentrated on chair making in the 17th century, established the craft which attained such perfection in the Queen Anne and

Georgian periods; the simpler and cheaper side of chair making remaining in the hands of the country turner. Another partnership, this time between chair makers and upholders (or upholsterers), developed during the 18th and 19th centuries. (*See also* **Stick Furniture.**)

Chair Rail

A name sometimes given to a dado rail in interior decoration, because that moulded projection stops the backs of chairs from coming into contact with a wall.

Chair Table

An armchair with a hinged, circular back, designed to swing over and rest horizontally upon the arms, thus forming a small, circular table. Chair table is a contemporary term, and it was also known as a table chairewise or a table chair. A 'table-chaire' valued at 2s., is included in the inventory of the goods of Alexander Reynoldson, of Writtle, Essex, dated February 28th, 1671. (*Farm and Cottage Inventories of Mid-Essex*, 1635–1749. Essex Record Office Publications, No. 8, p. 120.) The name monk's seat or monk's bench is a modern term. The chair table was introduced during the mid-17th century. (*See also* Section I, page 15.)

Chair table.

Chaise Longue

This was a form of chair with an elongated seat, supported by additional legs, which was introduced in the latter part of the 18th century. During the 19th century it gradually became almost indistinguishable from a sofa, except that one end was usually left open. It is called a chaise longue in *The Practical Cabinet Maker, Upholsterer and Complete Decorator* (1826), where it is described as 'a kind of sofa'. Sheraton illustrates two types of chaise longue on Plate 37 of *The Cabinet Maker's and Upholsterer's Drawing Book*, 3rd edition (1802).

Chalons

A mediaeval name for woollen coverlets or blankets. In *The Canterbury Tales* there is a reference to chalons in 'The Reve's Tale' (lines 4139-40):

> And in his owne chambre hem made a bed
> With shetes and with chalons faire y-spred.

The name was derived from Châlons-sur-Marne in France, where the material was originally manufactured. The word shalloon, for light woollen lining material, is an anglicised version of *chalons*.

Chamber Chair, *see* **Bedroom Chair**

Chamber Horse

A device which allowed the motions of horse exercise to be simulated in a bedroom. It consisted of springs encased in a concertina-like leathern envelope that was framed in mahogany, and was sometimes called a horse exercising machine. It was introduced during the first half of the 18th century, and in an advertisement published in *The London Daily Post and General Advertiser* on March 5th, 7th, and 10th, 1739–40, Henry Marsh of Clement's-Inn Passage, Clare-Market, describes himself as the inventor. Sheraton illustrates such a device on Plate 3 of *The Cabinet Maker's and Upholsterer's Drawing Book* (3rd revised edition, 1802), and in the Gillow records there is an order for one of these machines, dated January 1st, 1790. (E. & S. Book, No. 559.)

Chamber Table

An alternative name for a plain dressing table with a toilet glass, used in the late 18th century. Gillows' records include one, dated 1790. (E. & S. Book, No. 564.)

Chamfer

A flat surface formed by planing or smoothing-off the angle made where two surfaces meet. This term is used chiefly for wood or stone surfaces. (*See* illustration, *also* **Bevel**.)

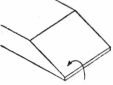

Chamfer.

Chandelier

A hanging frame of wood, metal or glass, with branches to hold candles or lamps. (*See also* **Candle Beam**.) Brass chandeliers were in use during the 17th century, and crystal chandeliers began to be made in England towards the end of that century. (*See* illustration, *also* page 57.)

Brass chandelier with eight lights, late 17th century. (From a drawing by E. J. Warne.)

Channel

A continuous groove or depression in a surface.

Charpoy

The Indian name for a bedstead, from the Hindu word *charpai*. From this word the slang term, charping, for lying in bed or idling, has been derived and has become popular in the British Army.

Chasing

The ornamentation of metal surfaces by embossing or engraving.

Two mediaeval chests. *Above:* Chest for storing jewels and other valuables. *Below:* A clothes chest. Both illustrations are copied from MSS. of the 14th century, and are included in *The Homes of Other Days*, by Thomas Wright. (*See* pages 180, 181, and 182.)

Cheeks

A contemporary term for the wings or side pieces of a high-backed easy chair, of the type introduced during the second half of the 17th century.

Cheese Waggon

A small trough, used on a table, with movable racks, in which cheeses could stand upright. Used in the second half of the 18th century.

Cheffonier, *see* Chiffonier

Chenille

A pile furnishing cloth. The yarn is either specially twisted on a chenille machine before weaving, or woven and cut, and then woven into the warp to form the pile.

Chequer

Decoration, usually inlaid, in the form of squares of alternate colours; like the pattern of a chess board.

Cherrywood (*Prunus avium*)

One of the fruit woods used in the 17th and 18th centuries for the turned members of chairs and tables, occasionally for chair seats, and for table tops and chests.

Chess Table

A table with the top inlaid or painted with the 64 black and white squares of a chess board.

Chest

The earliest form of wooden receptacle for the storing of various articles, clothes and linen, or the safe keeping of treasure. The mediaeval chest was usually in the form of a large rectangular box with a hinged lid, and progressive refinements of this basic form were made up to the end of the 17th century, when it was supplanted by the chest of drawers. (*See* **Dug-out Chest, Mule Chest,** *and* **Chest of Drawers**.) Although some authorities have suggested that chest and coffer are interchangeable terms, the coffer had a separate function and was made by a specialised craftsman (*see* **Coffer** *and* **Cofferer**), the chest being made first by the carpenter and later by the joiner. (*See* **Joiner**, also illustrations on pages 179, 181.) Chippendale designed what he called clothes chests, which were supported on four feet, and had sliding shelves. The various types of chests are entered under their respective names, as follows:

Armada Chest	Cassone
Bachelor's Chest	Chest of Drawers
Blanket Chest	Clothes Chest
Candle Chest	Coffer
Canteen	Commode
Casket	Connecticut Chest

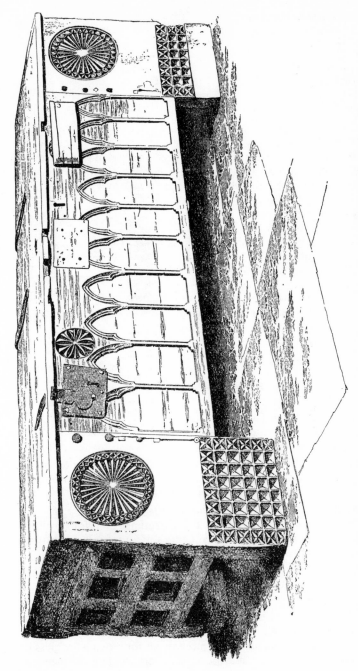

Chest from Clemping Church, Sussex: late 13th or early 14th century. (From Shaw's *Specimens of Ancient Furniture*.)

Cypress Chest	Lowboy
Danzig Chest	Mule Chest
Dower Chest	Nest of Drawers
Dressing Chest	Nonsuch Chest
Dug-out Chest	Standard Chest
Flanders Chest	Tallboy
Forcer	Trunk
Lobby Chest	Trussing Coffer
Locker	

Chest of Drawers

The chest of drawers was introduced in England in the mid-17th century, having evolved from the mule chest. At first, it was mounted on a solid plinth or a stand with legs, but the form known today, with two or three long drawers below and two smaller drawers above, with the carcase supported on feet, was perfected during the 18th century. The term is contemporary, and occurs in the inventory of the goods of Francis Taverner of Writtle, in Essex, dated January 25th, 1673, and was probably in common use much earlier. (*Farm and Cottage Inventories of Mid-Essex*, 1635–1749. Essex Record Office Publications, No. 8, p. 127.) (*See also* **Dressing Chest** *and* **Dressing Commode**.)

The final form of the chest of drawers. (This early 19th century example is from Loudon's *Encyclopaedia*, 1833.) This is the simple type which came into common use in the previous century. Variations on this basic form are shown on pages 197 and 236.

Chest-on-Chest, *see* **Tallboy**.

Chesterfield

A large, overstuffed couch with double ends. It is not known whether the name is taken from the town in Derbyshire, or was, like the Chesterfield overcoat, originated by one of the Earls of Chesterfield.

Chestnut Wood (*Aesculus hippocastanum*)

The wood of the horse chestnut is sometimes used for furniture making, but it is not satisfactory, being soft and woolly in texture. White in colour, it is used occasionally for carving and inlaying in cabinet work. (*See also* **Sweet Chestnut**.)

Cheval Screen Libraire, *see* **Library Screen**

Cheval Glass

A long mirror, swinging between two vertical columns which are supported upon long feet. The word cheval arose from a pulley or horse, which was part of the mechanism for moving the glass in some examples. By the end of the 18th century, improvements in the manufacture of plate glass allowed mirrors to be made sufficiently long to give a complete reflection of a man from head to foot. (*See* illustration.) This mirror is sometimes called a swing glass or a horse dressing glass. Sheraton includes it in *The Cabinet Dictionary* (1803), under the word Horse, and gives this description: 'A kind of tall dressing glass suspended by two pillars and claws' that 'may when hung by two centre screws, be turned back or forward to suit the person who dresses at them'.

Cheval glass or horse dressing glass. (From *The Prices of Cabinet Work*, 1797 edition.)

Cheveret, *see* **Sheveret**

Chevron

An heraldic term for a device resembling an inverted V. It was originally supposed to represent the rafters in the gable of a house. It is used as a carved zigzag enrichment on walls, and occasionally on surfaces, and for inlaid decoration.

Chiffonier

This is occasionally spelt cheffonier, and was a piece of furniture introduced in the late 18th century, consisting of open shelves for books, with a drawer and sometimes a cupboard, below. A contemporary description was: a moving library, 'chifoniere', or bookstand. Loudon calls the type with a cupboard below, a chiffonier pier table. It became more elaborate in the second half of the 19th century, and its original proportions were destroyed. (*See* illustration *and* page 184.)

A moving library, chifoniere, or book stand. (From *The Prices of Cabinet Work*, 1797 edition.)

Child's Chair

Chairs for children, specially designed to be stable, have been made since mediaeval times. During the late 17th century and throughout the Georgian period, replicas in miniature of fashionable models were produced by chair makers for the children of wealthy and modish people. The nursery chair of turned wood followed the form of the 18th-century stick back chair, and adaptations of this, with machine-turned rails and spindles, have been made since the middle of the 19th century, with various additions, such as hinged trays.

Chimera

A fabulous animal, used in Greek and Roman ornament, with

Above: A drawing-room chiffonier of the mid-Victorian period. (From *Hints on Household Taste*, by Charles L. Eastlake, 4th edition, 1878.)

Right: A chiffonier pier table, first half of the 19th century. (From Loudon's *Encyclopaedia*, 1833.) (*See* previous page.)

the wings of an eagle, the head and body of a lion, and the tail of a serpent, though occasionally the body and legs are those of a goat. (*See* illustration.) These hybrid monsters were occasionally used

A chimera. (From Ralph N. Wornum's *Analysis of Ornament.*)

in carved and gilded decoration on early Georgian and on late 18th and early 19th century furniture, and were usually based on some classical prototype. (*See also* **Griffin** *and* **Sphinx**.)

Chimney Glass

A looking glass hung above the mantel-shelf on a chimneypiece. Chimney glasses came into general use in the latter part of the 17th century. (*See also* **Mantel Mirror**.)

Chimneypiece

The ornamental structure of wood or stone that surrounds the fireplace and includes the chimney breast into which the fireplace is built. A contemporary term, in use during the 18th century, and probably introduced earlier.

China Cabinet

Cabinets designed for the display and accommodation of china were introduced in the late 17th century, when the taste for collecting Oriental china became fashionable. Chippendale uses the term china case. (*See* illustration on next page.)

China Case, *see* **China Cabinet**

China Shelves

A contemporary term for open hanging shelves, *q.v.*

China Table

A term used by mid-18th century cabinet makers for a table with a gallery round the top, usually of fretwork. (*See* page 187.)

Chinese Chippendale

The name subsequently given to a fashion popular in the 'fifties

185

A china case, or china cabinet. (Illustrated on Plate CXXXIV of Chippendale's *Director*, 3rd edition.)

China table. (From Plate LI of Chippendale's *Director*, 3rd edition.)

and 'sixties of the 18th century, arose from a craze for Chinese ornament that was particularly marked in the seventeen-fifties, when it affected architecture, garden design, and furniture. Thomas Chippendale, by his extensive use of Chinese ornamental *motifs* in furniture, was a conspicuous exponent of the fashion. Many plates in the first and subsequent editions of his *Director* are devoted to Chinese designs. (*See* illustrations on pages 102 to 107, *also* 282.)

Chinese Taste

Two waves of taste for Chinese ornaments and decoration have affected the design of English furniture. The first occurred in the latter part of the 17th century, and lasted well into the early part of the 18th: the second arose in the middle years of that century. (*See* page 63, *also* **Lacquer-Work** *and* **Chinese Chippendale**.)

Chinoiserie

A generic term for Chinese ornamental *motifs*, whether printed, inlaid, painted, or applied.

Chintz

Calico furnishing cloth, with a highly glazed stiff finish. There

187

are two types of finish: fully glazed, which is produced by the application of starch and pressure; and half glazed, where only pressure is used. Chintzes are either in plain self-colours or embellished with printed designs. First introduced from India, in the mid-17th century, and derived from the Hindu word *chīnt*.

Chip Carving

A simple and very early type of carving used to decorate wooden surfaces in the 13th, 14th, and 15th centuries. The patterns, which were usually geometrical, were first set out with compasses and then chipped out, probably by the joiner who made the chest, for it was not highly skilled work that required the services of a carver. (*See* illustration of roundel on page 399.) Chip carving persisted through the 16th and early 17th centuries.

Chippendale Style

The term Chippendale is used rather loosely to describe the style of furniture that originated with the work of Thomas Chippendale and his contemporaries (*see* List of Makers on p. 521) and was fashionable during the middle years of the 18th century.

Chromium Plating

The process of depositing, electrolytically, a thin skin of chromium upon another metal, thus increasing surface resistance to corrosion.

Circassian Walnut (*Juglans regia*)

Sometimes called Black Sea walnut. A wood with a fine wavy figure and an open grain. It is used for veneers.

Clarichord, *see* Clavichord

Classical Style

A generic term loosely applied to furniture, or other objects whose design is derived, directly or indirectly, from the classical orders of architecture.

Clavichord or Clarichord

A stringed musical instrument, with or without legs, of rectangular shape, with a simple keyboard. Mediaeval in origin, it evolved from the dulcimer, and eventually developed into the pianoforte.

Claw-and-Ball or Talon-and-Ball Foot

A device consisting of a claw or talon grasping a sphere. (*See* illustration.) This termination for chair and table legs was introduced into England late in the 16th century, though it was known and used earlier on furniture. The term is derived from the *motif* of an eagle's claw grasping a ball; alternative designs were a paw foot or a French scroll toe. (*See also* **Web Foot.**) In a contemporary oil painting of King Edward VI, an X-shaped chair with a carved frame and

Claw - and - ball foot: early 18th century

claw-and-ball feet is shown. It was reintroduced in the reign of Charles II, and was absent for a time, reappearing late in the second decade of the 18th century, and remaining in fashion until about 1760. It is probably of Oriental origin, and may have evolved from the paw foot resting on a cone. (*See* illustration of the Assyrian king, Sennacherib, on p. 352.)

Claw Table

An 18th century term for a tripod table with feet in the form of elaborate claws.

Clock

A generic term for a time-measuring machine that is actuated by a spring or weights, regulated by a pendulum, or today by electrically driven mechanism, which records the time by means of hands moving round a dial, divided into spaces which represent hours and minutes. Portable clocks were used in England in the early 16th century, but they were rarities until the second half of the

Claw table. (From the 2nd edition of *Genteel Household Furniture in the Present Taste*, by the Society of Upholsterers, Cabinet-Makers, etc. The 1st edition was dated 1760, the 2nd edition, which was undated, was probably published about 1765.)

17th century. The various types of clocks are entered under their respective names, as follows:

Alarm Clock	Long case Clock
Balloon Clock	Lyre Clock
Banjo Clock	Mantel Clock
Birdcage Clock	Mural Clock
Bracket Clock	Night Clock
Coach Watch	Sunray Clock
Coaching Inn Clock	Table Clock
Grandfather Clock	Travelling Clock
Grandmother Clock	Wall Clock
Lantern Clock	

Close Chair or **Close Stool Chair**

A close stool in the form of a chair with a back and arms. R. W. Symonds quotes an advertisement of the stock-in-trade of Alexander Perry, cabinet maker of King Street, Bloomsbury,

London, in *The Daily Post*, March 15th, 1733, in which 'Close-stool Chairs' are included. The accompanying illustration of a close stool chair is taken from a sketch in the Gillow records, dated 1788. (E. & S. Book, No. 257.)

Close Stool

An enclosed stool, or box, containing a pewter and later an earthenware vessel. Sometimes called a necessary stool. These were in general use before the invention of water closets, and continued in use throughout the 19th century. They were sometimes called night stools, and in the Victorian period increasing regard for delicacy favoured the name of night commode. The use of the word commode may arise from Sheraton's definition of a balance night stool in *The Cabinet Dictionary* (1803). These, he says, 'are made to have the appearance of a small commode, standing upon legs: when it is used the seat part presses down to a proper height by the hand, and afterwards it rises by means of lead weights, hung to the seat, by lines passing over pullies at each end, all which are inclosed in a case'.

Close stool chair.
Circa 1788.

Clothes Chest

A chest supported on four feet, either with a hinged lid (like a blanket chest, *q.v.*) or with sliding shelves and doors which open in front. (*See* illustration on opposite page.)

Clothes Horse

Rails, framed and hinged like gates, from which clothes may be spread to dry.

Clothes Press

An enclosed piece of furniture with sliding trays, or shelves, on which clothes were laid. (*See* illustrations on pages 192, 196, and 197.)

Cloven Foot

A short foot in the form of a cloven hoof, terminating a cabriole leg, introduced in the early 18th century from France, but originally derived from Roman furniture. The alternative name is *pied de biche*.

Club Fender, *see* Fender Stool

Club Foot.

Club Foot

A foot that rests upon a turned circular base, generally in connection with a turned chair or table leg. (*See* illustration.) Introduced in the early 18th century, it was used both with turned and cabriole legs for plain tables and chairs.

Clothes chest. (From Plate CXXVIII of Chippendale's *Director*, 3rd edition.) Alternative designs are shown. Compare this with the blanket chest in the Fitzwilliam Museum, Cambridge, illustrated on page 145.

Clustered Column

In Gothic architecture, this is a column consisting of four or more conjoined shafts, springing from a common base and terminating in a common capital.

Clustered Column Leg

The clustered column of three or four separate shafts was used from the mid-18th century onwards, for the legs of chairs and tables, and occasionally for bedposts. (*See* illustration.) The clustered column leg is of Chinese origin, its shafts being copied from bamboos.

Coach Watch

The forerunner of the 19th century carriage clock was the 18th century coach watch, which was really a large-scale watch, sometimes as much as 7 ins. in diameter. (*See also* **Travelling Clock**.)

Coaching Inn Clock

A hanging weight-driven clock of plain design, with a large wooden dial, generally japanned black with gilt figures on it, with a short trunk or case below. Such clocks have been misnamed Parliament or Act of Parliament

Clustered column leg.

Clothes press, mid-18th century. (From Plate CXXIX of Chippendale's *Director*, 3rd edition.)

clocks, on the assumption that they were introduced and used extensively by innkeepers after Pitt's Act of 1797 (under which clocks and watches were taxed) presumably to save customers the double expense of first buying a watch or clock and then paying a tax on it—not a plausible theory. Clocks of this design were in use in the coaching inns from the middle of the 18th century, when mail coaches began to run to a definite time table. They were also known as tavern clocks. This form of mural clock was adapted in a more elaborate design for domestic use, and was also used in coffee-houses and other public places. (*See* illustration.)

Coaching inn clock.

Coal Scuttle

A wooden box, with a detachable metal lining, hinged lid, and a slot at the back for a shovel, introduced during the 19th century. Although brass or copper cauldrons or scuttles were used in the 18th century, they were not recognised as permanent articles of furniture, as it was then customary for servants to carry coals into a room in some receptacle, which was removed when the fire had been made up. As domestic labour was less plentiful and more expensive in the 19th century, the coal bucket or scuttle became a permanent article in rooms where there were fires. During the second half of the 19th century the coal scuttle was sometimes called a purdonian or purdonium, *q.v.*

Coaster or Slider

Contemporary term for a small tray with baize underneath, or rollers, used on a dining table, chiefly for circulating bottles and decanters. Introduced during the 18th century.

Cob-Iron, *see* Andirons

Cock-Fighting Chair

A modern and misleading term for a chair with an adjustable desk at the back of it, described and illustrated as a reading chair in Sheraton's *Cabinet Dictionary* (1803). (*See* **Reading Chair.**)

Cocked Bead

A bead of semi-circular section, which projects beyond an edge or surface. It was generally used around drawer fronts.

Cod

An old name for a pillow, which frequently occurs in 16th century inventories of household furniture.

Coffee Table

A small, light, occasional table. What is often known today as a coffee table was originally a tea kettle stand, *q.v.* Modern coffee tables are sometimes made in sets to nest into each other, so that three or four tables could fit into each other. (*See* **Nest of Tables**.)

Coffer

In mediaeval England a coffer was a portable receptacle, a trunk, for valuables and clothes, and was a piece of luggage. It was usually a wooden box, covered with leather, and was made by a cofferer who was a leather worker. (*See* **Cofferer**.) The word is derived from the archaic French word *coffre—coffre-fort* meaning a safe. Chaucer uses the word *cofre* in two senses, as follows: In *The Canterbury Tales* it is a treasure chest, as it occurs in lines 1571-72 of 'The Frankeleyn's Tale':

> With herte soor he gooth un-to his cofre,
> And broughte gold un-to this philosophre . . .

In *The Legend of Good Women* (the later version) he uses the same rhyme and the same meaning in lines 380-81:

> And is his tresour, and his gold in cofre,
> This is the sentence of the philosophre . . .

In *The Parlement of Foules*, line 177 refers to an elm coffin: 'The piler elm, the cofre unto careyne . . .' (Careyne means a corpse.) In German and Dutch the word *koffer* means a box, a chest, or a travelling trunk.

Coffer Maker's Chair

A term for chairs (also stools) which are entirely covered with material, generally fabric or leather. The coffer maker's chair had a frame of beech, wholly covered with fabric or leather, with the edges garnished with nails. It had an open frame seat with a platform of webbing and canvas upon which a down cushion rested. The finials or pomels to the uprights at the back and arms were usually of gilt metal, sometimes enamel. Chairs of this type, which date back to the 15th century, if not earlier, were made by coffer makers; and this branch of their work has been identified by R. W. Symonds in two articles: 'The Craft of the Coffer Maker' (*The Connoisseur*, Vol. CVII, Jan.-June 1941, p. 100) and 'The Craft of the Coffer and Trunk Maker in the 17th century' (*Connoisseur*, Vol. CIX, Jan.-June, 1942, p. 40). The chair in the illustration on the opposite page was originally covered with fabric and leather and preserved in the vestry of York Minster, and is included in Shaw's *Specimens of Ancient Furniture*.

Cofferer

A coffer maker: a craftsman who was primarily a leather worker, who made the leather-covered receptacles called coffers, and leather-covered chairs. (*See* **Coffer** *and* **Coffer Maker's Chair**.) Cofferers are mentioned in the records of the Brewers' Company as early as 1422.

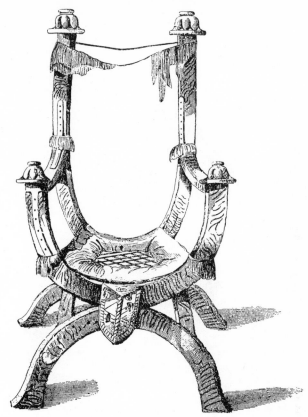

Coffer maker's chair. (From Shaw's *Specimens of Ancient Furniture*.)

Coffin Clock, *see* **Long Case Clock**
Coffin Stool

A term incorrectly used to describe a joint stool. The origin of the name is suggested by an entry in Pepys' *Diary*, July 6th, 1661: 'My uncle's corps in a coffin standing upon joynt-stooles in the chimney in the hall . . .' (*See* **Joint Stool.**)

Collar, *see* **Necking**

Collie, *see* **Crusie**

Colonial Georgian Style

The regional variations of Georgian architecture, interior decoration and furniture design in the American colonies from the accession of George I to the Declaration of Independence, are described as Colonial, or Colonial Georgian.

Commode clothes press. A design showing alternative doors and feet, illustrated on Plate CXXX in Chippendale's *Director*, 3rd edition. Compare this serpentine-fronted press with the design from Plate CXXXI, shown in a reduced and simplified drawing on page 197.

Column or **Pillar**

A vertical member, circular in section, which acts as a support. In classical architecture, it consists of a base, a shaft and a capital. (*See* **Order of Architecture.**)

Comb Back Chair, *see* **Windsor Chair**

Comb Piece

The shaped top rail of the comb back type of Windsor chair. (*See* **Windsor Chair.**)

Commerce Table

A small folding oval card table, with an X-shaped underframe, which could be folded together when the top was not in use. Gillows record commerce tables of mahogany, dated 1790 (E. & S. Book, No. 585). They were presumably used for the card game called Commerce.

Commode

Originally a French term, used to describe chests of drawers; and adopted in England during the 18th century, but used generally to describe ornate examples of chests. Chippendale describes some elaborate chests on legs as commode tables. (*See* illustration.) In the Victorian period the term commode was also used to describe a close stool, *q.v.*, or night stool.

 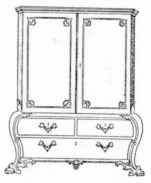

A commode table. A simplified drawing of a design described by Chippendale as a French commode table in Plate LXVI of the *Director*, 3rd edition.

A commode clothes press. A simplified drawing of a design on Plate CXXXI of Chippendale's *Director*, 3rd edition. (*See* page 196.)

Commode Clothes Press

A clothes press mounted on a chest of drawers. The term is used by Chippendale. (*See* illustrations above and opposite.)

Commode Table, *see* **Commode**

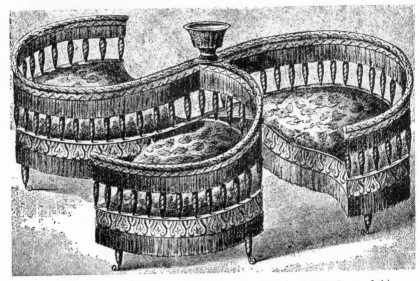

The companion chair, shown at the Great Exhibition of 1851. Seats of this type were popular in France in the eighteen-seventies and were called by an older name: confidante. (*See* page 199.) From Tallis's *History and Description of the Crystal Palace*, Vol. II.

Companion Chair
Three conjoined upholstered double seats to accommodate six people, intended for use in the centre of a drawing room. Introduced during the early Victorian period. (*See* illustration.)

Compass Seat
A round seat on a chair, introduced in the early 18th century: it is sometimes called a pincushion seat or a pincushion chair. Such round seats were often used on bended back chairs.

Compass Table
A term occasionally used to describe round-topped tables throughout the 18th century.

Compo, *see* Composition

Composite Order
A Roman order of architecture, combining the characteristics of the Ionic and Corinthian orders. (*See* illustration on next page.) Sir Henry Wotton in *The Elements of Architecture*, published in 1624, calls it 'the Compounded *Order*: His *name* being a brief of his *nature*'. He adds: ' For this Pillar is nothing in effect, but a *medly*, or an *amasse* of all the precedent *Ornaments*, making a new kind, by stealth, and though the most richly tricked, yet the poorest in this, that he is a borrower of all his Beauty'.

Composition or Compo

A plastic material that may be moulded or carved. Sometimes called stucco, and introduced in the latter part of the 18th century. It consists generally of whiting, glue, and resin, and may be cast in a mould and used as a substitute for wood carving.

Compounded Order, *see* Composite Order
Concertina Side

A modern term for a constructional device used in the second half of the 18th century on card tables with hinged tops. When the movable legs of such tables were pulled out, the horizontal member to which they were hinged straightened out in line with the side framing, folding back like a concertina when the table was closed. (*See* illustration below.)

Cone

A spiral spring, shaped like a cone; an individual member in a spring unit for an upholstered seat or back. A double cone consists of two spring cones, joined at the apices.

Confidante

A term used occasionally in the second half of the 18th century, for a small sofa. It always denoted an intimate type of seat; but it lost its initial simplicity of form in the following century. Giedion describes and illustrates a French confidante, of the late eighteen-seventies, formed by three chairs joined on an S-plan. (*Mechanization Takes Command*, by Siegfried Giedion, Oxford University Press (1948), page 373, Fig. 215.) This rather involved design had been used and shown in England at the Great Exhibition of 1851, where it was called a companion chair, *q.v.*

Roman Composite Order.

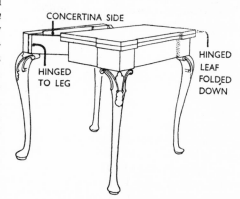

CONCERTINA SIDE

HINGED TO LEG

HINGED LEAF FOLDED DOWN

Connecticut Chest

The name given to a regional type of chest made in the second half of the 17th century in the Connecticut valley in New England. These were often mule chests, and the panels and drawer fronts were carved in low relief, the characteristic ornamental *motif* being a conventionalised tulip. Some of these chests have been identified as the work of Nicholas Disbrowe, the first known American furniture craftsman. (*See* page 526.) Split balusters are occasionally applied as ornaments on the stiles of these chests.

Console

A projecting bracket, generally in the form of a scroll, used to support the upper members of a cornice in the Corinthian and Composite orders of architecture. Occasionally used to support tables or marble slabs or shelves. (*See also* **Corbel** *and* **Modillion**.)

Console Cheffonier

An elaborate form of mid-19th century chiffonier with open, shelves below a marble slab, which is supported at table height by a carved frame; the whole being surmounted by a tall glass in an ornate frame. (A model in English walnut was shown at the Great Exhibition of 1851, made by Trapness & Son of Bristol.)

Console Table

A table fixed to a wall and supported on curved S-shaped legs, which act as brackets. (*See also* **Eagle Table** *and* **Pier Table**.)

Contour

The section or profile of a moulding.

Conversation Chair

A single chair with a padded top rail. The occupant sat facing the back, with his arms resting on this rail. Sheraton, in *The Cabinet Dictionary* (1803), said that this type of chair was 'peculiarly adapted for this kind of idle position, as I venture to call it, which is by no means calculated to excite the best of conversation'. The chairs were originally designed to allow the ample skirts of

Conversation chair. (From Plate 29 of Sheraton's *Cabinet Dictionary*, 1803.)

gentlemen's coats to remain uncrushed while they conversed. (*See* illustration on previous page.)

Convoluted

Material that is twisted or fluted, or rolled into the form of a scroll.

Coopered Joints

These resemble the joints that are used in the making of barrels and tubs by coopers, and are employed in curved work.

Corbel

An architectural term describing a projection from a wall which acts as a support for a beam. It is sometimes used instead of the terms bracket or console.

Cordwain or Cordovan

Leather of fine quality prepared from goatskin, named after Cordova in Spain. It was one of that Moorish kingdom's most famous products during the Middle Ages, and was known in England as cordwain.

Cordwainer or Cordonnier

A worker in cordovan leather, or cordwain. Cordwainer was the English name for this craftsman. The earliest reference to cordwainer is in 1272: a charter was granted to the Cordwainers' Company in 1439 by Henry VI.

Core

A term used to describe the internal parts of furniture; for example, the inside of a column.

Corinthian Order

One of the Greek orders of architecture, which was adopted and slightly altered by the Romans. (*See* illustrations on next page, *also* Section II, page 41, on origin of the Corinthian capital.)

Cork

The outer layer of a species of evergreen oak (*Quercus suber*), which is used occasionally for the seats and table tops of bathroom furniture. The insulating and absorbent properties of cork have long been recognised. John Evelyn in his *Sylva* (3rd edition, 1679) describes its use in Spain, where the cork tree has been cultivated for many centuries. 'The poor People in *Spain*', he writes, 'lay broad *Planks* of it by their Beds-side, to tread on (as great Persons use *Turkie*, and *Persian* Carpets) to defend them from the *floor*, and sometimes they line, or *Wainscot* the Walls, and inside of their Houses built of Stone, with this *Bark*, which renders them very warm, and corrects the *moisture* of the Air . . .' (chapter xxv, p. 127).

Corner Chair, *see* **Smoker's Bow** *and* **Writing Chair.**

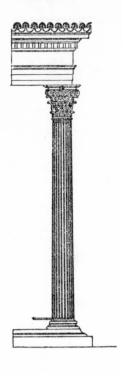

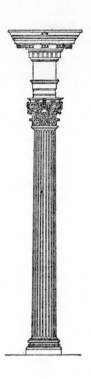

Left:
Greek Corinthian
order.

Right:
Roman Corinthian
order.

Mid-18th century hanging
corner cupboard.

Fitted corner cupboard.
(From Loudon's *En-
cyclopaedia*, 1833.)

Corner Cupboard

Such cupboards probably originated as fixtures, in the form of shelves fitted across the corner of a room and either left open or protected by a door. At some time late in the 17th or early in the 18th century they were made as free standing cupboards, occasionally having open shelves for the display of china and ornaments, with a door in the lower part. This type was elaborated during the 18th century, and Ince and Mayhew included alternative designs on Plate XLVII of *The Universal System of Household Furniture* (1760). (*See* pages 204 and 205.) Hanging corner cupboards were also made, chiefly in the countryside, throughout the 18th and early 19th centuries. (*See* page 202.)

Corner Ottoman

A type of ottoman that fitted into the corner of a room was introduced in the early 19th century. One illustrated in 1833, in J. C. Loudon's *Encyclopaedia* (and reproduced here), appears to be a forerunner of the cosy corner, *q.v.*, that

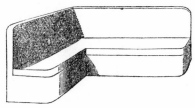

Corner ottoman. (From Loudon's *Encyclopaedia*.)

became fashionable over fifty years later. (*See* **Ottoman**.)

Corner Posts

The vertical members which support tiers of shelves and are placed at the corners for this purpose. (*See* illustrations of Bookstand, page 147, and Whatnot, page 502.)

Corner Stool, *see* French Corner Chair

Cornice

In architecture, the upper projecting portion of an entablature. The projecting moulded member at the top of a cabinet, bookcase, tallboy, or other large piece of furniture, or above the tester of a bed or the head of a window. (*See* illustration below and page 248.)

Bed or window cornice. (From Plate XXXVII of Chippendale's *Director*, 3rd edition.)

To the right and on the opposite page are alternative designs for corner cupboards by Ince and Mayhew. They are included in *The Universal System of Household Furniture*, published in London in 1760. They represent the fashionable cabinet maker's elaboration of a simple space-saving piece of furniture, humble in origin and made primarily for use in the farmhouse and cottage. (*See* page 203.)

Cornucopia

The horn of plenty, used as a decorative *motif* in the form of a curved goat's horn, from which ears of wheat and fruits are flowing out.

Cornucopia Sofa

An elaborate form of sofa, with scroll arms, introduced in the early years of the 19th century. The arms were carved to resemble a cornucopia.

Coromandel Wood (*Diospyros marmorata*)

Also known as calamander wood. Both names refer to variegated ebony, which is striped with black and yellow, and to Andaman marblewood, which is sometimes wrongly called zebrawood, *q.v.* Coromandel wood was used in the late 18th and early 19th centuries, and Sheraton, in *The Cabinet Dictionary* (1803), describes it as 'a foreign wood lately introduced into England, and is much in use amongst cabinet makers for banding. It resembles black rose wood, but is intermingled with light stripes, which produce a good effect in banding. . . . In texture it is close, and in weight about equal to black rose wood.'

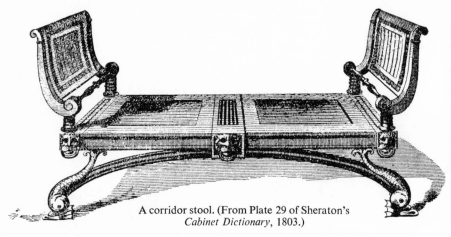

A corridor stool. (From Plate 29 of Sheraton's *Cabinet Dictionary*, 1803.)

Corridor Stool

A term used by Sheraton for a backless seat with two ends, without cushions or upholstery. (*See* illustration.)

Corset Back

A name sometimes used in America to describe a type of elbow chair with an upholstered back that curves inwards between the top and the seat, giving a waisted effect. These chairs were popular in the mid-19th century, and were clumsy variations of the French chairs illustrated in Chippendale's *Director*. (*See* pages 89 and 90.)

Coster

A wall cloth for hanging. This is a mediaeval term which is sometimes used to describe arras or tapestry.

Cosy Corner

A corner seat, with a high upholstered back, which fitted into a corner, enabling two or more people to sit side by side. Buttoning was used for the upholstery of the back, and gave to the whole the likeness of an old-fashioned railway compartment. It became extremely popular in the eighteen-nineties. Occasionally called a Turkish Corner.

Cot

A single bed, used at sea, made of canvas, and suspended from the beams of a ship. The sea cot probably gave its name to the swinging cribs or cradles used for children. The child's cot today is seldom designed to swing, and is usually in the form of an open-topped cage, the sides and ends being formed by vertical bars, with one side made to slide down.

Late Victorian cosy corner. (From a trade catalogue, 1895.)

Cottage Piano

An upright piano, originating with the upright grand piano of the 18th and early 19th centuries. The first upright pianos were very high (*see* **Giraffe Piano**), but the crank action perfected by Robert Wornum and patented in 1826 enabled the vertically strung piano to be accommodated in a lower and more agreeably proportioned case. This small, upright piano became known throughout the 19th century as the cottage piano; and a characteristic of its case was a fretwork panel in front, above the lid of the keyboard, backed with coloured, pleated silk. (*See* next page.)

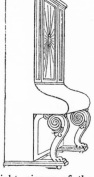

Two examples of upright pianos of the cottage type, by Wornum, London, 1833. (From Loudon's *Encyclopaedia*, 1833.)

A grand cottage pianoforte, shown at the Great Exhibition of 1851, and made by Moore & Co. (From Tallis's *History and Description of the Crystal Palace*, Vol. II.)

Cottage Weave

The term used to describe certain types of loosely woven furnishing materials made from coarse yarns. Sometimes called folk weave, village, or peasant weave.

Couch

A long upholstered seat with a back and one or two ends. The original chairback upholstered couch was really a double seat, like two conjoined armchairs. (*See* page 230.) These were first introduced during the reign of Charles II. The term couch was in use earlier. Evelyn, in describing the 'banquetting house of cedar' belonging to a Mr Tombs, mentions that 'the couch and seats were carv'd *à l'antique. . . .*' (*Diary*, May 8th, 1654. *See* pages 210, 211, *also* **Box Ottoman, Chesterfield, Corner Ottoman, Cosy Corner, Double Chair, Divan** *and* **Ottoman.**) Couche was a mediaeval term for a bed. (*See* description of 15th century bedroom furnishing in Section II, pages 44, 46.)

Couch Bed

Chippendale uses the term for a couch with a canopy and curtains which could, if desired, be converted into a bed. Such couches were designed expressly for alcoves or deep recesses in large apartments. (*See* illustrations on pages 212, 213.)

Couch Bedstead

A term used in the mid-19th century for a couch with a hinged end that could be folded down, thus becoming level with and giving additional length to the seat, so that it could be used as a bed. (Couch bedsteads are described and illustrated in Heal's Catalogue for 1854.)

Couching

A method of embroidery applied when using yarn which is too thick or heavy to be threaded in a needle. Continuous lengths of these yarns or cords are secured to the material by almost invisible 'over and over' stitches in a matching thread, the ends of the yarn being folded in and stitched down firmly. Couching is used for arabesque patterns, and to outline padded parts of an embroidered design.

Counter

A board marked with squares or covered by a cloth so marked, supported upon a chest or a frame. The counter was in use as early as the 14th century and as late as the 16th, and was known as a 'counter board', though it was sometimes called a 'conter cheste'. Some authorities suggest that it was a form of rent table, and that when it was a chest, the landlord sat at the plain side to receive rents from his tenants; the other side, which faced the room, being decorated. 'The top slid backwards and forwards on bearers so that the well underneath was accessible for money and papers.' (R. W.

 [*contd. on page* 214.

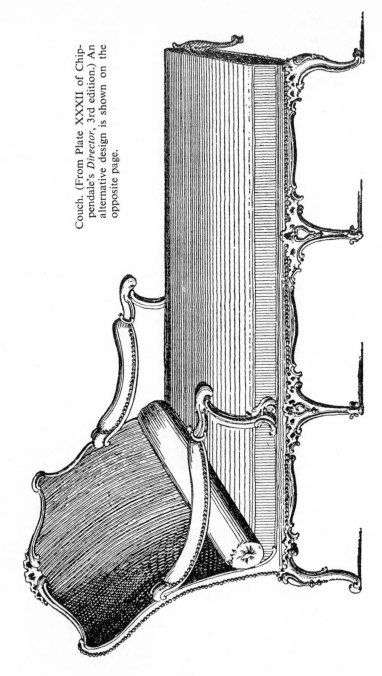

Couch. (From Plate XXXII of Chippendale's *Director*, 3rd edition.) An alternative design is shown on the opposite page.

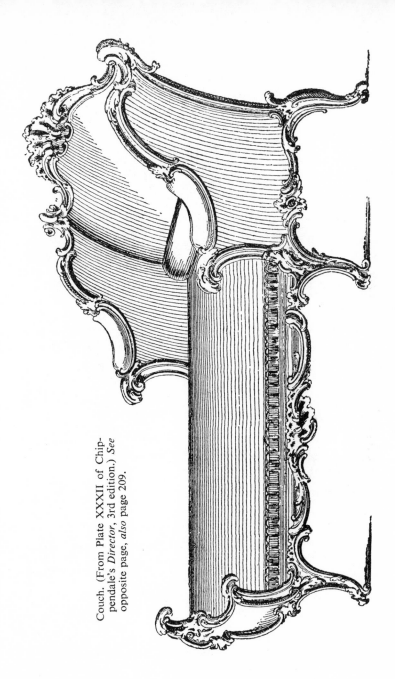

Couch. (From Plate XXXII of Chippendale's *Director*, 3rd edition.) *See* opposite page, *also* page 209.

A couch bed. From Plate XLVI of Chippendale's *Director*, 3rd edition.
A more elaborate example is shown opposite. (*See* page 209.)

Another example of a couch bed designed by Thomas Chippendale and illustrated on Plate L of his *Director* (3rd edition). *See* opposite page, *also* page 209.

Symonds in a paper entitled 'Modern Research and Old English Furniture', given before the Royal Society of Arts, April 19th, 1950.)

Counterpane

The light cover placed over the blankets and quilt of a bed. Also called a coverlet—an old form being coverlid—or bedspread. Sheraton, bracketing coverlet with counterpane, describes them as 'the utmost of the bed clothes; that under which all the rest are concealed'. Coverlets are generally plain, but are sometimes ornamented with embroidery or *appliqué* work. Some are made of specially woven white honeycomb material called 'Marcella' cloth. Coverlet is also used to describe a light-weight wrap used to cover anyone resting on a sofa.

Countersink

The term used for making a conical depression in a surface to receive a screw head.

Country Chippendale

A modern term, used to describe chairs made in the countryside during the middle years and second half of the 18th century, with simplified versions of the pierced splats and shaped top rails that were characteristic of the designs of Thomas Chippendale and his contemporaries. In such chairs, the country craftsman, working with materials that were readily available to him—ash, beech, elm, oak, and various fruit woods—skilfully edited the forms invented by the fashionable makers in the towns, but was content to use the chair backs only as models, and provided solid wooden seats and sturdy, square sectioned legs with stretchers, of his own design. (*See* illustration of Wheatsheaf Back.)

Country Turned Furniture

The type of furniture made by turners, and generally known as stick furniture, in which chair and table legs are plainly turned, also the spindles in chair backs. (*See also* **Stick Furniture**.)

Coupled Columns

Columns arranged in pairs. The columns shown at the right hand side of the illustration on page 54 are coupled columns; and this device was sometimes used in elaborate cabinet work, and on chimneypieces and overmantels.

Court Cupboard

An open cupboard for the display of plate, introduced during the 16th century, and representing a stage in the evolution of the cupboard. It consists of two open tiers with a pot board at the base. This type of court cupboard is sometimes, though perhaps wrongly, called a buffet. Some court cupboards have a small central cupboard in the upper part. (*See* **Livery Cupboard**, and accompanying illustrations.) Court cupboards were made throughout the early part of the 17th century, becoming less fashionable in houses of the wealthy after the reign of Charles II. Oliver Brackett refers to them as sideboards, though they were not the

Two types of court cupboard.

ancestral prototype from which the sideboard of the late 18th century developed. (*See* **Sideboard** *and* **Side Table**.) The true nature of the court cupboard has been convincingly suggested by R. W. Symonds (*see* Section I, pages 18 to 20, *also* **Press Cupboard** *and* **Plate Cupboard**).

Courting Chair

A small seat, introduced during the Carolean period, designed for two people to sit closely side by side. In the early 19th century, such double seats, of greater amplitude, were sometimes called *tête-à-tête* seats, *q.v.* (*See also* **Love Seat**.) This does not appear to be a contemporary name.

Cove

A large concave moulding, used in the cornices of large pieces of furniture; sometimes employed as an alternative term for a niche or any other curved recess in a flat surface.

Cover Fillet or Cover Strip

A thin strip of flat or moulded bead, used to cover a joint in a flat surface.

Coverlet or Coverlid, *see* Counterpane

Crabwood (*Carapa guianensis*)

Sometimes incorrectly called Brazilian or Demerara mahogany, this wood comes from the West Indies and tropical South America. It is reddish-brown in colour, and is straight-grained with a ribbon figure. It is used for cabinet making and joinery.

Cradle or Crib

A bed for a child, either suspended from a bar, or mounted on rockers, with or without a hood or canopy. Cradles with rockers

215

have been used from the earliest times and the basic form has remained unchanged since the Middle Ages. The 15th century example in the accompanying illustrations was apparently a light structure, easily carried, with an open wooden frame. Basket or wicker work cradles were probably in common use in mediaeval times, and have been used ever since. Hooded basket work cradles are usually mounted on wooden rockers.

Credence

A term variously applied to late mediaeval cabinets or cupboards containing shelves on which food was placed, ready to be tasted before being served. John Britton describes a credence as 'a shelf-like projection placed across a piscina or within a niche, as a place for sacred vessels used

Mediaeval cradle with rockers. (From Douce MS. 195 in the Bodleian Library, as reproduced in Parker's *Some Account of Domestic Architecture in England.* Oxford: 1859. Part I, pp. 106 and 166-67.)

at mass: also a buffet, or sideboard for plate'. (*A Dictionary of the Architecture and Archaeology of the Middle Ages*, 1838.)

Credence Table

A name in current use for a type of late 16th or early 17th century domestic flap table, which, when closed, is either half circular or has a three-sided front. In Parker's *Glossary of Architecture* (enlarged 5th edition, 1850), it is defined as 'the small table at the side of the Altar, or Communion-table, on which the bread and wine were placed before they were consecrated. This was a very early custom in the Church, but in many instances the place of the credence-table was supplied by a shelf across the fenestella or niche in which the piscina is placed: this shelf was either of wood or stone, and is to be found in many of our churches. The word also signifies a buffet, cupboard, or side-board, where in early times the meats were tasted before they were served to the guests, as a precaution against poison' (pp. 148-9). In Britton's *Dictionary of Architecture* (1838), it is stated that credence meant 'also a buffet, or side-board for plate'. (*See* previous entry.) It is certainly not a contemporary term for a side table; and the secular use of the term may date from the early 19th century, and particularly from the illustration of a small, semi-circular, early 17th century table at Chipping-Warden, Northamptonshire, which accompanies Parker's definition. R. W. Symonds in an article entitled 'The Renaming of Old English Furniture', published in *The Antique Collector* (Vol. 19, No. 4, August 1948, p. 127), states that no such name as credence table occurs in contemporary inventories.

Creepers, *see* **Andirons**

Cresset

An open lamp, usually in the form of an iron basket with a spike for a candle or a piece of combustible material soaked in oil. Cressets were generally mounted on the end of a pole, and could be carried about in the open, or fixed in sockets or clips inside a hall. (*See* illustration.)

Cresting

The carved decoration on the top rail of a chair, settee, or the back of a day bed. (*See* illustration.)

Cretonne

A strong, plain-weave cotton cloth, produced in dyed plain colours or printed by various processes. It is sometimes made with a printed warp that gives a shadow pattern to the finished cloth. The word may have been derived from the village of Creton in Normandy, where linen was manufactured, as cretonne was originally made with a hempen warp and a linen weft.

A cresset, 16th century. (From *The Homes of Other Days*, by Thomas Wright.)

Crib, *see* **Cradle**

Cricket

A low, wooden stool. The term was in use as early as the 17th century, and in the 18th century it was defined by Bailey as: 'A low stool, such as Children use to sit upon'. Windsor cricket is a term occasionally used in America for a low wooden stool with turned legs and stretchers; but this is probably a modern, made up name.

Cresting on the back of a Carolean chair.

Cricket Table

A modern term for a small, plain three-legged table, of a type made throughout the 17th century. The name may have arisen through the use of the word cricket for a plain wooden stool, or because the three legs resembled the three stumps used in the game of cricket, an origin suggested by Mr. F. Gordon Roe, F.S.A., in his book, *English Cottage Furniture* (London: Phoenix House Ltd., 1949. Section 7, p. 71). Although the word cricket was used for the game as early as the middle of the 16th century, the use of three stumps dates from the latter part of the 18th, and the term cricket table is certainly not contemporary, and, as Mr Roe concludes, is merely collectors' jargon.

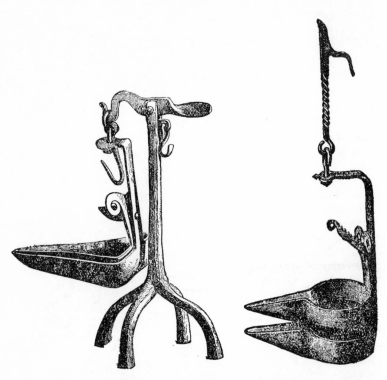

Early 19th century crusies. *Above:* A crusie with a stand. *Right:* A crusie from the Shetland Islands, where it was called a collie. (From *The Past in the Present*, by Sir Arthur Mitchell. Edinburgh: David Douglas, 1880.)

Cromwellian Chair

A type of chair made in the mid-17th century, severe in outline, seated and backed with leather, and garnished with brass-headed nails, supported on turned legs which were tied with turned stretchers. Hard and angular, it represented the 'utility' furniture of the Puritan period. Sometimes decorative spiral turning was used for the legs.

Croquet Chair ˙

A large armchair made wholly of basket work, or wicker work, with the seat—which is semi-circular in plan—and the upper part of the back of buttoned upholstery. Such chairs are similar in general shape to the mid-19th century example shown at the top of page 130, but are much larger, the arms and back being continuous, and the wicker work closely plaited. They were introduced during the second half of the 19th century, and the name croquet, which is used in contemporary furniture catalogues, does not appear to have any special significance. (*See* **Basket Chair.**)

Cross Banding, *see* Banding

Cross-Grained Moulding

A moulding with the grain of the wood running across its width and not along its length. Cross-grained mouldings were a characteristic feature of walnut furniture in the second half of the 17th and the early part of the 18th centuries.

Cross Rail, *see* Slat

Crown Glass

The name given to early window glass that was made by the process of blowing and spinning, so that the glass became a flat, circular disc, which was cut up into panes, the bullion or bull's eye in the centre being used for inferior types of glazing.

Crusie

The name given in Scotland to a form of open-flame hanging oil lamp, suspended from a hook and a rod, or hung on a stand. (*See* opposite page.) In the Shetlands this type of lamp was sometimes called a collie. The crusie went out of use during the mid-19th century as paraffin lamps became popular.

Cuban Mahogany (*Swietenia mahagoni*)

Today, this is also known as Jamaican, San Domingo, and Spanish mahogany. It comes from the West Indian island of Cuba, and is light red when cut, becoming richer and deeper in colour with exposure: it does not darken with age. Hard, heavy, and close and straight in grain, it often exhibits extremely beautiful curls in the figure. In the 18th and early 19th centuries it was known as Cuba wood or Havanna wood, and Sheraton, on pp. 184 and 251, respectively, of *The Cabinet Dictionary* (1803), gives definitions for these terms. He describes Cuba wood as 'A kind of mahogany somewhat harder than Honduras wood, but of no figure in the grain. It is inferior to Spanish wood, though probably the Cuba and Spanish mahogany are the same. . . . That, however, which is generally distinguished by Spanish mahogany is finer than what is called Cuba, which is pale, straight grained, and some of it only a bastard kind of mahogany. It is generally used for chair wood, for which some of it will do very well.' In the course of his definition of Honduras wood, on p. 254, he describes the grain of Cuba wood, which, he says, is 'close and hard, without black speckles, and of a rosy hue, and sometimes strongly figured'. Under the heading of Havanna wood, Sheraton says: 'A kind of mahogany that grows in the island of Cuba, usually called Cuba wood—See Cuba wood '.

Cup and Cover

A form of carved ornamentation found on the melon bulbs, q.v., of late 16th and early 17th century table legs and bedposts. The top of the bulb resembles a cover for the lower, cup-shaped part. It is not a contemporary term. (It is used by Mr Edward H. Pinto in discussing the analogy between fashions in costume and furniture, in Part III of 'Construction and Design of Some English Oak Furniture', *Apollo*, Vol. L, No. 295, September 1949, p. 65.)

Cupboard

Originally cup board, from one of the specialised uses of the mediaeval word board, it occurs in 14th and 15th century inventories, variously spelt as coppebord, cupbord, and copborde. The early cup board had a dual function: it was a board on which to set drink and drinking cups, and also a board for the display of plate. (*See* **Plate Cupboard**.) William Harrison, in his *Description of England* (1577–87), refers to 'costlie cupbords of plate' to be found in the houses of the wealthy, and in the same passage mentions that many farmers have 'learned also to garnish their cupboards with plate'. During the 16th century the word cupboard also meant an enclosed space fitted with a door, and since then it has gradually become a generic term for all receptacles fitted with a door or doors, whether movable or fixed. The various types of cupboards are entered under their respective names as follows :

Almirah	Hanging Cupboard
Armoire	Kas
Aumbry	Linen Cupboard
Bedside Cupboard	Linen Press
Clothes Press	Livery Cupboard
Commode Clothes Press	Plate Cupboard
Corner Cupboard	Press
Court Cupboard	Press Cupboard
Credence	Tri-ddarn
Deu-ddarn	Wardrobe
Dole Cupboard	

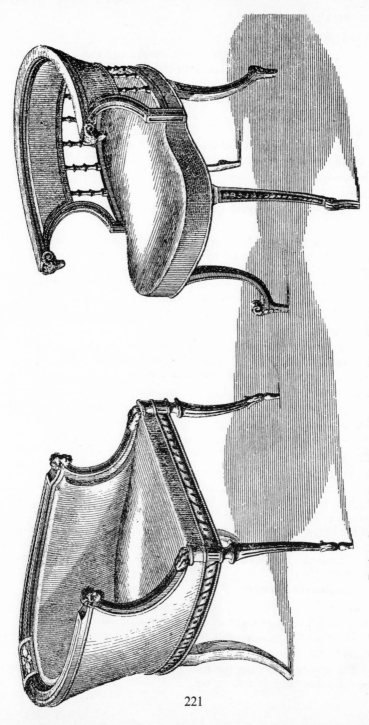

Designs for curricles by Thomas Sheraton. (From Plate 6 of *The Cabinet Dictionary*, 1803.)

Cupboard Stool

A rare form of joined stool with a hinged top and a small receptacle below, made in the late 16th and early 17th centuries. The term, which is not contemporary, is sometimes used to describe a low table, about the size and height of a stool, with a small cupboard below the top.

Cupid's Bow

Some mid-18th century chair backs have a top rail shaped like a cupid's bow, to which this term applies.

Curb, *see* Fender Curb

Curl

Feather-like markings in the grain of wood are known as curls.

Curricle

This term was used by Sheraton to describe a type of armchair whose shape was suggested by the lines of an open carriage. He described such chairs as 'well adapted for dining parlours, being of a strong form, easy and conveniently low, affording easier access to a dining table than the common kind'. (*The Cabinet Dictionary*, p. 48. *See* illustrations on previous page.)

Curtain

A length of fabric acting as a screen, which may be contracted or expanded at will, and suspended to cover a window, door, recess, or to surround a fourpost bedstead.

Curtain Rail

A rail, grooved or flanged to engage curtain runners.

Curtain Rod

A rod of wood or metal upon which curtain rings are threaded.

Curtain Tape

Woven tape through which two lines of strong cord are threaded, which can be drawn so that the tape gathers. It is made in various widths and colours, and is designed to simplify the making of curtains. The tape is sewn to the reverse side of the curtain material, at the top, the gathering cords are drawn up to the desired width and securely tied together (not sewn) to hold the gathers in place. The cords can be untied when the curtain is cleaned, washed, and ironed.

Cushion

A bag or case of fabric, round, oblong, square, or cylindrical, and stuffed with feathers or other forms of soft material. The mediaeval term was quisshin.

Cusp

The points separating the foils in Gothic tracery, that project at the intersection of two curves.

Cuspidor, *see* **Spittoon**

Cylinder

This term is used to describe the curved fall of a bureau or writing table. Sheraton, in *The Cabinet Dictionary* (1803), describes and illustrates a writing table entirely cylindrical in form. (*See* illustration.)

Cyma Recta, *see* **Ogee**

Cyma Reversa, *see* **Reverse Ogee**

Cypress Chest

Chests made of this wood have been used since the 16th century, for accommodating textiles, as the wood affords protection from moth.

Cypress Wood (*Cupressus*)

An aromatic wood, hard, close-grained, and reddish in hue. It was introduced into England in the early part of the 16th century. It is a durable wood, and in ancient Egypt was used for mummy cases.

Lady's cylinder writing table. (Drawn from Plate 40 of *The Cabinet Dictionary*, by Thomas Sheraton.)

* D *

Dagswain

A rough, coarse material used as a coverlet in the 15th century, and probably earlier. Dagswain coverlets are mentioned by Harrison, in his *Description of England* (1577–87), as being in common use in the previous generation.

Dais

A slightly raised platform at one end of the hall in a mediaeval house, where the master and mistress of the household sat at the high table for meals, together with the members of their family and guests. (*See* illustration.)

Damascening

Sometimes spelt damaskeening. A term used to describe the inlaying of thin wires of gold, silver, or copper into iron, steel, or bronze in arabesque patterns. The craft originated among the goldsmiths of Damascus, and is named after that city.

Damask

A figured fabric that takes its name from the city of Damascus. Its characteristic appearance is derived from the contrast between the figured weft weave and the warp weave of the ground.

Damaskeening, *see* **Damascening**

The mediaeval dais. (This illustration is copied from a MS. of the romance *Meliadus*, in the National Library at Paris, and is included in *The Homes of Other Days*, by Thomas Wright.)

Damassin

A term sometimes used for a damask in which gold, silver, or coloured metal threads have been used in the weave.

Dan Day Chair, *see* **Mendlesham Chair**

Danzig Chest

Chests of coniferous woods, such as spruce, were made in large numbers in Danzig during the 15th and 16th centuries, and were imported into England. They were known throughout Europe as Danzig chests.

Darby and Joan Chair

A seat wide enough to hold up to four persons. The name originated from a song called 'The Joys of Love Never Forgot', first published in the 'Poetical Essays' section of *The Gentleman's Magazine* for March 1735, Vol. V, p. 158. Two characters in that song, a devoted but physically repellent old couple, became accepted as symbols of cosy devotion during the rest of the 18th century, and thereafter, as a result of these lines:

> Old Darby with Joan by his side,
> You've often regarded with wonder,
> He's dropsical, she is sore-eyed,
> Yet they're ever uneasy asunder. . . .

Davenport

A name given to a type of small, kneehole writing desk, popular in the early part of the 19th century. The prototype was made by the firm of Gillow for a Captain Davenport, and was described

Two varieties of davenport, from Loudon's *Encyclopaedia* (1833), where the name is spelt devenport. (*See* Section I, page 33.)

as a desk. Repeat orders for this type of desk were recorded in the Gillow E. & S. Books under the name of the original customer. (*See* Section I, page 33.) In the latter part of the 19th century the name davenport in America was sometimes used for an upholstered sofa.

Davenport Bed

An American term for a couch which may be extended to form a bed. The term was probably introduced during the late 19th century.

Davenport Table

A term sometimes used in the United States to describe a long, narrow table; it does not refer to any specific style or type.

Day Bed

A long seat with an end that was adjustable, so that it could be lowered to form a bed. Introduced in the Carolean period, it was the forerunner of the sofa. (*See also* **Reading Seat**.)

Deal

A general term for the wood of various coniferous trees. Pepys records a proposition put to him by Sir William Penn for 'fetching timber and deals from Scotland, by the help of Mr Pett upon the place; which, while London is building, will yield good money'. (*Diary*,

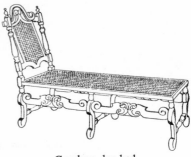

Carolean day bed.

September 28th, 1666.) Deal is used for carcase work, drawer

Deception table. (From Sheraton's *Cabinet Dictionary*, 1803, Plate 46.)

linings, and backs of case furniture. Deal is also a term for a small plank. (*See also* **Pine**.)

Death-watch Beetle

The popular name for a sinister insect called *Xestobium rufovillosum*. It attacks oak and chestnut, where such woods have

226

been used in structural work or panelling, and occasionally the larvae burrow into solid pieces of oak furniture. These beetles appear during April and May, and their characteristic tapping noise, which is really a mating call, has been given an eerie and superstitious significance in the past.

Deception Table

A type of table used in the late 18th and early 19th centuries, made to imitate a Pembroke table, but, as Sheraton explains in *The Cabinet Dictionary* (1803), 'to answer the purpose of a pot cupboard, or any other secret use which we would hide from the eye of a stranger'. (*See* illustration on page 226.)

Deck Chair

A chair with a light folding wooden frame, from which a continuous seat and back of canvas is slung.

Dentil

A small square block used in series in Ionic and Corinthian cornices.

Derby Folding Chair, *see* Steamer Chair

Derbyshire Chair

Derbyshire, Lancashire, and Yorkshire chairs are modern terms, loosely applied to chairs associated with those regions. These names

Dentils.

are usually given to a type of chair, made during the 17th century, with an open back rest framed by straight uprights, terminating in scrolls; with the top or both cross rails arched. Sometimes the upper part of the back is filled by a carved panel. Occasionally, split balusters are used to ornament the uprights of the back. (*See* illustration, *also* **Mortuary Chair**.)

Desk

A piece of furniture designed primarily for writing. The term covers a variety of forms, ranging from the mediaeval table desk, with a sloping lid for writing, to the Georgian bureau. It is also the term for the superstructure of a plate cupboard, upon which the plate was placed. (*See* **Davenport**, **Kneehole Desk**, *and* **Pedestal Desk**, *also* **Plate Cupboard**.)

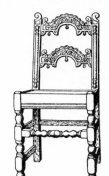

Chair with arched back rests: a mid-17th century type, regionally associated with Yorkshire and Derbyshire.

Desk and Bookcase, *see* Bureau Bookcase

Deu-ddarn, or Deu-darn

A Welsh form of press cupboard, *q.v.*, having two tiers for the display of plate. (*See also* **Tri-ddarn**.)

227

Diamond Ornament, *see* **Lozenge**

Diaper

Ornamentation consisting of repetitions of small squares or lozenges, forming an all-over pattern on a surface. This form of repeating pattern is used in marquetry, and for low relief carving in wood and gesso.

Digestive Chair, *see* **Rocking Chair**

Dinner Wagon

A small, wheeled table with two or three tiers to accommodate dishes. It is a simplified form of the supper canterbury, *q.v.*

Dipped Seat, *see* **Dropped Seat**

Dischbank, *see* **Bench Table**

Dishing

The shallow depressions sunk in the surface of a card table, to hold money or counters.

Distressed

The term used when the grain of the wood is torn in cutting a veneer: also used as a fancy term by some ingenious antique furniture dealers to describe surfaces that have been rendered rough and uneven, either by age or artifice.

Divan

A long, low, upholstered seat without back or arms, usually supported on feet or castors without visible underframing. The term and the design are of Turkish origin.

Divan Easy Chair

A name used in the late 19th century for a type of armchair with a high back, rollover arms, *q.v.*, and a very long seat, projecting beyond the arms in the form of a bow. Such chairs were usually finished in buttoned upholstery.

Dog Grate

A movable iron frame or basket for burning logs or coal on an open hearth.

Dole Cupboard

A modern name sometimes given to hanging cupboards used in churches, with bars or pierced openings in their doors. Such cupboards were used for bread that was distributed to the poor of a parish.

Divan easy chair.

Dolphin Foot

A foot in the form of a dolphin's head: a device that was occasionally used in the late 18th and early 19th centuries, both in the designs of Thomas Hope and Thomas Sheraton. (*See* illustrations of Corridor Stool, page 206, Library Table, page 317, and Sarcophagus, page 408, all from Sheraton's *Cabinet Dictionary*.)

Dolphin Hinge

A fanciful name given to the type of hinge used for the flaps of secretaires, from their supposed resemblance to the shape of a dolphin.

Dome or **Hood**

A term used to describe the semicircular, hooded tops of cabinets or bookcases, which were introduced early in the 18th century. It also applies to the wooden framework that surrounds the dial and encloses the mechanism of a longcase clock.

A dome bed, mid-18th century. (Drawn from Plate XLIII of Chippendale's *Director*, 3rd edition.)

Dome Bed

A bed with a tester or canopy in the form of a dome, from which draperies depend.

Domed Top, *see* **Dome**

Dorcer

Sometimes called a dorsal. A mediaeval term for a hanging, suspended upon the lower part of a wall at the back of a bench, to protect those who were seated from the coldness of the wall.

Doric Order

The earliest order of Greek architecture, which was adopted with modifications by the Romans. (*See* illustrations.)

Dorsal, *see* **Dorcer**

Dote

Patches or streaks in the surface of wood, lighter or darker than

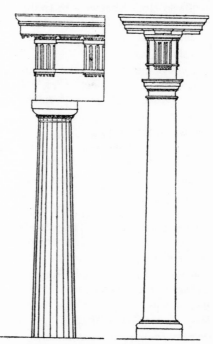

The Doric order of architecture. *Left:* Greek. *Right:* Roman.

its normal colour, indicative of the early stages of decay, when the wood is attacked by timber-destroying fungi.

Double Back, *see* **Double Chair**

Double Chair

A form of chair or settee for two people, with the back formed by two conjoined chair backs. (*See also* **Chair Back Settee** and **Couch**.) Introduced during the reign of Charles II, and popular in the first half of the 18th century.

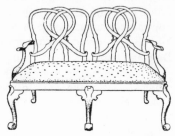

Double back or chair-back settee: mid-18th century.

Double Chest, *see* **Tallboy**

Double Cloths

Two or more cloths that are simultaneously woven on one loom, being held together during weaving by binding threads, or by the use of a special binding warp. This method produces cloths that may be similar on both sides or with a different structure or design on either face.

Double Domed

Twin domes forming the top of a bureau bookcase or a cabinet. (*See also* illustration of early 18th century bureau on page 157.)

Double Gate Leg Table

A gate leg table with two hinged leaves. (*See* illustrations on pages 266 and 294.)

Use of double domes for modern painted china cabinet.

Double Open Twist, *see* **Open Twist**

Double Plain

A double cloth with two different plain weaves on either side. The interplay of these weaves makes the design which binds the two cloths together.

Double Twist or **Double Rope Twist,** *see* **Barley Sugar Twist**

Dovetailing

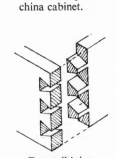

Dovetail joint.

A method of jointing wood, in which a fan-shaped projection at the end of one member fits into a corresponding slot cut at the end of another member. (*See* illustration.) Evelyn, in describing Clifden, writes: 'the house a stanch good old building,

and what was singular, some of the roomes floor'd dove-tail-wise
without a nail, exactly close'. (*Diary*, July 23rd, 1679.)

Dowel

A peg or pin of wood.

Dower Chest

A chest in which the
clothes, household linen,
and other fabrics and articles that formed a bride's
dowry were stored.

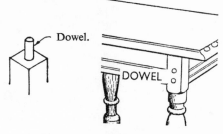

Dowel.

DOWEL

Draught Chair

A fanciful name sometimes given to a wing chair, based presumably on the protection from draughts afforded by the high,
forward-curving sides. (*See* **Tub Chair** *and* **Wing Chair**, *also*
Sheraton's description of an adjustable wing chair under the entry
Chair Bed.)

Draw Slip

The slip or strip of grooved wood to take the bottom of a
drawer in a chest of drawers.

Draw Table

An extending
table with the top
divided into three
leaves, those at each
end sliding under
the centre leaf when
the table is closed;
when open, the
centre leaf occupies

Draw table, with one leaf extended. Mid-17th
century.

the space left by drawing out the end leaves, thus forming a continuous surface. Such tables were known in the early 17th century, and were sometimes called drawing tables.

Drawer Runner

The rail that acts as a form of bearer for the drawers in a chest,
cabinet, or table. (*See* **Bearer.**)

Drawers

Sliding receptacles or drawers in food aumbries and tables were
introduced during the 16th century, and probably earlier. Drawers
fitted in cupboards were used in the 17th century, and 'one Cupboard with Drawers' is an item in an inventory, dated March 2nd,
1663. (*Farm and Cottage Inventories of Mid-Essex*, 1635–1749.
Essex Record Office Publications, No. 8, p. 98.) The terms for a
drawer in the 16th century were: a till; boxes to shoot in and out;

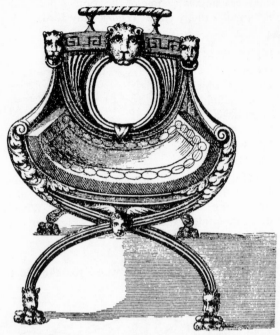

Drawing-room chair. (From Plate 47 of *The Cabinet Dictionary*, 1803, by Thomas Sheraton. *See* opposite page.) Compare this inept use of the lion *motif* with the chair designed by William Kent on page 319.

or drawing boxes—and it is from the last-named that the word drawer is derived.

Drawing Box, *see* **Drawers**

Drawing Table, *see* **Draw Table**

Drawing-Room Chairs

Sheraton uses this term. Such chairs, he says in *The Cabinet Dictionary* (1803), 'should always be the product of studied elegance, though it is extremely difficult to obtain to any thing really novel'. (*See* illustrations above and on opposite page.)

Dresser

A mediaeval term for a table that was used for dressing food: a dressing board. Lickfinger, the Master Cook in Ben Jonson's play, *The Staple of News*, says:

> A boiler, range, and dresser were the fountains
> Of all the knowledge in the universe. . . .
> (Act II, Scene 2)

By the 17th century it had developed into a side table with drawers and cupboards or open shelves, or a pot board below, usually

232 [*contd. on page 235.*

Drawing-room chair. (From Plate 47 of *The Cabinet Dictionary*, 1803
by Thomas Sheraton. *See* opposite page.)

Dresser with pot board. Such types were made during the late 17th and
early 18th centuries.

233

A free standing dresser with drawers and cupboards: an 18th century type often found in the North Country.

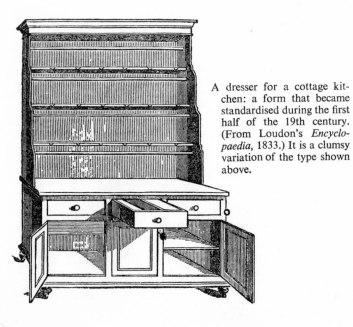

A dresser for a cottage kitchen: a form that became standardised during the first half of the 19th century. (From Loudon's *Encyclopaedia*, 1833.) It is a clumsy variation of the type shown above.

A dressing commode. (From Plate 43 of *The Cabinet Dictionary*, 1803, by Thomas Sheraton.) Like the dressing table on page 239, this is elaborately fitted and has a hinged top that rises with a quadrant. (*See* next page.)

with a range of narrow shelves set back above the table level and rising to the ceiling. The dresser with several drawers and cupboards was the forerunner of the kitchen cabinet. It was often a fixture. In Loudon's *Encyclopaedia* dressers are described as 'fixtures essential to every kitchen, but more especially to that of the cottager, to whom they serve both as dressers and sideboards'. (*See also* **Welsh Dresser** *and* **Yorkshire Dresser**.)

Dressing Board, *see* **Dresser**

Dressing Chest

Chippendale first used this term for a small chest of drawers, really a variation of the dressing commode. Sheraton, in his *Cabinet Dictionary* (1803), describes it as containing four drawers.

Sometimes a dressing chest would have a kneehole in the front, and occasionally the top was hinged and made to rise with a quadrant. The terms dressing chest and dressing commode were used according to the whim of individual cabinet makers in the late 18th and early 19th centuries.

French commode dressing chest. (From *The Prices of Cabinet Work*, 1797 edition.)

Dressing Commode

A low chest of drawers or cupboard on short legs or bracket feet, introduced in the mid-18th century, and called a French commode by Chippendale. In *The Prices of Cabinet Work* (1797) it is described as a 'French commode dressing chest'. Sheraton produced a most elaborate form, with a kneehole, drawers, and a fitted top with a toilet glass. (*See* page 235 *and* **Dressing Chest**.)

Dressing Glass, *see* Toilet Glass

Dressing Stand

Described in *The Prices of Cabinet Work* (1797) as a gentleman's dressing stand, this was a compact version of a dressing commode, almost square in plan, being 1 ft. 10 ins. long, and 1 ft. 8 ins. wide. Details of the fitted drawers and construction are given as follows: 'One for a night stool, one for a square bidet to take out of the carcase and to stand on four fly feet, one for a bason and two cups, one for a water bottle, the other empty, a glass frame hing'd to a sliding piece supported by a horse, and four loose covers inside, a tea-chest top miter dove-tail'd, plain taper legs, and an astragal round the bottom of the frame.' (*See* illustration.)

Gentleman's dressing stand. (From *The Prices of Cabinet Work*, 1797 edition.)

Dressing Stool

A stool designed as a seat at dressing tables was introduced during the 18th century. Ince and Mayhew describe these as ladies'

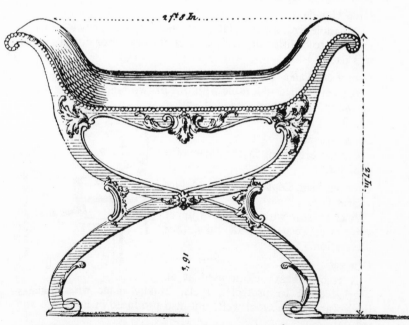

Ladies' dressing stools. (From Ince and Mayhew's *The Universal System of Household Furniture*, Plate XXXIV. London, 1760.)

237

dressing stools, and two with X-shaped underframes are illustrated on Plate XXXIV of their *Universal System of Household Furniture* (1760). (*See* previous page.)

Dressing Table

A table designed and fitted for the toilet, the extent of its elaboration depending on whether it was designed for ladies or gentlemen. (*See also* **Lowboy** and **Toilet Table**.) Fixed toilet mirrors were introduced in the first half of the 18th century. The type with the easel or swinging toilet glass was the most common. (*See* **Bureau Dressing Table**, *also* Section I, page 22.)

Walnut dressing table, early 18th century. (From a drawing by A. B. Read.)

Drinking Table

Probably an alternative name for a wine or social table, *q.v.* It is a contemporary term, and occurs in an advertisement in the *Bristol Journal* (1782), which lists for sale: 'Mahogany Dining, Drinking and Pillar Tables'.

Drop Front

The board of a desk, which is lowered to form the writing surface: sometimes called a fall front.

Drop Handle

A handle with a back plate, suspended by one or two joints, to enable it to be lifted up easily to open the drawer or door to which it is fixed.

Drop Leaf Table

A term applied to a table with one or two hinged leaves, which are supported, when extended, either by hinged legs or arms.

Drop Ornament

Carved ornament in the form of a pendant.

Dropped Seat, Dipped Seat, or Hollow Seat

A chair seat with a concave upper surface between the side rails. (*See* illustration.)

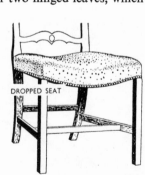

DROPPED SEAT

Drugget

A coarse, heavy cloth used as an overlay cover to protect carpets, usually made with a heavy linen warp and a wool weft, but also produced in both jute and cotton.

Drum Table

A type of tripod table, made in the late 18th century, with a

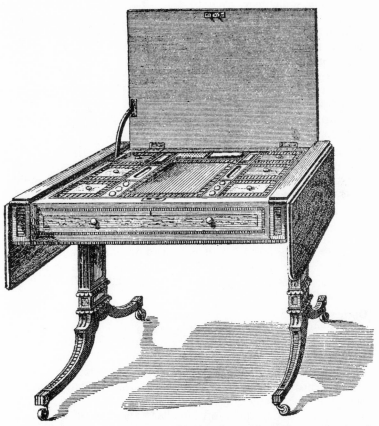

Early 19th century dressing table, with hinged top rising with a quadrant and side leaves that may be extended or folded down as shown. (From *The Cabinet Dictionary*, 1803, by Thomas Sheraton, Plate 42.) *See* entry on opposite page.

circular top and a deep frieze rail with drawers in it. (*See* illustration, *also* **Rent Table**.)

Drunkard's Chair

A name sometimes given to a broad type of chair, introduced early in the 18th century; a fanciful term, probably of Victorian origin. Such chairs, with their ample breadth of seat, were not necessarily designed only for sprawling gentlemen overcome with wine; they formed a comfortable seat for two people.

Drum table.

Duchesse

A duchesse consists of two easy chairs, with a stool between them. It can form three separate pieces of furniture, but when the chairs are placed at either end of the stool, it forms a kind of bed. (*See* illustration from Hepplewhite's *Guide*, 1788). Composite chairs and stools of this kind were in use during and after the mid-18th century, and probably earlier. In the will of Celia Fiennes, dated November 6th, 1738, there is mention of two 'square stools that have hook and staples to hang on to the chair as a couch', the chair referred to being an 'easy chair on wheels'. (*The Journeys of Celia Fiennes.*)

Duchess Bed

A bed made by erecting a canopy over a duchesse, *q.v.*, the two easy chairs, which form the ends of the duchesse, having sockets at their backs into which four posts are inserted to support the framework of the canopy. Sheraton shows what he calls a 'duchess' bed on Plate 16 of *The Cabinet Dictionary* (1803). The canopy is elaborately draped, and curtains hang down over the backs of the chairs which form the head and foot of the bed.

Duck-bill Joint

A descriptive term for the joint between the outer spindles and the horizontal top rail of a rare type of early 19th century American Windsor chair. After meeting, the upright members and the top rail curve gently outwards to a point, the junction resembling in outline the form of a duck's bill. The term was invented and first used by Wallace Nutting in his short survey of American Windsor chair types, *A Windsor Handbook* (Boston: Old America Company, 1917).

Dug-out Chest

An early type of chest formed by hollowing out a tree trunk with an adze. Such chests were bound externally with iron bands,

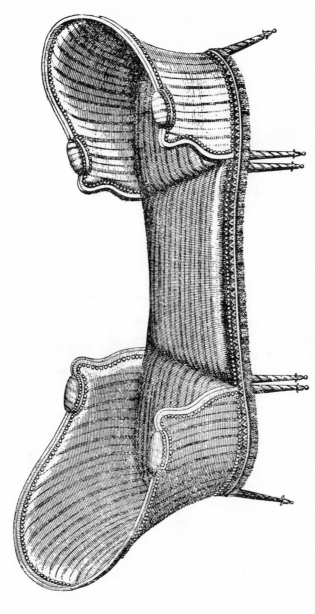

A duchesse. (From Hepplewhite's *Guide*, 1788.) When separated into its three component parts, the duchesse consisted of two easy chairs and a stool. In the illustration, the engraver has carelessly shown the line of braid and fringe as horizontally continuous, but it would have been used on all four sides of the stool and on the front of the chair seats.

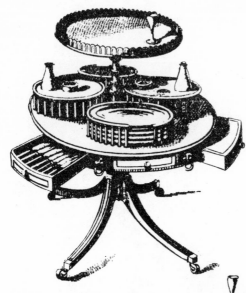

Two types of early 19th century dumb waiter. (From *The Cabinet Dictionary*, by Thomas Sheraton, 1803, Plate 44.)

both for additional strength and to prevent them from being broken open. (*See also* **Trunks.**)

Dulcimer

A mediaeval forerunner of the piano, which consisted of a sounding board, across which strings were stretched. These strings, varying in length, were struck by hammers.

Dumb Waiter

A movable mahogany stand with two or more circular trays supported on a three or four legged base. Described by Sheraton as 'a useful piece of furniture to serve in some respects the place of a waiter'. Some designs had four legs that were also corner posts, *q.v.* (*See* illustrations.)

Dust Board

The board between two drawers in the carcase of a chest of drawers, to protect the contents from being rifled and also from dust.

* E *

Eagle Table

A side table with the top supported upon the outspread wings of an eagle, carved in wood and usually gilded. Introduced during the first half of the 18th century, eagle tables were typical of the lavish decoration and furnishing of the early Georgian period.

Ears

The shaped or carved ends of the comb piece, *q.v.*, of a Windsor chair; sometimes called horns. Both are American terms, and they are probably modern.

Ease-and-Comfort, *see* **Leg Rest**

Easy Chair

Eagle table.

A term now applied to nearly every form of upholstered armchair. Originally it was the name for the winged, upholstered armchairs introduced in the late 17th and early 18th centuries. (*See* illustrations of Saddle Check, page 405, and Wing Chair, page 508.)

Ebonise

The process of staining and polishing wood to give a surface finish resembling ebony.

Ebonist

An anglicised version of the French term, *ébéniste*, meaning a cabinet maker who worked in ebony as well as other precious woods. (*See* **Cabinet.**)

Ebony

A heavy wood of deep black colour, provided by trees of the genus *Diospyros*. The best types of ebony are provided by *D. ebenum*, which occurs in southern India and Ceylon; ebony is also obtained from *D. reticulata*, of Mauritius. Ebony was known and used in antiquity as a precious and valuable wood. (*See also* **Coromandel Wood.**)

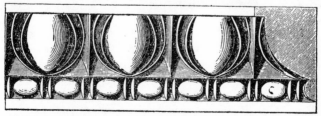

Echinus and Astragal. (From *Analysis of Ornament*, by Ralph N. Wornum, 1855.) *See* entry on next page.

243

Echinus

A curved projecting moulding, which supports the abacus in a Greek Doric capital. As this moulding was sometimes decorated with egg-and-dart ornament, *q.v.*, it is the term generally used for that type of enrichment. (*See* illustration of Roman variety on previous page, and Greek variety below.)

Edging

This term applies to the small, solid square let in on the edge of a veneered face when it forms the top of a piece of furniture, this solid square acting as a protection to the veneer.

Egg-and-Dart or **Egg-and-Tongue**

This form of enrichment is sometimes called egg-and-anchor ornament, but it is really based on the echinus, and in furniture is usually carved on ovolo mouldings, and occasionally associated with the astragal or bead. (*See* illustration, *also* **Echinus**.)

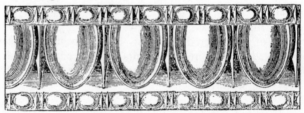

Echinus, commonly called egg-and-tongue or egg-and-dart. (From *Analysis of Ornament*, by Ralph N. Wornum, 1855.)

Elbow Chair

The term usually employed to distinguish the armchair in a set of dining room chairs, from the single chairs. It probably originated in the 17th century, and in the inventory of the goods of William Eree, of Writtle, Essex, dated May 28th, 1677, the contents of the parlour included 'one elbow chair, & one litle chair, 15s.' (*Farm and Cottage Inventories of Mid-Essex*, 1635–1749. Essex Record Office Publications, No. 8, p. 143.) It was probably a common term at that date. In the opening years of the 18th century Celia Fiennes records 'an elbow chaire tentstitch'. (*See* **Armchair**, *also* **Carver Chair**.)

Elbows

A term sometimes used for the hinged arms which support the flaps of Pembroke tables, *q.v.* Chippendale uses it in the *Director* (1762) to describe the open, padded arms of French chairs. (*See* illustration on page 87.)

Electrolier

A hideous word that enjoyed a brief currency in the early days of electric light, when chandeliers were first designed to take carbon bulbs.

Elizabethan Style

A loose but common term used to describe English Renaissance architecture and decoration of the second half of the 16th century.

Elm (*Ulmus procera*)

The common elm is probably a native of Britain, and provides a coarse-grained, light brown timber that is used for chair seats and table tops, though its most general use is for coffins. It is durable and hard-wearing, though it tends to warp easily. John Evelyn, in his *Sylva* (3rd edition, 1679), includes among its uses: '*Trunks*, and Boxes to be covered with *leather* . . .' also '*Dressers*, and Shovelboard-Tables'. (*See* **Shuffle Board.**)

Embattled

An heraldic term for a line formed like battlements on a wall. It was used occasionally to describe some types of furniture made in the second half of the 18th century, to reflect the fashionable taste for so-called Gothic forms. (*See* illustration on next page, of an embattled bookcase.)

Embossing

The projection of a raised pattern on some malleable material such as metal, leather, or cloth, so that it stands out in relief.

Embroidery

The application, by hand or machine methods, of decorative needlework to the surface of a textile fabric. Designs vary from simple outlines to extremely complicated patterns, in which a variety of stitches may be employed, as well as padding and couching. Every kind of textile thread, and metal thread, may be used in embroidery. It is widely applied: to household linen, furnishing fabrics, and ecclesiastical furnishings and vestments. Hand embroidery, which produces a higher degree of excellence than machine methods, is often executed by means of an embroidery frame, of which the round 'tambour' is the simplest, so that the fabric is kept tightly stretched and firmly held while the embroidery is worked.

Empire

The name given to the style that was invented by furniture designers and decorators in France during the early 19th century, after Napoleon became Emperor. It is characterised by the extensive use of gilded bronze ornament, with classical and Egyptian *motifs*.

Enamel

An enamel finish on furniture is prepared by coating the wood surface with whiting and size, then rubbing it down and finishing off with a transparent French polish. Another form of enamel,

Embattled bookcase. (From a plate in the 2nd edition of *Genteel Household Furniture in the Present Taste*, by the Society of Upholsterers, Cabinet-Makers, etc. The 1st edition was dated 1760; the 2nd, which is undated, was probably published about 1765.)

used on metal surfaces and on metal mounts, is a vitrified, glass-like substance that provides a very hard, smooth coating.

Endive Marquetry

A modern dealers' term for a very small type of marquetry which resembles the endive leaf.

Endive Scroll

A scroll used in mid-18th century carved ornament, based on the leaf of the endive.

English Empire

A modern name, given to the Regency style that arose from the Greek revival, *q.v.*, and was popular during the Regency period. (*See* **Regency Style.**) It is sometimes suggested that English Empire was the English equivalent of the Empire style which flourished in France: but, save for the uneasy peace of Amiens, England was at war with France for the first fifteen years of the 19th century, and the influence of French taste and fashion was thus diminished.

English Oak (*Quercus robur*)

Supplied by a tree native to the British Isles and Europe, English oak is the most durable and reliable of the oaks. Varying from light yellow to warm dark brown, its colour deepens with age. Hard and strong, it has been used for many centuries for ship-building and structural joinery, though it is not always suitable for panelling and furniture, because of its coarse and uneven texture.

English Renaissance, *see* Renaissance

English Walnut (*Juglans regia*)

The walnut tree was probably introduced to Britain by the Romans. It supplies a brown wood which is sometimes marked by dark streaks and is occasionally finely figured. It is apt to be a poor wood constructionally; and although it was employed by English cabinet makers from 1660 to about 1720, the scarcity of good English walnut in the reign of Charles II led to the use of beech for chair making, and in the last decade of the 17th century French and Italian walnut was imported. After 1720 Virginia walnut, *q.v.*, was used, and English walnut employed only for country-made furniture and work of inferior quality. (See *English Furniture from Charles II to George II*, by R. W. Symonds, chapter i, p. 45.) English walnut is seldom used today, for supplies are limited.

Engraving

A term used in marquetry to describe the relief effect made by engraving fine lines on the veneers, and filling them with black composition.

Enrichment

A general term that in architecture and cabinet making refers specifically to the carved or inlaid ornament with which mouldings are decorated.

Entablature

The upper part of an order of architecture, *q.v.*, supported by the columns, and consisting of an architrave, frieze, and cornice.

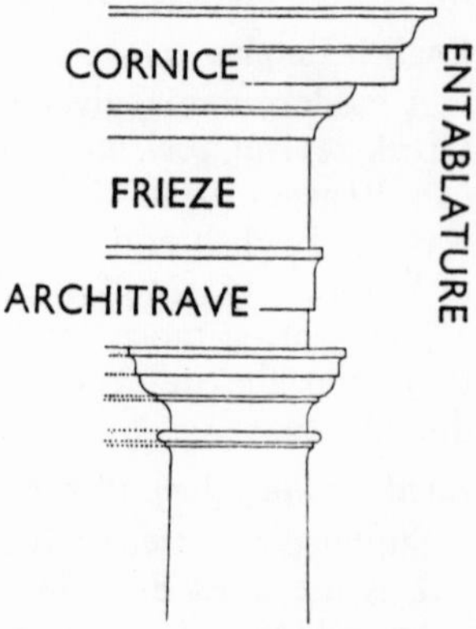

Entasis

A slight convex curve on the vertical line of a column, which corrects the optical illusion of the outline being concave which straight sides would produce.

CORNICE
FRIEZE
ARCHITRAVE
ENTABLATURE

Epergne

A decorative stand, usually of silver, used on the centre of a dining table to support a large dish.

Escallop or Scallop

A form of ornament, based on the escallop shell, and frequently used to decorate the edges of surfaces. It began to be used extensively in the early 18th century.

Escritoire, Secretaire, or Secretary

A piece of furniture that has a pull-out writing drawer, with a hinged front that lies flat. (*See* illustrations on the opposite page, which show this drawer open and closed.) Introduced during the 18th century.

Escutcheon or Scutcheon

In heraldry this word means either the whole coat of arms or the field upon which the arms are painted. The form of a small escutcheon has been used in cabinet making as a pivoted cover for a keyhole. (*See* illustrations on page 250, *also* **Key Plate.**)

Étagère

The French name for the tiers of shelves, supported by columns, that in England were called whatnots. (*See* **Whatnot.**)

Ewer and Basin, *see* Basin and Ewer.

Extending Table

Any table that may be lengthened with additional leaves. (*See* **Draw Table.**)

Above: An escritoire, mid-18th century, showing the fitted writing drawer open and closed. *Below :* An escritoire which is described as a writing table in *The Prices of Cabinet Work*, 1797 edition. This is 3 ft. long and 2 ft. wide, 'the drawer front to represent two, the top one to turn down, supported by quadrants. . . .'

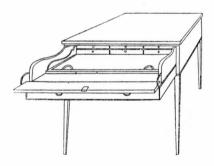

Escutcheon pivoted
over a keyhole.

Left: An elaborate
escutcheon, or key
plate, illustrated,
among other de-
signs for brasswork,
on Plate CC of
Chippendale's *Di-
rector*, 3rd edition.

250

* F *

Fabric

A term generally used for cloth when employed for the covering of furniture. Furnishing fabric is a generic term which includes a great variety of cloth.

Facia, *see* **Fascia**

Facing

A term in furniture construction, meaning a thin covering of wood, such as mahogany or walnut, not necessarily a veneer, upon a ground of whitewood. The term faced-up is sometimes used.

Faking

The practice of reproducing antique designs of furniture, using old wood or treating the surface to simulate the effects of age, is known as faking.

Faldstool

A mediaeval stool that could be folded. John Britton describes it as 'a folding stool or desk provided with a cushion for a person to kneel on' (*A Dictionary of the Architecture and Archaeology of the Middle Ages*, 1838). Faldstools are recorded as early as the 12th century, and were used in churches before the introduction of permanent stools or seats for the congregation. (*See* illustration.)

Fall

The falling front of a bureau, a writing desk, or a piano. (*See* **Drop Front.**)

Falling Table

Probably the earliest term used to describe a gate leg table, *q.v.* An inventory of the year 1600 includes this item: 'A little Table of wainescott with two fallinge leaves'. The term was still in use in the latter part of the 18th century, and appears in an advertisement ·published in the *Manchester Mercury*,

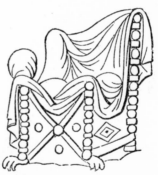

A faldstool. (This drawing, copied from the Trinity College Psalter, is included in *The Homes of Other Days*, by Thomas Wright.) The Psalter was written by Eadwine in the earlier part of the 12th century.

April 1st, 1766, for the stock-in-trade of 'the late Mr William Wells, cabinet maker, deceased, at his late shop opposite the Rose and Crown in Deansgate, Manchester, consisting of Dining Tables, Falling Tables, Chests of Drawers of different Sizes. . . .'

251

Fan Back Chair

A chair or settee with a fan-like design filling the back. The term is also used in America to describe a type of Windsor chair that has the spindles of the back slightly inclined outwards on either side of the central spindle.

Farmhouse Furniture

A loose and inconclusive term, variously applied to such articles as kitchen furniture, dressers, kneading troughs, and so forth, and also to furniture of the countryside made by rural craftsmen.

Farthingale Chair

Not a contemporary term: probably invented by some romantic Victorian. It is applied to a type of side chair or back stool, *q.v.*, with a broad seat, used in the latter part of the 16th and early part of the 17th centuries. It is assumed that such chairs were made specially to accommodate the hooped dresses or farthingales of the period. (*See* illustration.)

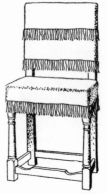

The so-called farthingale chair.

Fascia or Facia

An architectural term describing the flat band that projects slightly from an architrave. (*See also* **Entablature**.)

Fauteuil

A French term for an armchair with open sides and upholstered arms.

Feather Banding, *see* Banding

Feather Bed

One of the earliest forms of bed; its use was common in mediaeval times, though for the working class it was a luxury until the 16th century. There is a reference to a feather bed in Chaucer's *The Book of the Duchesse*, lines 250-51:

> Of downe of pure dowves whyte
> I wil yive him a fether-bed. . . .

It occurs as part of a description of luxurious furnishing. In *The Homes of Other Days*, Thomas Wright quotes the will of Agnes Hubbard of Bury St. Edmunds, made in 1418, which includes 'one feather-bed'. William Harrison's *Description of England* (1577–1587) records that the usual type of bed was a straw pallet 'covered only with a sheet'. Writing of the early 16th century, Harrison says: 'If it were so that our fathers or the good man of the house had [within seven years of his marriage purchased] a matteress, or flocke bed, and thereto a sack of chaffe, to rest his head upon, he thought himself to be as well lodged as the lord of the town [that peradventure laie seldome in a bed of downe or whole feathers]. . . .' During the 17th century feather beds were normal items of furnishing.

Feather Edge

Sometimes called feathering, a term used to describe planing-off to a point or fine edge.

Fender

A metal guard of iron or brass, introduced in the latter part of the 18th century, to surround the hearth in front of a fireplace, in order to protect the floor, carpet, or hearthrug.

Fender Curb or Curb

A shallow variety of fender, raised only two or three inches above the level of the hearth.

Fender Stool

A long, low stool for use in front of a hearth. The term is not contemporary, although such stools have been made since the second half of the 17th century, sometimes with six legs, and cane-work or upholstered seats. The modern fender stool is much lower than the Carolean and Georgian types, and just under a foot in height. A distinct type of fender stool, incorporated with the structure of the metal fender, came into use during the latter part of the 19th century, consisting of a padded seat supported by vertical metal bars which rise from the curb. This is known both as a seat curb and a club fender. The club fender usually has a continuous seat upholstered in leather: the seat curb is not continuous, being broken in the middle, or consisting only of padded box seats at each end of the fender, which provide receptacles, one for coal and the other for slippers.

Festoon

Sometimes referred to as a swag, and consisting of a suspended wreath, generally used on a frieze or a panel.

Fiddle Back Chair

A contemporary term, which in the 18th century referred to a bended back chair, *q.v.*, when the vertical frame of the back had a concave curve near the seat, producing a waisted effect which resembled the form of a violin, while the spaces between the frame and the splat suggested the sound holes. The term also appears to have been used to describe a ladder back chair, *q.v.*, with pierced spaces in the back slats, presumably

Fiddle back.

because the shape of those open spaces suggested the sound holes of a violin.

Fiddle Brace Back Chair, *see* Stays

Fiddleback

Figured veneer which resembles the markings of the wood used for the backs of violins.

Fiddleboard

A board with apertures cut to receive the stems of glasses, and used at sea during rough weather.

Field Bed

An elaborate form of camp bed, with an arched tester, and the framework wholly concealed by curtains and draperies. (*See* accompanying illustration, *also* Section II, page 49.)

Early 19th century field bed.

Fielded Panel

A cabinet-making term that describes a panel with the central space raised so that it projects slightly beyond the surface of its frame.

Figure

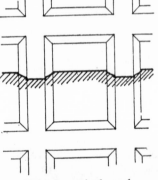

The natural, decorative markings of wood are known as figure, or figuring.

Filigree

Ornamental metalwork, in gold or silver wire, formed into delicate, lace-like patterns.

Filing Cabinet

A piece of office furniture, either of wood or metal, with drawers and divisions for the filing of documents.

Fielded or raised panel.

Filler

A wet paste made from whitening or very fine plaster of Paris, mixed with dye, and rubbed into the grain of wood after it has been sandpapered and before it is polished. Dye is used to prevent the filler from turning white in the grain after polishing, and the colour is determined by the colour of the wood: red dye being used for mahogany and sienna for oak. The paste is very wet when it is applied, so that it soaks into the grain of the wood.

Fillet

A small ledge which supports a shelf: also a small, square member, and an alternative term for band, *q.v.*

Filling

The material used for stuffing upholstered furniture, such as flock or hair.

Finial

A terminal ornament on chairs, pews, settees, beds, and other pieces of furniture. (*See* illustration of Poppyhead on page 370.) Sometimes called a pommel when rounded or in the form of a knob. (*See* illustration of Coffer maker's chair on page 195, *also* X-shaped, early 17th century chair on page 517.)

Fire Back

The cast iron plate at the back of an open fireplace. Cast iron fire backs were introduced in the late 15th century.

Fire Dogs, *see* **Andirons**

Fire Guard

A high screen of vertical metal bars, or, more generally, of wire mesh, used in front of a fire to prevent coals from flying out and children from falling in.

Fire Irons

Implements used for tending a fire. As early as the 17th century they were made in sets, consisting of tongs, poker, and shovel. During the 18th century fire irons were designed to match fenders.

Fire Screen

A screen, consisting of a panel of tapestry, needlework, or painted wood, which is moved vertically up and down a pole that is supported on a tripod. Sometimes called a pole screen or banner screen. During the 18th and 19th

Fire screen or pole screen, mid-18th century. (From the 1st edition of Chippendale's *Director*, 1754.) A screen of this type appears in Hogarth's 'Marriage à la Mode', Plate II. (*See* Section II, page 54.)

centuries a large variety of types was introduced, supported on feet and with fixed screens, with sliding or swinging leaves. These were sometimes called horse fire screens. (*See* accompanying illustrations.) Wood or wicker work was used for fire screens in

255

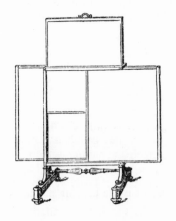

Above: A sliding fire screen. (From Plate 72 of *The Cabinet Dictionary*, 1803, by Thomas Sheraton.) *Right:* A fire screen with sliding and swinging leaves. (From Loudon's *Encyclopaedia*, 1833.)

mediaeval times; and a circular screen on an iron pole was of early origin. A screen of this type is portrayed in a painting of 'The Virgin and Child' by the Flemish artist, Robert Campin (1375–1444).

Fitment and Fittings-up

This modern term is probably derived from the clumsy expression, fittings-up, current in the early 19th century, that referred to any article made and fixed to a wall in a room. It occurs in chapter xxviii of *The Pickwick Papers*, when 'old Wardle informed Mr Pickwick how they had all been down in a body to inspect the furniture and fittings-up of the house. . . .' Loudon in his *Encyclopaedia of Cottage, Farm and Villa Architecture and Furniture* (1832) says: 'By Fittings-up are commonly implied the putting up of wooden closets; the fixing of shelves; of seats and basins in water-closets. . . .' He includes plumbing and the hanging of bells, and 'such other articles in a house, as cannot be taken down without deranging in some way or other the finishing of the apartments'. (Book I, chapter iii, p. 258.)

Fitted Furniture or Built-in Furniture

This term covers such things as built-in dressers, cupboards and wardrobes, bookshelves and cabinets, that are fixed permanently in recesses or on walls in a house.

Flanders Chair

Chairs elaborately carved were imported into England from the Low Countries in the 15th and 16th centuries, and were known as Flanders chairs. There are references to them in contemporary inventories.

Flanders Chest

The name given to chests with highly elaborate carved decoration that were probably imported from the Low Countries in the 15th and 16th centuries.

Flap and Elbow Table

An alternative name for a Pembroke table, derived from the elbows or hinged arms that are used for supporting the flaps.

Flap Table

A term sometimes used for a single or double gate leg table, and applied to any table with a hinged flap or flaps that may be raised on supports to extend the area of the top.

Fleur-de-Lis

In heraldry this device is supposed to represent the garden lily, and it is the bearing of the Bourbons of France. (See *The Manual of Heraldry*, edited by Francis J. Grant, 1924.) It is frequently used as a decorative device.

Flock

Wool refuse used in upholstery and for stuffing mattresses.

Floreated

Ornamental forms in which leaves and flowers are used in flowing lines, are said to be floreated.

Florentine Mosaic Work, *see* Pietra-Dura

Florentine Stitch, *see* Point d'Hongrie

Flower Stand

An upright stand in wood, metal, or marble, used as a support for a pot containing flowers. Those designed in the mid-18th century accommodated single large pots; but the flower stand became larger and more elaborate during the 19th century.

Mid-19th century flower stand in cast iron. (From the *Art Journal*, 1862.)

Flush

Any member or feature that is level with an adjoining surface is said to be flush with that surface.

Flush Bead

A bead moulding that is sunk in a surface.

Fluting

Shallow, concave grooves on a surface are called flutes, and flutes used in a parallel series are known as fluting—such as the fluting on a column. (*See* illustration of **Gouge Work**.)

Flush bead.

Fly Rail

The side rail on a flap table, which opens out to support the flap.

Folding Furniture

This term covers a considerable range of articles, including such early forms of folding furniture as gate-leg tables, complicated devices like the bureau bedstead, dressing tables with flaps, and modern dual-purpose furniture, like the bed-settee.

Folding Table

A contemporary term for a type of table with a hinged leaf which rested on the fixed leaf of the top. Folding tables were in use in the late 16th century.

Foliated

In architecture, foliation denotes tracery formed by an arrangement of cusps and foils; and the term foliated describes the use of foils and leaf-shaped ornament.

Folk Weave, *see* **Cottage Weave**

Food-Hutch, *see* **Hutch**

Foot

A foot is the usual termination of the leg of a table, chair, stool, or stand. Furniture without legs, which is raised slightly above floor level, also rests on feet of various forms, such as bracket feet and French feet, *q.v.* The various types of foot are entered under their respective names, as follows:

Ball Foot	Lion's Paw Foot
Bracket Foot	Pad Foot
Bun Foot	Paw Foot
Cabriole Bracket	Scroll Foot
Claw-and-Ball	Splayed Foot
Cloven Foot	Stump Foot
Club Foot	Tern Foot
French Foot	Web Foot
Hoof Foot	Whorl Foot
Leaf Scroll Foot	

Foot Warmer

A small wooden box, perforated at the top and sides, with a metal container for hot cinders. In the 19th century, a new form of foot warmer, consisting of a flat metal case which could be filled with boiling water, was introduced by the railway companies for the comfort of passengers.

Footboard

The solid or panelled end of a bedstead, framed into posts which are continuous with the legs, and rising above the level of the mattress.

Footman

A metal stand with a barred top, high enough to be level with a fire in a grate, and used in front of the fire, to keep plates hot.

Footstool

A low stool, used originally to increase the comfort of those seated in the rather high chairs of the 16th and 17th centuries. They became very elaborate in form during the 19th century, and sometimes contained a small receptacle with a hinged lid.

Forcer

A small coffer, usually covered with leather, bound with iron bands, and furnished with a substantial lock or locks. It was a small, portable safe for jewels, valuables, and documents. The following reference from *The Paston Letters* shows the use of the forcer: '. . . as for the broke sylver that my mastres wend for to a sent yow whan she dede wryte her letter, ther is none in your forcer . . .' (Introduction, Supplement XII, p. 18, letter from James Gloys to John Paston, A.D. 1448, 3 Dec.)

Forest Chair

A term sometimes used in the 18th century to describe rustic furniture, *q.v.* The term occurs in an advertisement in *Jackson's Oxford Journal*, July 13th, 1754, by William Partridge, cabinet maker, which includes 'Garden Seats, Windsor and Forrest Chairs and Stools, in the modern Gothic, and Chinese Taste. . . .' (*See also* **Rural Chairs.**)

Form

A long, backless seat or bench: one of the earliest kinds of seats.

Fourpost Bedstead or **Fourposter**

A term that somewhat loosely covers all types of beds which have a canopy or tester, supported either by four posts or by two posts at the foot and a back board at the head. An older term is posted bed, *q.v.*

Frame

The supporting and protective structure of a picture or a looking glass, a term that came into use in England during the 17th century. Also the structural woodwork (or metalwork) of a piece of furniture or part of a piece of furniture, such as the seat frame of a chair. Chippendale uses the word frame in his *Director* to describe designs for marble-topped tables, calling them frames for marble slabs. His use of the term suggests that the old mediaeval description of 'a table with a frame' may have survived in 18th century cabinet-makers' shops. (*See* **Marble Table** and illustrations on pages 329 and 330, *also* **Table.**)

Free Standing

A piece of furniture which stands independently on legs, feet, or a base.

French Chair

The term is used by Chippendale in the *Director* (1762) for elbow chairs with upholstered seats and backs: in some of the designs he illustrates the back and seat are joined, in others they are separated by a gap. The latter, Chippendale writes in describing Plates XX to XXIII, 'are intended to be open below at the Back: which make them very light, without having a bad Effect'. (*See* illustrations of six examples of French chairs on pages 87 to 92.) The term has since been used extensively to describe various types of chairs with upholstered seats and backs, with open sides and padded arms.

French Commode, *see* **Dressing Commode**

French Corner Chair

A term used by Ince and Mayhew for a broad seat with a back and a curved side: an upholstered seat which resembled a short sofa. (*See* illustration.)

French corner chair. (From Plate LVII of *The Universal System of Household Furniture*, by Ince and Mayhew. London, 1760.)

French Foot

A bracket foot which curves outwards.

French Polishing

A process introduced in the late 18th century, but not generally adopted until the early years of the 19th. In this process a wood surface is thickly coated with transparent gum, and this gum surface becomes identical with the appearance of the wood, giving a highly glazed effect to the colour and marking. In *The Practical Cabinet Maker, Upholsterer and Complete Decorator*, by Peter and Michael Angelo Nicholson (1836), it is still described as 'a new and admirable mode of polishing or varnishing, by which means it is not so much necessary to polish the surface of the wood itself'.

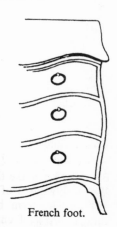

French foot.

French Scroll Foot, *see* Whorl Foot

French stools. (From Plate LXI of *The Universal System of Household Furniture*, by Ince and Mayhew. London, 1760.)

French Stools

A term used by Ince and Mayhew for a seat with curved ends and six or four legs, with or without a back. (*See* accompanying illustrations of both types.) They were usually called window seats, *q.v.*

French Walnut (*Juglans regia*)

French walnut was imported into England in the last decade of the 17th century, for it supplied a well-marked, rich brown wood, that, unlike English walnut, was reliable for construction. Walnut from Grenoble was particularly prized by English cabinet makers of the late 17th and early 18th centuries, because of its fine quality and figuring.

Fret

Geometrical ornament used on a flat surface, generally as a band, and formed by vertical and horizontal straight lines.

Fretwork

Woodwork, cut to represent frets or trellis, and used as perforated decoration, applied to a background or backed by some other material.

Frieze

An architectural term denoting the plain or sculptured member on an entablature between the architrave and the cornice. (*See* illustration of Entablature.) It is also used to describe the upper part of a wall in a room, immediately below the cornice.

Frieze Rail

The horizontal member immediately below the top of a table or a cabinet stand.

Fringe

A trimming used either for curtains or upholstery, consisting of a close and firm top band, from which hang lengths of thread or fine twisted cord, made of silk, cotton, rayon, or wool, and often given an admixture of metal threads. Fringes may consist entirely of metal threads.

Fumed Oak

A method of finishing oak furniture, that was popular during the first two decades of the present century. The process of fuming was to expose the furniture to the fumes of ammonia in an airtight chamber before polishing: this toned the oak to a greyish-brown colour, which gradually faded to a yellowish-brown.

Furnishing

A term that embraces the complete process of equipping a house, or any sacred or secular building.

Furnishing Fabric, *see* Fabric

Furnishing Tweed

A furnishing cloth that is similar in type to dress tweed, but woven from heavier and coarser yarns. It is used generally for upholstery, and also for curtains.

Furniture

The comprehensive term that covers movable articles in a dwelling, an office, or a public building. Derived from the French word *fourniture*.

Furniture Beetle

The common furniture beetle (*Anobium punctatum*) that lays its eggs in the cracks and crevices of furniture. The larvae eat their way through the wood, boring small holes that finally reach the surface, and then emerge as beetles. This insect is often confused with the death-watch beetle, *q.v.*

Furniture Pests, *see* Death-watch Beetle, Furniture Beetle, House Longhorn Beetle, Powder Post Beetle

Fustic or Fustick

A yellow coloured wood supplied by the tree *Chlorophora tinctoria*, which grows in the West Indies and tropical America. It has long been used for inlaying, and Evelyn includes it in his list of materials for such ornamental work. (*Sylva*, 3rd edition, 1679, chapter xxxi, p. 220.) Also known as yellow wood.

* G *

Gadroon, *see* **Nulling**

Galleried Table

A table with a narrow protecting edge, raised above the level of the top, and completely surrounding the surface. (*See* **Gallery**.)

Gallery

A raised curb or railing of wood or metal, bordering the edge of a table, a tray, the top of a cabinet, or a shelf. Sometimes a miniature balustrade is used, but more often a decorative fret.

Galloon

A corruption of the French *gallon*, meaning a braid. This word formerly described various kinds of decorative braid used in upholstery and on curtains.

Games Table

Tables with inlaid reversible tops, with a chess board on one side and a backgammon board on the other, were introduced during the 18th century. Chess boards were in use in mediaeval times. (*See* **Table**.)

Garde du Vin

A cellaret designed to stand under a sideboard or sideboard table. This was the name used by Hepplewhite, but Sheraton uses the term sarcophagus. It was designed to accord with the style of the sideboard.

Garden Furniture

A term of wide application, covering as it does the rustic furniture designed in the latter part of the 18th

Garden chair designed for a grotto. (From Plate XXIV of Chippendale's *Director*, 3rd edition, 1762.)

century, and the metal garden furniture, made of cast iron or wrought iron rods, of the Victorian period. Chippendale devoted one of the plates of the *Director* (3rd edition) to designs for garden seats for arbours, summer houses, and grottoes. (*See*

265

accompanying illustration.) Today, the term includes all varieties of metal, cane, canvas, and wooden furniture which is used out of doors.

'Garnished with Nails', *see* **Nail Head**

Gaselier or Gasolier

An atrocious word coined to describe a chandelier designed for gas lighting. (*Art Journal*, 1873, page 374.)

Gate Leg Table

A table with drop leaves which are supported by hinged gates, either single or double. They were introduced in the late 16th, and were in general use during the 17th century. The contemporary term was falling table, *q.v.*

Double gate leg table, with barley sugar twist legs. Second half of 17th century.

Gentleman's Dressing Stand, *see* **Dressing Stand**

Gentleman's Repository

This term is used by Ince and Mayhew in *The Universal System of Household Furniture* (1762) to describe a large and commodious piece of furniture, which they illustrate on Plate XXI of that work. The caption for the plate reads thus: 'The upper part of Middle is a bookcase, on each side is Draws, the Top of the under Part or Middle, is a Desk Drawer; under that either Draws or Clothes Press; on each side Cupboards'. Illustrations of such large pieces designed to perform several functions were probably included in the books of 18th century makers, with the idea of starting trains of thought with potential customers, rather than as models to be executed.

Georgian Style

The name Georgian is used to describe the characteristic architecture, interior decoration, and furniture of the long Georgian period, which lasted from 1714 until the death of George IV in 1830. Although the term embraces the whole period, it is subdivided into early Georgian, which extends approximately from 1714 to the seventeen-thirties; mid-Georgian, covering the seventeen-fifties and -sixties; while late Georgian, although it could be applied to the closing decades of the period, is seldom used. The underlying characteristic of all phases of the Georgian style was the use of the rules and proportions and conventionalised ornament of classical Roman and Greek architecture.

Gesso

A composition of whiting, linseed oil, and glue, that was applied thickly as a decorative coating on wood. When it had set it could easily be carved, and was usually gilded or painted. It was not used extensively in England until the early 18th century.

Gilding

The decoration of surfaces with gold leaf or gold dust is known as gilding. The practice of gilding furniture, particularly the stands of cabinets, became popular in the time of Charles II, and there was a revival of the use of this form of decoration in the early Georgian period. Thomas Sheraton, in *The Cabinet Dictionary* (1803), defines gilding as 'the art of spreading or covering thin gold over any substance'. (*See also* **Water Gilding.**)

Gingham

A plain-weave cotton cloth, produced in a variety of woven single and multi-coloured checks, large and small. The derivation of the word is uncertain. It may have come from the Malay word *gingan*, meaning striped; or from the town of Guingamp, in Brittany, where it may have been made originally.

Giraffe piano. Early 19th century.

Giraffe Piano

An early 19th century type of upright piano, with a high vertical case and a concave curve on one side which gradually diminishes the width above the keyboard.

Girandole or **Gerandole**

An elaborate wall sconce for holding one or more candles. The candles are supported by projecting branches. (*See* illustration on next page.)

Glacé

A term used to describe any plain or figured cloth that has a highly lustrous surface finish.

Glass

A transparent or translucent material, made by melting together sand, soda, and limestone. Transparent glass for window glazing was not used in England until the late 15th century, and then only in small panes. It was not used for the doors of cabinets and bookcases until late in the 17th century. (*See also* **Looking Glass.**)

Glastonbury Chair

A name given to a type of folding chair in use in the early 17th century. The design is supposed to be based upon the chair of the

Girandole or gerandole, carved and gilded. Mid-18th century. (From the 1st edition of Chippendale's *Director*, 1754. *See also* detail of girandole in use, Section II, page 56.)

last Abbot of Glastonbury, executed in 1539. The term probably originated in the mid-19th century.

Glazed Chintz, *see* **Chintz**

Glazing Bars

The members in the doors of a bookcase or cabinet, which frame the panes of glass. (*See* illustration below.)

Glazing Bead

A narrow wood or metal section, fixed inside or outside a window frame, to hold the glass: occasionally such beads are used in large expanses of glass in the doors of bookcases or cabinets.

Early 17th century folding chair, of the so-called Glastonbury type.

Gobelin

This was the name of a famous family of dyers, who established works in the Faubourg Saint-Marcel in Paris, about the mid-15th century. In the following century, the family added tapestry making to their activities, and grew very wealthy. In 1662 Colbert bought the Gobelin works in the Faubourg Saint-Marcel on behalf of Louis XIV, and established a manufactory for general upholstery, where designs for tapestry were executed under the supervision of Le Brun. After the restoration of the Bourbons, early in the 19th century, the manufactory was revived—its work having been suspended during and after the French Revolution—and carpet making was added to its other productions. The word Gobelin has become associated with tapestry, but should apply only to the actual products of the Gobelin factory, which is still a state-owned concern.

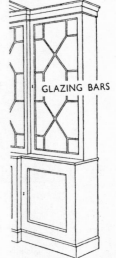

GLAZING BARS

Gobelin Stitch, *see* **Petit Point**

Goose-neck Pediment

The term is sometimes used in America as an alternative to Swan-neck, *q.v.*

Gothic Chippendale

A name given to the furniture designed by Chippendale and his contemporaries, that incorporated Gothic ornamental *motifs*, such as tracery in chair backs or bookcase doors. (*See* illustration on next page.)

Gothic Furniture

A loose term that was used without much discrimination from

Part of a Gothic bookcase. (From Plate C of Chippendale's *Director*, 3rd edition, 1762.)

the middle years of the 18th century until the late Victorian period to describe almost any type of furniture which incorporated good, bad, or indifferent Gothic ornament. How good and bad such furniture could be is shown opposite and on pages 272, 273. It was often known as Old English Furniture, and in a technical book published in 1826 it was predicted that 'There is a wide scope for novelty in this style, and if ever it be taken up by a person of good taste, who is perfectly familiar with the habitudes of the ancient artists, we may expect it to predominate among people of fashion; but such furniture cannot become common, so long as Greek and Roman architecture are so prevalent'. (*Practical Carpentry, Joinery, and Cabinet-Making; Being a New and Complete System of Lines for the Use of Workmen.* London: printed for Thomas Kelly, 17, Paternoster Row. Book III, Cabinet-Making, p. 10.)

Gothic Revival

The revival of taste for the various mediaeval styles associated with the name Gothic began as a fashionable diversion in the middle years of the 18th century. It was much encouraged by the antiquarian activities of Horace Walpole, but it was not until the early years of the 19th century that it became a powerful emotional movement with a spiritual rather than a fashionable momentum. It led to the imitation of Gothic styles in all sorts of incongruous ways. (*See* Section II, pages 60, 65 to 76.)

Gouge Work

The name given to gouge carving, a method of ornamenting surfaces by scooping out regularly spaced shallow depressions with a gouge. The resulting pattern was a form of fluting, that was used extensively in the last half of the 16th and throughout the 17th centuries.

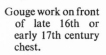

Gouty Chair

A self-propelled easy chair on wheels is described in Gillows' records as a gouty chair. (Dated 1789, E. & S. Book, No. 547.)

Gouty Stool or **Gout Stool**

A stool with an adjustable seat. Hepplewhite's *Guide* (1788), from which the illustration on page 274 is reproduced, discreetly

Gouge work on front of late 16th or early 17th century chest.

praises the device, 'the construction of which, by being so easily raised or lowered at either hand, is particularly useful to the addicted'. (*See* illustrations on page 274.)

Graining

The highly skilled imitation of the grain of wood in painted work is known as graining. During the 19th century, the practice

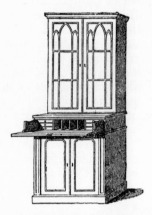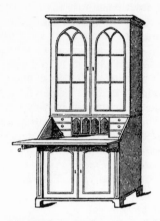

Gothic furniture in the second quarter of the 19th century. The two examples shown above are from Loudon's *Encyclopaedia* (1833), and are described therein as 'bureau bookcases in the Gothic style' (p. 302). The description can be applied accurately only to the design on the *right*: that on the *left* is an escritoire with a bookcase.

A Gothic sideboard, with a *garde du vin* or sarcophagus in the same style. (From *Furniture with Candelabra and Interior Decoration*, designed by R. Bridgens. London, William Pickering, Chancery Lane, 1838.) The proportions acceptable to the taste of the late 18th century are still preserved: compare this with the example on the following page, where those proportions have been abandoned.

A sideboard shown at the Great Exhibition of 1851, made by Hindley of London, and described as being in 'the later Gothic style' and 'peculiarly appropriate for one of those mansions in which that form of decoration predominates'. (From *The Art Journal Illustrated Catalogue*, 1851, p. 302. *See* previous page, *also* Gothic Chippendale bookcase on page 270.)

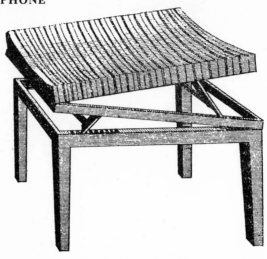

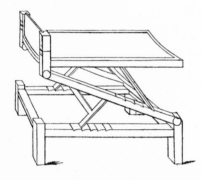

Above: A gouty stool. (From *The Cabinet Maker and Upholsterer's Guide*, by Hepplewhite, 1788.) *Left:* A gout stool. (From *The Prices of Cabinet Work*, 1797 edition.) *See* entry on page 271.

was debased and became associated with the cheapest and often the nastiest types of furniture, which were painted and grained to simulate oak or mahogany or walnut.

Gramophone

What is now known as a gramophone was originally a phonograph, the gramophone being patented by Emil Berliner in 1887, in the United States. During the early years of the present century, the gramophone, with its large, amplifying, trumpet-shaped horn, was a characteristic item of luxurious furnishing; but during the nineteen-twenties it became a more compact appliance, accommodated in a large box or cabinet, without any exposed mechanism. (*See* **Phonograph**.)

Grand Piano

The term now applies generally to a pianoforte enclosed in a horizontal case. (*See* **Cottage Piano** *and* **Pianoforte**.)

Grandfather Chair

A sentimental name introduced about 1880 for a winged or easy chair. There are no references to grandfather chairs in the early works of Charles Dickens, nor does Washington Irving mention them, although both writers delighted in the use of sentimental, antiquarian terms, and it may be assumed that this use of the name was not current during the first two-thirds of the 19th century. It may have become popular concurrently with grandfather clock—a term which can be dated. In Heal's catalogues the first reference to 'Grandfather's' easy chair occurs in September 1895. (*See* **Easy Chair, Grandfather Clock**, and **Wing Chair.**)

Grandfather Clock

This name for a long case clock appears to have come into general use after 1878, the year when a popular song called 'My Grandfather's Clock' was first published. The song was composed by Henry C. Work, and the opening lines of the first verse run thus:

> My grandfather's clock was too large for the shelf,
> So it stood ninety years on the floor;
> It was taller by half than the old man himself
> Though it weighed not a pennyweight more.

Grandmother Clock

A modern name, probably of American origin, for a miniature long case, weight-driven clock, about two-thirds the size of the standard long case clock. Comparatively few of these small-scale long case clocks were made, and existing examples date generally from the period 1690–1730. Some of these so-called grandmother clocks are equipped with repeating mechanism that made it possible to tell the time in the dark by pulling a cord which made the clock strike the last quarter, followed by the last hour; a device which suggests that they were used in bedrooms, though it does not explain their small dimensions. They were expensive and not cheap clocks.

Grate

Baskets consisting of iron bars, that were supported between andirons or fire dogs, were introduced in the 17th century; and the fixed fire basket, flanked by metal hobs, came into use during the 18th century.

'Grecian' Furniture, *see* Greek Revival

Greek Fret

A form of geometric repeating pattern, used on flat, narrow surfaces such as the frieze rail of a table or the frieze of a bookcase. Sometimes called a labyrinth. (*See* next page.)

275

Greek fret. (From *The Analysis of Ornament*, by Ralph N. Wornum.)

Greek Revival

The Grecian and neo-Greek revivals began about 1795, and developed in the opening decades of the 19th century. Architects and designers were skilful in their use of Greek decorative *motifs*, both in furniture and interior decoration; and such *motifs* were used by designers like Thomas Sheraton and Thomas Hope. Various articles of furniture which incorporated such ornaments were often labelled Grecian. (*See* illustration of Grecian sofa on page 277.)

Green Ebony, *see* **Ash**

Gresaille, *see* **Grisaille**

Greywood, *see* **Harewood**

Griffin

An heraldic term for a fabulous beast with the head and wings of an eagle. Its front legs and talons are those of an eagle, its hind legs and tail those of a lion. Such fantastic monsters were used in Greek and Roman ornament, and were oc- casionally incorporated in the carved decora- tion of early Georgian furniture, and during the second half of the 18th century on work designed under the influence of the brothers Adam. (*See* illustration, *also* **Chimera** *and* **Sphinx.**)

A griffin. (From *Fictitious and Symbolic Creatures in Art*, by John Vinycomb. Chapman and Hall, 1906. Reproduced by permission of the publishers.)

Grille

Brass lattice or trellis work used in the doors of bookcases and

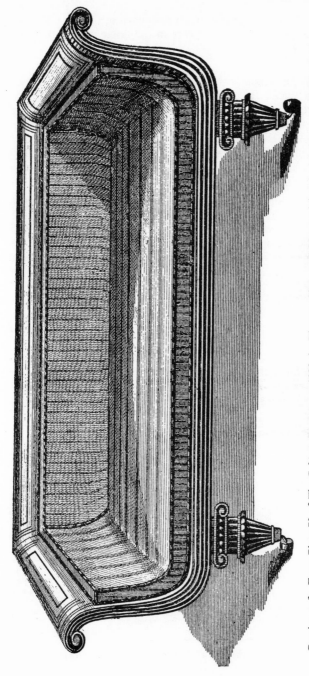

Grecian sofa. From Plate 73 of *The Cabinet Dictionary*, 1803, by Thomas Sheraton, who explains the label by saying, 'The Ionic volutes on the legs are in conformity to the title of the sofa, that being a Grecian order'. (P. 305, under entry Sofa).

cabinets is known as a grille: metal-work of this type occasionally replaced glass in such furniture in the latter part of the 18th and early 19th centuries.

Grisaille

Sometimes spelt gresaille. A form of decorative painting in tints of grey, usually in simulation of bas-reliefs, which was used on a large scale for mural decoration in the late 17th and throughout the 18th centuries, and, towards the end of the latter, on painted furniture of the type designed by the brothers Adam and Thomas Sheraton. *Grisaille* panels and medallions were occasionally used to decorate japanned or satinwood furniture.

Grog Table

A term sometimes used in America to describe a tripod table, with a gallery, and a hinged curved handle in the centre of the top, to allow the table to be lifted and moved easily. A grog table of this type, made in the mid-18th century, and subsequently used by Lord Nelson in the *Victory*, was described and illustrated in an article by Helen Comstock entitled 'The Connoisseur in America', published in the *Connoisseur*, Vol. CXI, Jan.-June, 1943, pp. 134-5. The word grog is supposed to have been derived from the nickname of Admiral Edward Vernon (1684–1757), who originated the custom of mixing rum with water, and was given that nick-name by the sailors because he wore a boat cloak made of a material called grogram, which is a coarse cloth made from silk and mohair. It seems unlikely that any particular type of table should be associated with the custom of serving and drinking rum and water, and the term appears to be modern.

Groove

A narrow, shallow channel sunk in a surface.

Gros Point

A form of cross-stitch embroidery carried out in wool on canvas,

Guilloche ornament. (From *The Analysis of Ornament*, by Ralph N. Wornum.)

and used decoratively in upholstery. The effect is similar to *petit point*, but is coarser and more rigid. (*See also* **Petit Point.**)

Grotesque

A term used to describe carved ornamentation that was deliberately fantastic and even monstrous. Grotesque masks and figures were sometimes used in woodwork of the late 16th and early 17th centuries. (*See also* **Arabesque.**)

Guilloche

A form of ornament based on interlaced circles, and used either to enrich a moulding or a plain surface. The device is of Greek origin, and is capable of considerable variation.

* H *

Haldu (*Adina cordifolia*)

A pale yellow wood that comes from India and Burma. It is strong, and is occasionally used for light-coloured furniture. It tends to darken with time, to a rich yellow.

Half-headed Bedstead

A bedstead with a headboard but no tester. The term is contemporary, and in an inventory dated April 20th, 1635, of the goods of William Coleman of Writtle, Essex, 'one halfeheaded bed-stedle' is included. (*Farm and Cottage Inventories of Mid-Essex, 1635–1749.* Essex Record Office Publications, No. 8, p. 71.)

Half-Tester Bedstead

Bedsteads with canopies bracketed forward from posts at the head, and with curtains depending from them, were known as early as the 15th century. (*See* illustration under **Bed**, on p. 134). They were reintroduced during the early part of the 19th century. The tester, or canopy, barely covered the area of the bed. These 19th century half-tester beds may have developed from the dome bed. (*See* illustration.)

Half-tester folding bedstead. (From Loudon's *Encyclopaedia*, 1833.)

Hall Chair

Hall chairs were single chairs, of rather severe design and not upholstered, put in the entrance hall of a house, 'for the use of servants and strangers waiting on business', as Sheraton says in *The Cabinet Dictionary.* They were not made for comfort. (*See* illustrations on page 281, *also* **Porter's Chair.**)

Hall Seat

A long, mahogany bench, usually with a low back, used in a hall. In the late 18th century such seats, together with hall chairs,

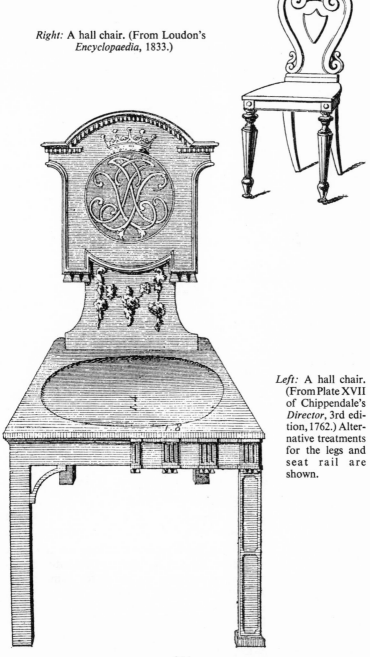

Right: A hall chair. (From Loudon's *Encyclopaedia*, 1833.)

Left: A hall chair. (From Plate XVII of Chippendale's *Director*, 3rd edition, 1762.) Alternative treatments for the legs and seat rail are shown.

Hanging shelves, designed in the Chinese style by Chippendale, and illustrated on Plate CXXXVIII of the *Director*, 3rd edition, 1762.

were generally of mahogany, and embellished with the arms of the family painted or carved on the back.

Hall Stand

A piece of furniture that accommodated hats, coats, and umbrellas, and was occasionally provided with a small shelf and a drawer beneath for clothes brushes. It was sometimes fitted with a small looking glass. During the middle years of the 19th century, hall stands were often made wholly of cast iron, extremely complicated in design, but also of mahogany and oak. As a piece of furniture it was seldom designed: it merely occurred.

Hammock

A slung couch or bed, the ends suspended from walls or upright supports. The word may have been derived from the Brazilian hamack tree, whose bark was used by the natives of that country for the nets from which their slung beds were made.

Handle

A comprehensive term applied to knobs or hinged drop handles used on drawers and doors.

Hanging Clock, *see* **Wall Clock**

Hanging Cupboard

A term generally applied to cupboards sufficiently high and deep to allow clothes to hang at full length. The term was in use in the second half of the 17th century, and occurs in an inventory of the goods of Andrew Hall, of Writtle in Essex, dated December 7th, 1665. The first item of furniture in the hall is: 'One Hanging Cubard, 8s.' (*Farm and Cottage Inventories of Mid-Essex*, 1635–1749. Essex Record Office Publications, No. 8, p. 103.)

Hanging Shelves

Small sets of open shelves, either for books or ornaments, which may be hung on walls. Chippendale describes them as 'shelves for books or china'. (*See* opposite page, *also* **China Shelves.**)

Hardwoods

Under the nomenclature of the British Standards Institution, hardwoods are supplied from broad leaved trees, belonging to the botanical group *Angiosperms*. 'The term hardwood has no reference to the physical hardness of the material' (B.S. 881: 1946).

A harlequin table with hollow tambour and cupboard below. (From *The Prices of Cabinet Work*, 1797 edition.)

Harewood

A name given to sycamore (*Acer pseudoplatanus*) or maple, dyed to a soft brown-grey. It is sometimes known as greywood.

Harlequin Table

A name sometimes given to a rather complicated dual-purpose table, designed in the latter part of the 18th century. It could be used either as a writing or a dressing table, and sometimes contained a hidden looking glass and various drawers and pigeon holes. (*See* illustration.)

Harmonica

A musical instrument consisting of a table containing 24 glasses, varying in size, each able to produce a note. The principle of the glass harmonica was known in the 17th century, but the invention of musical glasses has been associated with the name of Richard Pockrich, who gave a public performance on the instrument in Dublin in 1743. Benjamin Franklin, visiting London in 1757, was so impressed by the tone of these instruments and with the general possibilities of glasses as musical instruments, that he evolved a mechanical application of the principle which became the glass harmonica, which he produced in 1762.

Harmonichord

A form of upright piano invented at the beginning of the 19th century, in which the strings were set in vibration by friction, without the use of hammers. In tone, it resembled the glass harmonica.

Harmonium

A small organ without pipes and with one or two keyboards. It was invented during the latter part of the 18th century.

Harpsichord

A musical instrument with a keyboard resembling the piano. Instead of being struck by hammers, the strings are plucked by quills which catch and twang them when the keys are depressed. It was very popular during the 16th and 17th centuries.

Hassock

A thick cushion, covered in some strong, hard-wearing material, and generally used for kneeling in churches.

Haster

A device for keeping plates warm, consisting of a tall cupboard with an open back, usually made of deal and lined with metal. The open back is placed against a fire, and the doors in the front are shut, so that the plates in the cupboard may be kept warm. A haster is illustrated and described in the Gillow records, dated 1788. The dimensions given are 5 ft. high, 25 ins. deep, and 3 ft. 4½ ins. wide. (E. & S. Book, No. 400.)

Hat Stand

Hat stands of cast iron were made during the 19th century; but they were generally associated with umbrella stands. (*See* **Hall Stand**.) The independent hat stand, made of bentwood, was introduced in the mid-19th century, but was used chiefly for restaurants, hotel lobbies, and other places where accommodation for hats had to be provided.

Havana or **Havanna Wood**, *see* **Cuban Mahogany**

Head

The top of a mediaeval cupboard or plate cupboard was often called a head.

284

Headboard

The solid or panelled head of a bedstead, rising behind the pillow, and either framed into posts (as in the low post bedstead, *q.v.*) or forming part of the framework which supports a tester or canopy (as in a fourpost bedstead, *q.v.*). Sometimes called a back board in relation to a fourpost bed.

Heading

The top of a curtain which projects above the curtain rod after attachment to it: also that part of a ruffle or frill which projects above the gathering threads at the top.

Hepplewhite Style

A term used to describe the type of furniture made from the designs of George Hepplewhite, during the seventh, eighth, and ninth decades of the 18th century. Many designs attributed to Hepplewhite were probably originated by Richard Gillow: but Hepplewhite's designs were published posthumously in *The Cabinet Maker and Upholsterer's Guide* (by A. Hepplewhite & Co., in 1788), and his name has thus become associated with a style that was practised and partly invented by his contemporaries. (*See* List of Makers on page 251.)

Herculanium

A label used by Sheraton, for a type of early 19th century chair, which reproduced various classical *motifs* of the kind found in the specimens of Roman sculpture, paintings, and metal furniture recovered from the excavations at Herculaneum and Pompeii. (*See* illustrations on page 286.)

Herringbone

Patterns in the form of a herring bone were used on the banding of drop fronts on early 18th century walnut furniture.

Hessian

A plain-weave jute fabric: often used for the undersides of chair seats and settees.

Hickory

A native tree of North America, belonging to the genus *Carya*. It supplies a hard, tough, elastic wood, pale red in colour.

High Chair, *see* Child's Chair

High Daddy

An American term, interchangeable with highboy.

Highboy

The American name for a tallboy or double chest, usually of the type supported upon legs.

Hinge

A folding metal joint by means of which doors, gates, or lids are hung.

Sheraton's Herculanium chairs. (From Plate 7 of *The Cabinet Dictionary*, 1803.)

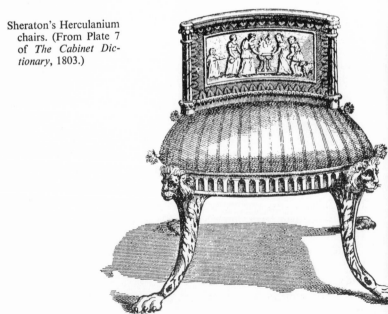

The hip or sitz bath in the mid-Victorian bedroom. (Reproduced by permission of the proprietors of *Punch* from the issue of December 26th, 1863.)

Hip Bath

A portable bath of painted metal. It was probably introduced during the early part of the 19th century. Also called a sitz bath. (*See* illustrations.) Models of the type shown here, were sometimes known as Oxford hip baths.

Hock Leg

A term sometimes used for a cabriole leg, when the curve on the inside of the knee is broken.

Hogarth Chair

A Victorian term for a bended back chair, adopted presumably because chairs of this type were often included by Hogarth in his

Hip bath. (From the *Family Cyclopaedia*.)

interior scenes. (*See* page 25 and illustrations on pages 27 and 28, *also* **Bended Back Chair**.)

Holland

An unbleached, plain-weave cloth, usually finished with an oil and starch glaze. It is used chiefly for roller window blinds, and is made in plain colours, such as buff, black, dark blue, and dark green.

Hollow Seat, *see* **Dropped Seat**

Holly Wood (*Ilex aquifolium*)

A hard, coarse wood, greenish-white or ivory in colour, that is used chiefly for inlaying. It is sometimes stained to imitate ebony.

Honduras Mahogany (*Swietenia macrophylla*)

This comes from Central America, and is a rich, reddish-brown, uniform in grain and colour, though of a softer texture than the West Indian varieties. It is a plain wood, having little figure, and becomes pale after exposure. Occasionally, finely marked veneers are obtained, but it is used chiefly for drawers and panels, for which it is very suitable. Sheraton says, on p. 254 of *The Cabinet Dictionary* (1803): 'From this province [Honduras] is imported the principal kind of mahogany in use amongst cabinet-makers, which generally bears the name of Honduras mahogany, and sometimes Bay-wood, from the bay or arm of the sea which runs up to it. The difference between Honduras and Spanish wood is easily perceived by judges, but not by others unskilled in wood. The marks of the former are, as to size, its length and width, which generally run much more than in the latter wood . . . the grain of Honduras wood is of a different quality from that of Cuba. . . . Honduras wood is of an open nature, with black or grey spots, and frequently of a more flashy figure than Spanish. The best quality of Honduras wood is known by its being free from chalky and black speckles, and when the colour is inclined to a dark gold hue. The common sort of it looks brisk at a distance, and of a lively pale red; but on close inspection, is of an open and close grain, and of a spongy appearance.'

Honeycomb Weave

This name accurately describes the appearance of a cloth woven in it. Honeycomb weave is often used to make heavy standard cotton materials for bedspreads.

Honeysuckle Chair, *see* **Anthemion Back**

Honeysuckle Ornament, *see* **Anthemion**

Hood

The movable part of the wooden case that encloses the mechanism and surrounds the dial of a clock is called a hood. (*See also* **Dome.**) The first long case clocks were low and the hood slid upwards to expose the winding: at the turn of the 17th century, when the long case clock had grown in height and it was no longer convenient to slide the hood up, the hood was fitted with a door. The term hood is also used for the semi-circular head of a mirror frame.

Hooded Top, *see* **Bonnet Top**

Hoof Foot

The use of a cloven or solid hoof as a termination for a chair, stool, or table leg, is extremely ancient. Specimens of chair legs in carved ivory resting on the hooves of bulls have been found in Egypt, and are ascribed to the early dynasties, over 2000 B.C. The hoof foot occurs on Roman furniture. It came into use in England during the latter part of the 17th century. (*See* illustration of Walnut Dressing Table, page 238, and Spindle Back Chair, page 444.)

Hooked Rug

A rug made by hooking evenly cut lengths of wool through a canvas foundation. A special rug hook is used, which automatically knots the tufts of wool in place as they are drawn through the foundation. Although the term means a hand-made rug, it also covers rugs made by the same method, but with evenly cut strips of old rags instead of wool tufts. This type of hooked rug is popular in the U.S.A., and is made either as a medley of bright coloured rags, or is designed in geometric or floral patterns.

Hoop Back Chair

A term sometimes used for a chair back in which the vertical members and the top rail form a continuous curve, which may be slightly broken near the seat level. A bended back chair was a form of hoop back. The term has a different meaning when referring to one of the two main classifications of Windsor chair, *q.v.*

Hornbeam (*Carpinus betulus*)

A wood, yellowish-white in colour, plainly figured, and, after staining, occasionally used for inlaying and decoration. Dyed black, it is used as a substitute for ebony. It is also used for turnery.

Horns, *see* Ears

Horse

This term describes the supporting feet of a screen, a tall dressing glass, or a desk. It was sometimes used to describe a cheval glass (*see* quotation from Sheraton under Cheval Glass). During the 19th century it was also applied to hinged frames for drying clothes, and to frames upon which towels could be hung. (*See* **Clothes Horse** and **Towel Horse**.)

Horse Dressing Glass, *see* Cheval Glass

Horse Fire Screen

A term used by Hepplewhite in the second half of the 18th century (*see* **Fire Screen**).

Horsehair

A material woven from the tail and mane hairs of horses, that was introduced about the middle of the 18th century, for covering chair seats. It became popular during the early part of the 19th century, and was used on all types of chairs, settees, and sofas during the early Victorian period.

Horseshoe Dining Table

Originally designed by Thomas Shearer, this was a table with flaps which could extend to form a half circle. The guests sat on the outer circumference, and were served from the inner. When not in use, the flaps were folded back on the top, and the table was then a segmental shape, with plain taper legs. (*See* illustration.) It is described and illustrated in Shearer's *Designs for Household Furniture* (1766), and in *The Prices of Cabinet Work*.

Horseshoe dining table, from the 1797 edition of *The Prices of Cabinet Work*, where it appears as this much simplified version of the original drawing in Shearer's *Designs for Household Furniture*, 1766.

Horseshoe or Kidney Table

A small, light table, usually designed for writing, or as a lady's work table, which became popular in the latter part of the 18th century. (*See* opposite page.) A small horseshoe or kidney-shaped table was used for dining and wine parties, and was called a social table, *q.v.*

Horseshoe Writing Table

A term used by Sheraton in *The Cabinet Dictionary* (1803) for a kidney-shaped writing table. (*See* illustration on opposite page, *also* **Kidney Table**.)

Hour Glass or Sand Glass

An early instrument for measuring time, consisting of two glass cones, conjoined at their apices and standing vertically. They contained sand, which trickled through the small aperture between the upper and lower cones, this process taking one hour. The instrument could then be reversed and another hour measured. Elaborate examples had three or four glasses fitted in a stand, each glass adjusted to a certain period of time.

Hour-glass seat. (From Loudon's *Encyclopaedia*, 1846 Supplement.)

Hour-Glass Seat

An upholstered seat in the form of an hour glass. Sometimes made of straw for use in summer-houses. Mid-19th century.

House Longhorn Beetle (*Hylotrupes bajulus*)

This insect, which is a serious pest on the Continent but not widespread in Britain, attacks seasoned softwoods only. The young

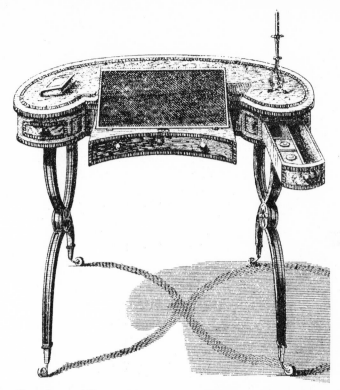

Horseshoe or kidney writing table. (From Plate 45 of Sheraton's
The Cabinet Dictionary, 1803.)

larvae emerge from the eggs, which are laid in cracks in the wood,
within fourteen days, and then bore into the wood, and feed on it
for a period of from three to eleven years. Further damage is
inflicted when the beetles finally emerge through exit holes.

Hunting Board

A high sideboard of simple design, with drawers and cupboards;
so called because it was used as a table at which hunters, after returning from their sport, could stand and help themselves to food.
Hunting boards were made in the second half of the 18th and early
part of the 19th centuries, and originated in the southern states
of North America. They were made of native woods, generally
walnut.

Hunting Chair

An armchair, described by Sheraton in *The Cabinet Dictionary*
(1803) as 'stuffed all over, except the legs, which are of mahogany'.
There was a sliding frame in front, which, when fully extended,

supported the loose back cushion, bringing it 'even with the seat of the chair', thus forming 'a temporary resting place for one that is fatigued, as hunters generally are'. This description occurs on page 19, under the comprehensive heading of Arm-chair, in *The Cabinet Dictionary*; but the term does not seem to have been adopted for general use.

Hutch

Derived from the French word *huche*, meaning a chest. Halliwell gives the old form, which was hucche, an ark or chest. The term is rather loosely applied to various types of small cupboard; but the food-hutch may have been a country-made successor to the mediaeval aumbry, *q.v.* Mr F. Gordon Roe has suggested that the food-hutch was the prototype of the modern larder-cupboard, with doors of perforated zinc or metal gauze. (*English Cottage Furniture*. London: Phoenix House Limited, 1949. Section 8, page 77.) The food-hutch had doors with ornamental perforations; and the term was apparently used for the small cupboards with pierced doors that were made during the 16th and 17th centuries, either hanging or supported upon legs. In an inventory of the goods of Alexander Reynoldson of Writtle, in Essex, dated February 28th, 1671, the items of furniture 'In the Chamber over the Hall' include: 'two good Hutches, 12s.; one old Hutch, 1s.' (*Farm and Cottage Inventories of Mid-Essex*, 1635–1749. Essex Record Office Publications, No. 8, p. 120.) In the early 18th century, hutch is defined as: 'A vessel or particular place to lay grain in; also a kind of hollow trap for the taking of weasels or other vermin alive' (*Dictionary of Husbandry, Gardening, Trade, Commerce, and all sorts of Country-Affairs*. London: printed for J. Nicholson, W. Taylor, and W. Churchill. 2nd edition, 1717). From mediaeval times a hutch has been associated with the storing of corn or foodstuffs. (*See also* **Chest** *and* **Livery Cupboard**.)

Hutch Table

An American term for a chair table, *q.v.*

Hylotrupes bajulus, *see* **House Longhorn Beetle**

Imperial Dining Table

The name given by the firm of Gillow in the late 18th century to an extending dining table that could be lengthened by inserting loose leaves.

'In the White'

This term is used in cabinet making to describe any piece of cabinet work in any wood in its unpolished state.

Incised Lacquer

Panels of lacquer used on the doors of cabinets or for screens are sometimes built up of different coloured layers, and ornamental patterns are formed by cutting down through the top layer and exposing the other colours.

Incised Ornament

Carved or cut ornament, sunk below the level of a surface.

India Back Chair

The name given in the late 17th century to a type of chair, probably of Dutch origin, that had a high hooped back with a central splat, pierced and carved with ornament derived from India.

Indian Chairs

A term sometimes used for chairs copied from Indian models, or lavishly decorated with ornament of Indian character. There was no established fashion for such Indian designs, as there was for Chinese furniture, at any time during the 17th, 18th, or early 19th centuries; apparently they aroused only sporadic interest. An example of an Indian chair is illustrated on Plate CXLVI of George Smith's *Cabinet-Maker's and Upholsterer's Guide* (1836 edition) under the heading of 'Antique Chairs'. (The plate was issued in 1827: *see* Section I, page 13.) It is described as a copy of an ivory chair, brought from India by Sir George Talbot, and with agreeable frankness the writer of the description admits that 'It is a chair not altogether adapted for ease on account of its form, nevertheless there is a considerable display of merit in the original composition'. The legs, uprights of the back, and the top rail are turned; the seat is upholstered; and the chair is squat and ill-proportioned.

Indian Laurel Wood (*Terminalia alata*)

A dark brown wood, diversified with wavy streaks of deeper brown. It takes a high polish and is used for cabinet making and panelling.

Indian Rosewood (*Dalbergia latifolia*)

Sometimes known as Bombay blackwood. A dark, purplish-black wood, hard and exceptionally tough. It is used for furniture, and occasionally for piano cases.

Indian Silver Greywood (*Terminalia bialata*)

This name refers only to the darker heartwood of this species. It comes from the Andaman Islands. The wood varies in colour from grey to a clouded yellow-brown hue, and is very decorative. It takes a fine polish, and is used for cabinet making and decorative furniture.

Ingle Nook

A fireside seat, placed within the chimney breast; the seat being usually in the form of a high-backed wooden settle. In wide fireplaces, two such settles would flank the fireplace opening. Such large-scale fireplaces were seldom built after the 17th century.

An ingle nook with high-backed settles, typical of farmhouse kitchens of the late 16th or 17th centuries. (From a drawing by E. J. Warne.)

Inlay

This term applies to a method of decorating a surface with various ornamental forms which are cut into a wooden ground and the cuts or grooves filled with other materials, either woods of different colours or metal, ivory, and mother-of-pearl.

Intarsia or Tarsia

A term of Italian origin, used to describe inlaid decorative work of a pictorial nature, when the design is cut out and inserted into prepared cavities.

Interlaced Chair Back, *see* **Ribband Back Chair**

Ionic Order

One of the orders of Greek architecture, easily distinguished by

294

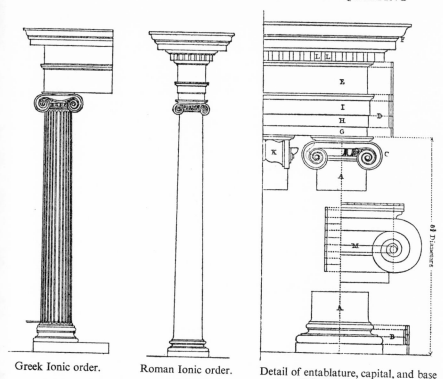

Greek Ionic order. Roman Ionic order. Detail of entablature, capital, and base of Roman Ionic order.

the volutes on the capitals. It was adapted, with modifications, by the Romans. (*See* illustrations.)

Irish Chippendale

A romantic name, which has nothing to do with Chippendale, arbitrarily given to the heavy and ornately carved furniture made in Ireland during the mid-18th century.

Ironing Board

A collapsible board with folding legs, either free standing or fixed at one end to a wall. The top is generally padded, and one end is pointed or rounded so that garments may be slipped over the board and ironed without creases.

Isle of Man Table, *see* Manx Table

Italian Quilting

A form of decoration applied chiefly to bedspreads and curtains. The material to be quilted is lined with a light, semi-transparent fabric, such as muslin, and the design is then outlined in double on the right side of the material in fine running stitches, which secure the lining at the same time: the thread used is generally of the same colour as the material. When the outline is completed, a piping cord is threaded, on the wrong side of the material, through the channels made by the double outline, this cord being of an exact thickness to fill the channels. The cord is stitched at each end to secure it to the material. The result is a raised design on a smooth flat ground.

Italian Walnut (*Juglans regia*)

This wood comes from southern Europe, and is light brown in colour, occasionally streaked with gold or stripes of darker brown. A hard, finely grained wood, it is used for furniture and occasionally for panelling. Burrs of Italian walnut are cut into veneers. Italian walnut was imported into England during the last decade of the 17th century, for it was more reliable for construction than English walnut.

Ivory

This material, provided by the tusks of elephants, was employed for the making and decorating of furniture even before the 1st and 2nd dynasties of ancient Egypt (3400–2980 B.C.). Ivory is easily turned, and has been used occasionally for the legs of furniture and also for inlaying and for covering surfaces.

Jacobean

This term is applied to furniture made during the reign of James I. (A revolting modern diminutive, occasionally employed in the furniture industry, is 'Jaco'.) Furniture made at the end of the Stuart period, during the short reign of James II (1685–88), is sometimes known as late Jacobean.

Jamaican Mahogany, *see* **Cuban Mahogany** *and* **Mahogany.**

Japanese Oak (*Quercus mongolica* var. *grosseserrata*)

This wood comes from Japan, and is lighter in colour than English oak. It is easy to work, and is used for furniture and panelling.

Japanning

The process of coating metal or wood surfaces with various varnishes, which are subsequently dried and hardened by heat. Japanning, when it was introduced into England in the second half of the 17th century, was an imitation of the Japanese lacquer-work which had been imported by merchant-adventurers, and this lacquer-work was often called japanning. (*See* **Lacquer-Work.**) A black background was characteristic of the original process, but the English imitative method included various coloured grounds, on which designs were painted. (*See* **Pontypool Japanning.**) This form of decoration was applied at first to furniture, as well as such smaller articles as drinking bowls, looking glass frames, and so forth, and, from about 1720–70 it was applied chiefly to long case clocks, its popularity for furniture having disappeared. From the last part of the 18th century until Victorian times the fashion for japanned furniture revived, culminating in the mass production of all kinds of goods finished in this way for the cheaper markets. True Japanese lacquer-work was carried out with the gum of trees, but in the imitative process, spirit varnish was used in good work to provide the necessary transparency. Cheaper forms of japanning employed an oil varnish. (*See also* **Varnish.**)

Jardinière

A stand for the display of flowers, which became an ambitious and even complicated article during the 19th century. Peter and M. A. Nicholson, in *The Practical Cabinet-Maker* (1836), describe it as 'a support for a small room garden'. (*See* illustration on next page.)

Jarrah (*Eucalyptus marginata*)

This wood comes from western Australia, and is reddish brown, occasionally so dark in colour that it resembles mahogany. It is sometimes used for parts of furniture.

Jardinère and aviary. (From a design published by Jones & Co. for George Smith, May 20th, 1826, and included in the first and subsequent editions of Smith's *Cabinet-Maker's and Upholsterer's Guide, Drawing Book, and Repository of New and Original Designs for Household Furniture, Interior Decoration*, etc.)

Joined or Joyned

During the 16th and early 17th centuries this term was used for furniture whose members were held together by mortice and tenon joints, fixed by dowels or pegs, without glue.

Joiner

The craft of the joiner, or 'joyner', evolved from carpentry. The joiner handled woodwork that was smaller in scale than structural woodwork, which was the carpenter's province, and he developed a careful and exacting technique, based upon firmness and accuracy in the making of joints, and skill in the smoothing of surfaces. By the early 17th century the joiner's craft was subdivided, so that some joiners were specialists in the making of movable furniture, and others in the interior woodwork of houses, such as stairs and staircases and panelling. Today, joiners' work is mainly concerned with fixed woodwork in buildings. (*See also* **Bed Joiner** *and* **Carpenter.**)

Joinery

A term covering all those branches of woodworking that are executed by joiners.

Joint or **Joyned Stool** or **Coffin Stool**

A stool of joiner's construction, with four turned legs held by rails above and stretchers below, with a rectangular seat. It was used during the 16th and 17th centuries as a seat at the dining table. The incorrect term coffin stool, which seems to have originated in Victorian times, may have been suggested by an entry in Pepys's *Diary* (*see* **Coffin Stool**). A contemporary reference to the use of joint stools by children, extracted from the writings of Sir Nicholas L'Estrange (1603–1655), is included in *Anecdotes and Traditions*, by W. J. Thoms (Camden Society, 1839, No. CXXVI, p. 70), as follows: 'One complain'd that Privy

Joined stool, early 17th century.

Counsellors multiplyed so fast as the table would not hold them. "Why," sayes another, "then some must sitt by like children at joynt-stooles"; for many in King James's time were very green and young.' (*See* illustration, *also* **Buffet Stool.**)

Juniper (*Juniperus communis*)

The common juniper was used occasionally in the late 17th and early 18th centuries for tables and chests, according to John Evelyn, who said 'it is *Timber* for many curious works', including 'small *carvings* and *images*', also '*spoons*, wholesome to the mouth . . .' (*Sylva*, 3rd edition, 1679, chapter xxvi, p. 137.) The wood, of a rich brown hue, was seldom available in large sizes, though it was used for furniture making as well as for small articles. Two inventories, made in 1672, include the following items: 'One Livery Cuuboard of Juniper & strip't Cloth, 4s.', and '1 Juniper Chist. . . .' (*Farm and Cottage Inventories of Mid-Essex*, 1635–1749. Essex Record Office Publications, No. 8, pp. 124 and 126.) (For the American variety, *see* **Pencil Cedar**.)

* K *

Kamassi (*Gonioma kamassi*)

Usually known as kamassi boxwood, and, incorrectly, as Cape boxwood. A South African wood, light yellow in colour, hard and close-grained. Used for turnery and cabinet work.

Kangaroo Sofa

A small curved sofa, designed to enable those reclining upon it to relax with the legs slightly elevated. This comfortable type of seat was introduced and used in the United States during the mid-19th century; its name being suggested by its contours, which resemble those of a kangaroo.

Kas or **Kasse**

A term of Dutch origin, applied to a large, upright cabinet, cupboard, or clothes press. Articles thus named were made during the second half of the 17th and throughout the 18th

Kangaroo sofa.

centuries in North America, and originated in the region that lies between the Delaware and Connecticut rivers, which was the Dutch colony of the New Netherlands until 1665, and is now incorporated in the states of New Jersey, New York, Connecticut, Massachusetts, and Vermont. These spacious pieces of furniture are made of various native woods, such as maple and walnut, and are often distinguished by heavy mouldings and bold and sometimes rather crude carved or painted decoration.

Kettle Front or **Kettle Base**

An alternative term for *bombé*, used both in England and America to describe particularly the lower part of a cabinet or bureau when it curves outwards. (*See* **Bombé**.)

Key Plate

The mount which surrounds a keyhole on a door, drawer, or chest. The word escutcheon is sometimes used to describe elaborate key plates. (*See* **Escutcheon**.)

K.D. Furniture, *see* **Knock Down Furniture**

Kidderminster

The name given to carpets manufactured at Kidderminster in Worcestershire, where they have been made since the first manufactory was established in 1735.

Kidney Table

Sometimes called a horseshoe table, *q.v.*, it was introduced during the mid-18th century. The top was shaped like a kidney, and was usually made for writing, or as a lady's work table, sometimes with a rising desk in the centre and tiers of drawers on either side. (*See* illustration, *also* **Horseshoe Table**.) A kidney-shaped commode table with a straight back is shown on Plate LXX of the 3rd edition of Chippendale's *Director* (1762).

Kingwood (*Dalbergia*)

Sometimes known as violet wood, being dark purple in colour, hard, and close-grained. It is used chiefly in the form of veneer for banding and inlaying.

Kneehole kidney-shaped library writing table. (From *The Prices of Cabinet Work*, 1797 edition.)

Kitchen Cabinet

A modern elaboration of the kitchen dresser, with cupboards in the lower part, a sliding enamelled metal shelf above them, which may be used as a table, and shelves and fitted cupboards in the upper part.

Kneading Trough

A common piece of country furniture, of boarded construction, resembling a chest on splayed legs; the receptacle splaying out-

Kneading trough. (From Loudon's *Encyclopaedia*, 1833.)

wards and being divided internally into compartments for dry flour and dough. Sometimes called a bread trough. (*See* illustration.)

Knee

The upper part of a cabriole leg. (*See* illustrations on page 162, *also* **Shoulder**.) That portion of a chair leg into which the seat rail is tenoned is also known as the knee, or knee-part.

Kneehole Desk or Table

Writing tables, dressing tables, desks, and bureaux with a central space or kneehole below the framework of the top, for the

Two types of kneehole. *Left:* A mid-18th century bureau table or writing table. (A simplified drawing of one of Chippendale's published designs.) *Right:* An early 18th century writing table. (From a drawing by E. J. Warne.)

comfort of those seated at them, were introduced in the early part of the 18th century. In *The Cabinet Dictionary* (1803) Sheraton defines a kneehole as 'a recess, convenient opening, or an aperture in any piece of furniture, to admit a person to sit to write or dress at'. (*See* illustrations.)

Knife Box

A receptacle for accommodating knives and spoons, used on a sideboard, and introduced during the latter part of the 18th century. With sloping tops, and curved or serpentine fronts, such boxes were highly decorative articles, made usually of mahogany, and inlaid with ivory and bands or lines of other woods, such as satinwood. (*See also* **Knife Urn**.)

Knife Pleats

A series of sharp-edged pleats, with the edges all turned in the same direction. The edge of each pleat may either just touch or overlap the preceding pleat.

Knife Urn

A knife box in the form of an urn. Such urn containers were probably introduced by the brothers Adam, for a pair of pedestals surmounted by bases or urns often flanked the sideboard tables of the type designed by Robert and James Adam. These urns were used for storing knives, forks, and spoons. (*See* illustration of side table on page 426.)

Knitting Chair

An armless, upholstered chair, supported on a wooden base

which contains a work drawer, and rests on slightly splayed feet. This is a modern article, originally designed by Charles Addison, and entered in a competition organised in 1948 by the Scottish Committee of the Council of Industrial Design, for the Scottish Furniture Manufacturers' Association.

Knob

A rounded protuberance, projecting from or affixed to the surface of a door or drawer front, or other hinged or sliding part of a piece of furniture, which is used as a handle. Knobs are sometimes used decoratively, either in rows to form a pattern, or as finials to upright members, such as the posts on a low post bedstead.

Knock Down Furniture

Furniture that may easily be folded or taken apart and packed flat for transport: for example, tables with hinged legs that fold up flat under the top. The term is often abbreviated by using the initials K.D. An alternative name is packaged furniture.

Knuckle

The small scrolls which terminate the arm rails of some types of Windsor chair are called knuckles. The term knuckle-arm is sometimes used in America to describe such types.

Knuckle Arm, *see* Knuckle

Knuckle Joint

A movable, interlocking joint used for the brackets which support the hinged leaf of a table, and for legs connected on fly rails, *q.v.*, which perform the same supporting function for a hinged leaf.

Knurl

A term sometimes used for a form of whorl foot, *q.v.*, on which the scroll is formed on the inner side of the leg and is not apparent from the front. It was used by chair makers during the mid-18th century.

Knurl foot.

Kokko (*Albizzia lebbeck*)

Also known as koko and occasionally, but incorrectly, as East Indian walnut. A dark brown wood, resembling walnut in colour, and sometimes richly marked. It provides good veneers and is used for turned work and cabinet work generally. It takes a fine polish after filling.

* L *

Laburnum (*Laburnum anagyroides*)

A hard, yellow wood, shading into light, almost pinkish brown. Used for inlaid decoration, occasionally for veneering, and, on some modern furniture, for drawer and door handles.

Labyrinth, *see* **Greek Fret**

Lace Box

A name given to a type of flat wooden box, square or rectangular in shape, with a hinged, overlapping lid, made in the late 17th and early 18th centuries. Such boxes were often decorated with marquetry, and one in the Victoria and Albert Museum (dated 1687) is decorated with cut paper work.

Laces

The braids used for trimming upholstery were called laces in the 17th and 18th centuries.

Lacquer

A term for varnishes, transparent or opaque, which are applied to the surfaces of wood or metal. The coating of polished metal with varnishes prepared from resin lac imparts a rich and lustrous finish to the surface, and the process is known as lacquering, resin lac being the basic substance from which all true lacquers are made. The lacquering of wooden surfaces as practised in the East, and imitated in Europe, is a different and distinctive decorative process. (*See* **Lacquer-Work**.) In connection with furniture, the term lacquer is also used to describe the translucent lacquer perfected by the French family of artist-craftsmen named Martin who worked in the early 18th century. (*See* **Vernis Martin**.)

Lacquer-Work

Lacquer- or lacker-work originated in China, where it was developed and practised with great skill. The art, derived from China, was also practised in Japan, where it acquired distinctive elaborations and characteristics. It flourished in both countries while Europe was still in the Dark Ages. Lacquer-work consists of the coating of wooden or papier-mâché surfaces with the prepared sap of lacquer trees. Many coats are applied, each being rubbed down to get a perfectly smooth surface. H. P. Shapland, in Vol. III of *The Practical Decoration of Furniture* (1927), suggests that between thirty and thirty-five separate processes are involved before the groundwork is ready for painting and gilding. Lacquer-work screens and cabinets were imported in great numbers from China and Japan during the latter part of the 17th century; and carcases of furniture, made in Europe, were shipped to China for lacquering. A European industry was established, and lacquered or japanned furniture, as it was then called, was made in Holland, France, and England at the end of the 17th and throughout the early part of the 18th centuries. (*See* **Japanning**.)

Ladder Back Chair

A modern term for a chair with a back formed by horizontal slats or rails between the uprights. Introduced first in country districts in the early years of the 18th century, it was adopted by fashionable town chair makers, who, among other refinements, introduced the pierced back slat. As these lateral apertures sometimes resembled the sound holes of a violin, the name fiddle back was in contemporary use. (*See* illustration, *also* **Fiddle Back Chair**.)

Ladder back chair: mid-18th century.

Ladies' Easy Chair

A small upholstered armchair with low arms and a high back, which was introduced in the mid-19th century. Buttoning was used for the upholstery of the seat, back, and inside of the arms: the seat was deep and the short, turned legs had castors. Sometimes called a pompadour chair.

Lady's Cabinet, *see* Sheveret

Lambrequin, *see* Pelmet

Laminated

Laminated materials are built up from layers of the same or alternating materials, such as plywood, or plywood faced with metal or plastic sheets.

Lamp

Until the 19th century, when gas lighting was first introduced, a lamp meant a vessel containing oil of animal or vegetable origin, into which a wick was dipped. (*See* illustrations of Roman Lamps, *also*

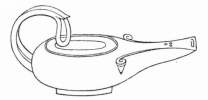

Roman lamps from Pompeii. *Left:* Earthenware lamp with two wicks. *Right:* Bronze lamp. (From Edward Trollope's *Illustrations of Ancient Art.*)

Betty Lamp *and* **Crusie**.) Improvements in the design of lamp mechanism were made in the closing decades of the 18th century, when the tubular wick was introduced, which rose between concentric tubes and was protected by a transparent chimney resting upon a perforated gallery. The moderator lamp was invented in 1836, and in this device the flow of oil from the reservoir to the wick was constantly regulated. The duplex burner was introduced in 1865. Sperm oil and refined rape oil were used until paraffin became commercially available in the latter part of the 19th century.

Lampshade

An opaque or translucent shield, partially or wholly enclosing the source of light, affixed to the lampstand or holder, and made of various materials—paper, parchment, glass, plastic, or fabric.

Lampstand

Lampstands and lamp standards are probably as old as lamps. (*See* illustrations of Roman Lampstands and Standards, *also* **Crusie**.) In England, before the end of the 18th century, lampstands were required only to accommodate shallow vessels, and resembled candle stands. When oil-burning lamps had larger reservoirs and their wicks were protected by glass chimneys, their weight and height increased, and they were mounted on vases which contained the reservoir, or were placed in metal baskets of brass, bronze, or iron, that varied in size and design with the strength and position of the lamp.

Lancashire Chair, *see* Derbyshire Chair

Lancet Clock Case

The term is used by F. J. Britten, in *Old Clocks and Watches and their Makers* (1904), to describe a table clock with a case that is shaped like the Early English Gothic type of pointed arch, known as a lancet arch. Such clock cases were made during the first half of the 19th century, and reflected the prevailing taste

for mediaeval forms, which arose from the Gothic revival in architecture.

Landscape Panel

A panel of wood, placed so that the grain is horizontal.

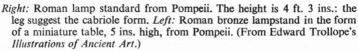

Right: Roman lamp standard from Pompeii. The height is 4 ft. 3 ins.: the leg suggest the cabriole form. *Left:* Roman bronze lampstand in the form of a miniature table, 5 ins. high, from Pompeii. (From Edward Trollope's *Illustrations of Ancient Art*.)

Lantern

A metal or wooden case, with transparent or translucent sides, enclosing a source of light. As horn was used in mediaeval times and as late as the 18th and early part of the 19th centuries, the old name, lanthorn, has, not unnaturally, been associated with this material, though the word lantern is adapted from the French *lanterne*, which was derived from the Latin *lanterna* or *laterna*. The metal used was generally brass or sheet iron, though 'a tinn lanthorne' is included in an inventory dated May 13th, 1680.

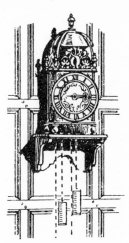

(Farm and Cottage Inventories of Mid-Essex, 1635–1749. Essex Record Office Publications, No. 8, p. 159.) Brass and bronze hanging lanterns of elaborate design were used during the late 17th century and throughout the Georgian period. By the close of the 18th century they were generally relegated to halls and staircases, for the chandelier and the wall sconce had supplanted them. (*See* **Moon**.)

Lantern Clock

A chamber clock with a bell. The type of small, brass chamber clock, surmounted by a dome-shaped bell that was protected by four arched ribs terminating in a decorative finial, is known variously as a lantern, bedpost, or birdcage clock; though these names are almost certainly of modern origin.

Mid-17th century 'lantern' clock. (From a drawing by E. J. Warne.)

Such clocks, driven by weights, were either hung against a wall or put on a bracket, to let the weights hang free. They were superseded by the pendulum clock, which was introduced in the second half of the 17th century. (*See* illustration.)

Late Georgian Style

The various fashions in furniture design and interior decoration that arose in the closing decade of the 18th and the first and second decades of the 19th centuries are sometimes described under this general heading; but the term, which is seldom used, properly describes the style that prevailed in the reign of George IV. (*See* **Georgian Style** *and* **Regency Style**.)

A lath back chair.

Lath Back

A simple type of Windsor chair, with a back formed by four

vertical laths, slightly curved, and flanked by stouter members, all socketed into the solid wooden seat and top rail. (*See* illustration on previous page, *also* **Stick Back** *and* **Windsor Chair**.)

Latten or **Laten**

An alloy of copper and zinc, not unlike brass, and used in mediaeval times for monumental brasses and figures, also for domestic articles such as candlesticks, plates, and spoons. Chaucer mentions it in the Prologue to *The Canterbury Tales*, line 699: 'He hadde a croys of latoun, ful of stones. . . .' Thomas Wright, in *The Homes of Other Days*, quotes the will of John Baret, of Bury, made in 1463, which includes a 'candylstykke of laten with a pyke'; also the will of the widow Agnes Ridges, of Bury, 1492, which includes a candle beam with six cups of latten, 'bellys of laton' as they were called. (*See* **Candle Beam**.) Shakespeare is alleged to have made a pun on the word at the christening of one of Ben Jonson's children, to whom he was godfather. The story is quoted from the writings of Sir Nicholas L'Estrange (1603–55) by W. J. Thoms in *Anecdotes and Traditions* (Camden Society, 1839). On the authority of L'Estrange, an avid collector of anecdotes, Shakespeare spoke of a gift to his godchild, in these words: 'I' faith, Ben, I'le e'en give him a douzen good Lattin spoones, and thou shalt translate them'.

Lattice Back

A type of late 18th century chair back, with the splat formed by slender members, crossing over each other with a net-like effect.

Lattice Work

A form of net-like tracery, either of wood or metal, used in the doors of cupboards, cabinets, and bookcases. Sheraton suggested the use of brass lattice work with pleated silk behind it for the cupboard doors in the plinth of a library bookcase.

Laurel

Carved laurel leaves were used for the enrichment of moulded detail, and for friezes in cabinet work, particularly during the early Georgian period. This form of ornament was based upon an architectural prototype of classical origin.

Laurel Wood, *see* **Indian Laurel Wood**

Leaf Scroll Foot

A scroll foot enriched with foliated carving.

Leather Furniture

Leather-covered stools, chairs, cushions, and beds were used in ancient Egypt, in the period of the Old Kingdom, 2980–2475 B.C., according to Breasted. (*History of Egypt*.) Leather was used for coffers and seats in mediaeval England (*see* **Coffer Maker's Chair**) and was popular during the Puritan period of the mid-17th century, when chair seats and backs were covered with leather and garnished with brass nails. Dyed leather was used in the 18th century, not only for upholstery, but in cabinet making, and particularly for the tops of desks, writing and library tables. (*See also* **Cofferer** *and* **Cordwainer**.)

Lectern

A reading desk used in churches in mediaeval England, and made of wood or metal, sometimes designed with the outspread wings of an eagle or a pelican supporting the desk. The name, aquila, derived from this eagle device, was sometimes used. Some mediaeval lecterns in brass or latten are extant. (*See* page 310.)

Leg Rest

An early 19th century device, sometimes known as an ease-and-comfort, used for increasing the comfort of old and elderly gentlemen, being carefully upholstered to fit the calves of the legs. J. C. Loudon, in his *Encyclopaedia* (1833), delicately suggests

Leg rest, or 'ease-and-comfort'. (From Loudon's *Encyclopaedia*, 1833.)

that it was 'used in dining rooms by old gentlemen after the ladies are gone'. (*See* illustration.)

Legs

Independent legs for stools, chairs, and tables are of ancient origin. Chair legs of ivory, carved in the form of a bull's legs, are placed by Breasted in the first two dynasties (3400–2980 B.C.) of Egypt, and in the ancient world the modelling of legs to represent those of animals was a common device. In the 6th and 5th centuries B.C., chairs with elegant, inward-curving legs were used in Greece; forms that were introduced during the Greek revival of the late 18th and early 19th centuries in England. (*See* pages 42 and 404.) The different types of legs evolved in chair making and cabinet making in England were broadly as follows: *16th century*, square-sectioned legs for chairs and turned legs for tables, often with large decorative bulbs: *17th century*, turned legs with decorative twisting, and scroll legs; and ultimately the cabriole leg, which was in use during the first part of the *18th century*. Round- and square-sectioned tapering chair legs of great slenderness were introduced in the latter part of the 18th century. The various types of legs are entered under their respective names, as follows:

Cabriole Leg	Scroll Leg
Clustered Column Leg	Swing Leg
Hock Leg	Taper Leg
Marlboro' Leg	Truss Leg
Sabre Leg	

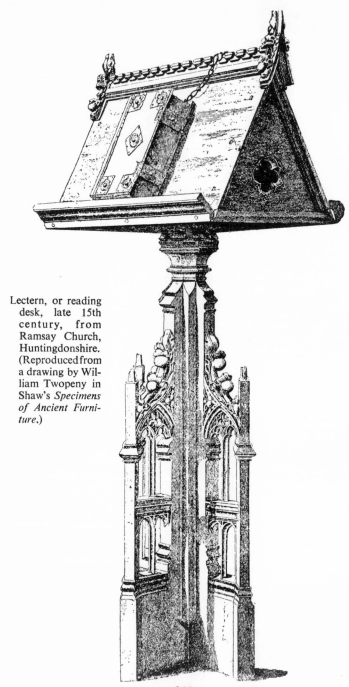

Lectern, or reading desk, late 15th century, from Ramsay Church, Huntingdonshire. (Reproduced from a drawing by William Twopeny in Shaw's *Specimens of Ancient Furniture*.)

Library Case

A name sometimes used in the 18th and early 19th centuries for a large library bookcase.

Library Screen or Library Fire-screen

A low, shallow bookcase, with a sliding adjustable fire screen, which may be raised to expose the bookshelves and to protect the user from the direct heat of a fire. The type illustrated in George Smith's *Cabinet Maker's and Upholsterer's Guide* (1836) is entered as a cheval screen libraire. (*See* illustration on next page.)

Library case: mid-18th century.

Library Stool

A term used by Sheraton for a rectangular stool, the seat being framed by a hinged lid over a receptacle which accommodates folding library steps. (*See* illustration on page 313.)

Library Table

In the mid-18th century, library tables were in the form of two large pedestals, with drawers and cupboards in them, supporting a top with drawers in the depth of the frieze rail. The kneehole space between the pedestals, and the great width of the table top, allowed two people facing each other to sit and write or read comfortably at the table. Many variations of this form were developed, and in the early 19th century Sheraton published designs for circular and oblong library tables. (*See* pages 314 to 317.)

Lignum Vitae (*Guaiacum officinale*)

An excessively hard wood, imported from Central America, dark brown or greenish-black in colour. Extremely durable, and used only where hard wear and tear has to be resisted.

Lime Wood (*Tilia vulgaris*)

An easily worked wood of a creamy white colour, used for turnery and particularly for carved decoration.

Limed Oak

Oak that has been pickled with a coating of lime, which is subsequently brushed from the surface, though it is usually allowed to remain in the grain. Limed oak surfaces are generally left unpolished.

Lincoln Rocker

A name occasionally used in the United States for a mid-19th century type of rocking chair, with a high, straight upholstered

A library screen, described as a 'cheval screen libraire' in *The Cabinet Maker's and Upholsterer's Guide*, by George Smith. (The plate from which this is reproduced was first published in 1827, and is included in the 1836 edition of the *Guide*.)

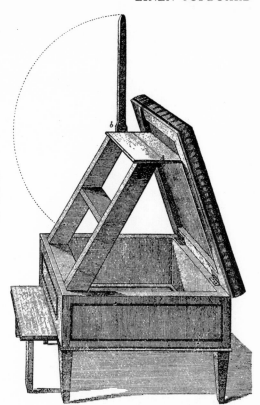

Sheraton's design for a library stool. (From Plate 57 of *The Cabinet Dictionary*, 1803.)

back and seat, and open arms with upholstered pads on the elbows. Chairs of this type were comfortable but clumsy; the arms were decorated with piercing, and occasionally carved cresting would be used on the top rail of the back. Abraham Lincoln is supposed to have liked this type of rocking chair, and his name has become associated with it; but it does not appear to have been a contemporary term.

Linen

The name given to all fabrics woven from flax fibre. Flax was cultivated in ancient Egypt, and the manufacture of linen is recorded as early as the Old Kingdom, 2960–2475 B.C. (Breasted's *History of Egypt*.) Bed linen in the form of large sheets was used in England in mediaeval times, and has become traditionally associated with bedding.

Linen Cupboard

A large cupboard, usually called a press, fitted with shelves. Such cupboards were in use in the 17th and 18th centuries, and

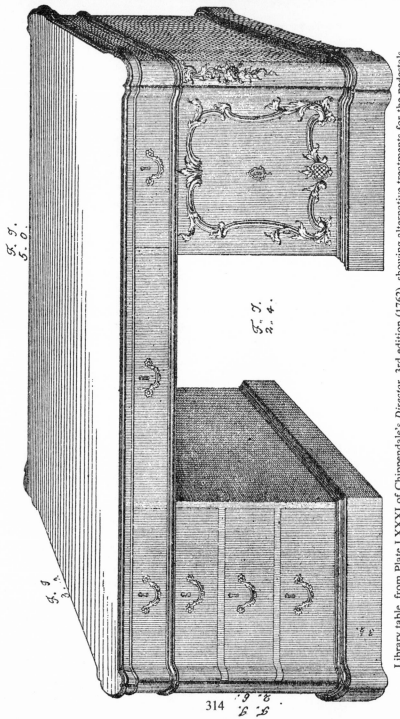

ft. y.
5. 0.

ft. y.
2. 4.

ft. y.
3. 2.

ft. y.
3. 6.

314

Library table, from Plate LXXXI of Chippendale's *Director*, 3rd edition (1762), showing alternative treatments for the pedestals. Compare with Sheraton's design opposite: *see also* illustrations on pages 316 and 317.

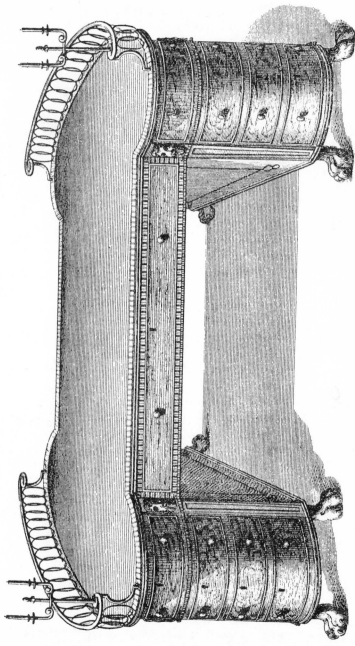

Library table. (From Plate 56 of *The Cabinet Dictionary*, by Thomas Sheraton, 1803.)

A library table, from Plate LXXXII of Chippendale's *Director*, 3rd edition (1762), which has a writing drawer that slides out of one end, and is supported on feet. Alternative treatments are shown for drawers or cupboards in the pedestals. (*See also* illustrations on pages 314, 315, and 317.)

replaced the chest as a receptacle for storing linen. (*See* **Linen Press.**)

Linen Press

This has a double meaning, being the term both for large standing cupboards, used for storing linen, and for a device specifically designed for pressing such articles of linen as sheets and table napkins. These linen presses, which were in use in the 17th and 18th centuries, resembled, upon a much larger scale, the old-fashioned letter-copying press used in offices: the sheets and other articles were folded and placed between flat boards, the upper board being pressed down by means of a screw until sufficient pressure had been exerted.

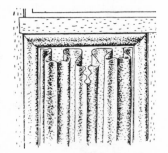

Linenfold panel.

Linenfold Panel or Parchment Panel

A form of ornament used on wall panelling and the panels of chests and on chair backs, consisting of vertical mouldings, ter-

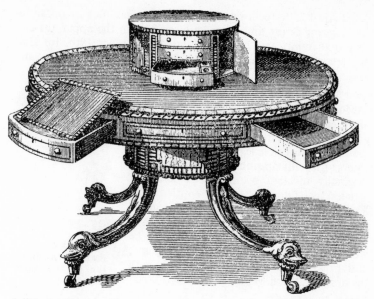

A library table from the upper part of Plate 55 in *The Cabinet Dictionary*, by Thomas Sheraton (1803). The toes and castors below the dolphin feet 'are of one piece cast in brass', and in describing this design Sheraton says: 'The nest of drawers in the centre, rise by two small springs . . .' (p. 260).

minating in folds. The device may originally have been suggested by folded linen or by scrolls of parchment. (*See* **Scroll Moulding**.) It was of Continental origin, and was introduced into England at the end of the 15th century. (*See* illustration on page 316.)

Lining

Thin lines of inlaid decoration are sometimes described as lining.

Lining Up

A cabinet-making term describing the practice of affixing a moulded frame below a table top, to increase its apparent thickness. Also known, rather clumsily, as thicknessing-up.

Linoleum

A hard-wearing material, variously patterned and coloured, made from oxidised linseed oil, ground cork, and certain resinous substances and pigments. It is used chiefly on floors, but also for covering table tops and shelves. It was first made by Frederick Walton, who took out a patent, No. 209, dated January 27th, 1860, for 'Improvements in the manufacture of varnish and in treating oils, also in the application of products obtained therefrom'. This was followed in 1863 by two further patents: No. 1037, dated April 25th, for 'Improvements in the manufacture of fabrics for covering floors and other surfaces, and in the apparatus employed therein': and No. 3210, dated December 19th, for 'Improvements in the manufacture of floor cloths and coverings and similar fabrics, and in pavements'.

Lion Mahogany or Lion Period

Modern terms, used to describe a phase of the early Georgian period that was distinguished by the lavish use of lions' masks on the knees of cabriole legs and on the arms of chairs. (*See* illustration.) Both terms were originally inspired by one of a series of articles by Haldane Macfall, entitled 'The Years of Mahogany: The Early Georgian', which was published in the *Connoisseur* (Vol. xxiv, May-August 1909), in which he wrote of 'The Lion Years of Mahogany', and began his subsequent paragraph with the heading: 'Lion Mahogany, 1720 to 1730'.

Lion's mask carved on the knee of a cabriole leg of the early Georgian period.

Lion's Paw Foot

The lion's paw has been used as a termination for the legs of stools and chairs since the early days of ancient Egypt; the device was common also in Assyria, ancient Persia, and the Roman Empire. (*See* illustrations of lampstands on page 306.) The lion's paw accompanied the lion's mask in the early Georgian period, as a form of carved ornament on chairs. It was used in subsequent periods, and reappeared in the early 19th century. (*See* illustration of Library Table by Sheraton on page 315.)

Listel

A narrow band or fillet. (*See* **Band**.)

Livery Board

A contemporary term, which occurs in 17th century inventories and was probably in use much earlier. It refers to a livery table, or a stand upon which a livery cupboard could rest. An inventory of the goods of Thomas Osburne of Writtle, Essex, dated February 24th, 1672, includes: '1 Livory board & Darnix Cloth & 2 Cusheons upon it ...' (*Farm and Cottage Inventories of Mid-Essex*, 1635–1749. Essex Record Office Publications, No. 8, p. 125.) This suggests that the livery board was occasionally used as a bench.

Livery Cupboard

A term for a free standing cupboard in which food was kept, the word livery denoting rations: food and drink given to people before retiring for the night: livery for the night. (An early precaution against night starvation.) The habit of keeping food in

Front and side views of a chair designed by William Kent, with the lion *motif* used on the back. (From *Some Designs by Mr Inigo Jones and Mr Wm. Kent*, published by John Vardy, 1744.)

319

bedrooms in special cupboards was of mediaeval origin (*see* **Aumbry**); but the term livery cupboard is not found earlier than the second quarter of the 16th century. It was probably, though not necessarily, used as a piece of bedroom furniture, for it was customary to take 'liveries', that is, food and drink, during the night time, until the first half of the 17th century. Mr F. Gordon Roe, F.S.A., regards a livery cupboard as a form of dumb waiter, used for displaying plate and serving food, and quotes contemporary evidence (the Contracts for Hengrave Hall, Suffolk, of 1537–38) that such cupboards were made 'without doors'. (*English Cottage Furniture*. London: Phoenix House Ltd., 1949, Section 8, p. 74.) The nearest identification of a livery cupboard is a two-tiered structure, similar to a court cupboard, with a small cupboard in the upper tier. Apparently, the aumbry went out of use when livery cupboards came in.

Livery Table, *see* **Livery Board**

Lobby Chest

Described by Sheraton, in *The Cabinet Dictionary* (1803), as a small or half chest of drawers, 'adapted for the use of a small study, lobby, or small lodging room'. The term was current in the late 18th century, and the dimensions of a lobby chest are given in *The Prices of Cabinet Work* (1797 edition) as follows: '3 feet 6 inches long, three long and two short drawers in ditto . . .', the chest being supported on a 'plinth or common brackets' (that is, bracket feet). Details are also included for round-fronted and serpentine lobby chests. (Pp. 13-17.)

Lock

A metal device used for fastening lids, doors, and drawers. Small, compact brass locks for the doors of cabinets and the drawers of chests and desk falls were gradually evolved from the large, cumbersome, and often highly complicated iron locks used on mediaeval chests and other receptacles. During the Georgian period, the key of a drawer or door lock often served as a handle, no other handles being provided. Sheraton gives details of the various types of locks in use for cabinet work, as follows: 'The common till lock, both spring and tumbler, used for drawers. The cupboard door kind, common, and spring and tumbler, used for bookcase and wardrobe doors. Box locks with link plates, such as for tea chests and wine cisterns. Mortice locks, some for doors, and others for sliders of cylinder writing tables. Those for inner doors are called spring locks, and are the most considerable, both in use and structure. The principal parts of a spring lock are the main plate, the cover plate, and the pin hole; to the main plate belong the key hole, top hook, cross wards, bolt toe, draw back spring, tumbler, pin of the tumbler, and the staples; to the cover plate belong the pin, main ward, cross ward, step ward or dap ward; to the pin hole belong the hook ward, main cross ward, shank, the pot or broad bow ward, and bit.' After referring critically to the claims made for various patent locks, he says that in general 'those of Mr Bramah have the preference'. (*The Cabinet Dictionary*, 1803, p. 262.)

Locker

A name originally given to a box or chest with a lid secured by a lock. The modern use of the word is nearly always confined to a lockable unit in a large fitment called a set of lockers, or, more briefly, the plural, lockers.

Locking Stile

The vertical frame of a door in which the lock is fixed.

Locust, *see* **Robinia**

Long Case Clock

Sometimes known as a tall case clock or, more popularly and since about 1878, as a grandfather clock, *q.v.* When weight clocks began to be regulated by a pendulum, they were enclosed in long cases which accommodated the weights. Pendulums were invented

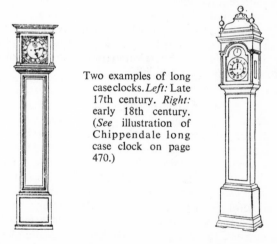

Two examples of long case clocks. *Left:* Late 17th century. *Right:* early 18th century. (*See* illustration of Chippendale long case clock on page 470.)

by Huygens in Holland in 1657–58, and the first long case clocks were made in England by the Fromanteel family of London immediately afterwards. It is the view of some authorities that the long case for weight clocks was invented by an English clockmaker. (*See* illustrations, and *A History of English Clocks*, by R. W. Symonds, p. 43.) The term 'clock with weights', that occurs in the late 17th century, probably refers to long case clocks. The name coffin clock does not appear to be contemporary.

Loo Table

A circular card table with a central pillar supporting the top and resting upon a base with three or four feet, introduced in the late Georgian and early Victorian periods, and designed specifically for the round game of cards that was known originally as lanterloo. (*See* illustration.) Sheraton shows a large loo table of

Loo table. (From George Smith's *Cabinet Maker's and Upholsterer's Guide*, 1836 edition.)

a totally different design in *The Cabinet Dictionary* (1803) on plate 57, which has a large rectangular top, hinged so that the table may stand against a wall when not in use. This top is supported on a base with a cupboard in it, resting on paw feet with castors. 'In this design', Sheraton writes, 'the intention of the cupboard is evident. . . .' (P. 338.)

Looking Glass

The use of the word glass in connection with mirrors is found as early as the 15th century; and a guild of glass-mirror makers was established at Nuremberg before the end of the 14th century. Glass mirrors were made in England by Sir Robert Mansell in the early 17th century, who brought in Venetian craftsmen as instructors. The Worshipful Company of Glass-sellers and Looking-glass Makers was incorporated in 1664. Until the mid-Victorian period, the term glass, prefixed by a specific reference to its function, was used for wall mirrors; the word mirror usually referred to hand mirrors, though glass and mirror were interchangeable terms. The term seeing glass was sometimes used in the 17th century. (*See* **Cheval Glass, Chimney Glass, Pier Glass,** *and* **Toilet Glass.**)

Loop Back

An alternative term for a hoop back Windsor chair, *q.v.*, sometimes used in America.

Loose Cover

Sometimes called a slip cover. A tailored and tightly fitting separate cover that may be slipped over a piece of upholstered furniture. One seam of the cover is usually left open to ensure a tight fit, and is fastened by means of hooks and eyes or press studs when the cover is in place.

Loose Seat

A stuffed seat with an independent frame, that fits into the framing of a chair or settee. Loose seats were in general use after the middle of the 18th century.

Loper

Sliding rails which pull out from the carcase of a bureau to support the fall are called lopers.

Lotus

A form of ornament based on the flower of the Egyptian lotus (*Nelumbium speciosum*), a water lily. Conventionalised representations of this lily occur with great frequency in Egyptian decoration and architecture, and were occasionally used in the ornamentation of furniture during the interest in Egyptian design that began in the Louis XVI period and was revived in the Napoleonic period, thus affecting the character of Empire furniture, on which the lotus flower is sometimes used. It was also used on Regency furniture, for in England the work of Thomas Hope stimulated interest in Egyptian decoration. (*See* Section II, page 67.)

Louis Style

A loose and misleading term used in the furniture trade to describe furniture that suggests the styles prevailing in France during the 18th century, before the Revolution. (*See* Section II, page 74.)

Lounge

A term that has become popular during the last half-century, which referred originally to the type of sofa that resembles a deeply sprung low-seated easy chair, with the seat extended to provide a leg rest. Lounges are occasionally made in canework, with a retractable leg rest, so that they may also be used as easy chairs.

Lounge Chair

A deeply sprung easy chair with a long seat, sometimes called a lounging chair. The term came into use in the mid-19th century. This type of chair is illustrated in A. J. Downing's book, *The Architecture of Country Houses*, published in 1850 in New York. (D. Appleton & Company.) The chair he shows is similar to the English variety, and he describes it as 'an easy chair—or lounge, better adapted for the siesta, than to promote the grace or dignity of the figure'. (P. 452, referring to Fig. 287. *See* illustration on next page.) Edward Bradley, who wrote under the pseudonym of Cuthbert Bede, described and illustrated a similar chair in his best known book, *The Adventures of Mr Verdant Green*, and

American lounge chair, *circa* 1850.

English lounge or lounging chair. (From *The Adventures of Mr. Verdant Green*, by Edward Bradley, published 1853-56.)

called it a lounging chair (p. 152). These lounge or lounging chairs usually had bobbin turning on the uprights of the back, on the horizontal and vertical members that supported the padded arms, and occasionally on the legs. They closely resembled, and may indeed have been the forerunners of the Morris chair, *q.v.*

Love Seat

A modern name given to a small seat designed for two people to sit close together. (*See* **Courting Chair.**)

Low Back Chair

A term sometimes used for a back stool.

Low Daddy

An American term, used as an alternative to lowboy.

Low Post Bed

An American term for a bed with four posts of approximately the same height as the top of the headboard and footboard. These turned posts and the cresting on head and footboards were elaborately carved. The term was probably introduced during the early part of the 19th century. (*See* illustration.)

Low post bed. American: early 19th century.

Low Relief

In the decoration of furniture, this term applies to carved ornamental detail, either in wood or gesso, which projects only slightly from the background.

Lowboy

An American term for a dressing table with several drawers, supported either on turned legs with stretchers, or cabriole legs. The lowboy was made to match the highboy, which was a chest of drawers supported on a stand of the same pattern as its companion lowboy. (*See* **Tallboy.**)

Lozenge

A diamond-shaped form of ornament, used both for inlaid and carved decoration, in the late 16th and early 17th centuries.

Lug Chair

A name, now obsolete, for the wing type of easy chair. (*See* **Easy Chair** *and* **Wing Chair.**)

Lug Support

An L-shaped stud or support for a shelf in a bookcase or cabinet. The vertical part of the L is inserted in a groove, and the horizontal part, which is usually rounded, projects so that the shelf rests upon it.

Lyre back chair. Late 18th century, American. Based on a design by Duncan Phyfe. (*See* illustration on page 356, where lyre device is used on an American type of Pembroke table.)

Lustre

A term used to describe candlesticks or chandeliers that are decorated with cut glass drops or pendants.

Lyctus Brunneus and **Lyctus Linearis,** *see* **Powder Post Beetle**

Lyre Back Chair

A name sometimes given to chairs when the back splat is in the form of a lyre. This device was used by Robert Adam, Hepplewhite, and more frequently by Sheraton. In America it was used by Duncan Phyfe. (*See* illustration on previous page.)

Lyre Clock

A spring clock in a lyre-shaped case, originating in France during the period of Louis XVI.

* M *

Madras Muslin

A furnishing material, used for curtains, with opaque figures on a plain-weave transparent ground.

Mahogany

This wood which, when polished, has a rich red colour, began to be extensively used for furniture during the reign of George I. There were several varieties, but the common source of supply was Jamaica, for the merchants in that island bought the Spanish mahogany from Cuba and Honduras and shipped it to England. (R. W. Symonds, *Connoisseur*, Vol. XCIV, July-Dec. 1934, pp. 216-217.) It has since become a generic term for the dinner table, which is spoken of as 'the mahogany'. (*See* **African, Cuban, Honduras**, and **San Domingo** or **Spanish Mahogany**.)

Mammy's Bench or **Mammy's Rocker**

A modern name used in America for a short stick back or Windsor bench on rockers, with a detachable fence occupying two-thirds of its length, so that a baby could lie on the seat without rolling off, while the mother or nurse sat beside it. This type of rocker bench became popular in the United States in the mid-19th century.

Mantel

The projecting shelf or ledge above the fireplace opening on a chimney breast. Also known as the mantel shelf. The term mantel or mantel-piece also embraces the lower part of a chimneypiece, including the surround of the fireplace and the shelf above it. It is derived from the term mantel tree, which was the name for a horizontal piece of timber laid across the jambs of a fireplace opening to support the breastwork of the chimney. Sir Henry Wotton refers to the mantel of a chimney in *The Elements of Architecture* (published in 1624). During the 19th century the term mantel-piece was regarded as synonymous with chimneypiece, *q.v.*

Mantel Clock

A Victorian name for a spring clock that was not normally designed to stand on a chimneypiece, but often did in the late 18th and 19th centuries.

Mantel Mirror

This term was introduced during the 19th century to describe what was formerly known as a chimney glass: that is, a looking glass resting upon the mantel shelf of a chimneypiece.

Mantel Tree, *see* **Mantel**

327

Manx Table

Also known as an Isle of Man table. A tripod table, with the three feet or claws carved to represent legs with knee breeches and buckled shoes; an adaptation of the three-legged device which is the arms of the Isle of Man.

Maple (*Acer saccharum*)

The maple grows in Canada and the eastern U.S.A., and supplies a light, yellowish-brown wood, diversified with dark brown lines. It has an elaborate, highly decorative figure, which takes the forms of fiddleback, bird's-eye, blister, and curly. The famous bird's-eye figure consists of a series of small spots, linked by undulating lines in the grain. It is used for ornamental veneers in cabinet making.

Maple Silkwood, *see* Queensland Maple

Marble Table

A table with a wooden frame, often elaborately carved, supporting a marble slab. Introduced in the late 17th century, such tables were used during the 18th century. (*See* **Frame**, and the illustration of a Table by William Kent opposite, frames for marble slabs by Chippendale on page 330, *also* the Eagle Table on page 243.)

Marcella Cloth

A woven white honeycomb material, used for counterpanes, *q.v.*

Marlboro' Bedstead

This term may refer to a type of bedstead with tapering Marlboro' legs, similar to those used on chairs and cabinet stands in the late 18th century (see following entry). R. W. Symonds has traced several references to this bedstead in advertisements appearing in the *Bristol Journal*. One of these, dated September 20th, 1783, reads as follows: 'For Sale. A neat Mahogany Marlboro' Bedstead.' It has been suggested that it may have been a form of camp or tent bedstead, named after the first Duke of Marlborough; but there is no evidence to support this, or illustrations that would give a clue to its appearance. The term does not occur in the Gillow records, and its use appears to be confined to the west country—where it may have taken its name from some maker in the Wiltshire market town of Marlborough—and to the late 18th century.

Marlboro' Leg

A trade term, used by cabinet makers in the latter part of the 18th century for a tapered leg of square section. In *The Prices of Cabinet Work* (1797) under the heading of 'General Observations' there is the following reference: 'All Table Work, to measure on

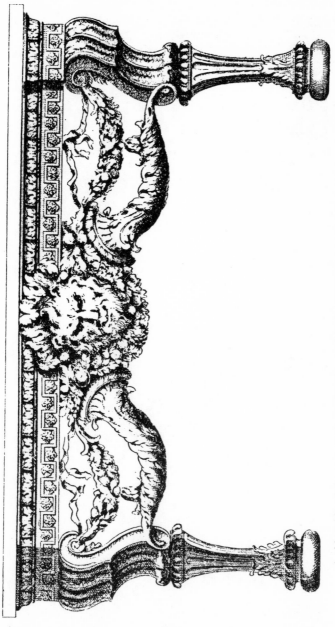

A side table of the type that supported a marble slab: designed by William Kent. (From *Some Designs by Mr Inigo Jones and Mr Wm. Kent*, published by John Vardy, 1744.)

Two examples of marble tables from the third edition of Chippendale's
Director (1762), Plates CLXXV and CLXXVI, where they are described as
frames for marble slabs.

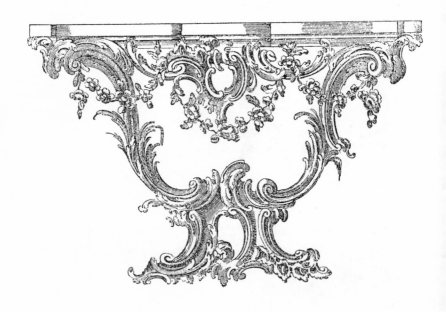

the tops, and to start with plain Marlboro' legs without castors, except otherwise mentioned in the preamble'. How this term arose is a matter for conjecture: it may have originated as a compliment to George Spencer, the fourth Duke of Marlborough, to whom Ince and Mayhew dedicated their book, *The Universal System of Household Furniture*, which was published about 1762. (*See* page 32.)

Marquetry or Marqueterie

An elaborate decorative process in which patterns are formed by various woods and other materials such as mother-of-pearl and ivory, which are inlaid into veneers, so that veneer and ornament form one sheet which is applied to a wooden surface such as a panel, a drawer front, or a table top. (*See also* **Endive Marquetry.**)

Marquise Chair

A broad chair with upholstered seat and arms, introduced in France during the latter part of the 17th century, and similar to the double chair back settee with a cane seat, used in the reign of Charles II. (*See also* **Love Seat.**)

Mask

The face of a human being or an animal, used as a form of carved decoration. (*See* illustrations on pages 286, 318, and 329.)

Matted

The background of carving was often matted or roughened to give it an even surface. (*See* **Stippled Background.**)

Matted Chair

A chair with a matted seat of rushes or straw. In an inventory, dated February 21st, 1686/7, five 'mated chaires' are mentioned. (*Farm and Cottage Inventories of Mid-Essex*, 1635–1749. Essex Record Office Publications, No. 8, p. 182.)

Mattress

A flat bag of cloth, stuffed with some soft material, such as straw, feathers, hair, or cotton, and laid upon a bedstead or a floor to form a bed. A straw-stuffed mattress was known as a pallet, and was the earliest form of bed. (*See also* **Feather Bed.**)

Medallion

A circular, oval, or rectangular plaque carved in low relief.

Medullary Rays

The lines that radiate outwards from the medulla, which is the pith or heart of a tree, and cut across the annular rings, are known as the medullary rays. They are strongly marked in oak and beech.

Meeting Stile

The vertical members or stiles of double doors, which adjoin when the doors are closed.

Melon Bulb

A melon-shaped bulbous form of ornament, used on the legs of tables, on bedposts, and occasionally for the supports of the upper parts of press cupboards and on court cupboards in the late 16th and early 17th centuries.

Melon bulb. Late 16th and early 17th centuries.

Mendlesham Chair

A chair of stick construction, with four rails in the back, a solid wide seat, and turned spindle legs. Such chairs, which are classified as Windsor chairs, *q.v.*, are said to have been originated by a chair maker named Daniel Day, of Mendlesham and Stoneham, in Suffolk. R. W. Symonds has recorded that Daniel Day 'began to trade as a wheelwright, and his son, about 1790, is said to have worked with Thomas Sheraton, after returning to his father's workshop'. (Article on the Windsor chair, Part II, *Apollo*, Vol. XXII, No. 131, November 1935.) Mendlesham chairs were made of fruit wood, with elm seats, and date from the beginning of the 19th century.

Mendlesham chair, sometimes called a Dan Day chair.

Metal Furniture

Furniture of bronze and iron was used by the Greeks and Romans, and metal receptacles were used during mediaeval times. A state chair of iron covered with purple satin is an item in an inventory taken at Ewelme in 1466. (Quoted in Parker's *Domestic Architecture of the Middle Ages*, Part I, chapter iv, p. 115.) During the 19th century, improvements in iron-founding led to the production of large quantities of highly ornamental cast iron furniture, *q.v.* The most ubiquitous form of metal furniture introduced in that century was the bedstead, constructed of brass or iron rods, and ornamented with innumerable knobs and finials. During the present century furniture made of sheet steel, pressed or welded, has come into use for office equipment, and also for domestic furnishing, chiefly for wardrobes and bed heads and ends. In the third decade of this century, chairs, tables, and beds with frames of steel or copper tubing or steel strip became popular; though some of the forms evolved by designers had been foreshadowed a hundred years earlier. (*See* accompanying illustration and Section II, page 72, *also* **Cast Iron Furniture**, **Flower Stand**, **Revolving Chair**, and **Rocking Chair**.)

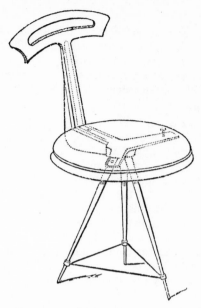

Early 19th century forerunner of a combined wood and metal chair with tubular iron legs, designed for the use of cottagers, by Robert Mallet. (From Loudon's *Encyclopaedia*, 1833).

Miniature Furniture

Small scale models of cabinets, wardrobes, bookcases, chests of drawers, and other pieces of furniture, were made with great skill and attention to detail and finish, by cabinet makers in the 18th century, for use in their shop windows to advertise their wares. Those windows were cut up into small panes by glazing bars, and it was not until plate glass was made in large sizes that the use of such models was discontinued. As H. P. Shapland points out: 'Having served their purpose as advertisements they have passed through the hands of antique dealers into those of collectors of old furniture.' (*A Key to English Furniture*, chapter xviii, p. 173. London: Blackie & Son Ltd., 1938.)

Mirror

Chaucer mentions mirrors, and in *The Romaunt of the Rose*, line 567 runs thus: 'She hadde [in hande] a gay mirrour. . . .' The word mirror meant a hand mirror, or any reflecting surface, and early mirrors were of polished metal. When glass was coated with amalgam of mercury, the term looking glass, or glass, replaced mirror. It was not until the late 19th century that the word mirror came back into general use, and was applied to all forms of looking glasses.

Misericord

A small ledge or bracket on the underside of a hinged seat in the choir stalls of a church, which protrudes sufficiently when the seat is folded back to give support to the occupant when standing. (*See* illustration, *also* **Stall** *and* **Subsellum**.)

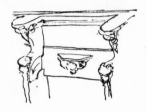

Mission Furniture

A name associated with the crude, heavy, unpolished furniture of native materials, used primarily for the furnishing of Spanish mission stations in Mexico, and often of Indian workmanship. In the first decade of the present century, the forms of this furniture were deliberately imitated in the

Misericord. (From Ware and Beatty's *A Short Dictionary of Architecture*.)

United States, and a so-called Mission style gained a transitory popularity. This taste for clumsy and all too obviously 'handmade' furniture may have been generated partly by the English arts and crafts revival of the 'seventies and 'eighties of the 19th century.

Mitre

The diagonal joint formed by two pieces of moulded woodwork when they intersect at right angles.

Mixing Table

A marble-topped side table for mixing drinks, with a superstructure containing drawers for decanters, and a tamboured rolltop, which descends to cover the marble slab when the table is not in use. Such tables were occasionally made in the United States towards the end of the 18th century, and the term may have originated in America, where the preparation of appetising drinks by mixing various ingredients was an established custom. There is an excel-

Mitred angle. (From Ware and Beatty's *A Short Dictionary of Architecture*.)

lent example of a mahogany mixing table in the room from Baltimore, Maryland, in the Metropolitan Museum of Art, New York.

Moderator Lamp, *see* Lamp

Modillion

A bracket used to support the upper members of a cornice in the Corinthian and Composite orders of architecture. Also known as a *console*, and a *mutule*.

Mohair

A cloth made from the hair of the Angora goat, used occasionally for upholstery. The word is derived from the Arabic *muhayyar*.

Mohair fabrics were used in early 18th century furnishing. Pope refers to mohair in his 'Moral Essays', Epistle II, lines 169 and 170:

> And when she sees her friend in deep despair,
> Observes how much a chintz exceeds mohair.

Moiré

Cloth with a very closely woven rib and a highly lustrous surface finish that gives a watered figure. The word *moiré* was adapted by the French from the English mohair.

Monk's Seat, *see* **Chair Table**

Moon

A spherical lantern with a brass frame and horn panes, fixed on the end of a pole. The moon was carried by servants to light their masters in lanes and dark roads, and could be used inside a house by fixing the pole into a socket. The moon was a 16th-century improvement on the cresset, *q.v.* (*See* illustration.)

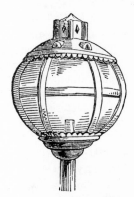

Moquette

A heavy upholstery velvet, usually woven as a double cloth, the two grounds with their connecting threads being cut apart after weaving. (*See* **Double Cloth.**) It has a wool or ramie pile, and a cotton ground. (*See* **Ramie.**)

Moreen

A strong woollen material, sometimes mixed with cotton, and occasionally used for upholstering furniture in the late 17th and 18th centuries. The word moreen,

A moon. (From a drawing in *The Homes of Other Days,* by Thomas Wright.)

which is sometimes spelt morine, is obsolete. It is a corruption of *moiré*, which was the French adaptation of the English word mohair, *q.v.*

Moresque, *see* **Arabesque**

Morris Chair

An easy chair with wooden arms padded on top, and an adjustable back. The term, particularly in the United States, is now applied chiefly to chairs of this type which have loose seat and back cushions; but the original type was produced by the firm founded by William Morris in 1861. (The origin and adoption of this term and the history of this particular type of chair has been traced by Mr Edgar Kaufman in his article on furniture in the *Architectural Review*, No. 644, vol. 108, August 1950.)

Mortice or **Mortise** (*verb*)

To join two members by means of a mortise and tenon: to cut a mortise in a member.

Mortice or **Mortise** (*noun*)

A cavity sunk in a member, cut so that it receives a projection called a tenon on another member.

Mortise-and-Tenon

A method of joining two members so that a projecting tenon on one fits exactly into a sinking of corresponding size in the other. (*See* illustration of Mortise.)

Mortise Lock

A lock fitted into a mortise. (*See* **Lock.**)

Mortlake Tapestry

The name given to the products of the tapestry works organised by Sir Francis Crane under the patronage of James I, at Mortlake, Surrey, in 1619. The products were not characteristically English, as foreign workmen were chiefly employed. The works were closed after the Civil Wars of the mid-17th century.

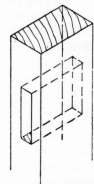

A mortise. (From Ware and Beatty's *A Short Dictionary of Architecture.*)

Mortuary Chair

A term used for a type of chair, made during the third quarter of the 17th century, with arched rails in the back, similar to the so-called Derbyshire (*q.v.*) and Yorkshire chairs, and identified with those regions. The name mortuary is suggested by the masks carved on the centre of the back rails, which are supposed to portray the head of Charles I, but it does not appear to be a contemporary term.

Mosaic, *see* **Tonbridge Ware**

Mother-of-Pearl

The lustrous, iridescent lining of the pearl oyster and various other shells. Mother-of-pearl has been used chiefly for inlaid decoration on furniture since the 17th century. It is translucent, and in Goa, India, Portuguese architects used it instead of glass in the windows of churches built in that city during the 16th and 17th centuries; but this particular property has seldom been used, its ornamental quality for surface decoration having attracted and held the attention of craftsmen and designers for centuries.

Motif or **Motive**

The basic theme of an ornamental surface pattern, or of the carved decoration used to embellish any article.

Mottled

A speckled grain in a veneer.

Moulding

A continuous projection or incision, curved or faceted in section, or with combined curves and facets, used as a decorative band. (*See* illustrations of various mouldings in section, such as bead, cavetto, flush bead, ogee, ovolo, reverse ogee, scotia and torus.)

Moulding Table

A mediaeval term for a table that was used for pastry making.

Mount

A term generally applied to metalwork—bronze, brass, or ormolu—used for the enrichment of furniture.

Moving Bookstand, *see* **Bookstand**

Moving Library, *see* **Bookstand** *and* **Chiffonier**

Muffineer

An early 19th century term for a small salt or sugar castor: used for sprinkling muffins. (Sydney Smith mentions muffineers in a reference to the work of Thomas Hope. *See* page 67.) Later in the century, it was used to describe a covered dish for keeping muffins and crumpets warm.

Mule Chest

A chest invented in the mid-17th century, with a plinth in which two or more drawers were fitted. It was a traditional design, partaking of the characteristics of the chest and the chest of drawers. It is not a contemporary term.

Mule chest, mid-17th century.

Muntin or **Munting**

The central vertical member of a door frame, which divides the panels above and below the middle or lock rail.

Mural Clock

An alternative term for a wall clock, *q.v.*

Music Desk, *see* **Reading Desk**

Music Rack

An open rack for holding music, usually of mahogany or rosewood. (*See* **Canterbury**.)

Music Stand, *see* **Reading Desk**

Music Stool

Adjustable music stool. (From Loudon's *Encyclopaedia*, 1833.)

Music stools with circular adjustable seats were introduced early in the 19th century. Stools with rectangular seats and a receptacle below for storing music came into use in the middle of that century. (*See* **Canterbury**.) Before that time stools were used for spinets, pianos, and other musical instruments with keyboards.

Muslin

A light-weight plain woven cotton cloth, in plain white or dyed colours: it is sometimes printed with patterns.

Mutule, *see* **Modillion**

Nail Head

The plain or ornamental boss or rosette forming the head of a nail used to secure leather or fabric to chairs. Leather-covered chests and chairs were often 'garnished with nails', a term for the decorative use of brass-headed nails. The use of dome-topped brass nails for fastening leather or fabric to a wooden carcase or a frame, such as a trunk or chair frame, dates from mediaeval times, for it was the cofferer's method of fixing the leather. It was also used by upholsterers from the 16th to the end of the 18th century. During the 18th century it was a common method to frame the upholstery of chairs with a row of closely set brass-headed nails. Sometimes the nails were used to make a decorative design. (*See* **Cofferer** *and* **Stud**.)

Necessary Stool, *see* Close Stool

Neck Mould

An architectural term for a small, convex moulding, encircling a column at the junction of the shaft and capital.

Necking or Collar

In architecture, necking is the term used for the space immediately below the capital in the Roman Doric order. In furniture, it is taken to mean any bead or small moulding that encircles some vertical unit, such as the leg of a table or cabinet stand.

Needlework

A generic term that includes plain needlework in all its utilitarian aspects, and art needlework, which is wholly decorative. For specific applications of decorative needlework to furniture, *see* **Appliqué**, **Embroidery**, **Gros Point**, *and* **Petit Point**.

Nef

Sometimes called a *cadenas*, the *nef* was an elaborate silver casket, shaped like a ship, a form that probably originated in the 13th century when Queen Margaret, wife of Louis IX, dedicated to St. Nicholas a silver model of a fully rigged ship,

A *nef*. This drawing, copied from a MS. in the French National Library, is included in *The Homes of Other Days*, by Thomas Wright.

in thanksgiving, after she and her three children had survived a great storm off Cyprus when they were returning to France from Palestine in 1254. (This origin is suggested by Mr Cyril G. E. Bunt in an article on 'The Silver Nef', published in the *Connoisseur*, Vol. CXI, Jan.-June, 1943, pp. 90-91.) The *nef* was the most conspicuous and important piece of plate, which took precedence over the great salt, and was brought to table and placed ceremoniously before the nobleman or prince who owned it. Within the hull, which was raised upon a stand, there were receptacles for spices, seasoning, and salt, and a place for a knife and spoon. The casket could be locked. The *nef* was, by its nature, a rare and costly article; and *nefs* were made and used from the 14th to the end of the 18th centuries. (*See* illustration on previous page.)

Nelson's Chairs

The name given by Thomas Sheraton to some complicated chairs that he designed to celebrate Nelson's victory at Trafalgar. The designs, published in 1806, consisted of an elbow chair, with the back in the form of an anchor, and two dolphins, tied together with ribbon, acting as the front legs; and a single chair with an anchor in the back. Easily the worst designs ever produced by Sheraton, they were clumsy, ill-proportioned, and repellently grotesque. (*See* **Trafalgar Chair.**)

Nest of Drawers

A name formerly given to a chest of drawers. It is a contemporary term and occurs in late 17th and 18th century inventories. It was used by cabinet makers in the late 18th and early 19th centuries to describe a group of small drawers on a writing or dressing table. Sheraton uses it in this sense in describing the circular library table shown on page 317.

Nest of Tables or **Nested Tables**

A set of three or four small tables, with tops at different levels, and with frames progressively diminishing in width, so that they may fit into each other and occupy the space of one table only. (*See* **Coffee Table.**) Sheraton describes them as work tables, and calls them trio tables, when they are in sets of three, and quartetto tables, *q.v.*, when there are four. In the Gillow records, 1811, they are called quarto tables. (E. & S. Book, No. 1895.)

New Art

New Art is the anglicised version of *L'Art Nouveau*, a style of decoration that originated in France during the eighteen-nineties and spread over Europe, affecting English furniture design and interior decoration in the opening years of the present century. It was characterised by the free use of naturalistic *motifs*, by the association of metal and enamel with woodwork, and the distortion of form in furniture to accommodate the floreated decoration, to which all functional needs were subordinated. (*See also* **Quaint Style.**)

New Zealand Red Pine, *see* **Rimu**

Niche

A term borrowed from architecture to describe a shallow concave recess in a wall, which was often a feature of panelled rooms during the late 17th and 18th centuries, sometimes filled with shelves for the display of ornaments and china (*see* illustration), and occasionally fitted with glazed doors. Niche also means a shallow recess in the front of a cabinet.

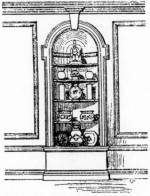

Nicking

A term sometimes used to describe the simplest kind of gouge work, *q.v.*, of the late 16th and 17th centuries.

Night Clock

A clock with a lamp and an additional set of hour numerals, which were pierced so that the light of the lamp shone through them, and they appeared in a curved aperture

Example of early 18th century niche in a panelled room. (From a drawing by E. J. Warne.)

above the dial. Pepys mentions such a clock when describing the bedchamber of Catherine of Braganza, Charles II's Queen. (*Diary,* June 24th, 1664.) F. J. Britten describes a 16th century lamp timekeeper with a cylindrical transparent glass reservoir for the lamp oil, which was fitted vertically into a pewter stand, and had hour numerals marked on one of the pewter uprights that framed the reservoir, so that as the oil sank the hours were recorded. R. W. Symonds points out that the unsatisfactory light devices of the 17th century caused the invention of the repeating movement, so that at night, by pulling a cord at any time, the hour and nearest quarter would strike on different sounding bells.

Night Commode, *see* **Close Stool**

Night Stool, *see* **Close Stool**

Night Table

A combined table and close stool. Sheraton, in *The Cabinet Dictionary* (1803), describes a night table as having a tray top, while 'the seat part draws out in front like a common drawer, and contains a pan hid from the eye by a deep front rail, which is sometimes made to appear like two drawers with knobs or handles. . . .' (*See also* **Close Stool.**)

Nomadic Furniture

A term used by Dr Siegfried Giedion to describe the various

341

types of collapsible and portable furniture: such as camp furniture of all kinds. (*See Mechanization Takes Command*, Oxford University Press, 1948.)

Nonsuch Chest

A name given to a type of chest, made in the late 16th and early 17th centuries, with the front decorated by an inlaid representation of the Palace of Nonsuch at Cheam, Surrey, that was built for Henry VIII. There is some doubt whether such chests were of English origin, as the character of the inlaid decoration often suggests Flemish workmanship.

Nosing

A general term for any projecting, rounded edge, applying particularly to the projecting edge of a stair tread.

Nottingham Lace

This term covers all varieties of woven laces made in Nottingham, and thus includes types used for dressmaking as well as for furnishing. In furnishing, the term applies to the boldly patterned, heavy-meshed and wide laces used for window curtains. They are usually made with a square mesh, and all-over or border patterns in solid Jacquard weaves, with floral and geometrical designs.

Nulling

Nulling.

A form of carved decoration resembling fluting, with alternating concave and convex flutes, and sometimes called gadrooning. Used on the flat or turned edges of tables and cabinet stands in the 17th and 18th centuries, and occasionally on the underframing of chests.

Nursing Chair

A single chair with a low seat, between 13 and 15 ins. high. The term appears to have been introduced during the 19th century, though it is probably much older.

* O *

Oak (*Quercus pedunculata*)

The common oak is native to Europe and the British Isles. It supplies a hard, reliable wood, pale yellow in colour, deepening to a rich brown with age and polishing. There are also American and Asiatic varieties of oak. The following are all used in furniture making and joinery, and are included under their respective names: American red and white oak, Austrian oak, bog oak, brown oak, English oak, and Japanese oak. (*See also* **Wainscot Oak**.)

Obeche (*Triplochiton scleroxylon*)

Sometimes known as African whitewood. A straw-coloured wood, varying to yellow. It is soft and light and works well, and is used for drawer linings and shelves in inexpensive furniture.

Occasional Table

A small, conveniently portable table that came into use during the 18th century. The term occasional table, though specifically mentioned by Sheraton, appears to have been adopted at some subsequent date as a general description for almost any small table. Sheraton's definition in *The Cabinet Dictionary* (1803) suggests that occasional tables were used chiefly for games, and that a concealed chessboard was one of their features.

Ogee

The common name for the moulding known in architecture as cyma recta. Sometimes written as O.G., and also known as ogive. In section it has a double curve, concave above, convex below. (*See* illustration, *also* **Reverse Ogee**.)

Ogee, or cyma recta.

Ogive, *see* **Ogee**

Old English Tail, *see* **Cascade**

Olive Wood (*Olea europaea*)

The Spanish and Italian olive supplies a decorative wood of a yellow shade, varying to greenish-brown, with a wavy, mottled figure. It was used for turnery, ornamental veneers, and occasionally, in the form of thin boards, for frames and boxes, and was very popular in the reign of Charles II. An olive wood chest of drawers and looking-glass frame are items in a late 17th century inventory.

Ombre Table

A small card table, probably introduced in the latter part of the 17th century. The game of ombre is mentioned in *The Man of Mode; or Sir Fopling Flutter*, a play by Sir George Etheredge, first acted in June 1676, and published in that year. Lady Townley, one of the characters, says in praise of a young man, that he is 'always ready to stop up a gap at ombre ...': a reference which suggests that it was by then a popular and established game. It was played throughout the 18th century. According to Strutt, it was brought into England by Catherine of Braganza, Charles II's Queen. (*The Sports and Pastimes of the People of England*, published in 1801.)

Omnium

A pretentious name for a whatnot, sometimes used in the mid-19th century. An omnium with three tiers, elaborately carved, designed and made by Arthur James Jones of Dublin, was shown at the Great Exhibition of 1851, and was illustrated and described in the *Official Catalogue*. (Vol. II, entry 78, p. 735.)

Open Back Chair, *see* **Derbyshire Chair**

Open Twist

A form of spiral turning, used for the legs of chairs, tables, and cabinet stands, also for balusters, in the second half of the 17th and the opening years of the 18th centuries. Known as double open twist when two members were turned, and as triple open twist when there were three. (*See* illustration above.)

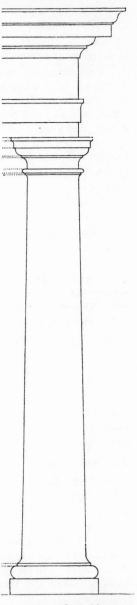

Double open twist spiral turning.

Order of Architecture

An order of architecture is a system of design by which the relative proportions of vertical and horizontal members may be determined. These members consist of a column, usually resting upon a base, with the shaft

An order of architecture, showing the column supporting an entablature, *q.v.* This example is the Roman order known as Tuscan.

344

terminating in a capital, surmounted by an entablature. (*See* illustration on preceding page.) The Greek orders of architecture were Doric, Ionic, and Corinthian; the Romans adapted them, and added two others: Tuscan and Composite. (The individual orders are described under their appropriate letter.)

Ormolu

An alloy of copper, zinc, and tin. It is gilded and used for mounts on decorative furniture. The name is also given to the gold leaf used for gilding bronze mounts on furniture. The use of ormolu is associated chiefly with the ornate furniture made in France during the 18th century.

Ornament

The definition given by Ralph N. Wornum, in his *Analysis of Ornament* (1855), cannot be bettered: 'Ornament is essentially the accessory to, and not the substitute of the useful; it is a decoration or adornment; it can have no independent existence practically'.

Orrery

An instrument for showing the motions of the planets round the sun by means of clockwork. The name was derived from Charles Boyle, Earl of Orrery, for whom the instrument was invented by George Graham. An octagonal orrery was made by Thomas Tompion and George Graham, in the first decade of the 18th century: it was 9 ins. high, and was enclosed in a case of veneered ebony with silver dials and mouldings.

Ottoman

A low, long, stuffed seat without a back, upon which several

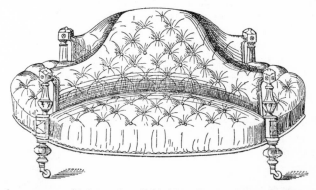

Circular ottoman with buttoning, divided into four seats: second half of 19th century. This is a modification of the more elaborate type shown by Balny of Paris at the Great Exhibition of 1851.

people could sit. This type of seat originated in Turkey, as the name suggests, but when introduced to England in the early part of the 19th century it acquired a variety of forms. Circular and corner ottomans were introduced, the latter being the forerunner of the cosy corner. (*See* **Corner Ottoman**.) The original backless type of ottoman was generally furnished with loose cushions, and was not so long or so wide as a divan. Another original type of ottoman was designed to allow people to sit back to back, and it was from this that the English circular and corner variants developed. (*See* illustration, *also* Section I, page 35.)

Ottoman Footstool

A footstool standing on four feet, with a thickly padded top of buttoned upholstery, which could also be used as a low seat.

Overmantel

A Victorian elaboration of the chimney glass, which included shelves for ornamental objects, and, resting on the mantel-shelf, rose to the height of the cornice. The area of looking glass was reduced in the late Victorian

Ottoman footstool. (From Loudon's *Encyclopaedia*, 1833.)

period, and the frame with its shelves and decorative fretwork and turning became the most important part of the overmantel. (*See also* **Shelf Cluster.**)

Overstuffing

The term used in modern upholstery practice for the use of thick padding or stuffing that is applied to the wooden frames of armchairs and settees, under the actual upholstery material. This padding or stuffing, which is much thicker than that used when upholstery was first introduced, provides additional comfort and also determines the external shape of the arms and backs of the furniture on which it is used.

Ovolo.

Ovolo

In architecture and cabinet making, the name for a wide convex moulding. (*See* illustration.) An alternative name is Quarter Round, which accurately describes the section of the moulding, which is the quadrant of a circle.

Oxford Easy Chair

A high-backed easy chair, with open arms and upholstered arm rests, introduced during the mid-19th century.

Oxford Hip Bath, *see* **Hip Bath**

Oxford easy chair.

Oyster Board

A mediaeval name for a table used for opening and preparing oysters for eating. (*See* **Board,** *also* **Table.**)

Oystering

Sometimes known as oystershell veneering. A descriptive term for veneers that are cut from the boughs of small trees, like laburnum, also from walnut and lignum vitae, the cut being made

Oystershell veneering on the drawer fronts of late 17th century chest of drawers.

at right angles to the length of the bough. Of Dutch origin, oystershell veneering was introduced into England in the late 17th century, and was used for drawer fronts and the doors of cabinets and bureaux during the early part of the 18th century.

Oystershell, *see* **Oystering**

Oysterwood

The name sometimes given to the small oval veneers of olive and laburnum used in oystershell veneering.

347

* P *

Packaged Furniture, *see* **Knock Down Furniture**

Pad Foot

An alternative term for club foot, *q.v.*

Pagoda

The word pagoda was originally introduced to Europe during the 16th century by the Portuguese adventurers in India, and has since become an accepted term in architecture for a many-sided tower, usually polygonal in plan, with projecting roofs, elaborately ornamented. Such towers, based on Indian prototypes, were perfected in China. The pagoda became familiar as a decorative form during the various waves of Chinese taste that influenced the design and ornamentation of furniture during and after the second half of the 17th century. It was much used by English furniture makers after the publication, in 1757, of Sir William Chambers' book, *Designs of Chinese Buildings, Furniture, Dresses, Machines and Utensils*. (He designed the pagoda in Kew Gardens soon after the book appeared.) Thomas Chippendale and his contemporaries adopted the pagoda roof with its upturned eaves and little pendant bells, and used it on cabinets, china shelves, and occasionally for the canopies of beds. (*See* illustration of hanging shelves on page 282, *also* **Chinese Taste**.)

Painted Furniture

Paint has been used for covering and ornamenting the surface of furniture since the earliest times. Painted chests were used in ancient Egypt. Painted furniture was known during and after the Middle Ages in England: and since the taste for japanned furniture developed in the second half of the 17th century (*see* **Japanning**), furniture with coloured or gilded surfaces and ornamentation has been made in every subsequent period. The brothers Adam, and their contemporaries, used japanned furniture, decorated with delicately drawn flowers and figures. Such furniture was fashionable in the second half of the 18th and the opening decades of the 19th centuries. Sheraton, in *The Cabinet Dictionary* (1803), says that 'the principal thing which constitutes this a distinct branch of painting is the general use of size and varnish colours, by which it is performed with much greater dispatch and effect'.

Pair of Tables

A pair of tables consists of two boards, hinged together, which, when opened, form a board for chess or draughts; and this term, mediaeval in origin, was in use as late as the 16th century, and was probably derived from the game called tables. (*See* **Table**.)

Pallet, *see* **Mattress**

Palliase or **Pailliasse**

A small mattress, usually stuffed with chaff or straw.

Palm Stand, *see* **Art Pot Stand**

Pan Back Chair

An abbreviation for a panel back chair.

Panel

A sunk or raised surface, framed by the stiles and rails of a door, or the front or lid of a chest.

Panel Back Chair

This term, which is not contemporary, is sometimes given to oak chairs with a panel framed in the back, of the type made in the 16th century and in the early Stuart period. They are sometimes known as wainscot chairs, which was a contemporary term. (*See* **Wainscot** *and* **Wainscot Chair.**)

Panelling

Panels framed in series on a wall.

Papier Mâché

A material made from paper pulp, pressed and moulded into various shapes, and used during the second half of the 18th century for trays and boxes. It was lacquered and varnished, and embellished with painted ornament. In the mid-19th century, there was a popular fashion for papier mâché furniture, and chairs and small tables of all kinds, and even beds, were made, profusely

Papier mâché work table: mid-19th century. (From *The Art Journal*, 1862.)

ornamented with painted flowers and mother-of-pearl inlay, usually with a black or dark coloured ground. (*See* illustration.)

Parchment Panel, *see* **Linenfold Panel**

Parliament Clock or **Act of Parliament Clock,** *see* **Coaching Inn Clock**

Parlour

The parlour, or private room for conversation, is of mediaeval origin. By the 14th century, the parlour had become a living room as well as a retiring room, and its exclusiveness was condemned by Langland as a social evil because it caused the lord and lady to desert the hall, where they no longer sat and had their meals with the household. He wrote:

Now hath uche riche a reule to eten bi hym-selve
In a pryve parloure. for pore mennes sake,
Or in a chambre with a chimneye. and leve the chief halle. . . .

(Quoted by D. Chadwick in *Social Life in the Days of Piers Plowman*.)

Parlour chair. (From Plate 31 of *The Cabinet Dictionary*, by Thomas Sheraton, 1803.) *See* example on opposite page.

From the Middle Ages till the early 20th century the term parlour has meant a well-furnished, private living room; in the 18th century it was often a dining room as well. William Hickey in his *Memoirs* refers to 'the new dining parlour' in additions made to his father's house in 1770. (Reprint of tenth edition, 1948.) In *The Cabinet Dictionary* (1803) Sheraton has an entry for parlour, but says: 'See Dining Room', although he illustrates what he calls parlour chairs on Plate 31. During the mid-19th century the word acquired a slightly snobbish meaning, particularly in small houses that were cramped miniatures of large and grander houses. In Loudon's *Encyclopaedia* (1833) the standing of the parlour is indicated by the directions for its decoration. 'Parlours', said Mr Loudon, 'ought to be painted in a medium style between that of a drawing-room and that of a dining-room.'

Parlour Chair

Parlour chairs were known in the second half of the 18th century, and are illustrated and described on Plate IX of Ince and Mayhew's *Universal System of Household Furniture* (1760). Sheraton also shows parlour chairs on Plate 31 of *The Cabinet Dictionary* (1803). *See* illustration. It was not until the early Victorian

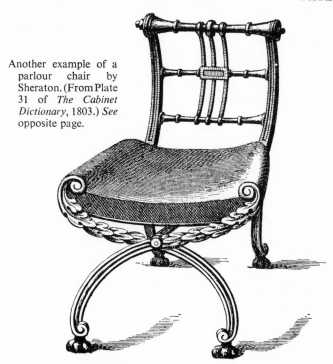

Another example of a parlour chair by Sheraton. (From Plate 31 of *The Cabinet Dictionary*, 1803.) *See* opposite page.

period that the term began to be used loosely to describe the cheaper varieties of what had formerly been called parlour, drawing room, or dining room chairs.

Parquetry or **Parqueterie**

A decorative use of various woods, which are pieced together to form patterns. In cabinet work, these patterns may be inlaid into a surface.

Partners' Desk

A large, flat-topped kneehole desk, at which two people may sit, facing each other. The term is probably of 19th century origin.

Patera

A small ornamental disc, with lightly carved decoration.

Four examples of paterae.

Patina

The surface colour and finish of wood, produced by age and wear and generations of polishing. The term is used also to describe the encrustation of the surface of antique bronze.

Partridge Wood (*Caesalpinia granadillo*)

A dark red-brown wood that is sometimes called brown ebony, though this name is misleading and should not be used. (B.S.I. recommend that it should be discontinued.) Supplied from Venezuela, and occasionally used for veneering and inlaid decoration.

Paw Foot

Carved representations of the paws of various animals were

Norman version of the paw foot on a stool of the 11th century. This drawing, representing William the Conqueror, was made by F. W. Fairholt from an original MS. by William, Abbot of Jumiéges, preserved at Rouen, and is included in *Costume in England* (1860).

Paw foot used on a stool of the 8th century B.C. Drawing of a bas-relief showing the Assyrian King Sennacherib on his throne, from *Discoveries in the Ruins of Nineveh and Babylon*, by Austen H. Layard (1853).

used as feet for the legs of stools and chairs in the civilisation of ancient Egypt, where the device probably originated. There are representations of paw feet on stools in Assyrian sculpture of the 8th century B.C., and such forms were common on Greek and Roman furniture. Paws and claws may have been used for the better type of furniture in pre-Norman England, but representations of them in contemporary manuscripts suggest classical designs, which the scribe may have seen and copied. (*See* illustrations under Table, on page 463.) The paw foot may have been known in England during the early mediaeval period, though its use was probably confined to such rare and exclusive articles as the stools of kings and prelates. Introduced as a fashionable form, probably from France, late in the 17th century, it remained in fashion until the middle of the 18th century. Paw feet came into fashion again at the end of the 18th and the beginning of the 19th centuries, and were used frequently by Sheraton. The two forms most favoured were the paws of lions and bears. (*See* illustrations opposite, *also* those on pages 233, 286, 306, 312, and 315.)

Peardrop Handle

A small pendant handle, in the form of an elongated pear, usually of brass, and hinged to the front of a drawer or door. It was introduced during the second half of the 17th century.

Pearwood (*Pyrus communis*)

This fruit wood, which is common to the British Isles and Europe, supplies a hard, close-grained, easily worked material, varying from pink to yellowish-white in colour. It is used chiefly for inlaying and for carved ornament.

Peasant Weave, *see* **Cottage Weave**

Pedestal

In architecture, the term means a moulded base that supports a column or a series of columns. (*See* **Plinth**.) Like many architectural terms it has been adopted by cabinet makers, who have used it to describe a solid support for such things as lamps, decorative objects like vases or sculptured figures, and those adjuncts to the side table based on designs by the brothers Adam, the free standing pedestals, which accommodated plates, and were surmounted by knife boxes in the form of urns. (*See* next page.) In the early 19th century the sideboard itself was supported by pedestals containing cupboards. (*See* **Sideboard**.)

Pedestal Desk or **Writing Table**

A kneehole desk or writing table, with the top supported by two pedestals containing cupboards or drawers. Small pedestal desks were introduced early in the 18th century (*see* illustration), and they were elaborated and enlarged by such cabinet makers as

Early 18th century pedestal desk. (From a drawing by E. J. Warne.)

Thomas Chippendale, so that two people could sit at them, facing each other, and they were then dignified by the name of library tables. (*See also* **Bureau Table, Kneehole Desk,** *and* **Library Table**.)

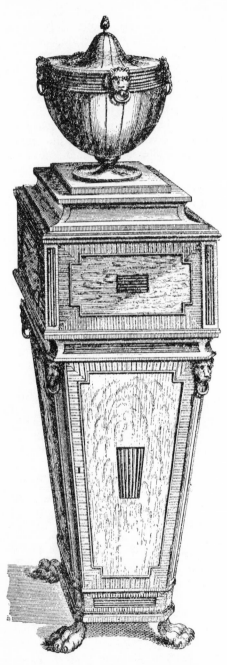

Pedestal and vase, designed by Thomas Sheraton. (From Plate 60 of *The Cabinet Dictionary*, 1803.) Compare the proportions with the pedestals and urns shown with the side table on page 426, which are based on designs by the brothers Adam.

Pedestal Table

A term sometimes used for round, oval, square, or rectangular tables that are supported by a single pillar or column which rests upon a stabilising base. (*See* illustration of Loo Table, page 322.)

PEDIMENT

Pediment

An architectural term for a triangular or segmental feature above the upper member of an entablature, and corresponding to some vertical feature below the entablature (such as a portico) or over a door or window opening. The pediment was occasionally used on bookcases in the late 17th century, and frequently by 18th century cabinet makers for such large, architectural pieces as library bookcases, and also as a termination for the upper part of cabinets and tallboys. (*See* illustration, *also* **Broken Pediment, Pierced Pediment,** *and* **Swan-neck Pediment.**)

Peg

A wooden spike; a crude form of dowel used in early joiners' work for fastening boards together.

Peg Leg

A plain turned tapering leg.

Pellets

Small plugs or studs of wood, used for concealing the heads of screws. This method of using plugs to make a level, unbroken surface is known as pelleting.

Pelmet

Originally known under the French name of *lambrequin*, the pelmet was introduced in the late 17th century as a stiff, three-sided case fixed across the head of a window to hide the top of the curtains and the curtain rod and rings. The word *lambrequin* also described the stiff, shaped cases, covered with fabric, that continued the pelmet down either side of a window, and framed the curtains. A pelmet may be made with straight or shaped edges, and of textile material, mounted on buckram, and trimmed with braids, fringes, or tassels; or of wood, metal, or plastic laminated sheets. (*See* illustrations on next page.)

Pembroke Table

A small, light table, with a drawer or drawers below the top, and two flaps which may be extended upon hinged brackets. Sometimes called a universal table. Sheraton, in *The Cabinet Dictionary* (1803), describes it as 'a kind of breakfast table, from the name of

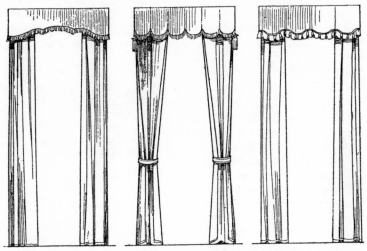

Three examples of pelmets. Such types were in use, variously elaborated, during the 18th century. (From a drawing by E. J. Warne.)

the lady who first gave orders for one of them', thus providing material for controversy, because some authorities believe that the Earl of Pembroke originated the design, which was certainly in use in the latter part of the 18th century. Henry, the tenth earl, a professional soldier, who wrote a book entitled *Method of Breaking Horses*, and died in 1794, seems unlikely to have been the creator of the design, though the ninth earl, who died in 1750, and was nicknamed 'the architect earl', is a more probable author for such an elegant idea. Duncan Phyfe in America evolved a distinctive type of Pembroke table, in which he introduced his favourite lyre device. (*See* illustrations, *also* **Flap and Elbow Table**.)

American type of Pembroke table, based on a design by Duncan Phyfe. *Circa* 1790–1800.

Pencil Cedar (*Juniperus virginiana*)

A fragrant softwood, also known as Virginian pencil cedar, that grows in the southern states of the U.S.A. It is brownish-red in colour, easy to work, but rather brittle, and used chiefly for interior cabinet work, such as drawers, pigeon holes, and divisions in desks.

Pendant

A term that applies generally to variously formed hanging ornaments.

Percale

A fine, plain-weave cotton furnishing cloth, that is usually printed and given a glazed finish.

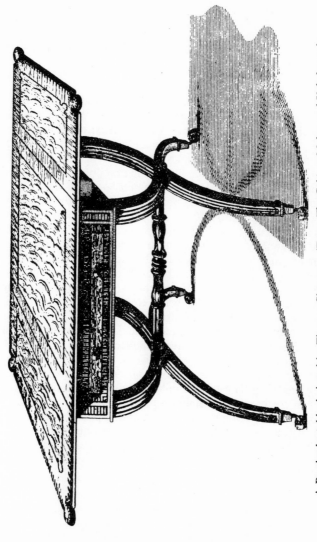

A Pembroke table designed by Thomas Sheraton. (From *The Cabinet Maker and Upholsterer's Drawing Book*, 3rd edition, 1802.)

Persian Carpet

Of all the carpets produced in the East, those of Persia have the highest reputation. One of their distinctive features is the arrangement of the warp on two levels, one set being behind the other. Their colouring is soft and rich, never emphatic, and the effect of softness arises from the use of graduated shades of the same colour, and the absence of massed colours: conventionalised floral forms predominate in the pattern.

Petit Point

A form of fine embroidery, worked upon fine-meshed canvas that is usually held in a frame during the work. What is known as tent stitch is nearly always used: it is the finest of all canvas embroidery stitches, and gives a closely and evenly filled surface that resists hard wear. Celia Fiennes, in one of her later journeys, 1701–3, describes in detail the furnishing of a house, and mentions 'an elbow chair tent-stitch', also 'Chaires, one red damaske the other crostitch and tent-stitch very rich'. (*The Journeys of Celia Fiennes*, Part IV, Section 10, p. 346.) The fineness of tent stitch makes it suitable for highly detailed pictorial designs. The stitch is worked diagonally over single vertical and horizontal threads of the canvas, and the stitch is always the same on both sides of the work, which gives a smooth and even effect. Fine woollen yarns are used, and also silk; sometimes both are combined in a single piece of embroidery, the silk being employed to point the high lights. The design is generally carried out in a mixture of colours against a background of a single colour. Dark grounds are usual in *petit point* that is intended for upholstery work. It is used for covering drop-in seats and chair backs, as well as for loose, separate cushions. In some old examples of *petit point*, Gobelin stitch is used. This is worked similarly to tent stitch, but over two threads of the canvas in height and one in width. It may also be used as a padded stitch by throwing a line of padding (generally a thread of yarn) across the canvas before working. Gobelin stitch is useful where fine shading forms part of the design, and is often used for this purpose where the rest of the design is executed in tent stitch.

Pew

A seat in a church, partly enclosed, to ensure privacy for members of the congregation. Its earliest form was a simple bench with a back, separated from the aisles of the church by end pieces which were usually embellished with carved decoration. (*See* illustration on opposite page, *also* **Bench End** and **Standard.**)

Pew Chair

A seat hinged to the end of a pew.

358

Pew End

Sometimes called a bench end, and sometimes a box end. The vertical end piece that separates a pew from the aisle of a church. During the 15th century, certain characteristic ornamental types were made, which have remained as basic designs. Of these, the poppy-headed pew end was the favourite, and variations of this are to be found in churches all over England. (*See* **Poppyhead.**) The finials on pew ends were sometimes surmounted by grotesque figures, and the surface of the ends

Pew at Headington, Oxfordshire.
(After J. H. Parker.)

was often carved with blind tracery, so that they resembled miniature church windows. (*See* illustration above, *also* **Bench End, Box End,** *and* **Standard.**)

Pewter

An alloy of tin and lead, tin forming about four-fifths of the composition. It was known as early as the 11th century, and the making and working of pewter became an important mediaeval craft in England, London having its own Worshipful Company of Pewterers. The earliest records of regulations for the pewterer's craft were made in 1348. It was used for plates, tankards, spoons, and occasionally for the tops of tables and bars in inns.

Philadelphia Chippendale

During the mid-18th century, cabinet makers and chair makers, working in Philadelphia (which was then the richest city in the American colony of Pennsylvania), developed a regional variation of the designs generally associated with the work of Thomas Chippendale. It was characterised by the lavish use of carved ornament on chairs and such articles as tallboys.

Phonograph

An instrument for recording and reproducing sound, words, or music: the name given to the first practicable 'talking machine' that was patented by Thomas A. Edison in January 1877. The records used for this early type were cylindrical. (*See also* **Gramophone.**)

Phyfe Furniture,

See Duncan Phyfe, American furniture maker, page 528.

Pianette

A small piano.

Pianino

A name originally used for an upright piano.

Piano Stool, *see* **Music Stool**

Pianoforte

A musical instrument with wires, enclosed in a horizontal or vertical case. The wires are struck by hammers which are moved by keys. The name is derived from the power this instrument gives the performer by playing soft (*piano*) or loud (*forte*). It was invented during the first decades of the 18th century, by Bartolommeo Cristofori, of Padua. The word pianoforte was shortened to piano after the instrument was introduced in England. (*See also* **Cottage Piano, Giraffe Piano, Grand Piano, Pianette,** *and* **Table Piano.**)

Pickled Finish

The pale, white-veined finish that follows the process of stripping from painted woodwork or furniture both the paint and the plaster filling that was used as a ground. (*See also* **Limed Oak.**)

Pie Crust Table

The name sometimes given to mahogany tripod tables when the top is bordered by a carved, scalloped, raised rim, which suggests the finish on the edge of a pie. Such tables were often used as tea tables in the middle years of the 18th century. (*See* illustration on page 144.)

Pier Glass

An upright looking-glass, designed originally for the pier walls

Pier glass frame from Plate CLXIX of Chippendale's *Director*, 3rd edition (1762).

dividing windows, introduced in the reign of William III, and remaining in fashion throughout the 18th century. Such glasses were nearly always used in conjunction with a pier table. (*See* illustrations.)

Pier Table

A side table, used for the piers between windows, usually with a pier glass above to form a decorative unit. Sheraton, in *The Cabinet Dictionary* (1803), describes them as being 'made to fit in between the architraves of the windows'.

Pierced Pediment

A pediment ornamented by unbacked fretwork.

Pierced Work

A general term, applied to ornamental woodwork, when part of the background is cut through and removed to produce an open-work pattern, and occasionally used to describe unbacked fretwork.

Pietra-Dura

A form of mosaic work, consisting of hard stones, agate, lapis lazuli, and fragments of precious marbles, inlaid into a surface and highly polished. Introduced in the 15th century, during the Italian Renaissance, it was sometimes known as Florentine mosaic work.

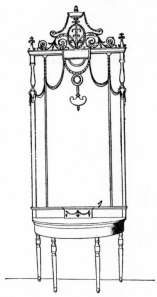

Pier glass and pier table, designed as a decorative unit. Such slender lines and delicate ornamentation were associated with the work of the brothers Adam.

Pigeon Holes

The small divisions and compartments in a bureau, escritoire, or scrutoire, for accommodating stationery and documents.

Pilaster

In architecture, a pilaster is a vertical feature, rectangular in section, projecting slightly from a surface, and reproducing the characteristic proportions of a base, column, and capital in one

A pier table, showing alternative finishes for front and sides: a hollow end on the left and an ogee end on the right. (From *The Prices of Cabinet Work*, 1797 edition.)

361

of the orders of architecture. Pilasters were used in cabinet work throughout the 18th century.

Pile Carpets

Carpets woven so that the threads are set vertically in innumerable short lengths and packed tightly together to form a nap. A highly skilled form of carpet weaving, which originated in the East and was known in Europe as early as the end of the 12th century, though pile carpets were seldom used in England, even in the 15th century, nor did they come into general use until the Georgian period.

Pile Fabrics

A term covering any fabric that has a plain ground, with an extra warp or weft that projects to give the surface a fibrous nap.

Pilgrim Furniture

A term that is sometimes used to describe the furniture made in New England in the mid-17th century: it was not a contemporary term, and is wide and vague enough to include most of the early furniture of simple design that was made by the Puritan settlers in North America.

Pillar

When a table rests upon a tripod, or circular or other form of stabilising base, the support is called a pillar. Bedpillar is an alternative term for bedpost. (*See* illustration of Claw Table, *also* **Column.**)

Pillar-and-Claw Table, *see* Claw Table

Pillow

A cushion covered with linen, and stuffed with feathers or some other soft, yielding material, used as a head rest. Although pillows were known and shown on Saxon beds in 9th century manuscripts (*see* **Bed** and illustration on p. 134), they were considered a luxury in mediaeval times. In the Prologue to the *Canterbury Tales*, Chaucer mentions a pilwe-beer, a pillow case, among the holy objects carried by the Pardoner. The reference occurs in lines 694-5:

> For in his male he hadde a pilwe-beer,
> Which that, he seyde, was our lady veyl . . .

In his *Description of England* (1577–87), William Harrison stated that in earlier generations 'Pillowes . . . were thought meete onlie for women in child-bed'. (*See* **Cod.**)

Pillow Back

The term used to describe the oval turned top-rail of a chair back. It applies particularly to single and elbow chairs made in the late 18th and early 19th centuries.

Pillow Beer

Sometimes spelt pillowe bere. A mediaeval term for a pillow case. (*See* Chaucer's use of the term quoted in entry for **Pillow**.) It was in current use in country districts in the late 17th century; and a reference to 'two paire of pillow beers' occurs in an inventory dated October 1st, 1681. (*Farm and Cottage Inventories of Mid-Essex*, 1635–1749. Essex Record Office Publications, No. 8, p. 165.)

Pin

An alternative name for a dowel.

Pinchbeck

An alloy of copper and zinc, which resembles gold in colour and ductility. It was invented in the first half of the 18th century, by a London clock and watch maker named Christopher Pinchbeck (1670–1732). (*See also* **Prince's Metal**.)

Pinched Head Pleat

A pleat that is creased into three folds of equal width. The pleat is stitched firmly in the centre, the stitches being drawn up to give the effect of a pinched-in waist, and a decorative button sometimes conceals this stitching.

Pincushion Chair or **Pincushion Seat**, *see* **Compass Seat**

Pine

This has become a general term for various softwoods supplied by coniferous trees in Britain, Europe, and North America. In the late 17th and early 18th centuries, cabinet makers frequently used Scots fir (*Pinus sylvestris*) for the carcasing of walnut furniture and for the panelling of rooms. The timber of this Scots fir was known as deal. In the American colonies, native varieties of pine were used for similar purposes. Of these, yellow pine (*Pinus strobus*) was known in England as Weymouth pine or New England pine. It was never called deal. After about 1760 it was used by cabinet makers for the carcasing of mahogany and satinwood furniture, as it was superior in quality to the deal hitherto employed. Only these two varieties of pine appear to have been used in England for furniture making.

Pitch Pine

A term applied generally to southern yellow pine (*Pinus palustris*) in North America, which supplies a close-grained, resinous wood that may be highly polished. It has a distinctive yellow colour, and during the 19th century it was used for pews and pulpits and other woodwork in churches, also for school furniture.

Plain Weave or **Tabby Weave**

This is the simplest form of interlacing, in which each warp thread interlaces alternately over and under each weft thread. The word tabby is derived from *Atabi*, the name of the street in

Baghdad where the makers of silken materials lived. (*See* Taylor's *Words and Places*. Nelson, abridged edition, 1925.)

Planted

A term used when a spurious antique, or fake, is put into surroundings that suggest an authentic atmosphere of age: generally a country house or cottage, to which some innocent tourist or amateur collector is introduced by the 'planter' or his collaborators.

Planted Moulding

A moulding cut independently, and applied to a surface.

Plaque

A flat piece of metal or porcelain, or decorative material such as lacquer, usually oval or rectangular in shape, applied as an embellishment to a surface. Plaques were used to ornament some of the furniture made to the design of the brothers Adam and their contemporaries, in the second half of the 18th century.

Plastics

A generic name for chemically produced resinous materials that may be moulded by heat or pressure or both. Plastics may be divided into three groups: thermoplastic materials that, when moulded, do not change chemically, and may be reheated and reformed; thermo-setting plastics that, when once they have been shaped by heat and pressure, are unchangeable and remain hard; and protein plastics, that are based on casein. This last group includes non-inflammable plastics that are easy to colour, polish, and fabricate. The contemporary plastics industry was founded in the mid-19th century by Alexander Parkes (1813–90), an English inventor who worked in Birmingham. In 1855 he took out the first patent bearing on 'celluloid', which is the oldest plastic and was commercially developed in the late 19th century. Parkes ultimately produced a plastic that he called 'Parkesine', and he described its properties in a paper before the Society of Arts, on December 20th, 1865. (*Journal of the Society of Arts*, Vol. XIV, No. 683, December 23rd, 1865.) Dr. Leo Hendrik Baekeland, who was born in Ghent in 1863, took out a patent in 1909 for the plastic known as 'Bakelite'. Dr. E. Frankland Armstrong, in a paper read to the *Royal Society of Arts* in January 1942, described plastics as forming 'a fifth class to the materials, metal, wood, glass and ceramics used in the past'.

Platband

A flat moulding, whose height exceeds its projection. Isaac Ware defines it as a square moulding which has less projecture than height or breadth. (*A Complete Body of Architecture*, 1767.) Also used for the fillets, *q.v.*, which separate the flutes of columns and pilasters.

Plate Basket

A mahogany case with a hinged hoop handle, for carrying plates, consisting of an octagonal base and seven vertical panels or facets, the eighth being omitted to enable the plates to be piled up and lifted out. (Gillow records, dated 1789. E. & S. Book, No. 516.)

Plate Cupboard

An early term for a court cupboard. A plate cupboard usually consisted of two or more open shelves on which silver, glass, and pewter vessels were displayed. The court cupboard evolved from the mediaeval plate cupboard that was used in the great hall of a mediaeval house. The superstructure of the cupboard, upon which the plate was placed, was called a desk. R. W. Symonds quotes an inventory dated 1558 (*Connoisseur*, Vol. CXII, December 1943, p. 94) as follows:

'In the hall. a skrene with a deske for plate.

'In the great parlour. a joyned cubberte, with a hall payse, and a deske for plate.'

Over a hundred years later, an entry in Pepys' *Diary* records that the habit of displaying plate on open cupboards still persisted. On May 15th, 1666, Pepys wrote: 'My new plate sets off my cupboard very nobly'. (*See* illustrations on pages 366 and 367 of 15th century plate cupboards.)

Plate Glass

Polished plate glass has both surfaces ground, smoothed, and polished, the object of the manufacturer being to render the two surfaces flat and parallel in order to secure clear and undistorted vision and reflection. The method of casting glass so that plates of large size could be made was perfected in 1691 by Louis Lucas de Nehou, who had been put in charge of the Royal Glassworks in France, by Colbert. (*See* McGrath and Frost, *Glass in Architecture and Decoration*.)

Plateau

A term occasionally used in the 19th century for the shelves or tiers of a whatnot or running sideboard. An omnium, *q.v.*, shown at the Great Exhibition of 1851, was described as 'containing three plateaus. . . .' (*Official Catalogue*, Vol. II, entry 78, page 735.)

Pleating

A method of drawing fullness in a material into a narrow compass, carried out by making and securing regular folds, either by sewing or by heat and pressure. Both sewing and pressing are used to pleat furnishing fabrics so that a sharp, straight edge may be obtained, the stitching being invisible. Various methods of pleating are used to give decorative forms to the edges of bed and window curtains and valances, and to frills on the edges of loose covers.

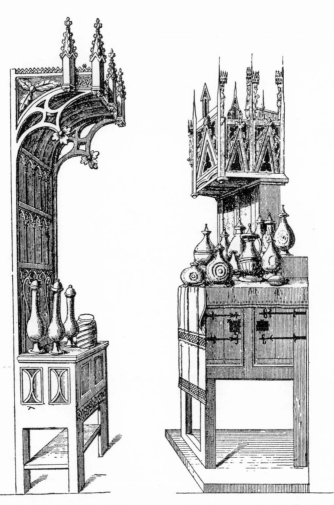

Plate cupboards of the late 15th century, each having an aumbry for food and drink fitted in the frame under the top, with an open space below the aumbry. The example on the left has a pot board below the aumbry. Both are reproduced from drawings in Shaw's *Specimens of Ancient Furniture*, and are copied from illuminated MSS. of the period.

Plate cupboard of the late 15th century, with an aumbry below the desk for the display of plate, and a pot board below the aumbry. This example, and those on the opposite page, are drawn from French MSS. and included in Shaw's *Specimens of Ancient Furniture*.

Plinth

An architectural term for the square member that forms the lowest part of the base of a column. In cabinet making, the term is also used to describe the moulded, projecting base of a piece of furniture. Sheraton says that 'It is also applied to mouldings mitered round the bottoms of table legs and bed pillars'. (*The Cabinet Dictionary*, 1803, p. 289.)

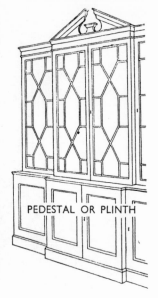

PEDESTAL OR PLINTH

Plum Mottle

A form of figuring sometimes found in mahogany veneers, when a small, dark mark, shaped like a plum, is repeated frequently.

Plumes

Interlacing feathers, generally used in a chair back, either three or five. (*See also* **Prince of Wales's Feathers**.) Plumes of real feathers were sometimes used as decorative features above the four corners of the canopies of state beds in the 16th, 17th, and early 18th centuries. (*See* **State Bed**.)

Plush

A pile fabric, usually made with a mohair pile warp on a cotton ground.

Plywood

A material composed of two or more wood veneers, cemented face to face with the grain of alternating veneers running in different directions.

Point d'Hongrie

Sometimes called Florentine stitch. A form of embroidery worked upon a fine canvas ground and often used for chair seats and backs, loose cushions and bedspreads. The designs, which are formal and flame-like in character, are nearly always carried out in 3- or 4-ply silk that may be worked horizontally or perpendicularly, usually over four threads of the canvas, the stitches of one row fitting between those of the next row. The design is always worked in a series of shaded lines of the same colour, followed by another block of similar shaded lines in a contrasting colour, and gold, silver, or black threads are sometimes worked between the blocks of colour in a kind of framework which follows the form of the pattern. By omitting a single mesh of the canvas at regular intervals, an openwork effect is obtained.

Poker Work

A method of burning ornamental patterns into a wood surface by means of a hot poker, or other metal instrument, and scrubbing out the charred grooves with sand.

Pole Lathe

A primitive device for producing turned work, used by the bodgers, *q.v.*, who turn chair legs in the woods of Buckinghamshire, and by other rural craftsmen. It is operated by a treadle, labour being reduced and power increased by a pliant wooden pole or sapling, fixed in the ground, which is kept in tension by a cord connecting its tip with the lathe shaft. (*See* **White Wycombe.**)

Pole Screen, *see* Fire Screen

Polishing

The name given to the treatment used for making a wooden surface smooth and glossy, to emphasise the figure and enrich the tone. Until the 17th century, wood surfaces were probably polished with beeswax and turpentine, but in the later part of that century, and throughout the 18th, spirit varnish was used. Recipes for three spirit varnishes, 'seed-lacc', 'shell-lacc' and white varnish, are given in Stalker's *Treatise of Japanning and Varnishing* (1688): surfaces which had been spirit varnished were subsequently polished, except some cheaper grades, to which 'shell-lacc' had been applied, and in some cases where only the front of a piece of furniture was polished, the sides were left varnished. (See *English Furniture from Charles II to George II,* by R. W. Symonds, The Connoisseur Ltd., 1929, pp. 122-4. *See also* **French Polish, Varnish,** *and* **Vernis Martin.**) There is a reference to the polished surface of English furniture in the *Mélanges sur l'Angleterre* of François de la Rochefoucauld. In the course of describing English houses of the time (1784), he says: 'The chairs and tables are also made of mahogany of fine quality and have a brilliant polish like that of finely tempered steel'. (Translated by S. C. Roberts and published under the title of *A Frenchman in England, 1784*: Cambridge University Press, 1933.)

Pollard Oak

A dark brown wood with a wavy grain, which is supplied from oak trees that have been 'polled' and their growth arrested.

Pommel, *see* Finial

Pompadour, *see* Ladies' Easy Chair

Pontypool Japanning

A handicraft devoted to decorating with paint and varnish such articles as tea-trays, candlesticks, urns, boxes, and numerous other utensils, which flourished at Pontypool in Monmouthshire during the 18th century. The characteristic groundwork of this Pontypool japanned ware was scarlet, green, yellow, blue, black, or white. The surface was heavily varnished to protect the paint, and the decoration consisted chiefly of floral swags, flowers, and landscapes, and was carried out on tin. The handicraft was originally established in the reign of Charles II, by Thomas Allwood, a native of Northampton, who invented the process and settled in Pontypool.

Poplar

The two chief varieties, black (*Populus nigra*) and white (*Populus alba*), are both trees native to Britain, supplying a softwood of a creamy white colour that is seldom used in cabinet making, though occasionally for decorative inlays, when it is stained.

Poppyhead

A characteristic form of decoration for the finials of 15th century pew ends. (*See* illustration, *also* **Pew End**.)

Porter's Chair

A high-backed, partly enclosed chair, with a semi-circular hood, completely upholstered in leather. Usually placed in the halls of houses, so that a porter may sit protected from draughts. Such chairs were introduced during the 16th century.

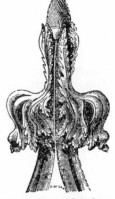

Poppyhead finial, from Kidlington Church, Oxfordshire, *circa* 1450. (After J. H. Parker.)

Portfolio Stand

A stand for the storing and examination of prints, usually made of mahogany or rosewood and popular as an article of drawing room and library furniture in the early 19th century. Such a stand is described and illustrated in Loudon's *Encyclopaedia* (1833). It was designed for portfolios or large prints, and could be locked. 'The two fronts fall down to any degree at pleasure', said Mr Loudon, 'till they become level' (*see* illustrations opposite), 'and thus admit to easily examining the prints or drawings.'

Post

A term for an independent upright member, such as a bedpost.

Posted or Post Bed

A term for a bed with bedposts that support a tester.

Pot Board

A term sometimes used for the lowest shelf of a dresser, that is just above floor level.

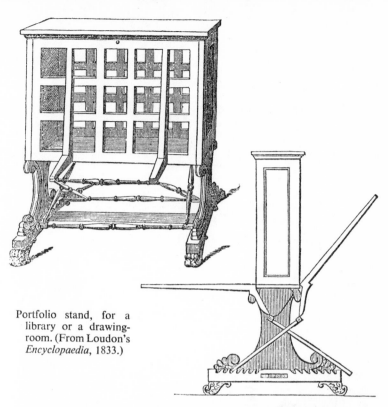

Portfolio stand, for a
library or a drawing-
room. (From Loudon's
Encyclopaedia, 1833.)

A portfolio stand, less elaborate than that shown by Loudon (*see* above),
appears in the background of this du Maurier drawing, and a far more
elaborate appliance occupies the foreground. Published on January 17th,
1880, and reproduced by permission of the proprietors of *Punch*.

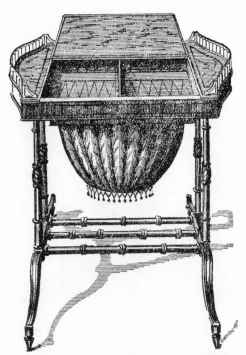

Above and to the *left:* Pouch tables from Plate 65 of *The Cabinet Dictionary*, by Thomas Sheraton (1803). *Below:* A lady's work table from Loudon's *Encyclopaedia* (1833).

Pot Cupboard

A small cupboard for a chamber pot, standing on tapered legs, occasionally with drawers above the cupboard, and sometimes finished with a tray top. Pot cupboards were also made to fit into a corner, and were then described as circular-front corner pot cupboards. The term was used in the 18th century. (*See also* **Bedside Cupboard.**)

Pouch Table

A small work table, with a fabric bag below the top, and a light under-frame, introduced towards the end of the 18th century. Sheraton describes and illustrates pouch tables with the bags, designed to accommodate needlework, suspended from a frame. (*See* illustrations on opposite page.) Pouch tables were popular during the first half of the 19th century.

Pouffe

A large, stuffed footstool, high enough to be used as a seat.

Powder Post Beetle

The two species, *Lyctus brunneus*, and *Lyctus linearis*, are found all over the world. The eggs, laid in May or June, are deposited in the cracks, crevices, and spores of hardwoods. The larvae hatch out within a few weeks, and remain in the wood for about a year, when they emerge as fully-grown beetles, and begin laying eggs at once. The larvae cause serious damage by burrowing inside the wood during pupation, and by the holes made when they come to the surface; they throw up a fine powder, which fills these burrows and holes.

Powder Table, *see* Wig Stand

Powdering Stand, *see* Wig Stand

Press

A term that has been applied to almost every type of cupboard, including wardrobes. It has not been used in this wide sense since about the middle of the 19th century.

Press Bedstead

A bedstead that could be folded up, and concealed in a receptacle that outwardly resembled a small press or a chest of drawers. Oliver Goldsmith, in *The Deserted Village* (1769), may have been describing one of these press bedsteads when he wrote those much-quoted lines:

> The whitewashed wall, the nicely sanded floor,
> The varnished clock that clicked behind the door,
> The chest contrived a double debt to pay,
> A bed at night, a chest of drawers by day.

They were used in the kitchens and parlours of cottages in the 18th and early 19th centuries, to supplement the limited bedroom accommodation. (*See* illustrations overleaf, *also* **Table Bedstead.**)

373

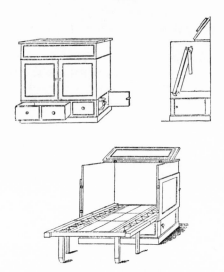

Press bedstead, shown closed and open, with a diagram illustrating how the folded parts are accommodated within the receptacle. (From Loudon's *Encyclopaedia*, 1833.) Press bedsteads for servants' bedrooms are shown in Heal's catalogues in the eighteen-fifties.

Press Cupboard

A large cupboard with a superstructure consisting of a shelf with smaller cupboards behind it. (*See* illustration.) This type of cupboard, often assumed to be a court cupboard, was introduced during the second half of the 16th century, and was made throughout the succeeding century.

Press cupboard, early 17th century.

Prie-dieu

A small praying desk, usually with a shelf close to the floor on which to kneel, and a desk at a convenient height for devotional books. Such praying desks were in use after the 14th century, but the basic form is probably earlier.

Prie-dieu Chair

A name used in the late 19th century for a type of upholstered chair without arms and with a very high, straight back.

Pricket

The thick spike on an altar candlestick which holds the large candles that are used.

Prince of Wales's Feathers

The three ostrich plumes that form the crest or badge of the Prince of Wales were used in chair

Prie-dieu chair.

374

backs in the second half of the 18th century, this device being characteristic of the work of Hepplewhite. The three plumes were also used on a smaller scale in the pierced central baluster splat of late 18th and early 19th century Windsor chairs, *q.v.*

Prince's Metal

An alloy of copper and zinc, a modified form of brass, which closely resembles the colour of gold. It was a forerunner of pinchbeck, *q.v.*, and was named after its inventor, Prince Rupert (1619–1682). During the late 17th and early 18th centuries this alloy was sometimes used for candlesticks.

Print Cabinet

A cabinet for storing prints, with sliding shelves to allow the contents to be examined easily. They were in use during and after the early 18th century.

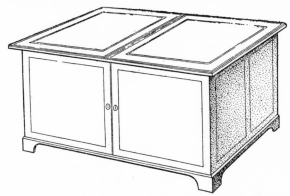

Walnut print cabinet, English, *circa* 1735, in the Fitzwilliam Museum, Cambridge.

Profile

The outline or contour of a moulding.

Projection

This term describes the overhang of the cornice or moulding at the top of a piece of furniture.

Pull Down Front

That part of a desk or a bureau which slides down or may be pulled down into place, to cover the interior. (*See* **Cylinder, Drop Front, Fall,** *and* **Roll Top Desk.**)

Pulpit

An elevated, enclosed platform, fitted with a desk, and sometimes covered by a canopy or sounding board. (*See* illustration on next page.)

Pulvinated

Used to describe the rounding or swelling of the frieze in the

375

Ionic order, *q.v.* This form of convex frieze was used occasionally in late 17th and early 18th century cabinet work.

Purdonian or Purdonium

A name introduced in the mid-19th century for a wooden coal box or scuttle, with a detachable metal lining, and a metal socket or slot at the back to take a small shovel with a wooden handle. It may have been suggested by the name of its inventor. (*See* **Coal Scuttle.**)

Purfled

A term for ornamental work in wood, that represents drapery, embroidery, or lace.

Puritan Furniture

A term used to describe the austere furniture made during, and in the years immediately preceding, the Commonwealth in England, and in the American colony of New England. Puritan furniture was characterised by plainness; leather was used on chairs, all frills and

Pulpit at Fotheringay, Northants. Mid-15th century. (After J. H. Parker.)

ornamental elaborations were omitted, though turners used decorative forms for the legs of chairs and tables, and the leather-work on chair seats and backs was garnished with brass-headed nails.

Puritan Period

A name occasionally used for the period of Puritan ascendancy and government during the fifth and sixth decades of the 17th century: it began before the Commonwealth and ended at the Restoration of 1660.

Purpleheart (*Peltogyne*)

Sometimes known in the United States as amaranth. Supplied from central and tropical South America and the West Indies, this wood assumes a purple colour shortly after it has been cut. It is hard and heavy, with an even texture. It is used for inlaying and turnery.

* Q *

Quadrant Drawer

A drawer that, as its name implies, is the fourth part of a circle in plan, and is pivoted below the top of a writing table or desk, so that it swings outwards when opened. Quadrant drawers were used by 18th century cabinet makers to accommodate ink and sand. (*See* illustration of Writing Table from Chippendale's *Director*, on page 512.)

Quadrant Stay

A curved metal band for supporting the fronts and falls of desks, and adjustable chair backs. (*See* page 249, *also* **Sleeping Chair.**)

Quaint Style

A fashion in furniture design, corresponding with the New Art movement at the end of the 19th and the opening of the present century, was known as the quaint style. It was characterised by naturalistic ornament; crude, elongated, and rather rigid shapes; and an excessive use of heart-shaped apertures in chair backs, doors, and framing. Much of this furniture was made in fumed oak, *q.v.*

Quaker Chair, *see* **Round Back Chair**

Quarry

A term used in glazing for a pane of glass, usually one that is cut in the shape of a lozenge or diamond, and lead glazed. Quarrell was the old English word for a pane of glass. Lead glazing was sometimes used for the doors of bookcases in furniture in the quaint and pseudo-Jacobean styles.

Quarter Round, *see* **Ovolo**

Quartered Oak

Oak from a log that has been cut into four quarters and the boards then cut from each quarter parallel with the medullary rays.

Quartering

The decorative effect obtained when veneers of similar grain are cut and laid so that the markings of four adjacent veneers are symmetrically disposed.

Quartetto Table

The name used by Sheraton for a nest of four small tables. Under this entry in *The Cabinet Dictionary* (1803) it is described as 'A kind of small work table made to draw out of each other, and may be used separately. . . .' (*See* illustration on next page, *also* **Nest of Tables.**)

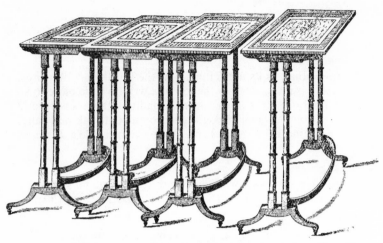

Quartetto table. Reproduced on a slightly reduced scale from Plate 75 of *The Cabinet Dictionary* (1803).

Quarto Table, *see* **Nest of Tables**

Quatrefoil

A form of Gothic tracery, used in woodwork as well as in architecture, consisting of four arcs enclosed within a circle and separated by cusps.

Quebec Birch, *see* **Canadian Birch**

Queen Anne Style

The name generally applied to the furniture designed and made in the opening decade of the 18th century. This furniture was characterised by the graciousness of its curves, the frequent use of the cabriole leg, and the increased use of walnut and decorative veneering.

Queensland Maple (*Flindersia brayleyana*)

Known also as maple silkwood, this is a decorative wood, varying from pink to rose-red in colour, with a bird's-eye figure. It takes an excellent polish, and is used for cabinet work and panelling.

Queensland Walnut (*Endiandra palmerstonii*)

A reddish-brown wood, streaked with black, used for cabinet work and veneering. It is sometimes incorrectly called Australian walnut.

Quilt

A thick coverlet for a bed, consisting of two pieces of cloth with a mass of soft material, wool or feathers, between them. Originally the quilt was a form of mattress. Quilts were in common use in the

17th century, and there is a reference to 'a painted callicoe quilt' in an inventory, dated May 26th, 1691. (*Farm and Cottage Inventories of Mid-Essex*, 1635–1749. Essex Record Office Publications, No. 8, p. 207.) The verb, to quilt, describes the process of stitching cloths together with something soft between them. (*See* also next entry.)

Quilting

A decorative method of holding a wadded interlining in place. The wadding is laid on the reverse side of the material, and secured by tacking threads, which are removed when the quilting is finished. When in position, the wadding and the material to which it is attached are stitched through and through by a series of very small, evenly spaced, running stitches, that are arranged to form a pattern, between which the wadding raises the material in a series of puffs. When the design is completed, the wadding is concealed by a lining material. Designs for quilting vary from the simplest type of diamond or chequer device to highly intricate floral or geometric patterns.

Bead and quirk.

Quirk

The groove sunk by the side of a bead.

Quirked Bead

A half round bead with a narrow, deep groove sunk between it and the adjoining flat surface. Sometimes called bead and quirk.

Quisshin, *see* **Cushion**

Rabbet or **Rabbit,** *see* **Rebate**

Rack

Sheraton defines this as a term used by cabinet makers for 'a brass plate with a number of square holes, into which a thumb spring catches, to support at any height, a glass made to rise in gentlemen's shaving tables'. He adds that it 'is likewise used to denote a slip of wood cut into notches for the purpose of supporting moveable book shelves'. (*The Cabinet Dictionary*, 1803, p. 294.)

Radio Set or **Wireless Set**

Like the gramophone, the wireless receiving set began as a piece of undisguised mechanism in the early 'twenties of the present century; but with the introduction of the amplifier, which replaced earphones, the radio set was accommodated in a cabinet, either of wood or plastic, or combinations of both materials.

Radiogram

A name used to describe a combined radio set and gramophone, both appliances using a common amplifier and being housed in the same cabinet.

Rag Rug, *see* **Hooked Rug**

Rail

The horizontal members in the frame of a door or the carcase of a receptacle, such as a chest, or a series of panels. The horizontal members of a table or chair frame are also known as rails.

Rain Mottle

A form of figuring in mahogany, resembling fiddle-back, but with elongated mottlings.

Ramie

Sometimes spelt ramee. China-grass that furnishes a strong fibre, comparable with silk for brilliancy. It is used as a component for some upholstery materials, such as moquette.

Ram's Head

A form of carved ornament of classical origin, revived during the latter part of the 18th century, and used extensively by the brothers Adam in furniture designed by them and their contemporaries.

Range Tables

A name occasionally used in the late 18th and early 19th centuries for sets of small tables, identical in size, that could be assembled to form one large table.

Reading Chair

A chair and desk combined, with broad arm rests and a reading desk fitted to the back, so that the reader could sit facing the back and resting his elbows upon the arms.
Reading chairs were made early in the 18th century, and have erroneously been called cock-fighting chairs, which is not a contemporary term. Sheraton illustrates an elaborate design for a reading chair, in *The Cabinet Maker and Upholsterer's Drawing Book* (3rd edition, 1802), with an adjustable book rest lit by a pair of candles. (*See* illustrations.)

Early 18th century
reading chair.

Reading Desk or Reading Stand

Stands with sloping tops on which books or sheets of music could rest were known in the 17th and were in use throughout the 18th century. Some were designed to rest upon a table. Generally, they were free standing, with a tripod and an

Reading chair. (From *The Cabinet Maker and Upholsterer's Drawing Book*, by Thomas Sheraton, 3rd edition, 1802.)

381

adjustable stem, which allowed the desk to be fixed at a height convenient for the reader. Ince and Mayhew illustrated a range of designs for 'Reading and Music Desks' on Plate XXVI of their *Universal System of Household Furniture* (1760). (*See* page opposite.) During the 19th century, reading desks acquired a multiplicity of forms, in metal as well as wood, and, because they often followed the prevailing taste for Gothic, occasionally resembled lecterns. A description of the furnishing of a wealthy undergraduate's rooms at Oxford, in *The Adventures of Mr Verdant Green*, by Edward Bradley (whose pen name was Cuthbert Bede), published 1853–56, indicates the variety of designs.

Music or reading stand with an adjustable desk rising from a pillar: a type that could be folded down flat and used as a small table. (From Loudon's *Encyclopaedia*, 1833.)

Late 18th century music or reading stand. (From *The Prices of Cabinet Work*, 1797 edition.)

'There were reading-stands of all sorts; Briarean-armed brazen ones, that fastened on to the chair you sat in,—sloping ones to rest on the table before you, elaborately carved in open work, and an upright one of severe Gothic, like a lectern, where you were to stand and read without contracting your chest.' (Part II, chapter vii, p. 154.)

Reading Seat

An early Victorian form of day bed, with a high end. It is described in the supplement to the 1846 edition of Loudon's *Encyclopaedia* as 'by no means elegant in form; but we can assert, from experience, that it is exceedingly comfortable to sit on; not only the back, but the head being supported by the peculiar form of the upper part of the end, or support for the back'. (*See* page 384.) Thirty-three years later this inelegant seat had become an accepted item of furniture, the back being slightly modified in form, to leave the head unsupported, so that those who used it could pass, almost imperceptibly, from the act of reading into a light doze. (*See* lower illustration on page 384, from *Punch*, January 18th, 1879.) In Heal's catalogue of the period, it is described as an Albany couch.

Rebate

Also spelt rabbet, and often pronounced and sometimes spelt

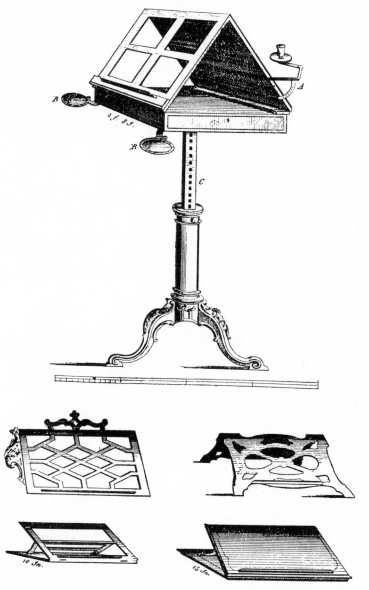

Alternative designs for reading and music desks. (From Plate XXVI of *The Universal System of Household Furniture*, by Ince and Mayhew, London, 1760.)

A reading seat for a drawing-room. (From the supplement of the 1846 edition of Loudon's *Encyclopaedia of Cottage, Farm and Villa Architecture*.)

A FASHIONABLE COMPLAINT.

Mamma. "PAPA DEAR, THE CHILDREN HAVE BEEN ASKED TO THE WILLOUGHBY ROBINSONS' ON THE ELEVENTH, THE HOWARD JONES'S ON THE FIFTEENTH, AND THE TALBOT BROWNES' ON THE TWENTY-FIRST. THEY'LL BE DREADFULLY DISAPPOINTED IF YOU DON'T LET THEM GO! MAY I WRITE AND ACCEPT, DEAR PAPA!"

Dear Papa (savagely). "OH, JUST AS YOU PLEASE! BUT, AS JUVENILE PARTIES SHOULD ALWAYS BE TAKEN IN TIME, YOU HAD BETTER WRITE TO DR. SQUILLS TOO, AND TELL HIM TO CALL ON THE TWELFTH, SIXTEENTH, AND TWENTY-SECOND."

A reading seat in use in a drawing-room, as recorded by *Punch*, thirty-three years after the prototype design had appeared in the supplement of Loudon's *Encyclopaedia*. (January 18th, 1879.) Reproduced by permission of the proprietors of *Punch*.

rabbit. A continuous rectangular channel or sinking, cut along the edge of a piece of wood or framework.

Recess

A depression in a surface, usually employed in cabinet making as a decorative feature. The term applies generally to any part that is set back from a main surface, whether it occurs on the front of a chest, cabinet, or cupboard, or in the wall of a room.

Recess Cabinet

This was not a contemporary term, and is used occasionally to describe tall, shallow, china cabinets, that may have been designed originally to fit into some recess in a room.

Recessed Front

A term occasionally used for a block front, when the central vertical panel is recessed. (*See* **Block Front,** *also* **Tub Front.**)

Recessed Stretcher

A stretcher that connects the side stretchers of a chair and is set back, or recessed, from the front legs. The term applies also to a similar arrangement for the underframing of tables.

Reed Top, *see* **Roll Top Desk**

Reeding

The decoration of a surface by a series of parallel convex mouldings of equal width: a form of inverted fluting. (*See* page 430.)

Refectory Table

This was not a contemporary term; but, with the growth of collectors' and antique dealers' jargon, it is often used to describe the long, oak tables with four, six, or eight turned legs, connected by square-sectioned stretchers, which were made during the late 16th and throughout the 17th centuries. As monastic establishments had been suppressed between 1536 and 1539, the inappropriateness of this description for large and often extravagantly carved Elizabethan and Jacobean tables is obvious. In contemporary inventories they were usually called long tables. (*See* 'The Renaming of Old English Furniture', by R. W. Symonds, *Antique Collector*, Vol. 19, No. 4, August 1948, p. 127.)

Reflecting Dressing Table, *see* **Rudd's Table**

Regency Style

This description applies to the furniture that was fashionable when George, Prince of Wales, was Regent, from 1811 to 1820. The Regency style was derived from the Greek revival, and was influenced particularly by the work of such architects as Thomas Hope, whose published designs aroused considerable interest in classical and Egyptian ornamentation. On Regency furniture, classical and Egyptian *motifs* were used with discretion, and never with the lavishness that occasionally made French Empire furniture rather overwhelming. Mahogany and sometimes rosewood were used; much of the furniture was japanned black, and decorated with gilded lines and ornamental devices; brass mounts and inlaid lines of brass and ebony were also used. The eccentrically ornate furniture that was made for the Prince Regent's Pavilion at Brighton was uncharacteristic of the Regency style and was seldom imitated. (*See* **Greek Revival.**)

Reglet or Regula

In architecture, this is a flat, narrow band below the triglyphs on the entablature of the Doric order. According to John Britton, it also means 'a flat, narrow moulding, employed to separate panels, or other members; or to form knots, frets, and similar ornaments'. (*A Dictionary of the Architecture and Archaeology of the Middle Ages*, 1838.)

Renaissance

Sometimes spelt Renascence. The term is used generally to describe the revival of interest in the learning, art, and architecture of the Graeco-Roman civilisation, that occurred during the 15th century in Italy and spread gradually to other European countries, reaching England early in the 16th century. The fall of Constantinople in 1453, that ended all secular continuity with the Roman Empire, was one of the principal causes of the Renaissance. Its effect upon architectural design was marked and far-reaching: the ten books of the Roman architect, Marcus Vitruvius Pollio, were reissued, and editions were printed in 1486 (at Rome), in 1496 and 1497; while nine editions were published in the 16th century. In England, the revived classical orders of architecture and their accompanying ornamental forms were regarded purely as a fashion, when they were first introduced early in the 16th century, and for over a hundred years after, much to the detriment of native domestic architecture and furniture design. They began to be used with real understanding by Inigo Jones during the first half of the 17th century. Thereafter the classic orders were recognised as a system of design, and not as a pattern book for ornamental forms. The English Renaissance thus falls into three periods: the Early Period, from about 1520 to 1620, when architects and furniture makers applied the classic orders ornamentally to houses and furniture, followed by a Transitional Period that began in the third decade of the 17th century, when architects and furniture makers gradually mastered the system of design represented by the classic orders and used their proportions correctly. The third, Late English Renaissance Period, passed through a Baroque phase in the late 17th and early 18th centuries, and received a fresh injection of inspiration by the classical revival that followed the excavation of the buried Roman cities of Pompeii and Herculaneum in the middle years of the 18th century. (*See* **Adam Style** *and* **Greek Revival**.) It survived until the third quarter of the 19th century, and has been resurrected spasmodically in the present century.

Rent Table

A type of office table made during the second half of the 18th century, with a round or octagonal top, with drawers immediately below. Sometimes the drawers would be labelled with the days of the week, and may have formed a rudimentary filing system for a rent collector: though this is only a supposition. The term does not appear to be contemporary. (*See* **Drum Table**.)

Rep or Repp

A silk, wool, or cotton cloth, woven in fine ribs: the wool and cotton varieties are used for upholstering furniture.

Repository, *see* Gentleman's Repository

Reproduction

A term for an honest copy of an antique design.

Restoration Chair

A name loosely applied to any Carolean chairs having high, cane-panelled backs and cane seats. Chairs of this type were introduced after the restoration of Charles II.

Restoration Period

A term sometimes used for the style of furniture made in the reigns of Charles II and James II (1660–88). (*See* **Carolean** *and* **Stuart**.)

Restore

The process of repairing a piece of antique furniture and supplying any parts that are missing or are worn or damaged beyond repair.

Restored

A term used to describe a piece of antique furniture that, by skilful repairs and renovation, has been brought back to its original form and appearance. An unscrupulous dealer may use it only when he feels that it is advisable to admit that repairs have been made; and its elasticity would allow such a dealer to describe as 'restored' a chair or a table of which one leg only was genuinely old. (*See also* **Faking**.)

Return

When a surface or a moulding is broken by a turn at right angles—as, for example, with the broken front of a bookcase—the sides of the break are called returns.

Reverse ogee.

Reverse Ogee

The common name for the moulding known in architecture as cyma reversa. In section it has a double curve, convex above,

387

concave below. (*See* illustration on previous page, *also* **Ogee**.) Sometimes called a talon moulding.

Revolving Bookcase

A small bookcase, circular or square in plan, with open shelves. It is pivoted on a central pillar, which rests upon a supporting base or on claws. The circular type, introduced in the late 18th century, resembles a circular dumb waiter. (*See* illustration.) A revolving bookcase with horizontal shelves was shown at the Great Exhibition of 1851, with the shelves loosely hung on pins to the circular ends, so that they remained level—in theory at least—when the ends revolved. The design may have been inspired by the treadmill: it never became popular. (*See* illustration on p. 389.) The revolving bookcase of table height has come into general use during the present century, its popularity increasing as the size of houses has progressively diminished.

Revolving bookcase, *circa* 1790.

Revolving Chair

Chairs with rotating seats were made in the 16th century, and were probably known and used in late mediaeval times; but they were rarities, and remained so until the middle years of the 19th century. A comb back Windsor chair with a circular seat that revolved upon a circular base was made for Thomas Jefferson in 1770. (Giedion gives this date in *Mechanization Takes Command*, p. 289, where he illustrates the chair.) The revolving music stool was in use in the early 19th century; but neither the revolving chair, nor the swivel, adjustable chair, developed or became popular until the middle years of that century. The revolving, adjustable chair was first popularised in the United States, and during the eighteen-fifties a type came into use that, with little modification of its basic design, has survived for a hundred years. It was patented in America in 1853, and Giedion names its inventor as Peter Ten Eyck (*Mechanization Takes Command*, p. 403, Fig. 237), who called it a sitting chair, and apparently regarded it as an improved form of rocking chair. It resembled a simplified form of smoker's bow, *q.v.*, with plain turned spindles connecting the back and arms with the seat. Below this seat were slightly curved steel rockers, which allowed the chair to be tilted backwards or forwards, and they were connected by a flat metal member; the seat revolved on a pivot, and was supported by four splayed legs, which were joined above, thus allowing a sufficient thickness of wood below the centre of the seat for the pivot to be

Revolving bookcase shown at the Great Exhibition of 1851. (From Tallis's *History and Description of the Crystal Palace*, Vol. II.)

socketed. A much simpler device for spring revolving chairs, as they were sometimes called, was used in the metal designs shown by the American Chair Company, of New York, at the Great Exhibition of 1851, two years before Peter Ten Eyck took out his patent. The illustrations and description on the pages following are reproduced from the *Art Journal Illustrated Catalogue* of the Exhibition. The early rocking and rotating chairs were not designed for the office. Although they were used by invalids, 'luxurious easiness' was, as the *Art Journal* records, the primary aim; but by the end of the 19th century they had become almost obligatory for the business executive, and were seldom used except in office furnishing.

Rib Pattern

An ornamental device, carved on panels in the late 15th and early 16th centuries, consisting of two curved ribs, generally set back to back, though occasionally interlaced, and enclosing various forms of ornament, such as vine tendrils and grapes.

Ribband Back Chair

Sometimes known as an interlaced chair back. Designs for ribband back chairs were published in the first edition of Chippendale's

America has long been noted for the luxurious easiness of its chairs, which combine in themselves all the means of gratification a Sybarite could wish. The AMERICAN CHAIR COMPANY, of New York, exhibit some novelties, which even

increase the luxury and convenience of this necessary article of furniture; instead of the ordinary legs conjoined to each angle of the seat, they combine to support a stem, as in ordinary

Text and illustrations to the right and on the page opposite are reproduced from the *Art Journal Illustrated Catalogue of the Great Exhibition of 1851*, p. 152. (*See* entry on **Revolving Chair**, page 388.)

music-stools, between which and the seat the SPRING is inserted; this we exhibit in our first cut. It will allow of the greatest weight and freest motion on all sides; the seat is also made

Text and illustrations to the left and on the page opposite are reproduced from the *Art Journal Illustrated Catalogue of the Great Exhibition of 1851*, p. 152.

to revolve on its axis. The design and fittings of these chairs are equally good and elegant, and certainly we have never tested a more easy and commodious article of household furniture.

Director (1754), the backs consisting of interlaced ribbons. (*See* illustration on opposite page.) Ribbon is spelt ribband by Chippendale, and was the contemporary form of the word.

Ribbon and Rosette, *see* **Rose and Ribbon Moulding**

Ribbon-and-Stick

An ornamental *motif*, consisting of a ribbon wound upon a rod, originating in France during the period of Louis XVI, but seldom used in the decoration of English furniture.

Ribbon Decoration

The use of ribbons in carved and painted decoration was characteristic of the rococo styles of the late 17th and early 18th centuries both in France and England. (*See* **Ribband Back Chair.**)

Rim

The raised edge that borders the top of a small table. (*See* **Gallery.**)

Rimu (*Dacrydium cupressinum*)

Incorrectly called New Zealand red pine, this supplies a light brown wood, straight-grained, and of even texture. The colour occasionally shades into a deep red, and burrs and figured logs produce veneers that are used for furniture and panelling.

Rio Rosewood, *see* **Rosewood**

Rising

A term used by cabinet makers in the 18th and 19th centuries to describe the motion given to various appliances or parts of furniture. Sheraton gives as examples a rising desk and 'a rising horse for the purpose of supporting a flap or top of a table to write at; a rising dressing glass, and various rising screens. . . .' (*The Cabinet Dictionary*, 1803, p. 297.)

Rising Stretcher

X-shaped stretchers that curve upwards to the point of intersection are known as rising stretchers. This form of decorative underframing was used on chairs and tables in the late 17th and early 18th centuries. (*See also* **Arched Stretcher.**)

Robinia (*Robinia pseudoacacia*)

Known formerly as acacia and locust. Native to Europe and the British Isles. A white, hard, durable wood. (*See* **Acacia.**)

Rocaille, Rococo, or **Rococco**

The word rococo is derived from the French *rocaille*, which means 'rock-work', a term used originally to describe the artificial grottoes and fountains in the gardens of Versailles. R. W. Symonds has suggested that '*Rococo* was, perhaps, coined to rhyme with the Italian word *barocco* and understood in a derogatory sense'. (*See* footnote to his introductory essay—on 'Rococo in the English

Ribband back chair. (From the first edition of Chippendale's *Director*, 1754).

Handicrafts'—to *The Ornamental Designs of Chippendale*. Alec Tiranti Ltd., 1949.) The rococo style was exuberant, light, graceful, and also revolutionary, because in an age of classical regularity and carefully balanced, symmetrical features, its delicate intermingling of ornamental forms was asymmetrical. Those forms included foliage, attenuated and involved exaggerations of the ubiquitous acanthus leaf, shells, scrolls, and a multiplicity of variously decorative objects. The initial inspiration of French rococo is attributed by R. W. Symonds to the work of Pierre Le Pautre, a designer and engraver. He was the eldest of the children of Jean Le Pautre (1618–82), a designer and engraver who had worked in the baroque style. The style developed in France during the early part of the Louis XV period, and it reached England in the middle years of the 18th century and influenced the work of Thomas Chippendale and some of his contemporaries. In France all forms of furniture, with the exception of chairs, were affected by rococo ornament. In England, the ornate tendency of French rococo was kept under control, and although Chippendale published many rococo designs in his *Director*, especially in the enlarged 3rd edition (1762), they were never overloaded with ornament. The rococo style had no outstanding or permanent effect upon English furniture design. (*See* illustrations on pages 150, 213, 250, 268, 330, 360, and 464.)

Rocking Chair

A chair with two curved members, known as bends, which connect the front and back feet, allowing the chair to be rocked. It is said to have been invented by Benjamin Franklin, at some time between 1760 and 1770, though it was probably in use earlier, and a Lancashire origin has also been claimed for it. Rockers have been used on cradles since the Middle Ages, and earlier, but the application of rockers, or bends, to chairs was not apparently thought of until the latter part of the 18th century. Since then, the rocker, or rocking chair, has become a national domestic institution in the United States, and is to be found in nearly every American home. The early rocking chairs were either of the Windsor or ladder- backed type. Rush seats or solid wood seats were used. Regional variations of form developed in America during the first half of the 19th century, notably the Boston rocker, which was evolved from the Windsor type, and had a curved seat, dipped from back to front, and

Rocking chair: American, late 18th century, with ladder back and rush seat.

a high back, with an ornamental panel or head rest in the top rail, usually painted with some floral device. Dr. Giedion records a patent for an improved rocking chair, taken out by D. Harrington in America as early as 1831, which was intended to increase the resilience of the chair by introducing wagon springs between the rockers and the seat. (U.S. Patent, April 23rd, 1831. Quoted in *Mechanization Takes Command,* by Siegfried Giedion. New York: Oxford University Press, 1948. Fig. 236, p. 402.) In the middle years of the 19th century two new types of rocking chair appeared which became popular both in Britain and the United States. They represented a complete break with the original American type, which, beginning simply as an ordinary armchair fitted with a pair of bends, never departed from the original basic form, despite subsequent refinements and ornamental variations. These new types were made of bent metal or bentwood, materials which allowed the function of the chair to be expressed by the whole design. Some English manufacturers had attempted, during the eighteen-forties, to make rocking chairs in cast iron, but that material was too brittle to resist the hard wear and tear to which the bends were constantly subjected in use; so steel or brass was used, and at the Great Exhibition of 1851 'a brass rocking or lounging chair, with morocco furniture' was shown by R. W. Winfield & Co., of Birmingham. This was entered and illustrated on p. 639 of the *Exhibition Catalogue* in Class XXII, General Hardware. (*See* accompanying illustration.) Some chairs of almost identical design, made from bent steel strips, were produced, apparently under the direction of a certain Doctor Calvert, who called them 'Digestive' chairs, and recommended them for ladies and invalids; but the design was not patented and any manufacturer could make them, and some did. At some time subsequent to the Exhibition, Dr Calvert's name became associated with this particular model of chair. It is debatable whether Dr Calvert may be identified with Frederick Crace Calvert, F.R.S. (1819–73), the industrial chemist, who was interested in industrial design,

Brass-framed rocking chair shown at the Great Exhibition of 1851. (From the *Exhibition Catalogue.*)

and delivered one of the first series of Cantor Lectures at the Society of Arts (1864). That the rocking chair was supposed to have some therapeutic properties is suggested by the following description of an exhibit by William Cunning, an Edinburgh manufacturer, at the 1851 Exhibition: 'Improved iron rocking chair, for the drawing room, in gold, and covered with French brocatel (from Whytock's, Edinburgh). In this chair the spine and neck rest in a natural

position. Exhibited as a useful invention for invalids and others.'
(An example of one of Dr Calvert's digestive chairs, which had
been repaired by Mr Ernest Race for its owner, Mr C. F. Colt, was
illustrated in the *Architects' Journal*, September 1st, 1949, p. 218.)
Metal chairs of the Dr Calvert type were exported to the United

States, and were also made there. Hans
Andersen's rocking chair, which is preserved in the Museum at Odense, Den-
mark, is of this type, with a loose fabric
seat slung from the top rail, instead of a
stuffed seat with buttoning; a bent iron
strip frame, the strips being flat in section
on the inside with a slight convex curve
on the outside; and a deep fringe hanging
from the front of the seat. (The accompanying illustration is based on a sketch,
made by the author, of the original chair
in the Hans Andersen Museum at

Hans Andersen's rocking
chair. A variation of the
metal type shown at the
1851 Exhibition.

Odense: compare it with the chair by R. W. Winfield & Co. shown
on the previous page.) Rocking chairs of bentwood were designed and produced in large quantities by Michael Thonet in the
eighteen-sixties. (*See* **Bentwood Furniture**.) These chairs with their
cane seats and backs and characteristic curved frames became

popular in Britain and America. By the
eighteen-eighties they were an accepted
and familiar item in the furnishing of
the Victorian home, and allowed ladies
to relax, perhaps a little inelegantly.
This bentwood type did much to popu-
larise the rocking chair in Britain, though
in America it did not succeed in diminishing the national affection for the
original models, which have retained
their popularity for over one hundred
and fifty years. The frames of some of
the steel tubular chairs, made in the

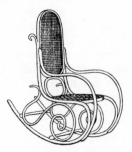

Bentwood rocking chair.

'twenties and 'thirties of the present century, have enough resilience
to bring them into the rocking chair category, though they are not
fitted with bends and afford only a limited rocking motion, which is
a by-product of their structural character. (*See* **Metal Furniture**.)

Rococo, *see* **Rocaille**

Roe

A name given to the regular appearance of dark flakes and spots
in figured mahogany, which give a mottled effect, like a fish roe. A
form of roe figure occurs in flowered, or East Indian, satinwood.

A simplified form of the bentwood rocking chair. The scroll in the frame below the seat, shown in the previous drawing, is dispensed with, but in gaining simplicity the design has lost its original vigour. (From *Judy Almanac*, 1886.) *See* opposite page.

Roll Top Desk

A desk with a top that is closed by means of a flexible pull-over shutter or fall, called a tambour or reed top, that is made by gluing thin strips or reeds of wood, of convex section, on to a linen or canvas back. The ends of this flexible panel fit into grooves or channels made for their reception in the inner sides of the desk, which guide the panel when the desk is being opened or closed. (*See* **Tambour**.)

Rollover Arm

A term for the arms of an easy chair when the upholstery is curved over in the form of a scroll, providing an elbow rest. (*See* illustration of Wing Chair on page 508.)

Roman Spindle

A simple type of Windsor chair with a back formed by five turned spindles, with beaded ornamentation, all socketed into the solid wooden seat and top rail. (*See* illustration, *also* **Stick Back** *and* **Windsor Chair**.)

Roman spindle.

397

Room Garden, *see* **Jardinière**

Rose and Ribbon Moulding

An elaborate form of decoration, in which roses or rosettes and ribbons were used to embellish the moulded edges of tables, particularly card tables in the mid-18th century. Sometimes known as ribbon and rosette.

Rosette

A rose-shaped ornamental disc: a patera carved to represent a conventionalised rose. (*See also* **Patera.**)

Rosewood (*Dalbergia nigra*)

Known also as Brazilian rosewood, Bahia rosewood, and Rio rosewood, it comes from Brazil, and furnishes a dark brown wood, marked with stripes of very dark brown, deepening almost to black. It has a fragrant smell when it is worked, hence its name. Rosewood also comes from India, Java, and the East Indies, and is known as Indian rosewood (*Dalbergia latifolia*), also called Bombay blackwood. Rosewood began to be used extensively in the early 19th century, and during the early Victorian period it was as much prized and as popular as mahogany. It is used for furniture of all kinds, and supplies richly marked veneers.

Victorian round back bedroom chair: a round back dining-room chair is shown on page 160.

Round Back or **Quaker Chair**

The commonest form of Victorian bedroom and dining-room chair, with an open, round back. The term Quaker appears to have been used in the furniture trade since the middle of the 19th century, though how it originated is unknown. (*See* illustration.) The name balloon back, which is sometimes used, is obviously descriptive.

Roundabout Chair

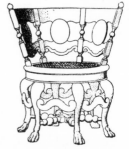

The term was not contemporary. The roundabout chair has a circular seat, either upholstered or caned, a semi-circular back, and six legs. (This term is also used in America, to describe what is properly a writing chair, *q.v.*) Such chairs were made by the Dutch in the East Indies for sale in Holland and other parts of Europe, in the 17th and early 18th centuries. They are sometimes known as burgomaster chairs, though that is probably a modern name for them. (*See* accompanying illustration, *and* that on page 64.)

Roundabout chair.

A roundel of chip carving on a mediaeval chest (late 13th or early 14th century). The complete illustration of this chest, reproduced from Shaw's *Specimens of Ancient Furniture*, is shown on page 181.

Roundel

The term has a wide application, and includes almost any form of ornament which occupies a circular space; for example, patrae, plaques, and medallions. The circular areas of chip carving on the fronts of early chests are called roundels, so too are the circular areas of stained glass, usually bearing heraldic devices, that were inset in the lead glazed windows of houses during the 16th and 17th centuries. It was also a mediaeval name for an iron ring for holding candles. Circular platters of beech, sycamore, or other woods were called roundels in the 18th century, and were in use during the 16th and 17th centuries, and probably much earlier. It is not known when they were first described by this name. Roundel is sometimes used as an alternative name for a bead, *q.v.*, or astragal. (*See* previous page.)

Roundels of coloured glass with heraldic devices. (From a drawing by E. J. Warne.)

Rout Chairs

These are defined by Sheraton in *The Cabinet Dictionary* (1803) as 'Small painted chairs with rush bottoms, lent out by cabinet makers for hire, as a supply of seats at general entertainments, or feasts; hence their name. . . .' Rout was formerly the common term for a large, fashionable evening party.

Ruching

A decorative form of trimming for cushions, bedspreads, curtains, and valances, made with a narrow band of material or ribbon. Throughout its full length, this band or ribbon has a series of running stitches down the centre; these are drawn up to give a tightly rucked effect, and are then securely fastened down. When the threads which run down the centre of the band are gathered, they cause the edges of the material to project with a double frilled effect. A more formal type of ruching is produced by using a series of box pleats throughout the length of the narrow band.

Rudd's Table or Reflecting Dressing Table

This elaborately fitted toilet table had various conveniently disposed receptacles and reflecting devices. It was first illustrated in Hepplewhite's *Guide* (1788), and was described as 'the most complete dressing table made, possessing every convenience which can be wanted, or mechanism and ingenuity supply. It derives its name from a once popular character, for whom it is reported it was first invented.' (*See* page 24.) A lighter variation of the design shown by Hepplewhite, based on a design by Shearer, is included in *The Prices of Cabinet Work* (1797), where it is described as 'A Rudd, or lady's dressing table'. (*See* illustration on next page.) Sheraton, in *The Cabinet Dictionary* (1803), devoted a few lines of description

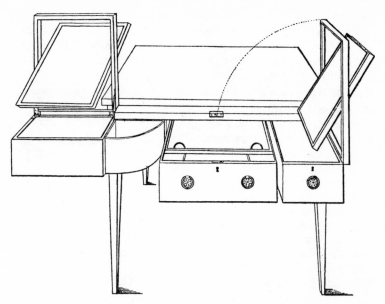

A Rudd, or lady's dressing table. (From *The Prices of Cabinet Work*, 1797 edition.) This is a simplified drawing of a design by Shearer: a more elaborate example of Rudd's table, by Hepplewhite, is shown on page 23.

to Rudd's table, prefaced by the statement that it was 'A kind of dressing table for ladies, not much in present use'.

Rudder

The name sometimes given to the solid, curved supporting wings of the type of drop-leaf table known in America as a butterfly table, *q.v.* These supports resemble a ship's rudder in outline.

Ruffle

A straight-edged band of material with the width diminished either by gathering or pleating along the upper edge, the lower edge being left free. It is used for furniture trimmings and for bed and window valances.

Rug

Derived from the Swedish word *rugg*, meaning rough, this has become a generic term for a rough woollen coverlet or blanket for a bed, or for a mat or a piece of carpet. Until the 19th century, the word carpet was generally used to describe all types of floor coverings. (*See* **Carpet**.)

Rule Joint

A hinged joint, used on table flaps and screens, which leaves no gap when the table flap is lowered. This device makes screens draught-proof, for no open space is left between the leaves.

Runner

The curved members at the base of a rocking chair are called runners. The term is sometimes used for drawer bearers. During the last half-century, the word has also been used to describe a strip of decorative material, placed on a table.

Running Scroll, *see* Scroll Ornament

Running Sideboard

Early 19th century running sideboard. (Drawn from Plate XXIX in Smith's *Guide*, 1826.)

A sideboard consisting of three tiers of open shelves surrounded by galleries and supported by brackets projecting from narrow, upright end members which rest either upon a base or feet, fitted with castors. Introduced during the early 19th century, and designed so that it could be used from both sides. In George Smith's *Cabinet-Maker's and Upholsterer's Guide* (1826) alternative designs for running sideboards are shown on Plate XXIX: the description that accompanies the plate says that they were 'sometimes vulgarly termed dinner wagons. Their use is for the purpose of bringing the dinner at once from the hall into the dining room at one opening of the door; and likewise for receiving and carrying away such dishes and plates as have been used.' (*See* illustration, *also* **Dinner Wagon.**)

Rural Chairs

The name given by Robert Manwaring to a type of rustic garden chair which he describes and illustrates in his book, *The Cabinet and Chair Maker's Real Friend and Companion, or the Whole System of Chair Making made Plain and Easy* (published in 1765). On Plate 26 of that book, he illustrates 'rural chairs for summer houses', and in the text he describes such chairs as 'made with the Limbs of Yew or Apple Trees, as Nature produces them, but the Stuff should be very dry and well seasoned; after the Bark is peeled clean off, shute from your Pitches the nearest Pieces you can match for the Shape of the Back, Fore Feet and Elbows; if you chuse to have strait Seat Rails, you may extend the small Bows over them, fastening them with Screws where it is necessary, the Bottoms let down with a Rabbett, some of them are usually blocked, provided the Seats are made in Wood; they are generally painted in various Colours'. (*See also* **Forest Chair** *and* **Rustic Furniture.**)

Rush Seating

The use of rushes for chair bottoms is of mediaeval origin; the weaving of rushes has been practised since very early times. Common rushes were used alike for chair bottoms, basket work, and mats, and rush-seated chairs were made throughout the 18th and 19th centuries, some being made by modern artist-craftsmen, like Ernest Gimson and Gordon Russell. (*See* List of Makers.)

Rustic Furniture

Chairs and seats, with the framework carved to resemble the branches of trees, were made in the middle years of the 18th century, and there was a popular fashion for this naturalistic rustic furniture. In the succeeding century, rustic furniture of every description was made, in wood and in cast iron. In the Victorian period, it became an accepted form for garden chairs and seats.

* S *

Sabicu (*Lysiloma latisiliqua*)

Supplied from the West Indies, chiefly from Cuba, and closely resembling rosewood in colour, being dark reddish-brown.

Sabre Leg

A hollow curved leg of rectangular section, so called because of its resemblance to the curve of a cavalry sabre. Copied from the *klismos*, the elegant chair depicted on Greek monuments and vases, it was introduced towards the end of the 18th century. After 1815, it was sometimes called a Waterloo leg. On chairs of cheap quality the front edge is usually rounded. (*See* illustrations, *also* page 42.)

Sabre legs on early 19th century chair.

A name sometimes used in the United States for a Windsor chair with a double bow back. (*See* **Windsor Chair.**)

Prototype of sabre leg. (From a vase in the Antichità Siciliane, engraved by Henry Moses and published in 1811 by J. Taylor.)

Saddle check or easy chair. (From Plate 15 of Hepplewhite's *Guide*, 1788.)

Saddle Back

A term used in the United States for a Windsor chair with a double bow back. It occurs in contemporary references to Windsor chairs. Thomas Hamilton Ormsbee quotes an advertisement in the *New York Gazette*, April 18th, 1765, by Andrew Gautier, the first American maker of Windsor chairs of whom there is any record, which lists saddle backed chairs and settees among other types. (*The Story of American Furniture*, the Macmillan Company, 1946 edition, chapter vi, p. 197.)

Saddle Check

A form of easy chair, described in Hepplewhite's *Guide* (1788), and illustrated on Plate 15 of that work. (*See* accompanying illustration.) Hepplewhite's description reads as follows: 'Plate 15 shows a design for a Saddle Check, or easy chair; the construction and use of which is very apparent; they may be covered with leather, horse-hair; or have a linen case to fit over the canvas stuffing'. There is some vague resemblance to the lines of a saddle in the form of the wings or ears to this type of easy chair. (*See also* **Wing Chair**.)

Saddle Seat

A solid wooden seat with two shallow depressions separated by a slight central ridge, suggesting the shape of a saddle. It is used on many types of Windsor chair.

Safe

The term includes practically all receptacles in which valuables may be securely kept and locked up; but specifically the word safe has, since the beginning of the 19th century, denoted a metal strong-box. Safes of cast iron were made in the early years of the 19th century, but wrought iron, and subsequently steel, were used, and safes were designed to resist fire as well as cracksmen. The word safe has also become a generic term for a strong-room built specially for the custody of documents and valuables.

Salt

The salt, or salt cellar, was an important piece of mediaeval plate, and when large, and richly decorated, its position on the table had social significance: the host, his near relatives, and privileged friends, sat above the salt; those of inferior degree sat below it. It was thus a social symbol, and 'It seems rather to have served this purpose than to hold salt for the meal, a supply of which was usually placed near each person's trencher, in a smaller salt-cellar, called a "trencher" salt'. (*Old English Plate*, by Wilfred Joseph Cripps. London, John Murray, 1901. Chapter X, p. 301.) There are many records of salt cellars in the Paston inventories. For example, in the inventory of Sir John Fastolf's goods (1489) there is this entry: 'Item, a saltsaler like a bastell [*a bastille or small tower*], alle gilt with roses, weiyng lxxvij unces'. Again, from the same inventory: 'Item, j. saltsaler, gilt, with a cover, weiyng xxxj. unces'. (*The Paston Letters*, Vol. I, pp. 468, 474.)

Saltire or Saltier

In heraldry, the saltire denotes two bands crossed diagonally, forming an X, called by Scottish heralds St Andrew's Cross. In furniture making, it is sometimes applied to X-shaped stretchers extending between the legs of chairs and tables. (*See also* **X-shaped Stretcher**.)

Samite or Samit

A word that in mediaeval times denoted some rich, silk-like material. It occurs in Chaucer's *Troilus and Criseyde* (Book I, line 109), and in the fragment of *The Romaunt of the Rose* that is attributed to him, where it is spelt samyt (lines 836 and 873). All three references are to its use for garments. It is not possible to identify this material, though it is conjectured that it may have been an early name for velvet.

Sampler

A generic name for some small piece of embroidery. The making of samplers was considered a proper employment for young ladies from the 17th century onwards. Dickens' description in *The Pickwick Papers* of the parlour at Dingley Dell emphasises, in a light-hearted way, the educational significance of the sampler. After describing Mr Wardle's mother, he says: 'Various certificates of her having been brought up in the way she should go when young, and of her not having departed from it when old, ornamented the walls, in the form of samplers of ancient date, worsted landscapes of equal antiquity, and crimson silk tea-kettle holders of a more modern period'. (Chapter vi.)

San Domingo or Spanish Mahogany (*Swietenia mahagoni*)

A variety supplied from the island of San Domingo. It is a deep red colour, which darkens after exposure, and though generally plain, occasionally exhibits great beauty of figure. The wood is very hard and smooth and takes a high polish. Under the heading of Hispaniola, on page 252 of *The Cabinet Dictionary* (1803), Sheraton says that the mahogany produced by San Domingo is 'of a hardish texture, but is not much in use with us'. (*See also* **Cuban Mahogany**.)

Sand Glass, *see* Hour Glass

Sandalwood (*Santalum album*)

An aromatic wood which comes from India. Occasionally used for boxes and small chests, and various items of Indian furniture, chiefly receptacles.

Santa Maria (*Calophyllum brasiliense*)

A hard, close-grained, pale red wood, supplied from the West Indies and Central America, with some of the properties of mahogany. Occasionally used for cabinet work.

Sarcophagus

Another term for a cellaret or wine cooler, which, as Sheraton points out in *The Cabinet Dictionary* (1803), 'is in some faint degree, an imitation of the figure of these ancient stone coffins, on which account only the term can with any colour of propriety, be applied to such wine cisterns'. They stood below a sideboard, were sometimes fitted with covers, and were generally made of mahogany with a lead lining. (*See* illustrations on next page, *also* the Sarcophagus below the Sideboard on page 428.)

Alternative designs for a sarcophagus, by Thomas Sheraton. (From Plate 66 of *The Cabinet Dictionary*, 1803.)

Sash Door

A mid-18th century term, used most probably to describe the glazed doors of bookcases and cabinets when rectangular panes were used. There is a reference to 'a new mahogany library bookcase with sash doors' in an advertisement of an auction sale, which appeared on November 4th, 1771, in the *Reading Mercury and Oxford Gazette*. Such glazed doors were often used on bookcases during the first half of the 18th century, and their resemblance to the contemporary sash window may have originated the term.

Satin

A material originally made of silk, with a very smooth and lustrous finish, usually woven with the warp forming the face. The weave is very close, and its structure is imperceptible in the finished cloth. Satin was certainly known in England in the 14th century, but it was a luxury, as described in Chaucer's *The Book of the Duchesse* (lines 251-6):

> I wil yive him a fether-bed,
> Rayed with golde, and right wel cled
> In fyn black satin doutremere,
> And many a pilow, and every bere
> Of clothe of Reynes, to slepe softe;
> Him thar not nede to turnen ofte.

The word *doutremere* means 'from beyond the seas'. Satin is of Chinese origin, and probably derives its name from the port of Zayton, which is mentioned by Marco Polo and was famous for the manufacture of a rich silk textile. The Chinese name of Zayton was Ch'üanchow. Zettani was the mediaeval Italian word for satin. Satin, although originally made of silk, is now also produced in rayon, and cheaper qualities are made with a silk or rayon surface and a cotton back.

Satin Walnut, *see* **American Red Gum**

Satinwood

There are two principal varieties, East Indian satinwood (*Chloroxylon swietenia*) and West Indian satinwood (*Fagara flava*). Both kinds supply rich, golden-yellow wood, often beautifully figured. Satinwood was used in the second half of the 18th century for luxurious, decorative furniture, and many of the designs drawn and published by Thomas Sheraton were intended for execution in this material. It is used for panelling, turning, veneering, and inlaying.

Satyr Mask

During the middle years of the 18th century, the mask of a satyr was occasionally used by some cabinet makers of the first rank as an ornamental *motif* on the frieze of a table, or on the knees of chair and table legs. (*See* illustration of Table by William Kent on page 329.)

Save-all

A candlestick designed to burn the ends of candles, so that nothing was wasted. In describing the parsimonious habits of Joseph Nollekens, J. T. Smith mentions 'a flat-candlestick with a save-all. . . .' (*Nollekens and his Times*, reprint of 2nd edition, 1920, Vol. I, chapter xiii, p. 296.)

Saucer Edge

A modern term for a table with a raised rim. (*See* **Piecrust Table.**)

Scagiola

An artificial marble, composed of cement, isinglass, and colouring matter, to which chips of real marble were occasionally added. It was used both for interior decoration and the tops of small tables and chests during the 18th century.

Early Georgian sconce with three branches, supported on a bracket of carved and gilded wood. (From a drawing by E. J. Warne.)

Scallop, *see* Escallop

Sconce

A wall fitting, with a branch or branches attached to it, each branch having a socket for the candle and a circular pan below to catch the candle grease. Sconces were made in silver, pewter, brass, pottery, sometimes in looking glass and japan ware (*see* **Japanning**), while those made by cabinet makers had wooden frames, usually with a panel of looking glass at the back, which magnified the light of the candle or candles. Occasionally, these wooden-framed sconces had needlework panels instead of mirrors. During the mid-18th century, sconces were made in the rococo style by carvers and gilders. (*See* **Girandole.**) Sconces are of mediaeval origin, and the 18th century looking glass became a sconce by adding candle branches to the frame. Glass sconces are mentioned in *The Journeys of Celia Fiennes* (Part IV, 1701–3, Section 10, p. 344). Although they were made throughout the 18th century, their use gradually declined. A modern term for a sconce which has been wired for electric light, is wall light. (*See* illustration above, *also* those on pages 56 and 268.)

Scotia.

Scotia

A concave moulding. (*See* illustration.)

Scratch Carving

The simplest form of incised carving, consisting of single lines scratched in the surface of woodwork. Found only in furniture made in the countryside, and seldom later than the 17th or early 18th centuries.

Screen

Screens of wood and leather have been used in England since mediaeval times, to secure privacy and to afford protection from the draughts which have always ventilated English rooms. During the latter part of the 17th century, screens of Oriental lacquer were introduced: and John Evelyn, describing the dressing room of the Duchess of Portsmouth, mentions 'Japan cabinets, screenes', in a list of the rich furniture she had collected. (*Diary*, October 4th, 1683.) Screens were used throughout the 18th century, and various specialised forms and adjustable types were designed. (*See* **Fire Screen**.) The basic type of screen, consisting of several hinged leaves of uniform height, has persisted until the present century.

Screen Table

A small writing table with a sliding screen of pleated silk in a mahogany frame at the back, so that the table could be taken near a fire, and the writer screened from the heat. (Gillow records, 1790, E. & S. Book, No. 642.) It was a lighter and simpler version of the writing fire screen, *q.v.*

Screen Writing Table, *see* Writing Fire Screen.

Scribing

A term describing the exact fitting of mouldings or framework to an irregular surface, when the material to be fitted is cut exactly to fit the irregularities. (*See* illustration.)

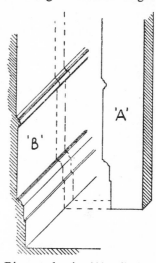

Diagram showing 'A' scribed to 'B'. (From Ware and Beatty's *Short Dictionary of Architecture*.)

Scrim

A very coarse fabric, generally used in building for covering and holding the joints between boards before plaster is applied. It is sometimes used for the underside of upholstered furniture.

Scriptoire, *see* Scrutoire

Scroll

Sometimes spelt scrowl. A spiral ornament. An alternative term for the volute of an Ionic capital. (*See* **Endive Scroll, Vitruvian Scroll,** *and* **Volute**.)

Scroll Foot

Used when the leg of a piece of furniture terminates in a

downward turning scroll. This type of foot was used occasionally in the late 17th and early 18th centuries. It is the reverse of the whorl foot, *q.v.*

Scroll Leg

A leg in the form of an elongated scroll, occasionally used for tables and cabinet stands in the second half of the 17th century. The silver table from Knole illustrated on page 433 has scroll legs.

Scroll Moulding

A moulding, derived from the Early English and Decorated periods of Gothic architecture, which resembles a scroll of paper. Scroll mouldings occur in some of the pseudo-Gothic furniture designed in the early 19th century. The term is sometimes incorrectly applied to the moulded detail of a linenfold panel.

Scroll leg.

Scroll Ornament

An ornament based on the use of a single scroll form, or a series of such forms. Single scroll is almost identical with the Ionic volute, and when the scrolls are used in series they are sometimes called running scrolls. (*See* **Vitruvian Scroll**.)

Scroll-over Arm

An arm in the form of a double scroll, curving inwards from the seat of a chair then breaking into a convex sweep before curving back to form an arm rest. (*See* illustration.) The scroll-over arm was fashionable among chair makers from the second to the fourth decade of the 18th century.

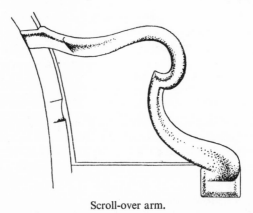

Scroll-over arm.

Scrolled Marquetry

Marquetry of intricate design, in which scrolls and tendrils of acanthus are intertwined. It is sometimes called seaweed marquetry, a doubtful term and not contemporary.

Scrolled Pediment, *see* **Swan-neck Pediment**

Scrutoire or **Scriptoire**

An obsolete term for a fall-down front writing cabinet, introduced in the reign of Charles II. (*See* accompanying illustrations showing a cabinet of this type closed and open.) The term was probably first used in the late 17th century, and continued in use

Late 17th century scrutoire, shown open and closed.

until the latter part of the 18th. Thomas Gray, in a letter to Dr Wharton dated July 10th, 1764, used it when referring to a paper called the *Scrutator*. In stating that he could not find anybody who had heard of the paper, he said: 'if anybody saw its name in the advertisements, I believe they only took it for a *scrutoire* to be sold'. (*Poems, Letters, and Essays of Thomas Gray*. Dent: Everyman Library edition. Letter CXIII, p. 261.) The term was also applied to the bureau bookcase, *q.v.*

Scutcheon, *see* **Escutcheon**

Seat

Although the term specifically refers to the solid or upholstered surface supported by the seat framing or seat rails of a chair, settee, or sofa, the word seat has, since the mid-18th century, been applied generally to garden seats, and to rather severely designed and purely utilitarian articles, such as hall seats.

Seat Back

A detachable, decorative covering for a chair or settee back.

Seat Curb, *see* **Fender Stool**

Seat Rail

The horizontal framework supporting a chair or settee seat.

413

Seating

A term for certain hard wearing cloths, such as haircloth, used in upholstery.

Seaweed Marquetry, *see* Scrolled Marquetry

Secret Drawer

A concealed drawer in a desk or writing table. Such a hidden receptacle for papers or valuables is an ancient device, and in cabinet making probably dates from the mid-17th century, when the increase of skill in woodworking facilitated the making of such carefully fitted hiding places. In the more elaborate cabinet work of the 18th and early 19th centuries, secret drawers were often hidden by pigeon holes, and the divisions between pigeon holes were sometimes hollow.

Secretaire or Secretary

A general term for a desk designed specially for writing, being employed among cabinet makers, as Sheraton says, 'to certain pieces of furniture to write at. . . .' It is also a term used for the piece of furniture for writing that is called an escritoire, *q.v.* (*See* next page.)

Section

A view disclosed by an imaginary cut made vertically or horizontally through an object, to show the variations of its surface and the profile of its mouldings.

Seeing Glass, *see* Looking Glass

Selour or Sellore

The mediaeval name for the panel at the head of a bed, usually of some rich fabric. It was one of the parts of which the bed was formed, and was often ornamented with arms of the owner. Also known as a celure, *q.v.* The selour and the tester were often of the same material. (*See* description of the apartments furnished for Prince Charles, Duke of Burgoine, in Section II, page 44.)

Serpentine-fronted dressing chests. *Left:* with ogee ends. *Right:* with straight wings. (From *The Prices of Cabinet Work*, 1797 edition.)

Serpentine Front

A convex curve, flanked by two concave curves, used on the fronts of cabinets, chests, commodes, sideboards, and tables, and

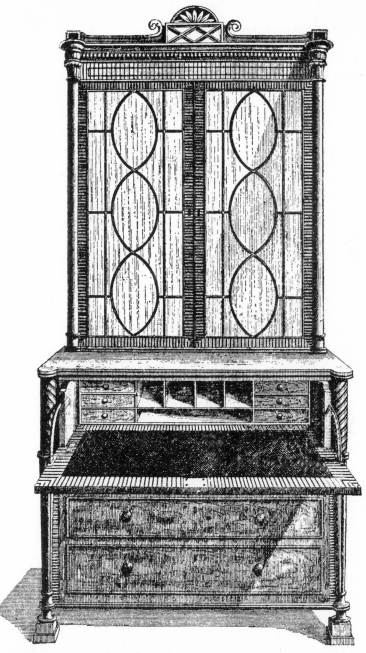

Secretary and bookcase designed by Thomas Sheraton. (From Plate 67 of
The Cabinet Dictionary, 1803.)

introduced during the mid-18th century. (*See* illustrations on page 414, *also* Hepplewhite Sideboard on page 427.)

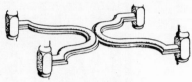

Serpentine Stretcher

An X-shaped stretcher, with the X formed by convex and concave curves. (*See* illustration.)

Serpentine stretcher.

Serpentine Top

A shallow convex curve, flanked by two concave curves, used on the top of a bookcase or cabinet. (*See* illustration below.)

Set of Chairs

The making of chairs in sets, particularly for dining, originated in the 17th century. A set would comprise six or more chairs, with an armchair for the host at the head of the table.

Settee

A long seat for two or more people, with a back and arms. The settee was introduced in the late 17th century, and often took the form of two conjoined chair backs. Settees with upholstered backs and arms were also introduced, and such seats, variously formed and decorated, became permanently established in English furnishing. (*See* **Bar Back Settee, Chair Back Settee,** *and* **Double Chair.**)

Serpentine top on a book case. (From *The Prices of Cabinet Work*, 1797 edition.)

Settle

A bench or seat for several people, of mediaeval origin, which was probably in use as early as the 12th century. There are two basic types of settle: the low-backed, with arms at either end, and the high-backed, usually with wings instead of arms, though the early high-backed settles had no wings. The high-backed settle was often a fixture against a wall, and was the type of seat used in the large fireplaces or ingle nooks of kitchens in farmhouses and taverns. High-backed settles made in the 18th and early 19th centuries occasionally had a couple of drawers

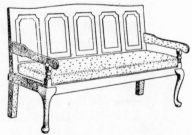

Early 18th century low-backed settle.

416

under the seat, though receptacles below the seat were introduced much earlier. In an inventory dated April 25th, 1638, there is a

Early 19th century high-backed settle with drawers. (From Loudon's *Encyclopaedia*, 1833.)

reference to 'one settle with 3 boxes in it'. (*Farm and Cottage Inventories of Mid-Essex*, 1635–1749. Essex Record Office Publications, No. 8, p. 73.) The low-backed type was introduced during the mid-17th century. (*See* illustrations, *also* **Box Settle** *and* **Ingle Nook.**)

Settle Table

A type of high-backed settle, with the upper part of the back hinged so that it may be lowered to rest horizontally upon the arms, thus forming a table. It is made on the same principle as the chair table, which was the contemporary name for it. (*See* **Chair Table.**)

Sewing Machine Table

The sewing machine, which came into general use during the second half of the 19th century, introduced a new, specialised piece of furniture, which was really a mechanised sewing table. The sewing machine was mounted on the table top, which was made of wood, while the underframing, which accommodated the treadle, was of cast iron, ornamental in form and painted and sometimes enlivened with a little gold paint. For the hand-operated machines, special sewing machine tables were made which allowed the machine to be clamped securely to the wooden top, which was supported upon a cast iron pillar resting either on a tripod or a circular plate of the same material; the weight of this underframing giving stability to the table. (*See* illustration.)

Sewing Table

A small work table fitted with drawers and a work bag. Introduced during the late 18th century. (*See* **Pouch Table**.)

Shagreen

Untanned leather with a granular surface, usually dyed green, and occasionally used for covering small receptacles, such as knife boxes and stationery cases. Although the skins of horses and asses were formerly used, shagreen is now generally prepared from sharkskin.

Shalloon, *see* Chalons.

Sewing machine table of the treadle type. (From *The Art Journal*, 1862.)

Shaving Chair

A chair with a high back, providing a head rest. Generally a corner chair, resembling in form an angle or writing chair. The type illustrated is early 18th century, though shaving chairs were known in the 16th century. (*See* illustration, *also* **Barber's Chair**.)

Shaving Glass

Small, concave shaving glasses were used in the 17th century and the adjustable types of 18th century toilet mirror, designed to stand independently upon a dressing table, are sometimes described as shaving glasses (*see* **Toilet Glass**). Today the term usually applies to small, metal-framed mirrors, attached to a hinged, extending arm.

Shaving Stand, *see* Shaving Table

Shaving Table

A toilet table with a wash basin, an adjustable shaving glass, receptacles for soap and perfume bottles, a cupboard below, and sometimes drawers also. Such tables were introduced during the mid-18th century, and examples are illustrated and described in

Shaving chair: early 18th century.

Chippendale's *Director* (1762) and Sheraton's *Cabinet Dictionary* (1803). *See* illustrations on pages 420, 421, *also* **Rudd's Table.** The very small types of shaving table without basins were often called shaving stands; and are described under that name in *The Prices of Cabinet Work* (1797). The size of the top of one of these stands is given as 1 ft. 4 ins. square, and it had one drawer, 'two holes for cups, a glass frame behind to rise with a rack and spring, and swing on centre screws . . .' (p. 168).

Sheathing

A term used in the United States to describe a primitive form of timber wall covering, consisting of vertical boards carried direct from the floor to the ceiling, with the edges of the boards joined, and the joints sometimes finished with a moulding. Occasionally, sheathing takes the form of boards laid horizontally against the wall surface, with the ends framed into upright members. Sheathing was used in American houses in the late 17th and throughout the 18th and early 19th centuries.

Sheet Glass

A transparent glass with a fire-finished surface, which is in general use for all kinds of glazing. As the glass is fire-finished, the two surfaces are never perfectly flat or parallel, although the flat drawn process, now used for its manufacture, has greatly diminished the amount of distortion of vision and reflection that used to be unavoidable with sheet glass.

Sheffield Plate

Copper that has been coated with a thin layer of silver is known as Sheffield plate, for the process was developed in Sheffield after it had been accidentally discovered in 1742 by a workman named Thomas Bolsover. Throughout the rest of the 18th century a great variety of articles was made in Sheffield plate, but the process was replaced by electro-plating at the beginning of the Victorian period.

Shelf

A platform of wood, metal, glass, or other material, supported by brackets and projecting from a wall or fixed within an open framework or a receptacle, upon which articles may rest.

Shelf Cluster

A mid-Victorian term for tiers of shelves, grouped above a mantelpiece, and used for the display of china and glass. (*See* illustration on page 422.)

Shelving

A generic term for shelves fitted to a wall or inside a cupboard.

Sheraton Style

A loose term, applied with misleading vagueness to much of the mahogany and painted furniture that was made in the last decade

[*Contd. on page 423.*

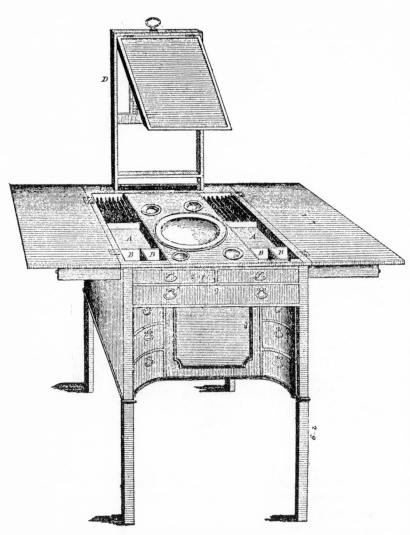

Shaving table designed by Thomas Chippendale. (From Plate LIV of the 3rd edition of the *Director*, 1762.) Compare with the design by Sheraton on the opposite page.

Shaving table designed by Thomas Sheraton. (From Plate 69 of
The Cabinet Dictionary, 1803.) *See* opposite page, and entry
on page 418.

Shelf cluster. (From *Decoration and Furniture of Town Houses*, by Robert W. Edis, F.S.A., F.R.I.B.A.: Kegan Paul, 1881.) *See* entry on page 419.

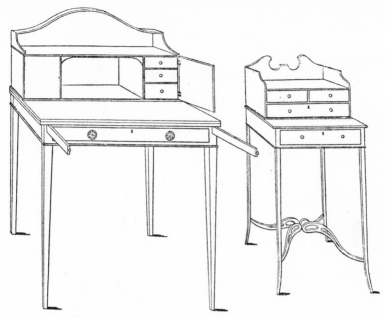

Left: A sheveret, described in *The Prices of Cabinet Work* (1797 edition) as a lady's cabinet. Designs of this type are described in the Gillow records as sheverets. *Right:* A lady's work table, which is a miniature of the sheveret form.

of the 18th and the first few years of the 19th centuries; it is even supposed to describe all furniture that was made of satinwood at that time. Thomas Sheraton's prolific pencil has been responsible for attaching his name purely as a label to the sort of furniture that was made by his numerous contemporaries. Little furniture can be directly attributed to him. (*See* List of Makers, on page 525.)

Sheveret

A narrow writing cabinet or desk, with taper legs and a shelf or shelves above a small set of drawers or pigeon holes. Gillows made many sheverets and an order for one in satinwood is recorded on July 5th, 1790 (E. & S. Book). It was similar to the lady's cabinet described and illustrated in *The Prices of Cabinet Work* (1797). *See* illustration. The word is sometimes spelt cheveret.

Shield Back Chair

Sometimes called a camel back chair, because the convex curve of the top rail in some types suggests a camel's hump. The shield back was characteristic of Hepplewhite's work (*see* List of Makers on page 523), and the shield-shaped frame of the back was elegantly filled with slender bars, delicately carved and curved to

Shield back chair with vase splat. (From Hepplewhite's *The Cabinet Maker and Upholsterer's Guide*, 1788.) Compare this with the example shown on the opposite page.

Shield back elbow chair with cane work. *Circa* 1780–90.

424

Another example of shield back chair. (From Hepplewhite's *Guide*, 1788).
See opposite page.

correspond or to contrast with the lines of the frame. (*See* **Prince of Wales's feathers**.) The back was sometimes filled with canework. (*See* illustrations on page 424 and above.)

Shoulder

An alternative name for the knee of a cabriole leg.

Show Wood

The exposed parts of the wooden frame of an upholstered chair.

Shuffle Board or Shovel Board

A large table, on which the game of shuffle-board was played. Robert Plot, in *The Natural History of Staffordshire* (published in 1686), describes one at Chartley as 'ten yards one foot and an inch long', and made up of about two hundred and sixty pieces, 'which are generally about eighteen inches long, some few only excepted, that are scarce a foot, which, being laid on longer boards for support underneath, are so accurately glewed together, that no shuffle-board whatever is freer from rubbs or casting'. John Evelyn, in his *Sylva* (3rd edition, 1679), mentions elm as the best wood for '*Shovelboard-Tables* of great length . . .' (chapter iv, p. 35). Joseph Strutt, who quotes Dr Plot, states that although these tables are of great length, the width seldom exceeds 3 ft. or 3 ft. 6 ins. (*The Sports and Pastimes of the People of England*, published in 1801.) The shuffle-board table was a conspicuous article in the homes of the nobility and gentry of the 17th century; but by the end of the 18th it had been relegated to the servants' hall, where it was used also as a dining table. Strutt described such a table which he had seen 'at a low public-house in Benjamin-street, near Clerkenwell-green, which is about three feet in breadth and thirty-nine feet two inches in length, and said to be the longest at this time in London'.

Side Chair

A chair without arms; a single chair. Sometimes called a small chair. (*See* illustration on page 252.)

Side Rail

The board or rail which connects the headboard with the foot-board of a bed.

Side Table

A large table used in a dining room, which served as a sideboard before that article in its now familiar form was invented. (*See* **Sideboard**.) Side or sideboard tables flanked by pedestals that were surmounted by urns, were designed by the brothers Adam (*see* **Pedestal**), and were the immediate forerunners of the sideboard fitted with

Side table with pedestals and urns.
Circa 1780–90.

drawers and cupboards; but to many cabinet makers in the late 18th century these terms were interchangeable.

Sideboard

Sideboard was a mediaeval term for serving table, and was in common use before the specialised type of side table with drawers and cupboards was invented in the second half of the 18th century, and which has since been known by that name. The invention of

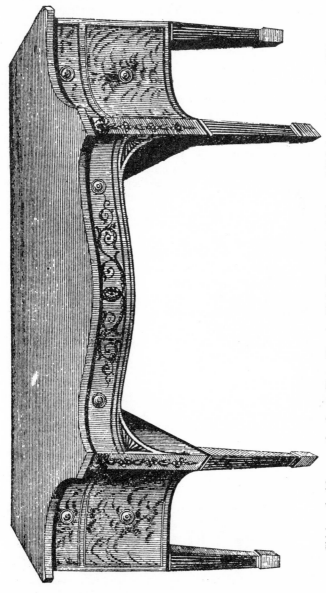

Sideboard with serpentine front. (From Hepplewhite's *The Cabinet Maker and Upholsterer's Guide*, 1788.)

this type of sideboard has been attributed to Thomas Shearer; but it may well have been invented by one of his contemporaries. In *The Journeys of Celia Fiennes*, this description occurs: '. . . when the table was spread I saw only spoones salts and forks and the side board plate. . . .' (Part III, 1698, Section 4, p. 171.) This suggests that at the end of the 17th century the mediaeval form of the term had persisted, for in the Middle Ages the word board meant almost any kind of table, and the sideboard was used largely for the display of plate. (*See* **Board**.) In Swift's *Directions to Servants*, written during the seventeen-thirties, the use of the sideboard for displaying glass is mentioned. In giving much facetious advice to the butler, he said: "When you dress up your Side-board, set the best Glasses as near the edge of the Table as you can. . . .' Sideboards with cupboards were in use during the second half of the 17th century, and probably much earlier, though the term may have been applied to the type of court cupboard, *q.v.*, that had a small central cupboard in the upper part. In an inventory dated August 20th, 1666, 'one sydboard Cuboard' is an item of the parlour furnishing; another inventory, dated November 4th, 1678, includes in the furnishing of two butterys 'one side boarde cubbord. . . .' (*Farm and Cottage Inventories of Mid-Essex, 1635–1749.* Essex Record Office Publications, No. 8, pp. 105, 156.) The ancestor of Shearer's design is most probably the dresser. Many makers adopted and developed the sideboard, and by the end of the 18th century it was made in a variety of forms and afforded the most comprehensive and convenient accommodation, with cupboards and drawers for glass, cutlery, and silver, and sometimes included an inconspicuous cupboard for a chamber pot. During the 19th century the sideboard became more commodious, and a popular type was made with the top and drawers immediately below it, resting upon pedestals with cupboards in them. (*See* illustration on page 427, *also* **Running Sideboard**.)

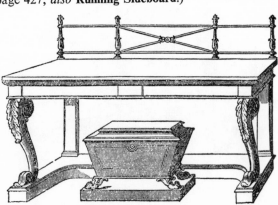

Sideboard with sarcophagus or cellaret below. (From Loudon's *Encyclopaedia*, 1833.)

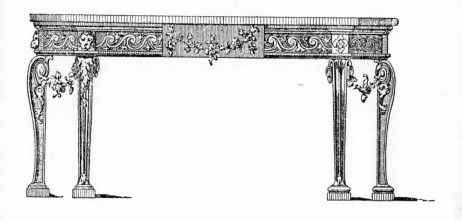

Two designs for sideboard tables from Plate LXI of Chippendale's *Director*, 3rd edition, 1762. (These are reduced in size from the plate.) On the plate, Chippendale describes them as sideboard tables: in his description, he calls them 'Side-Boards'—obviously the terms were at that time interchangeable. The design at the top has truss legs. (*See also* Chippendale's design on page 431.)

Sideboard table, decorated with reeding. (From Plate 71 of Sheraton's *The Cabinet Dictionary*, 1803.) This is reduced in size from the original plate.

Sideboard Table

In the first half of the 18th century, a sideboard table was a table with a marble top, without drawers in the frame. The name was used by cabinet makers in the late 18th century for a side table with one or more drawers in the frieze rail immediately below the top. Sheraton, in *The Cabinet Dictionary* (1803), says that such tables 'are used for a dining equipage, on which the silver plate is placed'. The term is sometimes used to describe the side tables of Adam design, which were used with a pair of pedestals. (*See* **Side Table.**) Both Chippendale and Hepplewhite regarded the term as interchangeable with sideboard. (*See* caption of illustrations on page 429.)

Sight Size

The visible area of the glass panes in the doors of a bookcase or cabinet; or the visible area of glass in a mirror.

Silk

A textile fibre which is made from the filaments produced by the larvae of the mulberry silk moth of China. The silk industry originated in China over four thousand five hundred years ago. The manufacture of silk was introduced into England during the 15th century, but it was not widely established until skilled weavers who were refugees from Flanders and the Low Countries settled

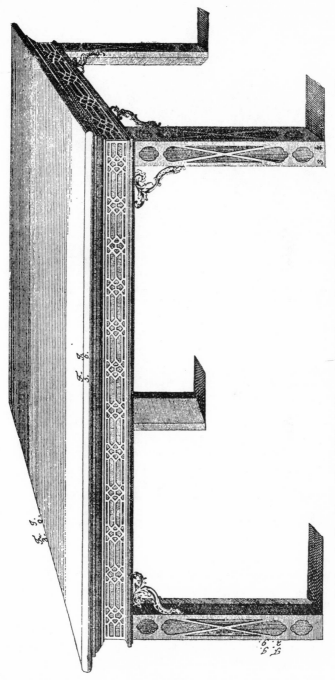

Sideboard table. (From Plate LVII of Chippendale's *Director*, 3rd edition, 1762.) *See* examples on page 429.

Looking glass frame of silver, from Knole Park, Sevenoaks, Kent. Second half of the 17th century. (From Shaw's *Specimens of Ancient Furniture*.)

in England late in the 16th century, and a hundred years after that first settlement Huguenot refugees from France extended and strengthened the industry, and made the name of Spitalfields famous for its products.

Silver Furniture

Furniture that was covered with thin sheets of silver, also furniture of solid cast silver, was made in England after the Restoration, in the reigns of Charles II and James II, though little of such extravagantly decorative work has survived. (*See* illustrations of silver furniture at Knole.) John Evelyn records that the Duchess of Portsmouth's dressing room contained 'screenes, pendule clocks, great vases of wrought plate, tables, stands, chimney furniture, sconces, branches, braseras, &c. all of massive silver, and out of number . . .' (*Diary*, October 4th, 1683.) Celia Fiennes, describing a house that belonged to the Earl of Chesterfield, mentions 'the bride chamber which used to be call'd the Silver roome, where the stands table and fire utensills were all massy silver', adding that 'when the plaite was in nomination to pay a tax, the Earle of Chesterfield sold it all and the plate of the house . . .' (*The Journeys of Celia Fiennes*, Part III, 1698, Section 4, p. 171.) This may account for the comparative rarity of such work.

Silvering

The term describes the use of silver leaf, which was a cheap method of gilding, for the silver was lacquered or varnished so that it turned to a gold colour. Carved cabinet stands and the frames of chimney glasses were sometimes silvered in the late 17th and early 18th centuries. Silvering is also the name given to the process of depositing silver on glass to make a mirror, and coating it with a

Silver table from Knole Park, Sevenoaks, Kent. Second half of the 17th century. (From Shaw's *Specimens of Ancient Furniture*.)

433

protective medium. Mirrors were formerly coated with an amalgam of tin and mercury, but this method has been superseded by the use of silver, chemically deposited.

Single Chair, *see* **Side Chair**

Sitz Bath, *see* **Hip Bath**

Skirting Piece

A horizontal strip of wood depending from the lowest member of the framework of a chest or cabinet, usually treated ornamentally, and extending between the legs or feet. It is a form of apron, and is sometimes described as a valance. (*See* **Apron** *and* **Valance**.)

Skiver

The top or grain layer of a sheepskin, about one millimetre thick, used occasionally for the lining of drawers and boxes.

Slat or **Cross Rail**

A flat, thin, horizontal rail in a chair back. An alternative term is horizontal splat. (*See* **Splat**.)

Slat Back

A name sometimes used for a primitive form of ladder back chair, with four or five slats between the seat and the top rail: a type made in the countryside.

Sleeping Chair

A high-backed easy chair with the back hinged and adjusted to fall by means of a quadrant stay, *q.v.*, so that it could be used as a reclining chair. An example of a late 17th century sleeping chair is in the collection of furniture at Ham House, Petersham, Surrey. The term is a contemporary one, and it occurs in the Lord Chamberlain's account for furnishing His Majesty's Service at Windsor (June 14th, 1675), when Richard Price was paid the sum of £2 'For a sleeping chaire to fall in the back of Iron worke'. (Public Records Office.)

Sleepy Hollow Chair

A name used in America for a type of mid-19th century easy chair with a continuous back and seat of fabric, forming a restful, inclined support for the back, and a hollow seat. The wooden frame is supported upon two arched members, so the side view of the chair resembles a mediaeval X-framed seat. The arms are open and not upholstered. The name was suggested by Washington Irving's tale, 'The Legend of Sleepy Hollow', in his *Sketch Book*; and presumably this type of chair was designed to encourage 'the listless repose' which characterised that 'sequestered glen' near the Hudson River.

Sleigh Bed

An American term for a type of early 19th century bed with the ends curving outwards in the form of a long S or elongated scroll, resembling the front of a sleigh.

Slides or Sliders

A small sliding shelf that is fitted into the carcase of a bureau, desk, table, or chest. The narrow slides, often used in desks, which could be pulled out and used as supports for candles, were called candle slides, *q.v.* Sliding shelves were used frequently in furniture made in the second half of the 18th and throughout the 19th centuries. Slider is sometimes used as an alternative term for loper, *q.v.*

Sliding Fire Screen

A fire screen, supported upon a stand, which may be extended by means of sliding leaves. (*See* illustrations *under* Fire Screen on pages 255-256.)

Slipper Bath

A tin bath, partly enclosed, and resembling a slipper in shape. Used during the 19th century before the general introduction of bathrooms and fitted baths.

Slipper Rocker

A type of rocking chair with low, pierced arms and a heavy mahogany frame, made in the United States after the mid-19th century. The seat and back were upholstered, usually with buttoning. The term slipper may have been used because the contours of the

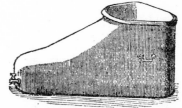

Slipper bath: mid-19th century. (From the *Family Cyclopaedia*.)

chair, with its curved arms, vaguely suggested the form of a slipper; though its comfortable upholstery may have prompted some tradesman to invent a name which evoked visions of slippered ease by a fireside.

Slot Screwing

A method of using screws, to secure a secret fixing, so that the screw heads may be concealed.

Small Chair

A term for a chair without arms. Small chairs, or little chairs as they were sometimes called, are mentioned in 16th and 17th century inventories. (*See* Side Chair.)

Smoker's Bow

A corner chair with turned legs, a shaped wooden seat, and a low back, semicircular in plan, with seven or eight plain spindles, or Roman spindles, *q.v.*, which are socketed into the seat and into the curved, horizontal member which forms both back rail and arms. The spindles incline outwards slightly, which gives a gentle rake to the back. This is a form of Windsor chair, which was first made at some time during the second quarter of the 19th century and became very popular as an armchair, not only for cottage furnishing, but for offices and institutions and particularly for public-houses. The name presumably originated from the bow-shaped back and its widespread use in smoking rooms and bars. (*See* illustration.)

Snakewood (*Piratinera guianensis*)

This decorative wood comes from central and tropical South America, and is rich brown, with darker mottled veins of the same colour running outwards from the heart. Used for veneering and inlaying.

Snap Table

A tripod table with a hinged oval, circular, or octagonal top that snaps back or folds back when not in use. (*See* **Birdcage**.) The term occurs in the Gillow records (1797, E. & S. Book, No. 1389; *also* 1798, E. & S. Book, No. 1428.) The term tip-top table is sometimes used in the United States.

Smoker's bow.

Snuffers

A pair of scissors for snuffing or trimming candles, with a closed box for receiving the charred wick. Snuffers generally stood on three small feet, and often rested on a tray with raised sides, shaped to follow the outline of the scissors. Snuffers were known in the early 16th century and were in general use in Elizabethan times and up to the middle of the 19th century. They were made of silver, pewter, brass, or iron.

Social Table

A small, kidney-shaped table with four legs, and a revolving, cylindrical receptacle for wine bottles, supported on a pillar-and-claw stand, which fitted into the concave curve of the table.

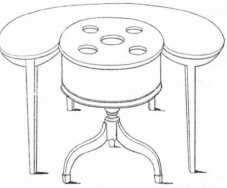

A gentleman's social table. (From *The Prices of Cabinet Work*, 1797 edition.)

Described as a gentleman's social table in *The Prices of Cabinet Work* (1797), it allowed two or three people to sit with their wine near a fire. A similar type of wine table, described rather misleadingly as a semicircular dining table, is illustrated in J. C. Loudon's *Encyclopaedia* (1833). 'It is chiefly used by gentlemen after the ladies have retired to the drawing room', Mr Loudon records. 'This table was then placed in front of the fire, with its convex side outwards, and the guests sit round that side, with their feet to the fire.' (*See* illustrations.)

Social table illustrated in Loudon's *Encyclopaedia* (1833).

Sofa

A long seat, stuffed and upholstered, with a back and two ends. The sofa combines the attributes of a day bed and a settee, which were both introduced in the latter part of the 17th century, but it did not become a distinctive article of furniture, known under that name, until the mid-18th century. In Bailey's *Dictionarium Britannicum* (2nd edition, 1736), a sofa is described as 'A sort of alcove much used in Asia; it is an apartment of state, raised from about half a foot, to two feet higher than the floor, and furnished with rich carpets and cushions, where honourable personages are entertained'. The word sofa is of Arabic origin. Chippendale includes some plates of sofas in his *Director* (1762). (*See* illustrations, *also* **Chaise Longue, Confidante, Cornucopia Sofa, Day Bed, Kangaroo Sofa, Lounge, Tête-à-tête Seat,** *and* **Tub Sofa.**)

Sofa Bed

A rather complicated piece of dual purpose furniture, which acted as a bed by night and folded up to become a sofa by day. Like the press bedstead and bureau bedstead, *q.v.*, it reflected a desire to conceal the bed or to make it become more compact in form during the daytime. Disguising the bed was apparently a popular habit in the late 18th and early 19th centuries. Sheraton published a design for a sofa bed in *The Cabinet Dictionary* (1803); and a less elaborate design, showing the various stages for converting the sofa into a bedstead, was included by Loudon in his *Encyclopaedia* (1833). (*See* illustrations on next four pages.)

Sofa Table

An oblong or rectangular table, introduced at the end of the 18th century. This development of the Pembroke table appeared in a variety of styles. Two shallow drawers were usually included, and many sofa tables had fly brackets. They were intended mainly for use beside the sofas of ladies or invalids, their height and size

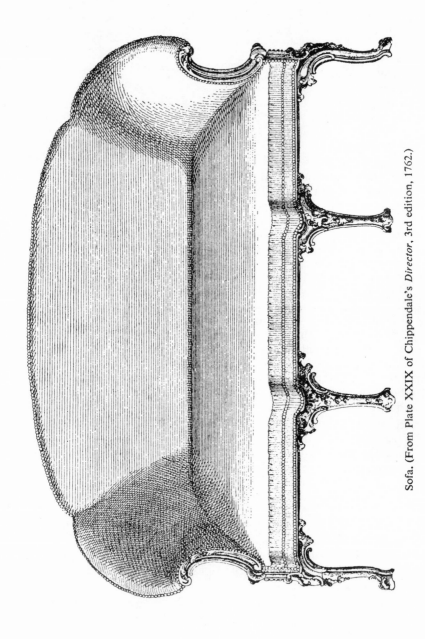

Sofa. (From Plate XXIX of Chippendale's *Director*, 3rd edition, 1762.)

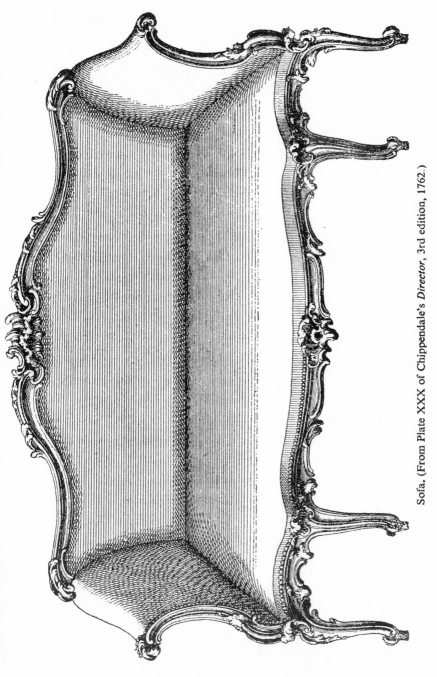

Sofa. (From Plate XXX of Chippendale's *Director*, 3rd edition, 1762.)

Sofa bed. From Plate 17 of *The Cabinet Dictionary* (1803), by Thomas Sheraton.

being convenient for this purpose. Occasionally, the top contained a chess board, hidden by a sliding panel, or a rising desk, for reading or writing. Sheraton describes this last type as a 'sofa writing table', and shows a sofa table used in conjunction with a sofa in *The Cabinet Dictionary* (1803), observing that 'The Ladies chiefly occupy them to draw, write, or read upon'. (*See* pages 442, 443.)

Softwoods

Under the nomenclature adopted by the British Standards Institution, softwoods are those woods supplied from trees belonging to the botanical group, *Gymnosperms*. Commercial timbers in this group are practically confined to conifers. (B.S. 589, 1946.)

Spade Foot, *see* **Therm** or **Thermed Foot**

Spandrel or **Spandril**

A triangular space enclosed between the curve of an arch, a horizontal line drawn through its apex, and a vertical line rising from its springing point.

440

Spanish Chestnut, *see* **Sweet Chestnut**

Spanish Mahogany, *see* **San Domingo Ma-**
  hogany

Span-rail

This term may be a corrupt form of spandrel, as it is sometimes used to describe a
curved rail between two upright members.

Sphinx

The Greek name for a fabulous monster
with the body of a lion, the head and bust of
a woman, and the wings of a bird. The
Egyptian sphinx was wingless and had the
head of a man, usually the portrait of a king,
with a lion's body, symbolising the Pharaoh's

The pedestal of a
Roman table of
white marble from
Pompeii. (From
Edward Trollope's
*Illustrations of An-
cient Art*.)

power. (*See* Breasted's *History of Egypt*, chapter vi, p. 120.) The
winged form was used ornamentally in the Graeco-Roman civilisation, and was reintroduced to Europe during the Renaissance.
The winged sphinx was used occasionally on furniture during the
latter part of the 18th century, and occurs as an ornamental *motif*

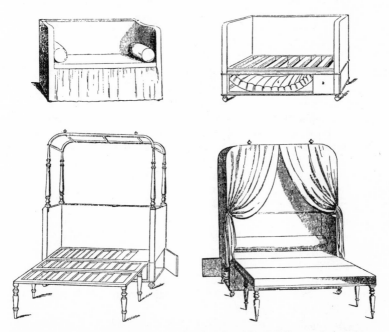

The sofa bed illustrated in Loudon's *Encyclopaedia* (1833) was designed as
a dual purpose piece of furniture for cottage dwellings. The four stages of
converting it from a sofa to a bed are shown above.

Sofa writing table, designed by Thomas Sheraton, and illustrated on
Plate 76 of *The Cabinet Dictionary* (1803).

on furniture designed by the brothers Adam. (*See* page 441.) The
wingless Egyptian sphinx appeared in France during the reign of
Louis XVI as a minor decorative item in a transitory fashion; but
the taste for Egyptian ornamental forms was not established until
it had been stimulated by the Egyptian campaigns of General
Buonaparte; thereafter the sphinx appeared on many types of
French furniture. During the opening years of the 19th century
it was used on English furniture, for Thomas Hope's published
designs for interior decoration and furnishing stimulated interest
in Egyptian ornament. (*See* **Regency Style.**)

Spindle

A thin, turned rod or baluster, either straight or varying in profile, used frequently as an upright member in a chair back. (*See*
illustration of Spindle Back Chair.) In architecture, the term denotes a small turned pillar used in a gallery. The name is obviously
derived from the spindle used in spinning yarn, which is a short
rod, tapering at each end.

Spindle-and-Baluster

Sometimes known as baluster-and-spindle. A descriptive term
for a simple type of Windsor chair, with a back composed of

442

Sofa table and sofa. (From Plate 74 of *The Cabinet Dictionary* (1803), by Thomas Sheraton.)

four spindles and a central splat in the form of a flat, pierced baluster.

Spindle-and-Bead

A form of enrichment used on mouldings of semi-circular section (*see* **Bead**), consisting of circular beads alternating with short, round-ended spindles. It is an enrichment used in architectural decoration, and occasionally on furniture.

Spindle Back Chair

A name sometimes given to chairs with backs consisting of spindles running from the seat to the top rail, or framed in a single or double row into horizontal bars between seat and top rail.

Baluster-and-spindle type of early 19th century Windsor chair.

Spinet

This was formerly a generic name in England for musical instruments with a small keyboard, having one string to a note that was plucked by a quill. Spinets were in use in England in the 16th century, but it was not until the latter part of the 17th century that the familiar wing-shaped form was introduced. (*See* illustration, *also* **Virginal**.)

Spinning Wheel

The hand wheel for spinning yarn was first known in Europe during the 16th century, and the spinning wheel with a treadle does not appear to have come into use until the late 17th century. These wheels, supported by stands with ornamental turning, were made in oak, beech, occasionally in yew, and, during the 18th century, in mahogany; for spinning was regarded as a polite as well as a practical accomplishment, and was practised alike by the farmer's wife and the squire's lady until the end of the long Georgian period. The spinning wheel was a light, compact, well designed piece of machinery.

Spindle back, rush-seated chair, with the front legs terminating in hoof feet. Mid-18th century.

Spiral Turning

A term for decorative turning in the form of a

A late 17th century spinet.

continuous ascending twist that began to be used on the legs and stretchers of chairs in the latter part of the 17th century, and was occasionally used in the following century for such members as the pillars of claw tables and for bed-posts. (*See* accompanying illustration, *also* page 125.)

Spittoon

A metal vessel for the convenience of those who smoke or chew tobacco and desire to spit. It was usually circular in form, and was sometimes encased by a wooden frame with a hinged lid, so that when closed it resembled a footstool. Spittoons were used in smoking-rooms during the 19th century, and probably much earlier in taverns; and the spit-box or spit-kid was used aboard ship to prevent seamen fouling the decks with tobacco juice. (*See* Marryat's *Peter Simple*, chapter xiv, where they are described as spitting-pans.) In the United States, the more refined name of cuspidor was adopted, derived from the Portuguese *cuspidore*, which presumably came from the Latin *conspuere*, to spit upon. This was not universally adopted in North America, for the term spittoon is also in common use, also the article itself in the Middle and Far West and South of the Union, where the habit of chewing tobacco persists.

Spiral turning on mid-18th century bed-post.

Splat or Splad

The central upright member occupying the back of a chair, between the seat and the top rail. (*See* illustration, *also* **Slat**.)

Splay

The outward spread of a member or a surface.

Splayed Foot

A foot with a slight outward curve. A French foot, *q.v.* is a form of splayed foot.

Split Baluster

A turned baluster split centrally, and applied ornamentally to a surface. Sometimes the split is not central, so that more than half the section of the baluster is used. This form of ornamental treatment for the surfaces of chests, cupboards, bed heads, chair backs, and chimneypieces was

Early 18th century rush-seated chair, with vase-shaped splat in the back.

used in the late 16th and during the first half of the 17th centuries. (*See* illustration of Derbyshire chair on page 227.)

445

Split Bobbin

Turned bobbins, split centrally and applied ornamentally to a surface. Used in the mid-17th century.

Split Handles

Drop handles of brass, cast hollow, with the visible surface of semicircular section, are known as split handles.

Split Turning

Turned work that is split either centrally or segmentally, and usually applied to a surface as a form of ornament. (*See* **Split Baluster** *and* **Split Bobbin.**)

Spoon Back

The bended back chair of the early 18th century is sometimes known by this fanciful name, which may have been suggested because the contour of the chair back when seen from the side resembles the curve of a spoon. (*See* **Bended Back Chair.**)

Sprig

A small, headless nail, used by glaziers in addition to putty, for fixing panes of glass to wooden frames.

Spring Revolving Chair, *see* Revolving Chair

Spring Spindles

A term sometimes used to describe the vertical spindles in the back of a Windsor chair when they are inclined outwards in a slight curve between the seat and the top rail or comb piece, *q.v.* (*See* **Fan Back,** *also* **Windsor Chair.**)

Spring Upholstery

Coiled springs, in mattresses, easy chairs, and other upholstered seats, came into general use during the middle years of the 19th century, though small springs may have been used in conjunction with stuffing in the previous century. The first patent for a coiled spring in a mattress and other upholstery was granted to Samuel Pratt, and signed and sealed on December 24th, 1828 (No. 5668). Pratt described himself as a Camp Equipage Maker, of New Bond Street in the Parish of St. George, Hanover Square, London. From the diagram attached to the patent, the springs do not appear to differ much from present-day springs. They were spiral, of iron or steel wire, twisted into circular or angular coils. The circular ones were shaped like an hour glass, the angular were triangular in form. These springs were attached to a foundation cloth of canvas or similar fabric, which was strengthened by whalebone or cane round the edges, and this strengthening material was also sewn diagonally across the foundation cloth, so that it crossed at junctions, and was firmly sewn in position. The springs were sewn firmly to the foundation cloth at spaced intervals, and then a similar cloth was fixed on top, the springs being sewn to this also.

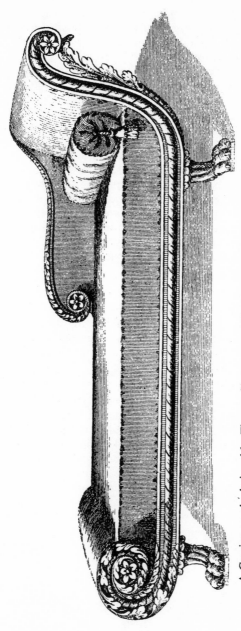

A Grecian squab,' designed by Thomas Sheraton, and illustrated on Plate 50 of *The Cabinet Dictionary* (1803).

The ends of the two cloths were then turned in to make a box containing the springs, and the top was padded externally. Only five years later, J. C. Loudon, in his *Encyclopaedia* (1833), refers to wire springs and illustrates a double cone spring, and his reference suggests that their use was well known, but that only recently had their possibilities been appreciated by upholsterers. He described the method of using them. 'These springs', he wrote, 'are placed, side by side, on interlaced webbing, strained to a frame of the intended size of the bed, cushion or seat; they are then all confined by cords to one height, and covered by a piece of ticken or strong canvass, strained tightly over them.' He concluded by saying: 'The effect of spiral springs as stuffing has been long known to men of science; but so little to upholsterers, that a patent for using them in stuffing was taken out, some years ago, as a new invention. Beds and seats of this description are now, however, made by upholsterers generally, and the springs may be had from Birmingham by the hundredweight.' Presumably Samuel Pratt's patent was that mentioned by Loudon as a 'new invention'. (*See* **Chamber Horse.**)

Spruce, *see* **Whitewood**

Spur Stretcher

A stretcher of bent wood, sometimes used to connect the front legs of Windsor chairs, and resembling the shape of a spur. (*See* illustrations of Windsor Chairs on centre of page 507.)

Squab

A small, independent cushion, used with wooden or cane-seated chairs. It is used either loosely on the seat or fastened by corner tapes, which are tied to the chair frame. It was introduced towards the end of the 17th century, but used almost exclusively on chairs with arms, and its use has survived to the present day. Sheraton calls a squab 'a kind of seat', and obviously regards the term as interchangeable with couch and sofa, for he brackets all three together under the entry for Grecian, in *The Cabinet Dictionary* (p. 247), and devotes one of the plates to 'a Grecian squab'. (*See* illustration on previous page.)

Stall

A fixed seat in a church, generally used by a priest or a member of a choir, with special and elaborate stalls for such dignitaries as bishops and deans. Stalls were usually made in series, and were architectural conceptions, carried out in wood and reflecting the characteristics, Gothic or Renaissance, of their period of architecture. (*See* illustrations on pages 450 and 451.)

Stamping

Steel punches in the form of circles, rosettes, and stars were used by carvers and joiners in the 16th and 17th centuries for stamping patterns on the surface of oak furniture, in conjunction with gouge work and sunk carving.

Stand

A generic term for a free standing frame which supports a chest or a cabinet, such as the heavily carved stands for lacquer cabinets in use during the late 17th and early 18th centuries, or the lighter independent stands which were used for candles. (*See* **Candle Stand.**) Sheraton, in *The Cabinet Dictionary* (1803), says that among cabinet makers the word stand 'is applied to different small pieces of furniture; as a music stand, bason stand, table stand, or small pillar and claw table stand, and a tray stand'.

Standard

The upright posts which support the frame of a toilet glass are called standards. (*See* **Toilet Glass.**) The term is also used for pew ends in churches.

Standard Chest

A mediaeval term for a large chest that was used for packing and storing goods. 'Standardes', as they are called in 15th-century inventories, were often bound with iron, fitted with one or more locks, and sometimes covered with leather.

Carved standard at Dorchester, Oxfordshire. (After J. H. Parker.)

Standing

The prefix generally used when describing a piece of furniture that is mounted upon a stand, such as a standing cupboard.

Standing Bedstead

A type of bedstead with a high panelled head and foot, connected above by a tester in the form of an open frame, across which a light tester cloth would probably be stretched. Such bedsteads were made during the 18th century, and probably originated much earlier. The term is contemporary.

Standish

A tray of silver or base metal, for inkstands, sand boxes, and pens, used upon a writing table. Originally, the term was confined to the inkstand, and as late as 1775 it was still defined by Bailey in the twenty-first edition of his *Universal Etymological*

Lower part of one of the wooden stalls in the chancel of Nantwich Church, Cheshire. 14th century. *See* view of chancel on opposite page. (From D. & S. Lysons' *Magna Britannia*, 1810.)

Choir stalls in the chancel of Nantwich Church, Cheshire. 14th century. *See* detail of stall on opposite page. (From D. & S. Lysons' *Magna Britannia*, Vol. ii, 1810.)

English Dictionary, as 'a standing Inkhorn Glass, etc., for a Table'.

State Bed

A term for a fully draped bedstead, with head and foot curtains and back cloth. State beds are of mediaeval origin. The term state bed or bed of state was current in the mid-17th century, and is used by Charles Cotton (1630–87) in his *Epigram de Mons. Maynard*, in the following lines:

> Anthony feigns him Sick of late,
> Only to show how he at home
> Lies in a Princely Bed of State,
> And in a nobly furnish'd Room . . .

In the great state beds of the late 17th and early 18th centuries no woodwork was visible; headboard and posts, tester and valance being covered with fabric, usually of the same rich damask used for the curtains. According to Sheraton's *Cabinet Dictionary* (1803) they were intended 'for the accommodation of princes and noblemen'.

State Chair

High-backed chairs with arms, covered with some rich fabric, are referred to in mediaeval records as chairs of astate, or state chairs. They were probably coffer maker's chairs, *q.v.*, and were made of wood and sometimes of iron. Parker quotes an inventory taken at Ewelme in 1466 as follows: 'A chaire of tymbre of astate, covered w^t blu cloth of gold, and 4 pomells of coper. . . .' Also: 'A chaire of astate of yren [iron], covered with purpell satyn. . . .' (*Some Account of Domestic Architecture in England*. Oxford: 1859. Part I, chapter iv, p. 115.)

Stays

Also called braces. The two spindles used in some types of Windsor chair which run from a projection at the back of the seat to the top rail, and form a V-shaped brace. Such chairs are sometimes known as brace back or fiddle brace back chairs. (*See* illustration of Comb Back chair at top right of page 507, and Wheel Back, page 503.)

Steamer chair with cane-work seat and slatted back. The Derby type had a canework back, but was otherwise identical.

Steamer Chair

A folding chair with six legs and a cane-work seat and back, or with four or five slightly curved upright slats in the back, usually furnished with a detachable leg rest, so that it may be used as a form of day bed. Such chairs were introduced during the mid-

A state bed in velvet, with ornaments of gold and silver, and plumed finials. Late 17th century. From Hardwick Hall, Derbyshire. (Illustrated in Shaw's *Specimens of Ancient Furniture*, from which this drawing is reproduced.)

453

19th century. Examples illustrated in Heal's catalogues (1858–60) are called Derby folding chairs. At some subsequent period the name steamer chair came into common use, for such chairs were often used on board ship for the comfort of passengers who wanted to sit on the upper decks.

Stepped curve.

Stepped Curve

A curve interrupted by a flat break or step, which continues for a short distance until the curve is resumed.

Steps

A term used by cabinet makers for the various forms of step ladder used in libraries. From the early 18th century, library steps were in use, usually of the folding type, and were occasionally elaborate contrivances, with shelves and adjustable writing tables, so that those who were using them could make notes without descending. (*See* **Library Stool.**)

Stick Back

The simplest type of Windsor chair back, consisting of three or four thin turned spindles, which are also known as rods or sticks, flanked by two stouter spindles, all socketed into the solid wooden seat and the top rail. (*See* illustration.) The term is also used for Windsor chair backs filled wholly by thin spindles, forming a bow or a double bow back. (*See* illustration of Double Bow Back chair on page 507.)

Stick back chair.

Stick Furniture

A term used broadly to describe chairs and stools which are made by socketing turned spindles into solid wooden seats, to form the legs and the chair backs. (*See* **Windsor Chair.**)

Stile

The vertical members in the frame of a door or the carcase of a receptacle such as a chest are called stiles. The relation of stiles and rails is shown by the sunk panel illustrated on page 460.

Stippled Background

In sunk carving of the type used on 16th and 17th century furniture, the background was often pricked with a pointed tool, and this peppering with tiny punctures created a stippled effect.

Stool

The oldest form of seat for one person, in use as early as the third to the fourth dynasties of ancient Egypt (2980–2476 B.C.),

Stove grate, from Plate CXCI of Chippendale's
Director, 3rd edition (1762).

and common to all subsequent civilisations. The various types of
stools are entered under their respective names, as follows:

Back Stool	Corridor Stool	Gouty Stool
Bidet	Cupboard Stool	Joint Stool
Box Stool	Dressing Stool	Library Stool
Buffet Stool	Faldstool	Music Stool
Camp Stool	Fender Stool	Ottoman Footstool
Close Stool	Footstool	Stool Table
Coffin Stool	French Stool	Tabouret

Stool Table

A term used to describe a large stool with a drawer fitted below
the seat: such hybrid types of stool were occasionally made in the
second half of the 17th century, but the term is not contemporary.
(*See also* **Box Stool** *and* **Cupboard Stool**.)

Stopped Channel Fluting

The name for fluting when the flutes are partially filled with
some convex ornamental device, such as bead and reel.

Stove Grate

A fire grate, complete with a cast iron fireback, which stands

455

independently upon the back hearth of the fireplace. The term is used by Thomas Chippendale in the 3rd edition of his *Director*. (*See* illustration on previous page.)

Straight Banding, *see* **Banding**

Straight Front

A term used for a flat-fronted chest, sideboard, or bureau, in contradistinction to a bow front, a broken front, or a serpentine front.

Strap and **Jewel Work**

A term sometimes used to describe a form of decoration on late 16th and 17th century furniture, consisting of turned balusters and bosses, split and applied to the stiles and rails of chests and cabinets.

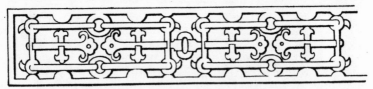

Late 16th century strapwork from a carved panel.

Strapwork

A form of decoration used on wood and plaster, consisting of flat interlacing bands, geometrically disposed upon a surface and carved or cast in low relief. It was popular during the late 16th and early 17th centuries.

Straw Chairs

Chairs made of woven straw were common in the 18th and early 19th centuries, and were probably in use much earlier, during mediaeval times, though the material was too perishable and the articles too commonplace for survival or record. Loudon described and illustrated a typical straw chair in his *Encyclopaedia* (1833), and stated that they were made of straw in the same way as beehives. (*See* illustration.) In the west of England such straw chairs were known as beehive chairs. John Donne's reference to a basket chair, *q.v.*, may have denoted one of these beehive straw chairs. In *Aubrey's Brief Lives* there is a description of Ben Jonson's 'studyeing chaire', which was made of straw and of a type used by old women.

A straw chair of the beehive type. (From Loudon's *Encyclopaedia*, 1833.)

Straw Marquetry

A method of decorating surfaces of wood or papier mâché by the application of tinted straw. It was introduced to England from

France in the late 18th century, and was used for the decoration of small caskets and boxes, and occasionally for the frames of looking glasses.

Stretcher or **Underbrace**

The horizontal rails which connect the legs of stools, chairs, and other seats, also tables and stands that support chests. Apart from the stabilising function of the stretcher, in the 16th and 17th centuries it provided a foot rest that was a pleasant alternative to a

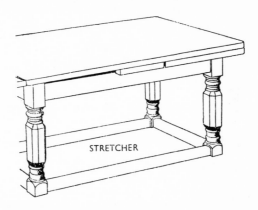

STRETCHER

possibly damp and dirty rush-strewn floor. During the second half of the 17th century, the stretcher became a decorative feature below chairs and tables; and although it survived throughout the 18th century, its use was discontinued by fashionable chair makers and cabinet makers towards the end of that century. (*See also* **Arched Stretcher**, **Rising Stretcher**, **Saltire**, **Serpentine**, **Spur** and **X-Shaped Stretcher**.)

Stretcher Mark

A thin, incised line, encircling the lower part of the turned leg of a Windsor chair, which marks the place where the stretcher should be inserted.

Stretching Rail

A term used by Chippendale for a stretcher, *q.v.* He uses it in describing one of his designs for breakfast tables. (*See* illustration on p. 152, *also* **Breakfast Table**.)

Striges

The channels of a fluted column or pilaster.

Strings

Very thin strips of coloured wood, square in section and used for inlaying. They are made up to $\frac{1}{8}$ in. square, and the smallest size is barely thicker than cartridge paper.

Struck Moulding

A moulding worked or struck directly upon solid members, such as the stiles or rails of panelling, as opposed to a planted moulding. The term stuck moulding is a corruption of the original term.

Stuart Period

A loose name for a long and varied period, extending from 1603 to 1688 and interrupted from 1649 to 1660, when England was a Puritan republic. The period thus named does not correspond with any specific style in furniture, for the period is subdivided into Jacobean (James I), Early Stuart (Charles I), Carolean (Charles II), Restoration, or alternatively, Late Stuart (Charles II and James II), with the further complication that Late Jacobean is sometimes used as a label for things made in the brief reign of James II.

Stucco, *see* **Composition**

Stuck Moulding, *see* **Struck Moulding**

Stud

A brass- or copper-headed nail, used for fastening leather or fabric to furniture. (*See also* **Nail Head.**) Also, a small, cylindrical piece of metal, with an enlarged head, which is used as a support for adjustable shelves in a bookcase.

Stuff-over

A term used when the framing of a chair or settee is almost completely covered by upholstery. It should not be confused with overstuffing, *q.v.*

Stump Bedstead

A bedstead supported on legs, without posts or tester, headboard or footboard.

Stump End Bedstead

A bedstead with a headboard but no footboard, the end of the bedstead being supported on legs.

Stump Foot

A turned foot which supports the underframe of a piece of furniture. (*See* illustrations on opposite page.) The leg of a piece of furniture that rests directly upon the floor, without any shaped foot or fitted castor, is sometimes described as having a stump foot.

Style

A term for any characteristic manner of designing and ornamenting furniture, arising from the taste of the designer and maker, or from some prevailing fashion related to the use of a particular kind of ornamentation or material. (*See* **Chippendale Style, Quaint Style, Regency Style, Sheraton Style,** *also* **Rococo.**)

Subsellum

A name sometimes used for a misericord.

Suite

The suite of furniture became fashionable during the 17th century, and gave to the salons of the nobility and gentry an air of decorative coherence. The suite consisted of chairs, stools, and couches, sometimes numbering as many as twenty-

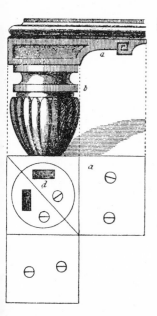

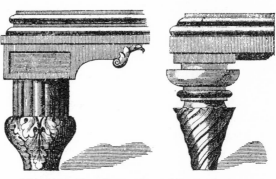

Three examples of stump feet, with a bracket foot above on the right. These are from Plate 23 of *The Cabinet Dictionary* (1803), where Sheraton shows seven designs for feet.

four chairs and stools, and two or four couches. Suites of upholstered chairs existed in Elizabeth's reign, but during the mid-17th and early 18th centuries they were used in the galleries and withdrawing rooms of the wealthy upper classes. Diminished modifications of the suite have persisted from the mid-18th century until the utility furniture period of the mid-20th.

Sunburst

A form of carved ornament, semicircular in outline, representing conventionalised sunrays. It is found on early and mid-18th century chests and tallboys and bureaux, and is characteristic of American colonial furniture of that period. The term itself is modern.

Sunburst.

Summer Bed

Twin fourposted single beds, separated by a narrow aisle, with the testers joined by a cornice which continues above the aisle. Originally designed by Sheraton, and illustrated in *The Cabinet Maker's and Upholsterer's Drawing Book*.

Sunk Carving

Carved decoration, executed by cutting away the ground from the pattern; a rather crude method of ornamenting surfaces, used during the 16th and 17th centuries.

Sunk Moulding

A moulding which covers a joint between two surfaces that are at different levels, but does not project beyond the most forward surface.

Sunk Panel

A panel with a surface set back from the level of the stiles and rails of the surrounding framework.

Sunk Top

A term sometimes used to describe tables with tops that are bordered by a raised rim or gallery.

Sunray Clock

A modern term used to describe a mural clock with the dial surrounded by a conventionalised representation of the sun's rays, carved and gilded.

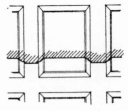

Sunk panel. (From Ware and Beatty's *Short Dictionary of Architecture*.)

Surbase

In architecture, the moulding on the upper part of a pedestal corresponding to a cornice: in cabinet work the moulded and often enriched portion of the upper part of a pedestal is sometimes known as a surbase.

Swag

A carved or painted representation of a festoon of flowers, fruit, foliage, or drapery. (*See* **Festoon**.)

Swag Drapery

A single or double draping of fabric, suspended across the top of a window instead of a pelmet or valance. It is attached to an ordinary pelmet board. Swag draperies are made by cutting a piece of material with a straight top edge, somewhat narrower than the bottom edge, which is shaped into a gentle curve. When the material is shaped, the two ends are gathered up and secured, and this gathering gives the drapery its characteristic scallop shell shape.

Swan-neck Pediment

A broken pediment formed by two S-shaped curves. Sometimes called a scrolled pediment. (*See* illustrations on opposite page.)

Two examples of the swan-neck pediment. *Left:* American colonial, mid-18th century. *Below:* from a design for a library bookcase on Plate XCII of Chippendale's *Director*, 3rd edition (1762).

Sweep

A term sometimes used in cabinet work for a gentle convex curve.

Sweep Front

A chest or sideboard with a slightly convex front, flatter and less pronounced than a bow front. Sometimes called a swept front. (*See* **Bow Front**.)

Sweet Chestnut (*Castanea sativa*)

Also called Spanish chestnut; native to Europe and the British Isles, and supplying a light brown wood, resembling oak in colour; occasionally used in panelling as a substitute for oak, and, more rarely, in cabinet work. John Evelyn, in *Sylva* (3rd edition, 1679), describes the sweet chestnut and states that 'The *Chestnut* is (next the *Oak*) one of the most sought after by the *Carpenter* and *Joyner*. . . .' After setting forth its various uses in building, he writes: 'This Timber also does well for *Columns, Tables, Chests, Chairs, Stools, Bedsteads* . . .' (chapter vii, pp. 45-6).

Swell Front, *see* Bow Front

461

Swept Front, *see* **Sweep Front**

Swing Glass, *see* **Cheval Glass**

Swing Leg

The leg attached to a swing bracket on a drop-leaf table.

Swords

The sliding supports of a draw-leaf or draw table.

Sycamore (*Acer pseudoplatanus*)

A tree native to Britain, supplying a hard, tough, white wood. It is used for turned work, and also for veneers in cabinet making, when it is stained in various colours. (*See* **Harewood**.) Dyed black, it is occasionally used as a substitute for ebony. In the United States the name sycamore is sometimes used for the American plane, *Platanus occidentalis*. (*See* **Buttonwood**.)

* T *

Tabby Weave, *see* **Plain Weave**

Tabernacle Frame

An ornamental frame surrounding a niche or recess, which came into fashionable use in the 18th century. Chippendale illustrates two tabernacle frames in the third edition of his *Director* (1762), describing them as 'proper for Staircases'. (*See* following page.) Such frames were examples of English rococo and resembled in their decorative treatment the frames of mid-18th century looking glasses and girandoles, *q.v.* The name is derived from tabernacle work (or shrine work); an architectural term denoting the elaborate tracery used on canopied niches in Gothic churches. Ince and Mayhew, in *The Universal System of Household Furniture* (1760), call them architectural frames.

Table

A flat slab, supported upon a frame consisting of legs and rails, pillars or trestles, variously shaped, and one of the basic articles of

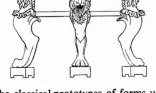

Two Roman tables which represent the classical prototypes of forms used in English furniture of the 18th century. *Left:* a table from a Pompeiian painting. *Right:* a circular table of white marble from Pompeii. (From Edward Trollope's *Illustrations of Ancient Art.*)

Circular table of the 9th century, with legs which suggest the cabriole form and which terminate in claw feet. (This drawing, copied from a 9th century MS., is included in *The Homes of Other Days,* by Thomas Wright.)

furniture in western civilisation. Tables have been known and used in Europe, certainly since the 5th and 6th centuries B.C., and

463

A tabernacle frame. From Chippendale's *Director* (3rd edition), Plate
CLXXXVIII.

earlier still in Assyria and Egypt, although in a rudimentary form.
In the Greek and Roman civilisations, tables of elegant design
were made in marble and bronze and wood. (*See* illustrations on
previous page, *also* on page 43.) From the Middle Ages until the
18th century the top of the table was regarded as being distinct
from the supporting structure, and the term table denoted the top
only, the legs and rails were called the frame, the complete article

often being described as a table with a frame. Derived from the Latin word *tabula*, a board, the word table occurs in England in the late 14th century, and is used by Chaucer in the Prologue to *The Canterbury Tales*, lines 99-100:

> Curteys he was, lowly and servisable,
> And carf biforn his fader at the table.

The laying of a table for dinner is described in 'The Shipmannes Tale', lines 1441-4:

> But hastily a messe was ther seyd,
> And spedily the tables were y-leyd,
> And to the dinner faste them hem spedde;
> And richely this monk the chapman fedde.

The wealth and hospitable character of the Franklin is suggested in the Prologue by a reference to the permanent or fixed side table, known as a table dormant, lines 353-4:

> His table dormant in his halle alway
> Stood redy covered al the longe day.

In *The House of Fame* Chaucer mentions 'a table sicamour' (line 1278). From such references it is clear that the word table was in general use in late mediaeval times, and was used concurrently with the old English word board, with its various descriptive prefixes, and this practice continued certainly as late as the 16th century. (*See* **Board**, *also* **Table Board**.) For example, in the will of William Tarbock, of Tarbock, made in 1557, the following bequests are recorded: '. . . the best bordclothe w'th vj napkins of the best for the table. . . .' Also '. . . all the meate bords and formes therunto. . . .' (*See Transactions of the Historic Society of Lancashire and Cheshire*, vol. xxxiv, Session 1881–92, 'Notes on the History of Huyton', p. 119.) In the inventory of the implements and household goods of Sir Henry Parkers (1551–60), there are references to 'Twoo square framed Tables, xxˢ' and, in the chapel, 'A yoyned [joined] table to sai masse on, xijᵈ.'

Trestle table, early 16th century.

Under the heading of 'utensyles for the chumber' there is an entry: 'A paier of playeng tables, vjᵈ.' (Quoted from *Society in the Elizabethan Age*, by Hubert Hall. London: Swan Sonnenschein & Co. 1901. Appendix I, pp. 149, 150, and 151.) The reference to 'playing tables' may refer to card tables, *q.v.*, or to the mediaeval game of tables, which appears to have been a form of backgammon and was played on a double board. This game is mentioned by Chaucer in 'The Frankeleyns Tale', line 900:

> They dauncen, and they plenen at ches and tables. . . .

Over two centuries later it was still being played, and Shakespeare refers to it in *Love's Labour's Lost*, Act V, Scene 2:

> This is the ape of form, monsieur the nice,
> That, when he plays at tables, chides the dice
> In honourable terms. . . .

The double board on which tables was played may have originated the hinged boards which were known as a pair of tables, *q.v.* Early in the 16th century, the word table also meant a painting framed for hanging on a wall, usually a painting on a panel; this particular meaning being derived most probably from the French word *tableau*. From the inventory of Henry VIII 'it would seem that the word "table" sometimes meant the frame of a picture and also that it was used for framed carvings or enamels or even needlework when hung up'. (See *In Shakespeare's Warwickshire and the Unknown Years*, by Oliver Baker: Simpkin Marshall, 1937, p. 156.) After the mid-16th century, tables developed a great variety of forms for specialised functions. But the term table dormant survived, and was in use during the 17th century. The first item of an inventory dated January 5th, 1638, is 'One planke Table with the Dormants, iijs. iiijd.'. (*Farm and Cottage Inventories of Mid-Essex*, 1635–1749. Essex Record Office Publications, No. 8, p. 79.) The various types of table are entered under their respective names, as follows:

Backgammon Table	Cricket Table
Basset Table	Deception Table
Bed Table	Double Gate Leg Table
Bedside Table	Draw Table
Billiard Table	Dresser
Birdcage	Dressing Table
Bookcase Table	Drop Leaf Table
Breakfast Table	Drum Table
Bureau Table	Eagle Table
Card Table	Extending Table
Carlton Table	Flap and Elbow Table
Chair Table	Flap Table
Chamber Table	Galleried Table
Chess Table	Games Table
China Table	Gate Leg Table
Claw Table	Grog Table
Coffee Table	Horseshoe Dining Table
Commerce Table	Horseshoe Table
Commode Table	Horseshoe Writing Table
Console Table	Imperial Dining Table
Credence Table	Kidney Table

Library Table
Loo Table
Manx Table
Marble Table
Mixing Table
Moulding Table
Nest of Tables
Night Table
Occasional Table
Ombre Table
Pair of Tables
Pedestal Table
Pembroke Table
Piecrust Table
Pier Table
Pouch Table
Range Table
Refectory Table
Rent Table
Rudd's Table

Screen Table
Settle Table
Sewing Machine Table
Sewing Table
Shaving Table
Shuffle Board
Side Table
Sideboard Table
Snap Table
Social Table
Sofa Table
Tea Table
Tiger Table
Toddy Table
Tray Top Table
Trestle Table
Trio Table
Tripod Table
Troumadam
Universal Dining Table

Table Bedstead

A piece of dual purpose furniture, in use during the late 18th and early 19th centuries, which served as a side table by day, a folding bedstead being accommodated in a cupboard. It was a smaller form of press bedstead, *q.v.* Two types are described in *The Prices of Cabinet Work* (1797), 3 ft. 6 ins. long by 3 ft. 6 ins. high, with 'top and front to lift up, supported by quadrants'.

Mahogany table clock, early 18th century.

Table Board

This term occurs in 16th century records, and may refer to boards placed on trestles to form a table. In the Darrell papers (1589) some itemised lists of money received and payments made in London include these entries: 'Received of his Worship, which he left on the Table-board ...' And under payments for furniture: 'His worship when he bought table-boards, £4'. (*Society in the Elizabethan Age*, by Hubert Hall. London: Swan Sonnenschein & Co., 1901. Appendix II, pp. 205 and 210.)

Table Chair or Table Chairewise, *see* Chair Table

Table Clock

The term table clock came into use during the 17th century, and refers to a spring-driven clock.

Table Cupboard

A contemporary term for a side table on which plate was displayed; the word cup-board being used in its original sense of a board for cups. (*See* **Cupboard.**) An inventory dated November 26th, 1638, of the goods of Henry Carr of Writtle in Essex, includes in the furnishing of the hall, 'one table Cuberd, 8s.'

(*Farm and Cottage Inventories of Mid-Essex*, 1635–1749. Essex Record Office Publications, No. 8, p. 77.)

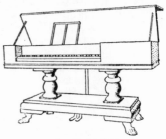

American table piano.
Period: 1830–50.

Table Dormant, *see* **Table**

Table Piano

A type of piano in a case made in the form of a heavy table, which became temporarily fashionable in the United States during the fourth and fifth decades of the 19th century. Apparently, table pianos were designed to conceal the fact that they

Table piano by Pape, shown at the Great Exhibition of 1851.
(From *The Art Journal Illustrated Catalogue*.)

were musical instruments: when closed they looked like clumsy and ill-proportioned tables. A form of table piano was shown at the Great Exhibition of 1851, more elaborate than the American type, and even more ungainly. (*See* illustrations on page 468.)

Tablet

· A small, flat surface, on which to write. In *The Cabinet Dictionary* (1803), Sheraton defines a tablet as 'a little table'.

Tablet Chair

An armchair of the Windsor type, with one flat, wide arm, which could be used as a writing tablet or desk. Such tablet chairs were occasionally produced by American makers in the late 18th and early 19th centuries.

Tabouret

A low, upholstered stool, introduced into England from France after the beginning of the 18th century.

Taffeta or **Taffety**

A plain woven fabric of delicate texture, usually silk, and used for cushion covers, curtains, and bedspreads.

Tallboy

Also known as a chest-on-chest or double chest, and in America as a highboy. A high chest with seven or more drawers, three or four in the lower part and three or four above, with a small pair of drawers immediately below the cornice. Introduced during the late 17th century, and made in various forms throughout the 18th and 19th centuries.

Tall Case Clock, *see* **Long Case Clock**

Talon-and-Ball Foot, *see* **Claw-and-Ball Foot**

Talon Moulding, *see* **Reverse Ogee**

Tambour

In cabinet making, this is the term for a flexible shutter or fall, which consists of thin strips of moulded wood, with the flat sides glued to linen or canvas, and the convex sides presenting a reeded surface. The ends of this flexible shutter run in guiding grooves. (*See* **Roll Top Desk.**) The tambour is used for desk tops and occasionally for doors; but only, as Sheraton says in *The Cabinet Dictionary*

Tallboy or double chest.
Mid-18th century.

(1803), 'when no great strength or security is requisite, as in night tables, and pot cupboards'. (A tambour front is shown on the Harlequin Table illustrated on page 283.)

Tantalus

A spirit case in the form of an open wooden framework with a lock, designed to accommodate two or three bottles.

Taper Leg

A leg of square section, sometimes called a thermed leg, gradually diminishing towards the foot, introduced in the second half of the 18th century for chairs, tables and sideboards. (*See also* **Marlboro' Leg.**)

Tapered Trunk

A term used to describe the trunk of a long case clock when it gradually diminishes in width from top to bottom. (*See* illustration.)

Tapestry

A generic term for richly woven fabrics used as wall coverings. (*See* **Arras** and **Gobelin.**) The name is also used to describe woven furnishing cloth, either all wool or partly wool, or woven with other and coarser yarns; or any furnishing fabric in which the colours of the design are wholly or partly to be found in the warp.

Tarsia, *see* **Intarsia**

Tassel

A group of cut cords or threads which are secured in a tight bunch at the top by means of a decorative band or by passing them through a pierced wooden ball, covered with the same material that is used for the threads.

Tavern Clock, *see* **Coaching Inn Clock**

Tea Board

A term used during the 18th century for a tea tray.

Tea Caddy

Originally the term caddy was applied only to porcelain jars imported from China and used as receptacles for tea. During the 18th century, caddies were made from a variety of materials, including metals and alloys, such as copper and silver, pewter and brass, also

Part of a clock case, showing the tapered trunk. From Plate CLXIII of Chippendale's *Director* (3rd edition).

tortoiseshell. When made wholly of metal, the tea caddy was sometimes called a tea canister. The ultimate form was a casket or box, usually of mahogany or rosewood, so the term tea caddy or tea chest came to mean a small chest which could be

Two tea chests. (From Chippendale's *Director* (3rd edition), Plate CLIX.)

locked, often lined with metal and fitted with special receptacles for tea and sugar. In his *Director* (1762), Chippendale describes various designs for these articles, as tea chests. (*See* illustrations.) Sheraton, in *The Cabinet Dictionary* (1803), states that the word caddy 'is now applied to various kinds of tea chests, of square, octagon, and circular shapes' (p. 120).

Tea Chest, *see* **Tea Caddy**

Tea Chest Top

A trade term, used in the late 18th century, for a hinged top with a rim on the underside. A tea chest top is specified for the gentleman's dressing stand described in *The Prices of Cabinet Work* (1797). *See* illustration on page 236.

Tea Kettle Stand

A low mahogany tripod stand, usually with a circular top, for holding the tea kettle and its spirit lamp. It stood under the tea table (*see* **Urn Stand**). It is often called, incorrectly, a coffee table.

Tea Table

A term used by mid-18th century cabinet makers for a table with a gallery round the top, usually of fretwork, to prevent tea cups from sliding off: sometimes called a china table. The first tea tables with rims were often japanned, and date from Queen Anne's reign. (*See also* **China Table**.)

Teak (*Tectona grandis*)

Supplied from Burma, India, Indo-China, Java, and Siam. A

Tea kettle stand from Plate LV of Chippendale's *Director* (3rd edition).

hard, durable wood, of a golden-brown colour, which darkens with age; used occasionally for table and counter tops, garden furniture, and frequently for chairs, chests, and fitted furniture on board ship. Its principal use is for joinery in building.

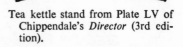

Teapoy

Derived from the Hindu word *tepai*, this name was given to a small pillar table supporting a tea chest or tea caddy, which was introduced during the mid-18th century. Its use continued into the Victorian period, and teapoys were decorative articles, made of various woods, and, in the 19th century, of papier mâché. The word is sometimes used for a large porcelain or

Early Victorian teapoy.

earthenware tea caddy, or the small type of bottle in which tea was actually kept, and which was one of the fitted receptacles in a tea chest or tea caddy.

Teaster, *see* **Tester**

Tenon

A projection cut at one end of a member to fit into a corresponding cavity called a mortise, in another member, in order to form a mortise and tenon joint.

Tent Bed

A bed with four posts which support a curved canopy, covered with fabric; it has deep valances and curtains, and no part of the wooden or iron framework is visible. It resembles a field bed, and is a much simplified version of some of Chippendale's published designs for field beds. In Horace Walpole's letter to Sir Horace Mann, dated July 27th, 1752, a tent bed is mentioned.

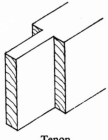

Tenon.

'Our beauties', he wrote, 'are travelling Paris-ward. . . . She [the Countess of Coventry] has taken a turn of vast fondness for her lord: Lord Downe met them at Calais, and offered her a tent-bed, for fear of bugs in the inns, "Oh!" said she, "I had rather be bit to death than lie one night from my dear Cov!" ' Boswell mentions 'a handsome tent-bed with green and white check curtains' which 'gave a snug yet genteel look to my room, and had a military air which amused my fancy and made me happy'. (*Boswell's London Journal*, 1762–1763. Heinemann, 1950, pp. 185, 189.) The tent bed is similar in form to Sheraton's design for a camp bed in *The Cabinet Dictionary* (1803).

It was so popular by the early 19th century that Loudon could say in his *Encyclopaedia* (1833): 'Tent beds are in universal use, and scarcely require description'. He illustrates and describes two models, one with a frame of wood, the other of iron. (*See* accompanying illustration, *also* pages 48 and 49.)

Tent bed, early 19th century.

Tent Stitch, *see* **Petit Point**

Term

A pedestal, gradually widening towards the top, and supporting a bust. In his *Director* (1762), Chippendale shows four designs for 'Terms for Bustos etc.'; Hepplewhite includes two in his *Guide* (1788). The name is abbreviated from terminal, or terminus, which in architecture means a trunk or pedestal that merges into a sculptured male or female figure, or a mythical creature, like a satyr. (*See* illustration on next page.)

473

Tern Foot

A foot that terminates in a triple scroll. It is of French origin, and is used occasionally in ornate examples of mid-18th century English furniture.

Tester

Sometimes spelt teaster. A flat canopy over a chair of state, a bed, or a pulpit. (*See* illustration below, *also* pages 46, 229, and 453.)

Tête-à-Tête Seat

A short sofa, or seat, with ends of different heights, with or without a back. It was a form of courting chair, *q.v.*, for two people to sit close together, but the name and the particular type of seat it described is of early 19th century origin. Two types are shown in George Smith's *Cabinet-Maker's and Upholsterer's Guide* (1826 and subsequent editions).

Therm or Thermed Foot

A tapered foot, of square section, sometimes called a spade foot. (*See* illustrations on opposite page.)

Therm or Thermed Leg, *see* Marlboro' Leg *and* Taper Leg

Therming or Thurming

The method used in the late 18th century for tapering or therming legs for chairs and tables. A lathe was used, with a drum on which the legs were placed and turned, one side at a time. This rather clumsy method was continued until mechanical saws came into general use.

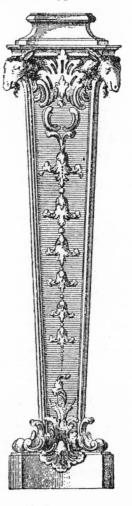

Right: Term for bustos. From Chippendale's *Director* (3rd edition), Plate CXLVIII.

Left: Bed with tester, mid-18th century.

474

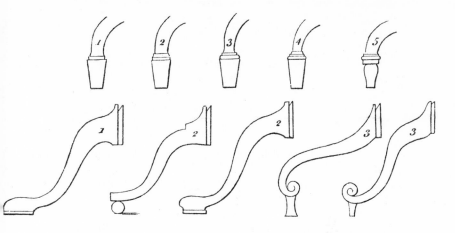

Ten designs for therms for claws. From *The Prices of Cabinet Work*, 1797 edition.

Thicknessing-up, *see* **Lining Up**

Three-Ply

Plywood consisting of three veneers cemented together, with the grain of the outer layers running in the opposite direction to that of the centre layer. (*See* **Plywood.**)

Throne

A chair of state, usually surmounted by a canopy or tester, for a monarch or prelate.

Thrown or **Throwne Chair**

A turned chair, from the old name for turning, which was throwing; a turner's lathe being called a throwe (Halliwell).

Thuya (*Tetraclinis articulata*)

Supplied from North Africa and Malta, thuya is known chiefly in the form of burrs, warm brown in colour, with spotted markings and a curly figure. Used for decorative veneers. (Thuya should not be confused with the botanical genus *Thuja*, to which the western red cedar and white cedar belong.)

Ticking or **Ticken**

A linen or very strong close-woven cotton cloth, used to cover mattresses and to make bed pillows. Ticking is usually woven with a white ground and dark blue or maroon stripes; those used for mattresses being either wide or narrow, while narrow stripes only are used for pillows. Ticking has been used, especially by modern American decorators, for upholstery or curtains in country houses; and for furnishing, variously coloured stripes are produced by

American manufacturers of the material. It is also used for awnings and tents.

Tigerwood, *see* **Zebrawood**

Tiger Table

A name sometimes used for tables with veneered tops of some decorative striped wood, such as zebrawood or tulip wood, the veneers being quartered and arranged in a pattern that resembles the markings of a tiger skin. The term was probably of late 19th century American origin.

Till

A 16th century name for a drawer where money is kept, in a cash desk or counter in a shop. From the till, with its locked and divided drawers, the cash register has been developed as a combination of a receptacle and recording machine. (*See also* **Drawer.**)

Tinder Box

Before the invention of friction matches, and their introduction and widespread use in the 'thirties and 'forties of the 19th century, the portable tinder box was as ubiquitous as the cigarette lighter

A brass tinder box with a candle socket on the lid: the inner lid and the steel and flint are also shown. Diameter: 4½ ins. Depth: 1¾ ins. (From *The Past in the Present*, by Dr Arthur Mitchell. Edinburgh: 1880.)

has since become. Usually made of iron or brass, it contained a flint and steel, and a supply of tinder, either a wad of charred linen or 'touchwood'. The flint was struck against the steel, and the resulting sparks ignited the tinder, which was then blown into a flame. (*See* illustration.)

Tip-top Table, *see* **Snap Table**

Toad Back Moulding

A term used by cabinet makers in the late 18th century. It occurs in *The Prices of Cabinet Work* (1797), and apparently refers to a type of moulding, used on chair legs, that consists of two shallow ogee mouldings separated by a bead, which vaguely resembles the contours of a toad's back: hence the fanciful name. (*See* illustration.)

Toddy Table

A name sometimes given to small, mid-18th century tables, on which a tray could stand, to hold the hot water, spirits, and sugar needed for making toddy, also the tumblers and the toddy ladle.

Toad back moulding, shown in section on two sides of a chair leg.

Toe

The lower end of the arm of a chair, where it joins the seat, is called a toe. Sheraton uses the term in *The Cabinet Dictionary* (1803), under the entry Arm, and recommends carved decoration for the toes of three of the designs on Plate 2 of that work.

Toilet Chair

A tub chair with a low semicircular upholstered back and a circular seat. The term was in use during the mid-19th century, and such chairs are illustrated in Heal's catalogues, 1858–60.

Toilet Glass

A free-standing looking glass, designed to set upon a dressing table or chest, swinging between two upright posts, or standards, supported upon a horse, like a miniature cheval or horse dressing glass; or with the uprights fixed into a box with one or more drawers in it. Introduced during the 18th century, they were called either toilet glasses or, if they had drawers, box toilet glasses. During the 19th century they were usually called dressing glasses. (*See* illustration.)

Toilet glass or dressing glass. (From Loudon's *Encyclopaedia*, 1833.)

Toilet Table

A table designed and fitted for the toilet. The term is used by Chippendale to describe dressing tables, either with drawers and a central kneehole recess, and a large adjustable looking glass above, or with drawers in the adjustable frame of the glass, the table being

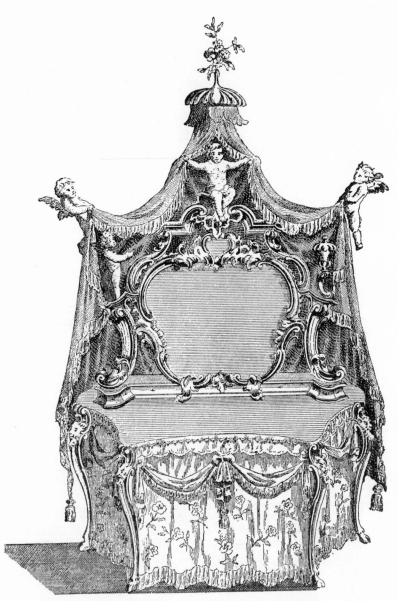

Toylet table. From Plate CXIX of Chippendale's *Director* (3rd edition), 1762.
Compare this with the 'toiletta' shown opposite.

Ladies' toiletta. From Plate XXXVI of Ince and Mayhew's *The Universal System of Household Furniture*. London: 1760.

supported on four legs, with elaborate draperies below the top. (*See* page 478.) The term, toilet table, was sometimes used as an alternative to dressing table, *q.v.*, and was occasionally called a toiletta. Ince and Mayhew illustrate a variation of Chippendale's draped design, but without an adjustable glass or any drawer accommodation, which they call a toiletta. (*See* illustration on previous page, *also* Section I, page 21.)

Toiletta, *see* **Toilet Table**

Tonbridge Ware

A form of marquetry consisting of a mosaic of various woods, the veneers used being cut from small rods of different coloured woods. It was made at Tonbridge in Kent, in the late 17th century, the taste for it being revived in the early 19th century.

Top Rail

The rail which connects the uprights at the top of a chair back.

Torchère, *see* **Candle Stand**

Tortoiseshell

The back plates of the hawksbill turtle supply the decorative material that is called tortoiseshell. These plates are flattened by heat and pressure, and formed into sheets, which are used for veneering and inlaying.

Torus

A large convex moulding.

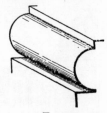

Torus.

Towel Horse or **Towel Rail**

A slender frame, supported upon two legs, usually with claw or trestle feet, having two or more horizontal rails upon which towels may be hung. Introduced during the mid-18th century.

Tracery

Pierced woodwork, resembling the ornamental stonework in the head of a Gothic window. It was imitated by the design of the glazing bars in the upper part of the doors of some of Chippendale's designs for Gothic bookcases, and was used extensively for the decoration of furniture during the Gothic revival in the first half of the 19th century, when the backs of chairs and hall seats were pierced with tracery. (*See* illustration under entry **Gothic Chippendale,** *also* **Blind Tracery** *and* **Foliated**.) Tracery is an architectural term which has been generally adopted since the late 17th century, when Sir Christopher Wren used it habitually in his reports. (*See* Parker's *Glossary of Architecture*.)

Trafalgar Chair

A name bestowed on various types of chairs made after 1805, when the Battle of Trafalgar had made the name particularly fashionable. A firm of upholsterers called Morgan and Saunders, whose address is recorded in Sheraton's *Cabinet Dictionary* (1803) as 16 and 17 Catherine Street, Strand, actually renamed their premises Trafalgar House. This habit of labelling articles of furniture was condemned by Richard Brown in *The Rudiments of Drawing, Cabinet and Upholstery Furniture* (1820), when he said: 'Many cabinet-makers for the sake of notoriety ridiculously give names to furniture, quite inconsistent, such as Trafalgar chairs, Waterloo feet, etc.' The Nelson's chairs, *q.v.*, designed by Sheraton, are sometimes called Trafalgar chairs.

Travelling Clock

Small travelling clocks in metal cases were occasionally made during the 18th century with a balance wheel movement. R. W. Symonds records that only a few examples are known, and mentions another type with a pendulum, which the traveller took with him and unpacked and set going upon his arrival at an inn. (*See Masterpieces of English Furniture and Clocks*, chapter vii, p. 136.) These clocks had a travelling box of wood with a hinged lid; the clock case being of plain lacquered brass. (*See also* **Coach Watch**.)

Tray

A large, flat plate of wood, metal, or papier mâché, rectangular, oval, or round in shape, with a raised edge or gallery, usually with handles. Trays came into general use with the habit of tea drinking during the late 17th century. In cabinet making, a tray is the term for a shallow, low-fronted sliding drawer, within the cupboards of a sideboard, used for cutlery. Sheraton, in *The Cabinet Dictionary* (1803), enumerates the following varieties: dinner; knife and butler's trays; also comb trays, the latter being used on dressing tables for ladies. (*See also* **Voider**.)

Tray Top Table

A small table with a gallery round the top. (*See* **Tea Table**.)

Treen and Treen Ware

A term now used for small utensils and articles of domestic use made from wood. Treen is derived apparently from the mediaeval use of the word *tre* or tree. Tree occurs in the fragments of *The Romaunt of the Rose*, which are continuations by other hands of Chaucer's translation; and is used to describe the shaft of an arrow, a carved figure, and a tower. An inventory of 1498, taken in the college at Bishop Auckland, includes 'x. old standis of tre'. (Quoted by J. H. Parker, in *Some Account of the Domestic Architecture of England*. Oxford: John Henry and James Parker, 1859. Part I, Chap. III, p. 70.) Tree has been used to describe things made of wood from the Middle Ages until the 17th century, and Spenser uses *treen* in *The Faerie Queene*:

> . . . The wanton loves of false Fidessa fayre,
> Bought with the blood of vanquisht Paynim bold;
> The wretched payre transformed to treen mould . . .
> (Book I, Canto VII, verse xxvi.)

In William Harrison's *Description of England* (1577–87) there is a reference which reads:

'The third thing they tell of, is the exchange of [vessell, as of] treene platters into pewter, and woodden spoones into siluer or tin. For so common were all sorts of treene stuffe in old time, that a man should hardlie find foure peeces of pewter (of which one was peradventure a salt) in a good farmers house. . . .' (New Shakspere Society edition, 1877, Part I, chapter xii, p. 240.) Whether 'treene stuffe' means wooden stuff is conjectural, for the word is used to describe platters in the same sentence as 'woodden' spoons are mentioned, and 'treene' here may refer to earthenware, which was known formerly as 'trenware'. Bailey lists trenware as an old word in his *Universal Etymological English Dictionary*, giving as its meaning 'earthen Vessels' and suggesting a derivation from the French word *terrine*. (From the 21st edition, 1775.) Halliwell spells it treenware, and gives the same meaning, but queries it. If treenware or trenware had been in common use during the 18th and early 19th centuries, to describe wooden utensils, neither Bailey nor Halliwell (whose work was separated by over one hundred and twenty-five years) would have failed to mention it, nor would William Cobbett in his *Cottage Economy* (1822), when he wrote: 'The plates, dishes, mugs, and things of that kind, should be of *pewter*, or even of wood. Anything is better than crockery-ware. Bottles to carry a-field should be of wood.' It seems doubtful if treenware was ever a contemporary term.

Trellis Work

A form of lattice work, *q.v.*, consisting of thin, wooden slats intersecting either at right angles or obliquely. The word trellis is sometimes used to describe the fretwork galleries on table tops, or the arrangement of horizontal and vertical or diagonal members in chair backs, particularly those made in the mid-18th century in the Chinese taste. (*See* illustrations of Chinese chairs, pages 102 to 107.)

Trencher

A wooden platter on which food was cut up. In mediaeval times, the word meant a slice of coarse bread, on which meat was cut and served and which became soaked with gravy. During the 18th century, flat earthenware plates were made which were called trencher plates. Wooden trenchers were replaced when dishes of pottery and porcelain came into general use.

Trendal

A mediaeval name for a circle of lights hanging before the rood in a church.

Trestle Foot

A broad base or foot, extending on either side of the end of a table leg to give it stability. (*See* illustration of Trestle Table on page 465.)

Trestle Table

The mediaeval table was usually a loose board, placed on folding supports called trestles, only the table dormant being supported upon a fixed frame. (*See* **Table**.) Early in the 16th century, permanent trestles were introduced, to act as a supporting frame at either end of the table, each resting upon a broad base or foot, and connected and stabilised by one or two stretchers. (*See* illustration on page 465.)

Trevit, *see* **Trivet**

Tri-ddarn or **Tri-darn**

A Welsh form of press cupboard, with a three-tiered superstructure above the cupboard for the display of pewter.

Trio Table

Described by Sheraton in *The Cabinet Dictionary* (1803) as 'a sort of small work table, made in three parts, to shut up into each other, and which may be used either jointly or separately'. (*See* **Nest of Tables**.)

Triple Domed

A cabinet or bureau bookcase with three domes forming the top.

Triple Open Twist, *see* **Open Twist**

Tripod Light

A form of candelabrum consisting of a standard, a tall pillar supported on a tripod, designed to hold three candles. (*See* illustration on next page.)

Tripod Table

A type of small table, usually of mahogany, introduced during the early 18th century, and better known as a pillar-and-claw or a claw table, *q.v.* It consisted of a round or square top, supported on a column or pillar, which rested upon three legs, either plain or terminating in eagles' claws. (*See* **Tea Kettle Stand**.)

Triptych

An altar piece consisting of three painted panels or leaves, joined by hinges. The term has been borrowed by cabinet makers to describe a type of looking glass flanked by hinged leaves, forming a triple, adjustable glass.

Tripod light. (From Plate 61 of *The Cabinet Dictionary*, by Thomas Sheraton, 1803.)

Trivet

A small stand, usually of brass or iron, with three legs, for use on a hearth, upon which a kettle or a teapot, or a bowl or dish, could be placed to keep warm. The term occurs frequently in 17th century inventories, and the alternative spelling trevet is generally used. Trivets were often elegantly designed during the 18th century, when they were in use in living rooms, and they continued in use throughout the 19th century.

Trophy

A group of weapons and armour, ornamentally disposed, and used as a subject for carved, painted, or inlaid decoration upon a surface. The term also includes the ornamental grouping of other objects, such as musical instruments.

Troumadam

A table with raised sides, specially made for a game resembling bagatelle, which was played with ivory balls. Troumadams occur in the Gillow records during the second half of the 18th century. (*See* illustration.)

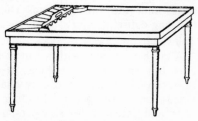

Truckle

A name sometimes given to a castor, *q.v.*, or small wheel.

Truckle Bed

In mediaeval times the terms truckle and trundle bed were interchangeable, and denoted a low bed, which could be wheeled below a

A troumadam, from a drawing in the Gillow records, dated August 4th, 1782.

bed of ordinary size, and used by servants who slept in the same room with their masters or mistresses. It was also used by children and page boys. The truckle bed was introduced as early as the 15th century, and it is mentioned by Shakespeare in *The Merry Wives of Windsor*, Act IV, Scene 5, when the host of the Garter Inn speaks of Falstaff's room: 'There's his chamber, his house, his castle, his standing-bed and truckle-bed; 'tis painted about with the story of the Prodigal, fresh and new'. Samuel Butler, in Part II of *Hudibras*, which was printed in 1664, includes this couplet:

> But first, with Knocking loud, and Bawling,
> He rouz'd the Squire, in Truckle lolling . . .

The old name trundle persisted in country districts, and occurs in 17th century inventories. Though long discarded in England, it is still current in North America. Such beds were in use until the early 19th century.

Trundle Bed, *see* **Truckle Bed**

Trunk

An early mediaeval name for a dug-out chest, which may have arisen because the arched lids of such chests were hewn from the solid trunk of a tree. It has become accepted as a name for a travelling coffer, and the arched lid form has survived; the rain fell off this lid when the trunk was strapped outside a vehicle. (*See* **Coffer.**) Also the name for the part of a long case clock between the dial and the base.

Truss

An alternative term for a bracket, corbel, or console.

Truss Leg

A leg in the form of a prolonged corbel or console. (*See* illustration of Chippendale Sideboard Table at top of page 429.)

Trussing Coffer

A mediaeval travelling chest: the word trussing is used in its old sense of packing. A list of deeds, made by Sir John Paston in 1471, states that the various items enumerated are 'In the square trussyng coffre'. (*The Paston Letters*, Vol. III, Item 679, p. 21.)

Tub Chair

A large easy chair with a concave back. The term was used by Sheraton and became popular after the mid-Victorian period. Sheraton describes a tub easy chair in *The Cabinet Dictionary* (1803), under the general heading of Arm-chair, as 'stuffed all over' and 'intended for sick persons, being both easy and warm; for the side wings coming quite forward keep out the cold air, which may be totally excluded from the person asleep, by laying some kind of covering over the whole chair' (p. 20). Sheraton illustrates a type of high-backed wing chair, with a seat almost semicircular in plan, and tapered legs on castors.

Tub Front

A form of block front, in which the front of a chest or bureau is vertically divided into three panels, the centre being concave and the flanking panels convex. This type of front is usually called a block front in the United States.

Tub Sofa

A small, early 19th century type of upholstered sofa with inward curving padded arms.

Tubular Furniture

Furniture with legs of tubular metal was designed as early as 1833 (*see* illustration on page 333), but the fashion for furniture made from manipulated metal tubing and fabric and plywood became popular towards the end of the nineteen-twenties. The first tubular steel chair of modern form was designed by Marcel

Breuer and made in 1925 at the Bauhaus Technical School at Dessau, in Germany. The term tubular furniture generally means furniture with a basic framework of drawn or extruded metal tubing, usually steel, and with a metal-plated or painted finish. (*See* **Metal Furniture**.)

Tudor Style

A term often loosely applied to any furniture made during the reign of the five Tudor monarchs. The design of furniture made in the early part of a period that lasted from 1485 to 1603, had distinct mediaeval affinities. Even before Elizabeth's reign, furniture was influenced by Italianate forms and ornamentation; by the end of the 16th century, foreign fashions had almost obliterated the native domestic style of England, both in furniture design and architecture. The Tudor style only covers the period between the accession of Henry VII in 1485 and the death of Mary Tudor in 1558.

Tulip Wood (*Dalbergia*)

Sometimes called after the country that supplies it, Brazilian tulip wood. A rose-coloured wood, paling sometimes to a pinkish hue, striped with yellow or grey. In the U.S.A. it is known also as pinkwood. It is used chiefly for bandings and inlaying.

Turkey Carpet

Carpets made in the hills of Anatolia, in Asia Minor, have for five centuries been imported into Europe under the name of Turkey carpets, and since the 14th century such imports have been considerable. The colours are usually pure and vivid; but are not greatly varied, shades of red and blue often predominating, the patterns being based upon geometric *motifs*, occasionally relieved with conventionalised floral devices.

Turkey Work

A name given to a knotting process, similar to that used in the making of Turkish pile carpets. During the late 16th and throughout the 17th centuries, carpets were made in this way in England. Panels of this 'Turkey work' were frequently used for covering the backs and seats of chairs in the late 17th century.

Turkish Corner, *see* Cosy Corner

'Turned All Over'

A term sometimes used to describe a turned chair, when every member of the frame is turned: legs, stretchers, seat rails, and all vertical and horizontal members of the back.

Turned Chair

Chairs with frames consisting entirely of turned posts and spindles were made in England from the earliest times. Some of the more elaborate forms made during the 16th and 17th centuries came from East Anglia. The early types often had three legs, with triangular seats, the apex of the triangle being socketed into the back leg, which continued above seat level as a vertical post from which spindles radiated to form the chair back, the front legs also rising above seat level as posts into which both seat and arms were socketed. The elaborate varieties, such as the example in the Fitzwilliam Museum at Cambridge, shown in the accompanying drawing, are erroneously called Henry VIII chairs. Wright, in *The Homes of Other Days*, describes and illustrates such a chair, stating that it was in the Ashmolean Museum at Oxford, 'where', he says, 'it is reported to have

Early type of turned chair with triangular seat. (From a drawing by A. B. Read.)

been the chair of Henry VIII', adding, frankly enough, 'on what authority I know not'.

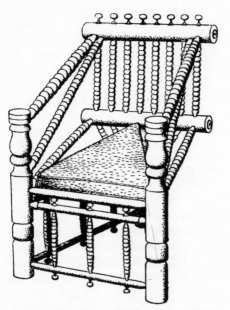

Turned chair of the type sometimes called Henry VIII. This example is of East Anglian origin, *circa* 1600. (In the Fitzwilliam Museum at Cambridge.)

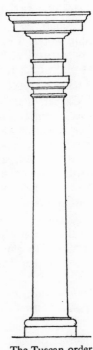

The Tuscan order of architecture.

Turnery and Turning

The craft of shaping wood by using cutting tools upon a rotating surface, the appliance for rotating or turning the wood being called a lathe. In England, legs, posts, balusters, and spindles for furniture were turned in the 16th century, and during the 17th century many refinements and ornamental forms were developed by English turners. (*See* **Barley Sugar Twist, Bobbin Turning,** *and* **Spiral Turning,** *also* **Bodger** *and* **Pole Lathe.**)

Tuscan Order

A Roman order of architecture, having some of the characteristics of the Doric order. (See opposite.)

Twiggen Chair

An early name for a basket chair, twiggen meaning made of twigs (Halliwell). Evelyn uses the word twiggie in *Sylva* (3rd edition, 1678) when discussing the various uses for oziers, including in his list cradles and chairs, and recommending oziers 'for all *Wicker*, and *Twiggie* works'. (Chapter xx, section 17, p. 86.)

Twist and Twisting, *see* **Spiral Turning**

* U *

Umbrella Stand

Introduced during the first half of the 19th century, and generally made of cast iron, with a tin draining pan for catching the drips from wet umbrellas. (*See* **Hall Stand.**)

Underbrace, *see* **Stretcher**

Undercut

A term applied to deeply carved ornamental woodwork and enrichment on mouldings, where parts of the carved ornament are separated from the ground or the moulded surface.

Underframing

The framework that supports a chair seat, a table top, or a cabinet, and which rests upon the legs of those articles. It may also apply to the whole supporting framework, as with a chair with an X-shaped underframe instead of legs. (*See* **Coffer Maker's Chair** *and* **X-shaped Chair.**)

Unit Furniture

A term that has come into use in the second quarter of this century to describe receptacles made in related units, so that wardrobes, chests, cupboards, bookcases, writing desks, and so forth, become available in standard sizes, and may be used as storage units in bedrooms and living rooms, and conveniently added to and rearranged.

Universal Dining Table

A small dining table, with taper legs, the top of which could be extended by pulling out leaves at each end. In the Gillow records, dated 1790, a universal dining table is described as having these dimensions: 5 ft. 2 ins. long when extended; 4 ft. wide; the length of the extending leaf being 14 ins. (E. & S. Book, No. 572.)

Universal Table, *see* **Pembroke Table**

Upholder

The 18th century form of the word upholsterer, which was still in use during the 19th century. In the list of Master Cabinet Makers, Upholsterers and Chair Makers included by Sheraton at the end of *The Cabinet Dictionary* (1803), both words are used, some firms being described as upholders, others as upholsterers.

Upholsterer

The craftsman who makes the padding and stuffing for seats of all kinds, also the cushions and coverings for chairs, settees and sofas, and draperies for beds and windows. Mattress makers are also included in the term upholsterer. It is derived from upholder, having passed through a transitional stage when it was known as upholdster. (*See* **Upholder.**)

490

Upholsterers' Chair

A term that is sometimes used for a chair with the back and seat wholly covered by fabric, so that neither the seat rail nor the frame of the back is exposed. Such chairs were made throughout the 17th century, and a contemporary term for them was imbrauderers' chairs. They were usually covered in leather or Turkey Work, *q.v.* They were made and sold by the dozen, and could be hired from upholsterers, when extra seating was needed in a dining-room. (An early type of upholsterers' chair is illustrated under the entry **Farthingale Chair**.)

Upholstery

A term which embraces the padding, stuffing, and covering of chairs and seats of all kinds. The practice of fixing padding to the seats of chairs was introduced during the 15th century, if not earlier. John Evelyn, in his *Sylva* (3rd edition, 1679), uses the word *upholsterer* in the sense that upholstery is now employed. (Chapter v, p. 39.) Upholstery was not seriously developed until after the Puritan period, when both the seats and backs of chairs were upholstered. The first patent for coiled spring upholstery was taken out in 1828. (*See* **Spring Upholstery**.) The term applies generally to all furniture and furnishings supplied by upholsterers.

Uprights

The vertical members of a chair back which are continuous with the legs.

Urn, *see* **Knife Box, Knife Urn,** *and* **Vase**

Urn Stand

A small table, on which the tea urn was placed. Introduced during the mid-18th century, these tables usually had a pull-out slide for the teapot. In *The Prices of Cabinet Work* (1797), three types of urn stand are described: square, oval, and serpentine, each with 'a slider for the tea-pot to stand on'.

Utility Furniture

During the second world war, the shortage of materials and labour made furniture rationing necessary in Britain, and on June 28th, 1942, the Board of Trade set up the Utility Furniture Advisory Committee, under the chairmanship of Sir Charles Tennyson. Furniture of simple design, which made the most economical use of materials and labour, became available to priority classes of purchasers after January 1st, 1943. A panel of designers was subsequently formed under the direction of Gordon Russell; and various types of utility furniture were made and put on the market during and after the war. Austere and well proportioned, utility furniture was unornamented, relying for its decorative effect upon the colour and character of the woods used in its construction.

* V *

Valance *or* **Vallance**

Any length of gathered or pleated material which is fixed horizontally to conceal some detail of framing or some empty or unsightly space. Pleated or gathered valances are hung from the cornices of testers on fourposted beds, to hide the attachment of the curtains to the rods; alike with windows, where valances may be used instead of pelmets, *q.v.*, to hide the top of the curtains. A valance may also be attached to a mattress on a bedstead, to conceal it when the bedspread is removed. In cabinet making, valance is an alternative term for apron or skirting piece, *q.v.* The term vallance or vallents often occurs in 17th century inventories in association with bed curtains; usually appearing as "curtains and vallance".

Varnish

A clear liquid, with an oil or spirit base, which dries and hardens after being applied to a surface, and retains its transparency. Spirit varnishes were employed by cabinet makers for polishing and good japanning, during and after the latter part of the 17th century, and their use is recorded in a contemporary technical book, by John Stalker and George Parker, published in 1688 and entitled *A Treatise of Japaning and Varnishing*. According to the authors, a shellac spirit varnish was used for polishing both the best and lower grade furniture, the differences being that to the former many coats of the varnish were applied, and after the application of each coat, the spirits of wine evaporated, leaving a thin film of shellac on the surface. When the surface had been bodied up by ten or twelve coats, it was then given a high polish with tripoli—a mineral substance which formerly came from North Africa. For the lower-grade furniture, a poorer quality of shellac was used, only two or three coats being applied, and it was not polished. For poorer quality japanning, and for varnishing pictures, oil varnish was used. Sheraton, in *The Cabinet Dictionary* (1803), pp. 324-8, gives directions for making various kinds of spirit varnishes and specifies the proportions for the various ingredients. (*See* **French Polish, Japanning, Lacquer, Polishing,** *and* **Vernis Martin.**)

Vase

A vessel used in the Greek and Roman civilisations for domestic purposes and in religious ceremonies, which has become a basic ornamental form in classical architecture. A vase usually rises from a narrow base, gradually increasing its diameter, so that it resembles in outline an inverted acorn: this form has an infinity of variations, and is occasionally reversed. The vase was used by turners in a slightly elongated form during the 17th century, and often with a bulbous base and a slender neck. Vase-shaped urns on pedestals and ornamental finials were used extensively by cabinet makers during and after the mid-18th century; and the urn was a device frequently employed in the architecture and furniture designed by the brothers Adam. (*See* illustrations on pages 354 and 426.)

Vase Baluster

A turned leg or baluster, based upon the form of a vase, used in furniture made during the late 16th and 17th centuries. Split vase balusters were applied ornamentally to the surfaces of cabinets or chests during that period.

Vase Splat

The broad splat in the back of some early 18th century chairs was shaped like a vase (*see* **Bended Back Chair**), and in the backs of some Windsor chairs an elongated vase splat was sometimes used. (*See* illustrations on pages 253 and 445.)

Vauxhall or Antique Bevel

The surface edge of a mirror or pane of glass when it is bevelled at an angle less than $7\frac{1}{2}°$, so as to give a very shallow and wide bevel and no clearly defined back edge. This is the definition approved by the British Standards Institution (B.S. 952; 1941). The term Vauxhall for this traditional type of bevel is probably derived from the glasshouse which was established at Vauxhall and worked under the direction of John Bowles in the second half of the 17th century.

Vauxhall Glass

A name sometimes given to the mirror glass with a pale blue tint, made in the 17th and 18th centuries at Vauxhall on the south bank of the Thames, where glassworks were established about 1670 by the Duke of Buckingham. Evelyn records a visit to Lambeth to see these works, where they made "looking-glasses far larger and better than any that come from Venice". (*Diary*, September 19th, 1676.) The works were closed in 1780.

Velvet

A rich silken textile, having a very close piled surface; its manufacture probably originated in the Far East. It was made in Italy, and was known in England as early as the 14th century. Chaucer mentions it in *The Romaunt of the Rose*, and describes its characteristic texture in this couplet, lines 1419–20:

> Sprang up the gras, as thikke y-set
> And softe as any velüet. . . .

It was used for vestments and robes and for hangings in the late Middle Ages. Although cushion covers might be made of velvet, it was rarely used on furniture, though some early 17th century chairs with X-shaped underframes had the complete framework, arms and back, covered with velvet and garnished with nails. (*See* **Coffer Maker's Chair**.) State beds were close covered with velvet during the 17th century, and it came into general use for upholstery after the Restoration.

Veneer

Wood cut into extremely thin sheets, or any thin sheets of material, such as ivory or tortoiseshell, applied to another surface, which is not necessarily of the same material. Up to the last half of the 19th century wood veneers were sawn: now they are knife cut.

Veneering

The highly skilled craft of applying thin sheets of wood or other decorative materials to a surface. Introduced to England from Holland in the second half of the 17th century, this new technique created and established the cabinet maker's craft, for its practice demanded the highest degree of skill. The commonly accepted notion that veneering is a rather shoddy way of covering up inferior material with a thin skin of some more expensive and showy substance dates from the 19th century, and is expressed by Dickens in *The Pickwick Papers*, chapter xiv, 'The Bagman's Story', when the old chair says to Tom Smart: 'Damme, you couldn't treat me with less respect if I was veneered'. In a later book, *Our Mutual Friend*, Dickens' description of Mr and Mrs Veneering makes them, and their name, sound particularly cheap and nasty. But veneering was and is a process which requires great skill and care.

Vernis Martin

A generic name for a particularly brilliant translucent lacquer, used for the decoration of furniture, which was perfected and patented by a family of French artist-craftsmen in the early 18th century. There were four brothers, children of Étienne Martin, a tailor: Guillaume, Simon Étienne, Julien, and Robert—the last named was born in 1706 and died in 1765—and they began as coach painters. By the middle of the 18th century they were directing at least three lacquer-producing factories in Paris, which were classed in 1748 as a 'manufacture nationale'.

Victorian Period

The term embraces the whole reign of Queen Victoria, and the period may be divided into three main sections, to which exact dates cannot be ascribed, though the following are broad indications of their duration:

> Early Victorian: 1837 to 1860–65
> Mid-Victorian: 1860–65 to 1880
> Late Victorian: 1880 to 1901

Some characteristics of the early part of the period were apparent in furniture during the late eighteen-twenties. In the two volumes on *Early Victorian England,* edited by G. M. Young (Oxford University Press, 1934), the first part of the period is given as 1830 to 1865.

Village Weave, *see* **Cottage Weave**

Vine Ornament

Carved representations of the leaves and tendrils of the vine have been used for the decoration of furniture since Greek and Roman times. The vine is an ancient ornamental *motif* and its use has been almost continuous in western civilisation. It was used in mediaeval carving, and was revived during the 18th century, when delicate, lightly carved vine leaves and bunches of grapes occasionally decorated the frieze rails of sideboards and side tables. Robert Adam made considerable use of this *motif.*

Violet Wood, *see* **Kingwood**

Virginal

An alternative name in England for a spinet, *q.v.,* so called because it was an instrument used chiefly by young girls.

Virginia Walnut (*Juglans nigra*)

Known as black virginia, it was used in the solid in England during the 18th century, sometimes for chairs and tables, and was often polished to imitate mahogany. It is a straight-grained wood, seldom finely figured. On p. 331 of *The Cabinet Dictionary* (1803) Sheraton says: 'The black Virginia was much in use for cabinet work about forty or fifty years since in England, but is now quite laid aside since the introduction of mahogany'.

Vitruvian scroll. (After J. H. Parker.)

Virginian Pencil Cedar, *see* **Pencil Cedar**

Vitruvian Scroll

The term for a decorative *motif* consisting of a band of undulating scrolls, which resembles a succession of waves. It is named after the Roman architect, Marcus Vitruvius Pollio. Originating as an ornamental form in classical architecture, its use was revived by architects during the 18th century, and it often appears as an enrichment, particularly on the frieze rails of tables.

Voider

A tray with two hand holes, and the edge of the rim and the bottom rounded. The term was current in the 18th and early 19th centuries.

Volute

The convoluted or spiral ornament placed at each side of the capital in the Ionic order of architecture. (*See* illustration, *also* **Angular Capital** *and* **Scroll**.) Small volutes also appear at each angle of the capitals in the Corinthian and Composite orders, *q.v.*

Ionic volute. (Detail from Plate 34 of *The Cabinet Dictionary*, by Thomas Sheraton, 1803.)

* W *

Wainscot

This term, of Dutch origin, which describes oak quarter cut (*see* **Wainscot Oak**), has become a generic term for wood panelling on the walls of rooms. It was employed in this sense in the late 17th century by John Evelyn, who in describing the uses of cork, *q.v.*, in houses in Spain, said: '. . . sometimes they line, or *Wainscot* the Walls, and inside of their Houses built of Stone, with this *Bark* . . .' (*Sylva*, 3rd edition, 1679, chapter xxv, p. 127). Deal panelling was also called wainscot. It is sometimes used to describe the dado, or lower part of wall panelling, and Sheraton, in *The Cabinet Dictionary* (1803), specifically defines it as 'The wooden work which lines the walls of a room as high up as the surbase'. (*See* **Surbase**.) During the latter part of the 16th, and throughout the 17th and 18th centuries, the term wainscot was often used to describe any article of furniture of solid wooden construction, especially in country districts. Thomas Wright quotes an inventory of the goods of Margaret Cottom of Gateshead, dated 1564, which included in the furnishing of the parlour 'one inner bed of wainscot' and 'a presser of wainscot'. (*The Homes of Other Days*, chapter xxv, p. 479.) The material, wainscot, is specifically named in those references, and follows the name of the article; in the 17th century this order was reversed. For example, an inventory of the goods of John Chalke of Writtle, Essex, dated July 21st, 1681, includes in the furniture of the hall, 'two wainscott formes'. In another inventory, dated July 7th, 1729, of the goods of Margaret Haward of Writtle, a 'pair of wainscot drawers' are valued at £1 : 1s. (*Farm and Cottage Inventories of Mid-Essex*, 1635–1749. Essex Record Office Publications, No. 8, pp. 164 and 264.) Other examples are quoted in the next two entries.

Wainscot Bedstead

A contemporary term used in the 17th century, and earlier, to describe bedsteads with solid panels at the head, or at both head and foot. (*See* previous entry.) The standing bedstead, *q.v.*, might qualify for this description. An alternative contemporary term was boarded bedstead, and both appear in 17th century inventories. 'One borded Bed with furniture belonging to same', is included in an inventory dated September 24th, 1638; and a 'wainscott bedsteadle' is mentioned three times in one dated July 21st, 1681. (*Farm and Cottage Inventories of Mid-Essex*, 1635–1749. Essex Record Office Publications, No. 8, pp. 75 and 164.)

Wainscot Chair

This is probably the contemporary name for the panel back chair, *q.v.*, though it may well refer to any solidly constructed chair of oak. (*See* **Wainscot**.) An inventory dated April 8th, 1663, includes 'one Wainsscott Chair'. (*Farm and Cottage Inventories of Mid-Essex*, 1633–1749. Essex Record Office Publications, No. 8, p. 95.)

Wainscot Oak

The two planks cut from the centre of an oak log supply the wainscot boards, and this term is usually applied to figured oak that is cut in this way.

Wall Clock

A clock designed to hang on a wall, because it was a weight-driven clock and the weights hung below: sometimes called a hanging clock. The lantern clock and the coaching inn clock, *q.v.*, of the mid-18th century, are popular types of wall clocks.

Wall Furniture

A modern term for built-in, fitted furniture; also a general descriptive term for all the varied articles of furniture that stand against a wall: cabinets, chests, sideboards, and so forth.

Wall Light, *see* **Sconce**

Wall Mirror, *see* **Chimney Glass** *and* **Pier Glass**

Walnut

This richly marked, golden-brown wood began to be used for furniture making during the second half of the 17th century, and continued in use during the 18th century, until it was superseded by mahogany. (*See* **American Black Walnut, English Walnut, French Walnut, Italian Walnut,** *and* **Virginia Walnut**.)

Wanded Chair, *see* **Basket Chair**

Wardian Case

A dome-topped glass case, under which ferns and other plants may be grown indoors. The Wardian case was used in conjunction with a stand, usually in the form of a table supported by a pillar resting upon claws or a solid base, which contained a large pot for the plants. Introduced during the mid-19th century, it was a popular item in Victorian furnishing, and was named after Nathaniel Bagshaw Ward (1791–1868), who in 1829 accidentally discovered the principle that led to this method of growing and transporting plants in glass cases. *See* Geoffrey Taylor's *Some Nineteenth Century Gardeners*. (Skeffington, 1951, chapt. ii, p. 60.)

Wardrobe

The word is used by Chaucer to describe a privy, and occurs in *The Canterbury Tales*, in line 1762 of 'The Prioresse's Tale'. In *A Dictionary of Archaic and Provincial Words*, James Halliwell gives it as wardrope, a house of office, and records that in Yorkshire it means a dressing room. In the late Middle Ages, the wardrobe was a special room or closet wherein clothes were hung in lockers and presses, or stored in chests. The term is used in Hepplewhite's *Guide* (1788) to describe the free-standing fitted cupboard for clothes; though during the 18th century it was usually known as a clothes press. Various types of clothes presses are described and costed in detail in *The Prices of Cabinet Work* (1797). (*See* **Clothes Press.**)

Wardrobe Trunk

A trunk large enough to take a number of coats or dresses on hangers, the hangers depending from an extending arm, so that the garments may be compressed without excessive folding, when the trunk is closed. Various drawers for other garments are included. A patent for a wardrobe trunk for travellers was taken out by Samuel Pratt on May 11th, 1815 (No. 3914). This was apparently the forerunner of the modern cabin trunk.

Warming Pan

A shallow, circular metal box with a lid, fitted with a long wooden handle. Hot cinders were put in the box, which was then put into a bed or moved about in it to warm the sheets. The pan was of brass, copper, or, more rarely, silver. Pepys records (*Diary*, January 1st, 1668–69): 'Presented from Captain Beckford with a noble silver warming pan'. Sometimes the lid was perforated with minute holes, arranged in a pattern. The warming pan was in use during the second half of the 16th century, and probably earlier. (*See* reference under **Bed Wagon** on page 136.)

Wash Hand Stand

An early 19th century elaboration of the basin stand, *q.v.*, designed to accommodate the large wash basins that were introduced at that time. It consisted of a table, often with a marble top, having a circular hole in which the basin rested, with two or three drawers immediately below the top of the frieze rail. (*See* illustration.) The mid-Victorian form consisted of a marble slab top, unpierced, with

Wash hand stand in mahogany with marble top. (From Loudon's *Encyclopaedia*, 1833.)

a marble splashback and sides, and a supporting framework of mahogany. Such wash hand stands were included as part of a bedroom suite and were made to match the dressing table and wardrobe. A form of wash hand stand, specially designed for offices, with a wooden cover which concealed the basin and jug and a cupboard below for a slop pail, was introduced during the 19th century, and was a much simplified version of the late 18th century wash hand table, *q.v.*

499

Wash Hand Table

A convenient but complicated piece of furniture, made in the latter part of the 18th century, and outwardly resembling a small chest of drawers when not in use. It contained a wash hand basin, a supply of water in a tank, a tap for filling the basin, and a

Wash hand table, with cylinder fall. (From *The Prices of Cabinet Work*, 1797 edition.)

shaving glass. The design shown in the accompanying illustration is described in *The Prices of Cabinet Work* (1797 edition) as 'two feet long, one foot ten inches wide, three real drawers and two sham ditto in front, cock beaded, a water drawer at one end behind the front drawer. . . .' The shaving glass slid down, the hinged flaps of the top folded over, and there was a cylinder fall in front to conceal the basin.

Wash Stand, *see* Basin Stand

Washing Stand

An alternative name for a corner washing or basin stand.

Water Gilding

Defined by Sheraton in *The Cabinet Dictionary* (1803), as that form of gilding 'generally termed burnished gold, and is only proper for internal works, and even in this situation requires much care to keep it from injury'. (*See* **Gilding.**)

Waterloo Leg, *see* **Sabre Leg**

Wave Moulding

An undulating moulding, consisting of a reeded band which resembles a series of waves. Used occasionally in cabinet work as an applied moulding in ebony, ivory, or some decorative wood.

Wave Scroll, *see* **Vitruvian Scroll**

Wax Polishing

A method of polishing the surface of wood by rubbing it with hard beeswax. This method of polishing was generally used on furniture made in the countryside before and throughout the 19th century, and is still employed. In *The Practical Cabinet Maker* (1826), P. and M. A. Nicholson state that 'This kind of polish is used in various stained articles, as also for chairs and bedsteads'.

Weathered Oak

The term was invented by Heal and Son Limited, a London firm of furniture makers, either during or just after the first world war, to describe the effect of a process for treating the surface of oak, which they had perfected. In this process, lime is used, among various other substances, to give an appearance similar to that of oak that has never been stained and has been allowed to weather and thus to acquire a natural patina. Weathered oak is finished with a wax polish and kept in condition with polishing cream. The term has since been adopted by various makers to include such a variety of finishes and shades that an exact definition of its meaning is now impossible. (*See also* **Limed Oak.**)

Web Foot

A modern term applied to the claw-and-ball foot when the claws are webbed. The fashionable London chair makers never made a webbed claw foot, such feet being peculiar to Irish and North Country furniture. (*See* **Claw-and-Ball Foot.**)

Webbing

Narrow bands of hemp, jute, or some other strong material, used in upholstery. These bands are interlaced, secured to the underside of the frame of a chair seat, and form a base for the support of springs or stuffing.

Welsh Dresser

A modern term, applied to free-standing dressers with cupboards in the lower part instead of a pot board, and shallow drawers above the cupboards, with open shelves in the upper part. Some dressers of this type can be regionally identified (*see* illustration of a dresser from Snowdonia); but the characteristics are too general for the term to be accurate, and are found in dressers made in Lancashire and the North Country. (*See* illustrations under **Dresser.**)

Western Hemlock (*Tsuga heterophylla*)

Supplied from British Columbia, Alaska, and the western U.S.A., it is also grown in the British Isles, and provides a straight-grained, light yellowish wood, deepening to warm brown. Used for the backs and bottoms of drawers and cabinets, and for furniture that is to be painted or enamelled.

Western Red Cedar (*Thuja plicata*)

Supplied from British Columbia and the U.S.A. Reddish brown in colour, this wood is occasionally used for cabinet making and panelling.

Welsh dresser from Snowdonia, early 18th century.

Whatnot

Tiers of three or more open shelves, held by corner posts or supported by two upright members which rest on feet or a solid base, and used for papers, books, ornaments, or whatnot. The fact that there is no specific use for this article may have been responsible

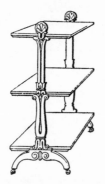

Two types of whatnot. (From *Designs of Furniture*, an undated trade catalogue issued by William Smee & Sons at some time between 1830 and 1840.) The design on the left is structurally identical with the running sideboard (*see* page 402).

502

for its inelegant name: its French equivalent was called an *étagère*, *q.v.* Whatnots are described and illustrated as early as 1790 in the Gillow records. A whatnot is shown consisting of four tiers, with slender corner posts: an elegant design compared with its Victorian descendant. (E. & S. Book, No. 579.) The whatnot became popular just before or during the early Victorian period. There is no reference to it in Loudon's *Encyclopaedia* (1833), but examples are shown in trade catalogues issued between 1830 and 1840. Victorian whatnots were sometimes triangular in plan, so they could stand in the corner of a room. (*See* **Omnium.**)

Whatnot Pedestal

A low cupboard, square in plan, with a shelf above supported by four turned columns: a late Victorian form of bedside or pot cupboard.

Wheatsheaf Back

A modern term for a type of chair back, made in the mid-18th century, with a waisted, pierced splat, which resembles the shape of a wheatsheaf.

Wheatsheaf chair back. (*See* illustration on page 62.)

Wheel back Windsor chair, with V-shaped brace.

Wheel Back Chair

Chairs made in the latter part of the 18th century occasionally had circular backs in the form of a wheel, the spokes radiating from a small central boss or plaque, and taking the place of splats or rails; a type of back used by Hepplewhite and his contemporaries. The term also applies to a Windsor chair with a wheel device pierced in the back splat.

White Wycombe

A term used for a Wycombe or Windsor chair, *q.v.*, 'in the white', unstained and unpolished. When all the work on these chairs used to be done in the Buckinghamshire beech woods around High Wycombe, by local craftsmen using pole-lathes and adzes, sales were made by stacking the 'White Wycombes' on farm wagons, and journeying through the Midlands and elsewhere, selling them from door to door.

Whitewood (*Picea abies*)

Supplied from northern and central Europe, and also grown in the British Isles, when it is called spruce. It varies in colour from white to pale yellow. Although used for joinery, it is seldom used for furniture of any kind. It should not be confused with the hardwood called American whitewood or canary wood, *q.v.*

Whiche or **Witche**, *see* **Ark**

Whorl Foot

Sometimes called a French scroll foot, and used when the leg of a piece of furniture terminates in an upturned scroll. This type of foot was used by mid-18th century cabinet makers and chair makers. (*See* illustration.)

Wicker Chair

A contemporary name for a basket chair, which occurs in 17th-century inventories. (*See* **Basket Chair.**)

Wickerwork, *see* **Basket Chair**

Wig Block

A shaped piece of wood on which a wig could be fitted when not in use.

Wig Glass

An 18th century looking glass designed to enable the back of the wig to be seen by the wearer.

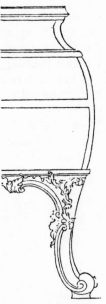

Part of French commode table, showing whorl foot. (From Plate LXIV of Chippendale's *Director*, 3rd edition, 1762.)

Wig Stand or **Wig Table**

A name sometimes given to a light tripod stand of mahogany which supports a small basin and is fitted with drawers. Sometimes called a powder table or powdering stand: these names are conjectural; the article is probably a wash stand. The top held a basin, and the ewer stood on the hollow platform below. (*See* opposite page.) A wig stand was the name for a small, turned baluster with a rounded top, smaller than a wig block, upon which a wig could rest when not in use.

William and Mary Style

A name used for furniture made during the transitional period of design, at the end of the 17th and the beginning of the 18th centuries, which roughly coincides with the reign of William III

(1689–1702). The style was influenced by the work of foreign craftsmen, Huguenot and Dutch. Men like Gerreit Jensen, a Dutchman who had supplied furniture to Charles II, settled in England. (Jensen changed his name to Gerard Johnson: *see* Section IV, page 523.) Such men worked throughout the period, and English furniture makers assimilated their ideas. Curved lines were increasingly used in furniture at this time, while formal dignity of shape was preserved. (*See also* **Queen Anne Style.**)

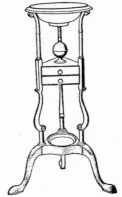

So-called wig stand or powder table: second half of 18th century.

Wilton Carpets

Pile carpets named after the town of Wilton, near Salisbury in Wiltshire, England, where they have been made since the early 18th century. A charter to weavers in Wilton and Axminster was granted by William III in 1701, though the industry was not established at the latter place until 1755, and by the end of the 18th century the Axminster industry, *q.v.*, had removed to Wilton.

Window Seat or Window Stool

A small, independent, upholstered seat with two ends, designed to fit into a deep window recess. Such seats were made during and after the mid-18th century. Ince and Mayhew called them French stools, *q.v.*

Windsor Bench

A long bench with four, six, or eight turned legs, and the back formed by upright spindles socketed into the seat and the top rail. It was an elongated form of the Windsor chair. Windsor benches were made in the late 18th and early 19th centuries in the United States, and far more rarely in England.

Windsor Chair

Windsor has now become a generic name for chairs and seats made in what is technically known as stick construction. (*See* **Stick Furniture.**) The name Windsor has been traced back to 1728, which disposes of the picturesque story that George III discovered chairs of this type in a cottage near Windsor when sheltering from the rain, and found them so comfortable that he ordered some to be made for himself, and that thereafter they were called Windsor in his honour. In the first of two articles on 'The Windsor Chair', R. W. Symonds quotes a sale catalogue of the furniture of Thomas Coke, sold on February 12th, 1728, in the Great Piazza, Covent

Garden, and Lot 41 included: 'Two cane Chairs, a matted Chair, a Windsor Chair, and a Table . . . 5s.' (*Apollo*, Vol. XXII, No. 128, August 1935, p. 69.) It is not known when or where Windsor chairs were first made; but the use of turned legs and spindles for chair making had created characteristic chair forms during the 16th century (*see* **Turned Chair**), and various elementary types of Windsor chair probably developed throughout the latter part of the 17th century. Early in the 18th century, bodgers, *q.v.*, were at work in the Buckinghamshire beech woods, turning the legs and spindles, which were assembled in and around the market town of Chepping Wycombe, now called High Wycombe, which became and remains the centre of a great chair-making industry. (*See* **White Wycombes**.) The manufacture of Windsor chairs spread to other parts of the country, and regional variations appeared, though the basic form remained. It consisted of a solid shaped wooden seat, into which the legs and vertical members of the back were socketed. It seems likely that the English Windsor chair was exported to the American colonies during the opening decades of the 18th century, and was soon copied by American chair makers, who gradually established their own traditions of design, un-influenced by contemporary English developments. The two main types of design in Windsor chairs are: the comb back and the hoop back. In the former, the top rail which surmounts the spindles of the back is shaped like a comb; in the latter, the back is shaped like a bow, into which the spindles are socketed. (*See* illustrations on page 507.) Throughout the 18th century the work of the fashion-able chair makers was reflected in the form of Windsor chairs, and various refinements of shape and decoration were introduced, such as cabriole legs and the double bow back. For the bentwood members of a Windsor chair, ash, elm, fruit-wood, or, more rarely, yew, were used, and beech for the legs and spindles. The seat was usually of elm. Occasionally, yew was used for all the members, including the seat. The simplest types of Windsor chair are classi-fied by the form of the back, and include: stick back, lath back, spindle-and-baluster, and Roman spindle. These are simple comb back types made during the 19th century, and are described and illustrated under those four names. Various terms have become current to describe some peculiarity of construction or decoration, such as brace back (*see* **Stays**) and wheel back, *q.v.*, and some regional types have been identified, and even traced to a special maker, such as the Mendlesham or Dan Day chair, *q.v.* But, with the exception of the last named and the smoker's bow, *q.v.*, all these variations fall into one or other of the two main categories of design: comb back or hoop back. (*See also* **Sack Back** *and* **Saddle Back**.)

Windsor Cricket, *see* **Cricket**

Above: Comb back Windsor chairs. *Left:* The back is bowed, with a plain baluster splat, and all four legs are of the cabriole type. *Right:* The front legs only are cabriole, there is a pierced baluster splat, and two stays forming a V-shaped brace for the back. (Mid-18th to early 19th century.)

Three hoop back Windsor chairs. *Left:* A plain double bow back, with plain turned legs and spur stretcher. *Centre:* A double bow back, with pierced baluster splat, cabriole legs in front, and a spur stretcher. *Right:* Simple type, with pierced baluster splat and turned legs. (Mid-18th and 19th centuries.)

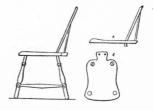

The shape and construction of the early 19th century Windsor chair. (From Figs. 643 and 644 of Loudon's *Encyclopaedia*, 1833.) Compare with illustration of wheel back Windsor on page 503.

Windsor Rocker

The name used in America for the Windsor type of chair on rockers. (*See* **Rocking Chair.**)

Windsor Table

A term used in America for a type of table, usually with a round top, supported by three or four turned legs, inclined outwards, with an underframe formed by one or two tiers of stretchers. Such tables were used chiefly in taverns during the late 18th and early 19th centuries.

Wine Cooler, *see* **Cellaret, Garde du Vin,** *and* **Sarcophagus**

Wine Table, *see* **Social Table**

Wing Bookcase

A large bookcase with a projecting central section, designed to give extra depth for accommodating big volumes, flanked by smaller sections or wings. (*See* illustration on page 311.)

Wing easy chair: mid-18th century.

Wing Chair

A type of upholstered easy chair introduced during the latter part of the 17th century, with a high back, flanked by wings or lugs, to give protection from draughts. Such chairs were described throughout the 18th century as easy chairs, though Hepplewhite uses the name saddle check, *q.v.* The term grandfather chair, *q.v.*, dates from the late Victorian period.

Wing Clothes Press

A contemporary term for a wing wardrobe (*see* next entry).

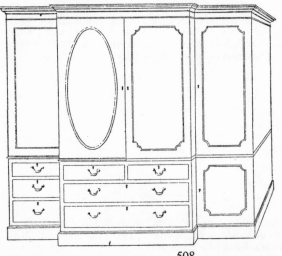

Wing clothes press, showing alternative treatments for cupboard doors. (From *The Prices of Cabinet Work,* 1797 edition.)

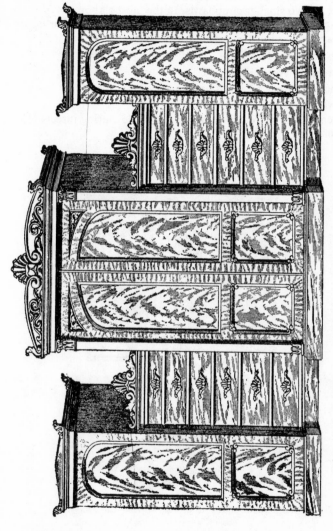

Wing wardrobe. (From a design first published in 1826 and included in George Smith's *Cabinet-Maker's and Upholsterer's Guide.*)

Wing or Winged Wardrobe

A large wardrobe, introduced during the latter half of the 18th century, consisting of three sections; a central hanging cupboard, flanked by two smaller cupboards. In the most elaborate types, the flanking cupboards are separated from the central section by sets of drawers. (*See* illustration on previous page.)

Wireless Set, *see* Radio Set

Woodware or Wooden Ware

Sometimes used as an alternative term for treen (*q.v.*).

Woodworm

A general term for the larvæ of wood devouring insects. (*See* **Furniture Pests.**)

Work stand: mid-19th century. (From *The Young Ladies' Treasure Book.*)

Work Stand

A small metal stand, supporting three or four movable leaves of card, covered with fabric, with loops and sockets, to accommodate sewing appliances—scissors, needlecases, pincushions, and reels of silk and cotton. Introduced during the mid-19th century, the work stand resembled a miniature screen. (*See* illustration.)

Work Table, *see* **Pouch Table**

Writing Arm

A broad, flat arm on a Windsor chair, designed to form a rest for a writing tablet. Probably of American origin.

Writing Chair

A chair with the seat placed diagonally so that one of the corners is in front if the seat is square, or with a curved front if it is fan shaped. Such chairs, dating from the early 18th century, are sometimes called corner or angle chairs. (*See* illustration.) Chairs of this type with a high back were also used for shaving. (*See* **Shaving Chair.**)

Writing chair in oak: early
18th century.

Writing Desk, *see* **Bureau Table, Desk, Kneehole Desk, Library Table, Partners' Desk** *and* **Secretaire**

Writing Drawer, *see* **Writing Table**

Writing Fire Screen or **Screen Writing Table**

A shallow writing desk with a fall front and a cupboard below. The carcase, which acts as the fire screen, is raised on curved or claw legs, so that a person seated at the table may warm his feet at a fire without being incommoded by the direct heat that it radiates.

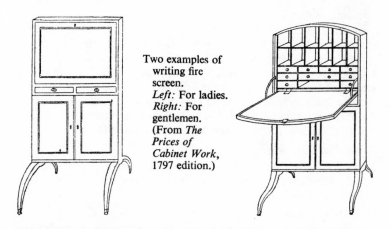

Two examples of writing fire screen.
Left: For ladies.
Right: For gentlemen.
(From *The Prices of Cabinet Work,* 1797 edition.)

Introduced by Thomas Shearer during the late 18th century, writing fire screens were luxurious additions to furnishing, and were made in two sizes: small for ladies, and a little larger for

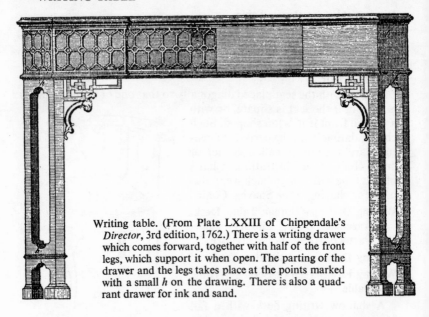

Writing table. (From Plate LXXIII of Chippendale's *Director*, 3rd edition, 1762.) There is a writing drawer which comes forward, together with half of the front legs, which support it when open. The parting of the drawer and the legs takes place at the points marked with a small *h* on the drawing. There is also a quadrant drawer for ink and sand.

gentlemen. Both types are illustrated, described and costed, in *The Prices of Cabinet Work* (1797), and are simplified versions of Shearer's designs. The illustrations on the previous page are from that edition. The gentlemen's size is 2 ft. 6 ins. wide and 6 ins. deep; the ladies' being 1 ft. 8 ins. wide and 3 ins. deep.

Writing Table

Writing tables were made during the middle years of the 18th century, and had a special device called a writing drawer, which pulled out and provided a flat, baize-covered surface. Writing tables were variously formed, and those specifically illustrated and described by Chippendale in the 3rd edition of the *Director* (1762) include the kneehole type with cupboards below, also tables surmounted by cupboards, drawers, and sets of pigeon holes. (*See* illustrations, *also* **Desk**, **Escritoire**, *and* **Kneehole Desk**.)

Wych Elm (*Ulmus glabra*)

Native to the British Isles, it supplies a pale, reddish-brown wood. It is hard wearing, and is used in chair making and occasionally in panelling.

Wycombe Chairs

A name that was commonly given to Windsor chairs during the 19th century, because of the extensive manufacture of all types of such chairs at High Wycombe in Buckinghamshire. (*See* **Windsor Chair**, *also* **White Wycombe**.)

512

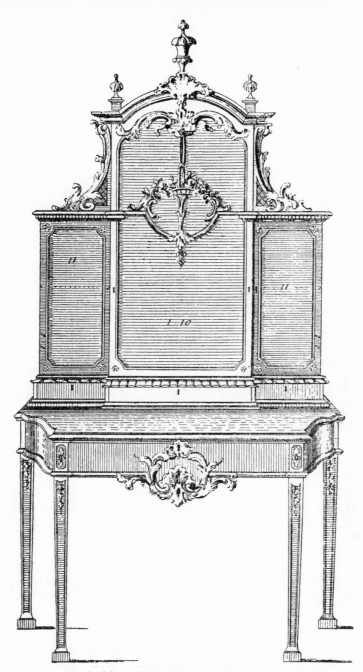

Lady's writing table with bookcase above.
(From Plate CXVI of Chippendale's *Director*, 3rd edition, 1762.)

Writing table. (From Plate LXXII of Chippendale's *Director*, 3rd edition, 1762.) The broad use of the term writing table by Chippendale and his contemporaries is indicated by the variety of designs shown on pages 512, 513, above and opposite.

Writing table. (From Plate LXXV of Chippendale's *Director*, 3rd edition, 1762.) Alternative treatments are shown for the left and right sides of the under part.

X-Shaped Chair

A chair with a supporting frame shaped like the letter X. These were originally coffer maker's chairs, *q.v.*, when the frames were covered with leather or fabric; but there were variations on the X-framework. The two 15th century examples illustrated here have

sides and arms formed by a continuous X-frame; but the early 17th century example, a velvet armchair from Knole, has the X-frame at the front and back, like the coffer makers' chair illustrated on page 195. This type of framework was used on mid-19th century metal chairs and on some modern metal furniture of manipulated metal tubing. (*See also* illustrations of Drawing Room Chairs by Sheraton, pages 232 and 233.)

Left: A 15th century chair with an X-shaped frame, a high back and a canopy. *Right:* Another example of a 15th century X-shaped chair. Both have the lower, supporting members of the X braced by stretchers. Both chairs are from the French MS. the 'Roman de Renaud de Montauban', and are illustrated in Shaw's *Specimens of Ancient Furniture*.

X-Shaped or X-Stretcher

Stretchers which run diagonally between the four legs of a piece of furniture. (*See also* **Saltire** *and* **Serpentine Stretcher**.)

X-Stool

Stools supported by an X-shaped underframe were known and used in Egypt as early as 1350 B.C. In the Graeco-Roman civilisa-

Early 17th century X-shaped arm-chair, covered with velvet and garnished with nails. (Drawn from a chair at Knole by Charles L. Eastlake and included in his *Hints on Household Taste*, 4th edition, 1878.)

A Roman stool, from a painting at Herculaneum. (From Plate XXII of Trollope's *Illustrations of Ancient Art*.)

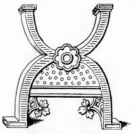

In the Middle Ages the X structural principle was used: the upper arms of the X becoming the arms of the chair or stool, as in this 15th century example. (From the 'Roman de Renaud de Montauban', illustrated in Shaw's *Specimens of Ancient Furniture*.)

517

tion many variations of this structural principle were used (*see* illustration on previous page), and it was known and used in the Middle Ages. (*See* **Coffer Makers' Chair** *and* **X-shaped Chair,** *also* illustrations of Ladies' Dressing Stools on page 237.)

Xestobium Rufovillosum, *see* **Death Watch Beetle**

* Y *

Yellow Birch, *see* **Canadian Birch**

Yellow Wood, *see* **Fustic**

Yeoman Furniture

A term sometimes used to describe furniture made in the countryside, which perpetuates the character and ornamental treatment of an earlier period. For example, it would apply to press cupboards and panel back chairs of mid-17th century type if they were made in the first half of the 18th century.

Yew (*Taxus baccata*)

A tree native to Britain, which provides a very hard, close-grained, durable wood of golden-brown, occasionally streaked with dark reddish-brown shading into purple. It is used for turned work, and frequently for the bow backs, spindles, and legs of Windsor chairs.

Yoke

The name sometimes given to the top rail of a chair back, from its resemblance to the shape of the yoke used for carrying milk pails. It may have been a contemporary term for cupid's bow cresting, *q.v.*, and yoke back was used in the 18th century to describe a plain type of cheap chair.

Yorkshire Chair, *see* **Derbyshire Chair**

Yorkshire Dresser

Dressers which incorporate clocks have survived in Yorkshire, which has suggested that such dressers were of local origin. Probably there is some truth in this suggestion; but dressers with clocks exist in other parts of the country, so this type cannot be associated only with Yorkshire. Regional labels of this kind, unsupported by specific evidence of origin, are unreliable.

* Z *

Zebrawood (*Astronium fraxinifolium*)

A decorative wood, sometimes known in the United States as tigerwood. It comes from Brazil; is of a reddish-brown colour, barred with dark stripes. It is used chiefly for banding and inlaying.

Zomno

A night-stand or small bedside cupboard. Mid-19th century American term, used by A. J. Downing in *The Architecture of Country Houses* (New York, 1850), Section XII, page 416.

Zoophorus

A term used for a frieze, *q.v.*, when it is carved with representations of animals.

SECTION IV

A Short List of British and American Furniture Makers and Designers, and British Clock Makers

*

BRITISH FURNITURE MAKERS

Adam, Robert (1728–92)

Architect and furniture designer. The second and the most famous of the four sons of William Adam of Maryburgh, Fife. Appointed sole architect to the King and the Board of Works in 1762. In partnership with his brothers James and William. Designed complete schemes of furnishing and interior decoration, employing contemporary cabinet makers, including Thomas Chippendale, to carry out his furniture designs.

Bradborn, John

Cabinet maker. Successor to William Vile as cabinet maker to the Crown; previously employed by Vile as foreman cabinet maker. When Vile died, in 1767, Bradborn took premises in Long Acre. London, where he remained until 1776, when he retired to Wandsworth, where he died in 1781.

Chippendale, Thomas

Cabinet maker and chair maker. Baptized at Otley Parish Church, Yorkshire, on June 5th, 1718. Died 1779, and buried in St. Martin-in-the-Fields, London, on November 13th of that year. He was the first cabinet maker to publish a book of designs. Entitled *The Gentleman and Cabinet Maker's Director*, the first edition was issued in 1754, the second, with the same contents, in 1755, the third, much enlarged, in 1762. It is not known when he first came to London, but in 1745 he was living in Conduit Court, Long Acre, and in 1752 at Somerset or Northumberland Court in the Strand. He moved to St. Martin's Lane in 1753 or 1754, and may then have taken into partnership James Rannie, a cabinet maker. Rannie died in 1766, and Chippendale continued his business alone until 1771, when Thomas Haig joined the business, which then became known as Chippendale, Haig and Company.

Sheraton, in the list of makers at the end of *The Cabinet Dictionary* (1803), gives the business of Thomas Chippendale, upholsterer, at the address of 60 St. Martin's Lane.

Cobb, John

Cabinet maker and upholsterer. He was a partner with Hallett and Vile, and remained in the business after Vile's retirement. He died on August 24th, 1778. He is referred to in *Nollekens and his Times*, by J. T. Smith. (*See* Section I, pages 25 and 26.)

Day, Daniel

Chair maker. Worked at Mendlesham and Stoneham in Suffolk, in the late 18th and early 19th centuries. (*See* **Mendlesham Chair**, Section III.)

Gibbons, Grinling (1648–1721)

Wood carver, probably of Dutch parentage. He came to London in 1666, and enjoyed the patronage of John Evelyn, and worked for Sir Christopher Wren. In 1714, he was appointed master carver in wood to George I. His work was used for the decoration of furniture, such as carved stands for cabinets.

The Gillows

Cabinet makers and chair makers. The firm of Gillow was founded by Robert Gillow, a joiner, at Gt. Singleton in the parish of Kirkham-in-the-Fylde, but in 1695 he removed to Lancaster, and set up in business there as a carpenter. He became a freeman of the borough of Lancaster, and in 1728 and thereafter practised as a cabinet maker. He had three sons, Richard, Robert junior, and Thomas, and in 1757 Richard was taken into partnership. Some time in the middle years of the 18th century the Gillows began trading in London, and about 1765 premises were built for the firm in Oxford Street, on the site of those now occupied by Waring and Gillow Ltd.

Gimson, Ernest (1864–1919)

Artist-craftsman and architect. The son of Josiah Gimson, an engineer, he was trained at Leicester Art School, and articled, in 1881, to Isaac Barradale, a Leicester architect. In 1884 he met William Morris, and was greatly influenced by his teaching. He came to London in 1886, and subsequently settled at Pinbury in Gloucestershire, where he practised as a cabinet maker, chair maker, and designer and worker in metal, plaster, and embroidery. In 1903, he moved to the neighbouring village of Sapperton. He died on August 12th, 1919. (*See* Section II, pages 76 to 78.)

Haig, Thomas

About 1771, he became a partner in Thomas Chippendale's firm, and remained in partnership until about 1796.

Hallett, William (1707–82)

Cabinet maker. Little is known of him as a furniture maker, though it is believed that he did work as such, and may have been associated with John Cobb. He lived in Newport Street from 1732 to 1753, when he moved to Long Acre, where he lived until 1769. He is described in contemporary records as an eminent cabinet maker.

Hepplewhite, George

Cabinet maker and chair maker. Apprenticed to the firm of Gillow of Lancaster, he came to London and opened a shop in Red Cross Street, Cripplegate. His book of designs, *The Cabinet Maker and Upholsterer's Guide*, was published after his death; the first edition appeared in 1788, and a second in 1789. His name is sometimes spelt Heppelwhite, and is entered thus in connection with his designs in the *Cabinet-Maker's London Book of Prices*. He died in 1786.

Hope, Thomas (1770–1831)

Amateur architect and furniture designer, and author of *Household Furniture and Interior Decoration* (1807). One of the leaders of the Classical revival of the late 18th century. (*See* Section II, page 67.)

Ince, William

Cabinet maker and upholsterer, who was in partnership with John Mayhew, and lived and worked in the second half of the 18th century. With Mayhew, he was joint author of *The Universal System of Household Furniture*, which first appeared in parts, and was published in 1760. The firm of Ince and Mayhew was established at Broad Street, Golden Square (*see* pages 33 and 68), and was still in existence during the first decade of the 19th century.

Jensen, Gerreit

A Dutch cabinet maker who settled in England in the latter part of the 17th century, and died apparently in 1715. He made furniture both for Charles II and William III, and his name was subsequently anglicised, so that he became known as Gerard Johnson.

Kent, William (1685–1748)

Architect and designer of gardens and furniture. He was born in Yorkshire, and began life as a coach painter's apprentice. Under the patronage of the Earl of Burlington, he had a distinguished career. He designed complete interior schemes, which included highly decorative furniture. (*See* Section II, page 52.)

Langley, Batty (1696–1751)

Architect and designer of furniture. With his brother, Thomas Langley, he established a school for teaching architecture and drawing, about 1740. Published various works, including *The City and Country Builder's and Workman's Treasury of Designs*. (*See* Section II, pages 53 and 60.)

Linnell, John

Upholsterer, cabinet maker, and carver. He began work about 1761, and his clients included many of the nobility. Best-known work is furniture and fittings at Shardeloes, which he supplied for William Drake. He died in 1796.

Lock, Matthias

Carver and designer of furniture, who worked during the middle and late 18th century. It is known that he was employed by Thomas Chippendale, and he published various works, which included *A New Drawing Book*, which is not dated; *A New Book of Ornament* (1768); *A New Book of Pier Frames* (1769), and *A New Book of Foliage* (1769). He was one of the English interpreters of the rococo style, introduced from France. (*See* **Rococo**, in Section III, page 392.)

Manwaring, Robert

Cabinet maker and chair maker, and a contemporary of Chippendale. He produced work both in the Chinese and Gothic manner, but many of his designs were heavy, and badly proportioned. In 1765, he published two books, *The Cabinet and Chair-Maker's Real Friend and Companion; or the Whole System of Chair-Making made Plain and Easy*, and *The Carpenter's Complete Guide to Gothic Railing*. In 1766, he published *The Chair-Maker's Guide*.

Mayhew, John

In partnership with William Ince, as a cabinet maker and upholsterer. Part author of *The Universal System of Household Furniture*.

Morris, William (1834–96)

Artist-craftsman, poet, author, and founder of the handicraft revival. Was originally articled to George Edmund Street, when he intended to become an architect, but gave up architecture, and became a painter and executant craftsman. He founded the firm of Morris, Marshall, Faulkner & Co. in 1861. (*See* pages 76, 77.)

Pugin, Augustus Welby Northmore (1812–52).

Architect, and occasionally a designer of furniture. One of the pioneers of the Gothic revival, in the second quarter of the 19th century. Such furniture as he designed had a strong Gothic flavour, and some of it is illustrated in his book, *The True Principles of Pointed or Christian Architecture*.

Seddon, George (1727–1801)

Cabinet maker. Master of the Joiners' Company in 1795. He was the founder of a prosperous business that was still in existence in the mid-19th century, and in which his sons, George and Thomas, and his son-in-law, Thomas Shackleton, were partners.

Shearer, Thomas

Cabinet maker and designer, who worked in the second half of the 18th century. Very little is known about him, but he was responsible for many of the plates in the *Cabinet Maker's London Book of Prices* (1788). He may have been the originator of the sideboard in its modern form.

Sheraton, Thomas (1751–1806)

Cabinet maker and furniture designer. Born at Stockton-on-Tees, he came to London about 1790, after being a journeyman cabinet maker for many years. In London, he settled in Wardour Street, Soho, where he taught drawing and architecture. He published many designs for furniture, and his principal works were *The Cabinet Maker and Upholsterer's Drawing Book* (which was published in parts between 1791 and 1794), and *The Cabinet Dictionary*, published in 1803.

Vile, William

At the beginning of George III's reign he was cabinet maker to the Crown: later, he entered into partnership with John Cobb, an upholsterer. (*See* Section I, page 25.) Together they rented premises on the corner of St. Martin's Lane and Long Acre, London, where they first paid rates in 1751. Vile's will was made in 1763 and there is no record of his accounts to the Royal Household after 1764–65. He was not a chair maker. Vile died in 1767.

Voysey, C. F. A. (1857–1941)

Architect and furniture designer. One of the pioneers of what came to be known as the modern movement in design. Strongly influenced by William Morris, he designed not only furniture, but wallpaper and textiles.

Webb, Philip (1831–1915)

Architect and designer of furniture. Met William Morris after he had entered the office of George Edmund Street. Worked as a designer for the firm of Morris, Marshall, Faulkner & Co. which Morris founded in 1861. His designs included stained glass, candlesticks, grates, table glass, and furniture. He built the Red House at Upton, in 1859, for William Morris.

AMERICAN FURNITURE MAKERS

Afleck, Thomas

Cabinet maker. Born at Aberdeen, and emigrated from London in 1763; died at Philadelphia 1785. A prominent member of the Philadelphia school of cabinet makers.

Ash, Gilbert

Chair maker. Established in New York during the sixties of the 18th century. In 1765 he owned a shop in Wall Street, and was a soap boiler as well as a chair maker.

Ash, Thomas (I)

Chair maker. Possibly a relative of Gilbert Ash, but not much is known about him. He was an early 19th century chair maker, and was secretary to the Tammanay Society for some years, and a person of some social importance.

Ash, Thomas (II)

Chair maker. Son of Thomas Ash (I), and a member of his father's firm, which made Windsor chairs during the early 19th century.

Chapin, Aaron

Cabinet maker. Known to have worked at East Windsor, Conn. He moved to Hartford in 1783. Famous for his highboy designs.

Connelly, Henry

Cabinet maker. Known to have lived and worked at Philadelphia, 1770–1826.

Cowperthwaite, John K.

Cabinet maker. Established towards the end of the 18th century, in New York. His name is still carried on by the business he founded in that city.

Delaplane, Joshua

Cabinet maker, 1681–1771. Worked in New York.

Disbrowe, Nicholas

Joiner. A famous maker of chests, and one of the earliest recorded furniture makers. Worked at Hartford, Conn., between 1639 and 1683. Sometimes known as the Connecticut joiner, and his chests as Connecticut chests.

Egerton, Matthew (I) (1739–1802)

Cabinet maker, of New Brunswick, N.J. His designs were influenced by the work of Chippendale.

Egerton, Matthew (II)

Cabinet maker. Worked in New York in the late 18th and early 19th centuries. Possibly a son of Matthew Egerton (I), of New Brunswick.

Folwell, John

Cabinet maker. Worked in Philadelphia during the latter part of the 18th century. Issued a prospectus in 1775 of a book of furniture designs, which was to have been entitled *The Gentleman and Cabinet Maker's Assistant*. It was based on Chippendale's *Director*, but was never published.

Gautier, Andrew

Born 1720, date of death unknown. Chair maker. Born in New York, of a Huguenot family, he became a maker of Windsor chairs and is one of the earliest known. He used press advertising, and illustrated his wares in advertisements; one such appeared in the *New York Gazette*, April 18th, 1765.

Gillingham, James (1735–91)

Cabinet maker and chair maker. Worked in Philadelphia. James Gillingham was also the name of his nephew.

Goddard, John

Born 1723/24, died 1785. Cabinet maker and chair maker. Son of Daniel Goddard, a shipwright, and his wife, Mary Tripp, of Dartmouth, Mass. After his birth his parents moved to Newport, R.I., where he was apprenticed to Job Townsend, a cabinet maker. Goddard was made a freeman of Rhode Island on April 3rd, 1745, and married Townsend's daughter, Hannah, in 1746. Two of his sons, Stephen and Thomas, followed him in his trade. By the early seventeen-sixties, Goddard was recognised as the leading cabinet maker in Newport. He has been specially identified with the development of the block front, or swell front, which he is supposed to have originated.

Gostelowe, Jonathan (1744–95)

Cabinet maker. The son of George Gostelowe, believed to have been a Swedish emigrant; his mother was an Englishwoman. He was born at Passyunk (now in Philadelphia), and learned joinery there. He made bureaux, dining and Pembroke tables, bedsteads, card tables, chairs and clock cases, and they were original in design and not imitations of contemporary English work. He was elected Chairman of the Gentlemen Cabinet and Chair Makers in Philadelphia in 1788. He retired from business in 1793, and died on February 3rd, 1795.

Hall, John

Architect and furniture designer. Author of *The Cabinet Makers' Assistant*, which he described as: "Designed, drawn and published by John Hall, Architect, Baltimore". It was published in 1840.

Hewitt, John

Cabinet maker. Worked in New York at the beginning of the 19th century.

Hitchcock, Lambert (1795–1852)

Chair maker. Worked at Riverton, Conn., in the early 19th century.

Lawton, Robert

Cabinet maker. Worked in New York in the late 18th century.

McIntire, Samuel (1757–1811)

Architect, carver and designer of furniture. The son of a house-wright, of Salem, Mass., where he was born. Entered his father's shop, and learned the family trade; married Elizabeth Field in 1778. Famous as a carver of furniture and woodwork. Many examples of his work exist in and around Salem.

Phyfe, Duncan (1768–1854)

Cabinet maker and chair maker. Perhaps the most famous of American furniture makers. The second son of a Scotsman named Fife, he lived as a child in Albany, N.Y., where he was apprenticed to a cabinet maker. When twenty-one, he moved to New York, where he had a joiner's shop at 2 Broad Street. In 1793/94, he changed his name to Phyfe, when he married a Dutchwoman, Rachel Lowzade. Moved in 1795 to larger premises at 35 Partition Street, and between 1802 and 1816 bought the adjoining houses and one opposite. Two of his sons entered his business. His early 19th century work was influenced by the French Empire style and the designs of Sheraton and Hope.

Randolph, Benjamin (1762–92)

Cabinet maker. An eminent Philadelphia craftsman. He worked in the manner of Chippendale.

The Sandersons

ELIJAH (1751–1825) and JACOB (1757–1810). Cabinet makers of Salem, Mass. Employed Samuel McIntire and other of Salem's fine handicraftsmen. Shipped furniture to the southern States and to South America.

Savery, William (1721–87)

Cabinet maker and chair maker. Descended from a French Huguenot family, and famous until well over a hundred years after his death, he is believed to have gone first to Philadelphia in 1740. He had a shop at 17 South Second Street. Like many of his contemporaries, he followed the designs of Chippendale.

Wadsworth, John

Chair maker. Worked at Hartford, Conn., in the late 18th century, and specialised in Windsor chairs.

BRITISH CLOCK MAKERS

The Clockmakers Company of London began its history in 1631, when it was granted a charter by Charles I, on the 22nd of August of that year.

The Easts

EDWARD EAST (c. 1610–75). London clock maker, contemporary with the Fromanteels. Watch maker to Charles I, and one of the ten original members of the Clockmakers Company. He was Renter Warden in 1639 and 1640, and Master in 1645 and again in 1652. He was made 'Chief Clockmaker and Keeper of the Privy Clocks' in 1662.

JAMES EAST. Probably a relative of Edward East. Both he and NATH EAST were watch and clock makers in the second half of the 17th century, working for the Royal Family.

The Ebsworths

JOHN EBSWORTH. Clock maker, a contemporary of Joseph Knibb (I). He was apprenticed to Richard Ames in 1657, was admitted to the Clockmakers Company in 1665 and was Master in 1697.

CHRISTOPHER EBSWORTH. Clock maker, probably the brother of John Ebsworth. Apprenticed to Richard Ames in 1662.

The Ellicotts

JOHN ELLICOTT (I). London clock maker; date of birth unknown. Apprenticed to John Waters, 1687; admitted to the Clockmakers Company in 1696, and was later Renter Warden. He died in 1733. In 1712, he lived in Austin Friars, near Winchester Street, and later in St. Swithin's Alley, Royal Exchange, where his son (*see* next entry) also lived and continued the clock-making business.

JOHN ELLICOTT (II) (*c.* 1706–72). The son of John Ellicott (I). Scientist and clock maker; elected a Fellow of the Royal Society in 1736. Invented a compensated pendulum in 1752. Clockmaker to George III.

Fennell, Richard

Clockmaker. Admitted a freeman of the Clockmakers Company in 1679.

The Fromanteels

A 17th century clock-making family of Dutch descent, who were responsible for introducing the pendulum into England.

AHASUERUS FROMANTEEL became a freeman of the Clockmakers Company in 1632, and in 1655 AHASUERUS (II) became a freeman. AHASUERUS (III) and JOHN FROMANTEEL were admitted in 1663.

Gould, Christopher

Clock maker, admitted a Brother of the Clockmakers Company, 1682, and was Beadle, 1713–18. Died in 1718. In 1701, he lived next door to the Amsterdam coffee-house behind the Royal Exchange, and in 1706 became bankrupt.

Graham, George (1673-1751)

Born at Kirklinton, Cumberland, in 1673. He became assistant to Thomas Tompion, and his nephew by marriage. He invented a compensated pendulum, with a jar of mercury for the pendulum bob; he also invented the 'dead-beat' escapement. He was elected a Fellow of the Royal Society. For some years before his death in 1751, he had a shop in Fleet Street.

Horseman, Stephen

Apprentice, and later partner, of Daniel Quare. Admitted to the Clockmakers Company, 1709. Carried on Quare's business after his death, but became bankrupt in 1733, and went out of business.

The Knibbs

SAMUEL KNIBB. Lived at Newport Pagnall, and later in London. Admitted to the Clockmakers Company in 1663.

JOSEPH (I) and JOHN KNIBB. Possibly the nephews of Samuel. They worked together at Oxford till about 1670. Joseph then went to London, and was admitted to the Clockmakers Company, and John continued to work in Oxford, where he became Mayor in 1700. Joseph Knibb (I) had important patrons at the Court of Charles II, including the King. He lived first at the Dial, Serjeant's Inn Gate, then (in 1693) at the Dial in Suffolk Street near Charing Cross. During the last years of the 17th century, Joseph left London and lived at Handslope, Bucks. He died 1711/12.

PETER KNIBB. Apprenticed to Joseph, and admitted to the Clock makers Company in 1677.

EDWARD KNIBB. Apprenticed to Joseph in 1693.

JOSEPH KNIBB (II). Apprenticed to Martin Jackson in 1710.

Martin, John

Clock maker, admitted to the Clockmakers Company, 1679.

Newsam, Bartholomew

Clock maker to Queen Elizabeth, working in the latter part of the 16th century.

Quare, Daniel

There is some disagreement about the date of his birth: 1632 and 1649 have been suggested. He was admitted a Brother of the Clockmakers Company in 1671, and to the Court of Assistants in 1697, becoming Warden in 1705–7 and Master in 1708. He was the inventor of the repeater watch mechanism, by which a spring was pressed and the nearest hour and quarter sounded, so that the time could be told in the dark. He also worked on barometers. He became clock maker to George I, and lived in St. Martin's-le-Grand, and in 1694 at the King's Arms, Exchange Alley. He died in 1724.

Tompion, Thomas (1639–1713)

The most famous English clock maker. He was the eldest son of a blacksmith, of Northill, Beds. In 1671, Tompion was admitted a Brother to the Clockmakers Company, and in 1691 to the Court of Assistants. He was Junior Renter and Senior Warden between 1700 and 1703, and Master in 1703–4. His nephews by marriage were his apprentices and assistants, George Graham and Edward Bangor. Tompion was closely associated with Dr Robert Hooke, the eminent 17th century scientist, whose horological discoveries were responsible for great improvements in clocks and watches at that time. Tompion and Graham both worked on barometers.

Vallis, N.

A clock signed by him is dated 1598. Believed to have been an English maker.

The Vulliamys

JUSTIN VULLIAMY. Dates of birth and death uncertain, but he worked in the latter part of the 18th century. The father of Benjamin Vulliamy.

BENJAMIN VULLIAMY. Date of birth uncertain. Probably died about 1820. The father of Benjamin Lewis Vulliamy. Employed by George III.

BENJAMIN LEWIS VULLIAMY. The most famous member of the family. Born 1780, died 1854. Son of Benjamin Vulliamy. Five times Master of the Clockmakers Company, and Court Clock-maker.

Webster, William

Clock maker, of Exchange Alley. Apprenticed to Tompion. Died 1735.

SECTION V

Books and Periodicals on Furniture, Furnishing and Design

*

This is a short list of works, grouped under centuries, with the names of the authors in alphabetical order

BOOKS

SEVENTEENTH CENTURY

Evelyn, John. *Sylva, or a Discourse on Forest-Trees* (originally published 1664, 1679, 3rd edition).

Stalker, John, and Parker, George. *A Treatise of Japaning and Varnishing* (1688).

EIGHTEENTH CENTURY

Chippendale, Thomas. *The Gentleman and Cabinet Maker's Director* (1754).

Darly, M. *A New Book of Chinese, Gothic and Modern Chairs* (1751).

Hepplewhite, A., & Co. *The Cabinet Maker and Upholsterer's Guide, or Repository of Designs for Every Article of Household Furniture* (1788).

Ince, William, and Mayhew, John. *The Universal System of Household Furniture: Consisting of above 300 Designs in the most Elegant Taste, both Useful and Ornamental* (1759–62. First published in parts).

London Society of Cabinet-Makers. *The Cabinet-Makers' London Book of Prices* (1788).

Manwaring, Robert. *The Cabinet and Chair-Maker's Real Friend and Companion; or the Whole System of Chair-Making made Plain and Easy* (1765).

Manwaring, Robert, and others. *The Chair-Maker's Guide* (1766).

Shearer, T. *Designs for Household Furniture* (1788).

Sheraton, Thomas. *The Cabinet Maker and Upholsterer's Drawing Book* (1791–93. Originally published in parts).

532

Society of Upholsterers, Cabinet-Makers, etc. *Household Furniture in Genteel Taste for the Year 1760* (1760).

NINETEENTH CENTURY

Downing, A. J. *The Architecture of Country Houses: including Designs for Cottages, Farm Houses, and Villas, With Remarks on Interiors, Furniture, and the Best Modes of Warming and Ventilating* (New York, 1850).

Eastlake, Charles L. *Hints on Household Taste* (Longmans, Green & Co., 1878, 4th edition).

Hope, Thomas. *Household Furniture and Interior Decoration Executed from Designs by Thomas Hope* (1807).

Loudon, John Claudius. *An Encyclopaedia of Cottage, Farm and Villa Architecture and Furniture* (1833).

Nicholson, Michael Angelo. *The Carpenter and Joiner's Companion in the Geometrical Construction of Working Drawings. Improved from the Original Principles of P. Nicholson* (1826).

Nicholson, Peter. *Practical Carpentry, Joinery and Cabinet-Making* (1826).

Nicholson, Peter, and Michael Angelo. *The Practical Cabinet-Maker, Upholsterer and Complete Decorator* (1826).

Pugin, A. W. N. *The True Principles of Pointed or Christian Architecture* (1841).

Shaw, H. (illustrator). *Specimens of Ancient Furniture Drawn from Existing Authorities, by H. Shaw, with Descriptions by Sir Samuel Rush Meyrick* (1836).

Sheraton, Thomas. *The Cabinet Dictionary* (1803).

Smith, George. *The Cabinet-Maker and Upholsterer's Guide* (1826).

TWENTIETH CENTURY

Bell, J. Munro, and Hayden, Arthur. *The Furniture Designs of Thomas Chippendale; a selection of plates from Chippendale's Director, arranged by J. Munro Bell, with an introduction by Arthur Hayden* (Gibbings & Company, 1910).

Brackett, Oliver. *An Encyclopaedia of English Furniture* (Benn, 1927).

Thomas Chippendale (Hodder & Stoughton, 1924).

Carrington, Noel, *Design in the Home* (Country Life, 1933).

Catalogue of English Furniture and Woodwork (Victoria and Albert Museum, 1923–31, 4 volumes):

Vol. I: Smith, H. Clifford, *Gothic and Early Tudor*, 1929.

Vol. II: Smith, H. Clifford, *Late Tudor and Early Stuart*, 1930.

Vol. III: Brackett, Oliver, *Late Stuart to Queen Anne*, 1927.

Vol. IV: Edwards, Ralph, *Georgian Furniture*, 1931.

Cescinsky, H., and Gribble, E. R. *Early English Furniture and Woodwork* (Routledge, 1922, 2 volumes).

Clouston, R. S. *English Furniture and Furniture Makers of the Eighteenth Century* (Hurst & Blackett, 1906).

Cornelius, Charles O. *Furniture Masterpieces of Duncan Phyfe* (Doubleday, Doran & Co., New York, 1928).

Edwards, Ralph. *Hepplewhite Furniture Designs, from the Cabinet-Maker and Upholsterer's Guide, 1794, with a preface by Ralph Edwards* (Tiranti, 1947).

   Sheraton Furniture Designs from the Cabinet-Maker's and Upholsterer's Drawing Book, 1791–94, with a preface by Ralph Edwards (Tiranti, 1946).

Edwards, Ralph, and Jourdain, Margaret. *Georgian Cabinet-Makers* (Country Life, 1946).

Ernest Gimson: His Life and Work (Memorial Volume) (Shakespeare Head Press, Oxford: and Benn, London, 1924).

Gibberd, F. *Built-in Furniture in Great Britain* (Tiranti, 1948).

Giedion, Siegfried. *Mechanization Takes Command* (New York: Oxford University Press, 1948).

Gloag, John. *British Furniture Makers* (Britain in Pictures, Collins, 1945).

   English Furniture (A. & C. Black, Library of English Art, 1951, 4th edition).

   The English Tradition in Design (Penguin Books, 1947).

   Time, Taste and Furniture (Richards Press, 1949, 3rd edition).

Harling, Robert. *Home: a Victorian Vignette* (Constable, 1938).

Hayden, Arthur. *Chats on Cottage and Farmhouse Furniture* (Fisher Unwin, 1912).

   Chats on Old Furniture (Fisher Unwin, 1905).

Holme, Charles (editor). *Modern British Domestic Architecture and Decoration, edited by Charles Holme* (The Studio, 1901).

Holme, R., and Frost, K. M. (editors). *Studio Year Book of Decorative Art, 1943–48. With Introduction by R. W. Symonds* (Studio, 1948).

Hooper, R. *Woodcraft in Design and Practice* (Batsford, 1948).

Jourdain, Margaret. *English Decoration and Furniture during the Later Eighteenth Century, 1760–1803* (Batsford, 1922).

   Regency Furniture, 1795–1820 (Country Life, 1948).

Kimball, Fiske, and Donnell, Edna. *The Creators of the Chippendale Style* (Metropolitan Museum Studies: Metropolitan Museum of Art, New York, 1929).

Lockwood, L. V. *Colonial Furniture in America* (Charles Scribner's Sons, New York, 3rd edition, 1926).

Logie, Gordon. *Furniture from Machines* (Allen & Unwin, 1948).

Macquoid, Percy. *A History of English Furniture* (Lawrence & Bullen, 1904–8, 4 volumes, covering The Age of Oak, The

Age of Walnut, The Age of Mahogany, The Age of Satin-wood).

Macquoid, Percy, and Edwards, Ralph. *The Dictionary of English Furniture* (Country Life, 1924–27, 3 volumes).

Merivale, Margaret. *Furnishing the Small Home* (Studio, 1948).

Nash, Paul. *Room and Book* (Soncino Press, 1932).

Ormsbee, Thomas Hamilton. *The Story of American Furniture* (New York: The Macmillan Company, 1934).

Pevsner, Nikolaus. *An Enquiry into Industrial Art in England* (Cambridge University Press, 1937).

Pioneers of Modern Design from William Morris to Walter Gropius (New York: The Museum of Modern Art, 1949).

Roe, Fred. *Ancient Coffers and Cupboards* (Methuen, 1902).

Old Oak Furniture (Methuen, 1905).

Roe, F. Gordon. *English Cottage Furniture* (Phoenix House, 1949).

Rogers, John C. *English Furniture* (Country Life, 1923).

Furniture and Furnishing (Oxford University Press, 1932).

Modern English Furniture (Country Life, 1930).

Schmidtz, H. *The Encyclopaedia of Furniture: An Outline History of Furniture Design, with an introduction by H. P. Shapland* (Benn, 1926).

Shapland, H. P. *A Key to English Furniture* (Blackie, 1938).

The Practical Decoration of Furniture (Benn, 1926, 3 volumes).

Simon, C. *English Furniture Designers of the Eighteenth Century* (A. H. Bullen, 1904).

Symonds, R. W. *Chippendale Furniture Designs, from the Gentleman and Cabinet-Maker's Director, 1762, with a preface and descriptive notes by R. W. Symonds* (Tiranti, 1948).

English Furniture from Charles II to George II (The Connoisseur, 1929).

A History of English Clocks (King Penguin Books, 1947).

Masterpieces of English Furniture and Clocks (Batsford, 1940).

Old English Walnut and Lacquer Furniture (Jenkins, 1923).

The Ornamental Designs of Chippendale, from the Gentleman and Cabinet-Maker's Director, 1762, with a preface by R. W. Symonds (Tiranti, 1949).

The Present State of Old English Furniture (Duckworth, 1921).

Veneered Walnut Furniture, 1660–1760 (Tiranti, 1946).

Tipping, H. A. *English Furniture of the Cabriole Period* (Cape, 1922).

Wells, Percy A., and Hooper, John. *Modern Cabinet Work, Furniture and Fitments* (Batsford, 1938).

Yates, Raymond and Marguerite. *A Guide to Victorian Antiques* (New York: Harper & Brothers, 1949).

PERIODICALS

AMERICAN

Antiques, published in New York, N.Y., established 1922.

Furniture Age, published in Chicago, Ill., established 1921.

Furniture Manufacturer, published in New York, N.Y., established 1879.

National Furniture Review, published in Chicago, Ill., established 1927.

Furniture Digest, published in Minneapolis, Minn., established 1921.

Furniture Field, published in Los Angeles, Cal., established 1945.

Furniture World and Furniture Buyer and Decorator, published in New York, N.Y., established 1870.

Southwest Furniture News, published in Dallas, Texas, established 1927.

BRITISH

Antique Collector, published in London, established 1930.

Apollo, published in London, established 1925.

Architect's Journal, published in London, established (under the title *Builder's Journal*) 1895.

Architectural Review, published in London, established 1896.

Art and Industry, published in London, established 1926.

Cabinet Maker, The, published in London, established 1880.

Connoisseur, The, published in London, established 1901.

Country Life, published in London, established 1897.

Design, published in London (the magazine of the Council of Industrial Design), established 1949.

Furniture Record and the Furnisher, published in London, established 1899.

Studio, The, published in London, established 1893.

Studio Year Book of Decorative Art, The, published in London, established 1906.

Periods, Types of Furniture, Materials and Craftsmen from 1100 to 1950

*

An outline of the development of furniture, with indications of the influences which affect its form, function and character, during the last eight and a half centuries

10TH, 11TH, AND 12TH CENTURIES

PERIOD	FURNITURE	METHODS OF CONSTRUCTION
Saxon and Norman	Beds (bedding as distinct from bedsteads) Bedsteads Benches Chairs Cradles Dug-out chests Forms Stools Tables—usually supported on trestles	Furniture making a branch of carpentry. Some furniture dependent on the wall—bedsteads often part of a wall. Receptacles formed by doors in front of recesses in the thickness of walls. Boards pegged to each other, and chests and boxes bound with iron bands

Materials	Makers	Styles and Fashions
Iron Leather Wood: Ash, Elm, Oak, and other native woods Probably straw and rushes Fabrics used for hangings and cushions	Carpenters Smiths Leather workers	Fabrics used to give decorative effects in furnishing

PERIOD	FURNITURE	METHODS OF CONSTRUCTION
Mediaeval	Andirons Arks (meal bins) Aumbries Basins and ewers Bath tubs (wooden) Beds (with testers) Benches Boards (for a variety of purposes, such as dressing boards for preparing food, cup boards for cups and drinks, and boards on trestles to act as tables) Candlesticks Chairs with rounded backs Chests (dug-out and iron-bound) Coffers Cradles Cressets Fire screens Forms Metal mirrors Plate cupboards Settles Stools Tables	Split boards, wedged and pegged Turned work — chairs made from turned members Increased use of fabrics and leather Bedsteads and their canopies structurally dependent on walls and ceilings, though more free standing furniture in use Doors used to enclose such receptacles as aumbries

Materials	Makers	Styles and Fashions
Leather Iron Iron banding Wood: Oak and other native woods Various fabrics used for cushions, dorcers, bed hangings and so forth	Carpenters Carvers Gilders Cofferers or coffer-makers (who were workers in leather) Joiners (or joyners) Smiths Turners The principal craftsmen responsible for furniture making were joiners and turners	Fabrics still used to give the decorative character to furnishing; but use of carved decoration increasing, which reflected prevailing ornamental forms used in architecture Increasing variety of articles in use in rooms

PERIOD	FURNITURE	METHODS OF CONSTRUCTION
Late Mediaeval	All the articles listed in the previous period, with certain elaborations and additions, such as: Coffer makers' X-shaped chairs Plate cupboards with many tiers Dressers (evolved from dressing boards) State beds Larger and highly ornamented chests Counters—or counter boards Hanging lights, the forerunners of the chandelier, called candlebeams More and larger receptacles with doors, called presses	Pegged and joined work Turned members Chairs with upholstered slung seats of fabric and leather Woven or 'wanded' chairs of rushes or straw

Materials	Makers	Styles and Fashions
Leather Iron Latten Wood: Oak, Elm, Ash, Beech, and other native woods Hair cloth and perforated tin used to protect apertures pierced in doors of aumbries Various fabrics used for furnishing accessories, cushions and curtains	Joiners Turners Coffer makers and leather workers Carvers Gilders Smiths	Increasing influence of contemporary architectural design on the form and ornamentation of chests. Lavish use of rich fabrics to create decorative background and on curtained furniture, such as beds Emergence of a domestic English style of architecture, related to the Perpendicular phase of Gothic

16TH CENTURY (1500–1558)

PERIOD	FURNITURE	METHODS OF CONSTRUCTION
Early Tudor	All the articles in use in the Mediaeval period, but with many improvements in design The trestle table is now larger and longer, with a fixed top Tables for specialised uses Bedsteads are larger and more decorative The livery cupboard begins to replace the aumbry X-shaped chairs richly upholstered The press comes into general use Clocks with bells, but only rarely used	Joined and turned work of good finish Pegs and dowels used Far greater skill in woodworking than in previous period

MATERIALS	MAKERS	STYLES AND FASHIONS
Oak and other native woods Leather Iron Latten Various fabrics, used for chairs	Joiners Turners Coffer makers and leather workers generally Carvers and gilders Smiths and other workers in metal	Native English style established, but gradually giving place to 'Italianate' fashions in the decoration of furniture

16TH CENTURY (1558–1600)

PERIOD	FURNITURE	METHODS OF CONSTRUCTION
Late Tudor or Elizabethan	All the basic articles of furniture, bedsteads, chairs, stools, tables, dressers, and receptacles, with ornamental variations and some additions The four-post bed is enlarged and highly carved The long table with six or eight legs appears, also the court cupboard and the press cupboard. Transition of the cupboard from an article *on* which things are placed to one *in* which things are stored Glass mirrors Back stools or single chairs. Suites of upholstered chairs Joined stools Clocks in use but still rare	Joined and turned work of good finish Upholstered chairs

MATERIALS	MAKERS	STYLES AND FASHIONS
Oak and other native woods. Ash, Beech, Elm, possibly fruit woods, and Walnut Leather Iron Latten Various fabrics used for chairs Glass	Joiners Turners Carvers and gilders Coffer makers and leather workers generally Smiths and other metal workers The coffer maker's place is being taken by the upholsterer, and the coffer maker is becoming a trunk maker	'Italianate' fashions predominate, and badly proportioned variations of the classic orders of architecture are used ornamentally on four-post beds, tables and other furniture

17TH CENTURY (1600–1640)

PERIOD	FURNITURE	METHODS OF CONSTRUCTION
Early Stuart or Jacobean	All the basic articles, with variations and some inventions, such as the table with hinged leaves and the mule chest Suites of upholstered chairs used in galleries and at dining tables Joined stools The press cupboard is enlarged and profusely carved Aumbries no longer used Glass mirrors Chandeliers of brass and other metals Weight-driven clocks	Joined and turned work showing increased skill and excellent finish Turned work more elaborate Upholstery

MATERIALS	MAKERS	STYLES AND FASHIONS
Oak, and other native woods. Ash, Beech, Elm, fruit woods and Walnut Leather, iron, brass and silver Glass Fabrics	Joiners and turners The turner is beginning to be chiefly a chair maker, though his work is used by the joiner for table legs and bedposts Carvers and gilders Leather workers Upholsterers Various metal workers Clock makers	The 'Italianate' fashions still inspire highly ornamental treatments for surfaces; but the classical *motifs* are used with greater skill The influence of Inigo Jones and his contemporaries promotes a better understanding of classical architecture, and this is reflected in furniture design

17TH CENTURY (1640–1660)

PERIOD	FURNITURE	METHODS OF CONSTRUCTION
Puritan	All the basic articles of the previous period, but no more elaborate X-shaped chairs of rich fabric Mule chests, press cupboards, court cupboards, cabinets Long tables, double-leaf gate leg tables, draw tables and leather-seated and leather-backed chairs are all in use Joined stools Settles Dressers Brass chandeliers Weight-driven clocks	Joined and turned work Leather work no longer used for a slung seat or merely for a covering, but in conjunction with seat and back frames for chairs Many new developments in turned work: bobbin turning and the barley sugar twist appear on legs

MATERIALS	MAKERS	STYLES AND FASHIONS
Oak and other native woods. Ash, Beech, Elm and fruit woods, also Walnut Leather Fabrics Iron and other metals Glass	Joiners Turners Chair makers (who were specialist turners) Clock makers Carvers Upholsterers	Fashion in abeyance during the Puritan period: no elaboration in ornament or fabrics—a period of 'utility' The native English style of the early 16th century was resumed from the point where it had been superseded by 'Italianate' modes; but it was resumed with greater skill than the Early Tudor wood workers enjoyed

17TH CENTURY (1660–1700)

PERIOD	FURNITURE	METHODS OF CONSTRUCTION
Restoration (Carolean and Late Jacobean) William and Mary	All the basic articles of furniture now show an exuberance of form and decoration, and a variety of specialised functions Upholstered furniture, chairs, settees, day beds, chests of drawers, chests on stands, cabinets on stands, scrutoires Easy chairs (at end of period) with high backs and wings Long case clocks, carved and gilded chandeliers Sconces Looking glasses and pier glasses Tables in great variety Lacquer work — screens and cabinets	Joined furniture, turned work, and the introduction of veneering Veneering demands greater skill, and cabinet making, as distinct from joiners' work, is practised by specially skilled craftsmen Marquetry inlay used to decorate surfaces Japanning introduced

MATERIALS	MAKERS	STYLES AND FASHIONS
Oak, Walnut, and native woods, including fruit woods Lacquer imported from the East Canework Leather Fabrics Glass Lime and pearwood used for carving	The cabinet maker, whose craft was established with the introduction of veneering Chair makers Japanners Looking glass makers Carvers and gilders Clock makers Upholsterers	Foreign influences affecting design, Portuguese and Dutch Architectural design influencing the embellishment of furniture Reaction from Puritan utility apparent in Carolean period—elaborate carving and gilding Rise of taste for Oriental things — lacquer, porcelain Increase in the general comfort of furnishing

18TH CENTURY (1700–1730)

PERIOD	FURNITURE	METHODS OF CONSTRUCTION
Queen Anne and Early Georgian	All the basic articles hitherto listed, with many variations of function for such things as tables (tea tables for example) Chests and cabinets Large architectural pieces —bookcases and cabinets Bureaux Buffets Use of marble slabs supported on carved and gilded frames Console tables Chairs and tables with cabriole legs Looking glasses in heavily carved frames Windsor chairs	Cabinet making, turning Bentwood used in back bow of Windsor chairs Veneering Marquetry inlay Japanning Standards of skill rising to levels never before attained

MATERIALS	MAKERS	STYLES AND FASHIONS
Walnut, Oak, Beech, Ash, various native woods Walnut and other timber imported from Europe and Virginia Mahogany introduced during the seventeen-twenties Gesso Marble Glass Fabrics Various metals	Cabinet makers Carvers and gilders Looking glass makers Japanners Chair makers Clock-case makers Clock makers Upholsterers Turners	Influence of architects on furniture design increases William Kent outstanding example of such influence Oriental taste enjoying fluctuating popularity Lavish use of carving and gilding Furnishing usually designed as a coherent scheme: generally under the direction of an architect Beginning of a genteel but romantic taste for 'Gothic' ornament at end of period

18th CENTURY (1730–1800)

PERIOD	FURNITURE	METHODS OF CONSTRUCTION
Georgian	The golden age of cabinet and chair making. Great increase in variety of functions performed by furniture Writing tables, desks, bureaux, escritoires, library tables, bookcases, china cabinets, toilet tables, chests, double chests, clothes presses, looking glasses, chairs in sets Stools, upholstered furniture, sofas and settees Beds in great variety— tent, field, and dome beds Wine coolers Sideboards, sideboard tables Adjustable screens, including screen writing tables Rocking chairs introduced, but used chiefly in America	Cabinet making Turning Veneering Japanning Ornate carved and gilded work, and inlaying Painted furniture Spring upholstery probably introduced at end of period

MATERIALS	MAKERS	STYLES AND FASHIONS
Walnut, Mahogany, Satinwood, Oak, Beech, Elm, Ash, Yew, Cherry and Applewood Virginia Walnut Gesso Marble Glass Fabrics Various metals Woven canework and bamboo	Cabinet makers Chair makers Japanned chair makers Looking glass makers Carvers and gilders Turners Clock-case makers Cellaret makers Upholsterers The age of the great cabinet makers and chair makers: Chippendale, Shearer, Ince and Mayhew, Hepplewhite and the Gillows	The architect is the master designer and influences every branch of furnishing The 'Chinese taste' of the seventeen-fifties and -sixties revives the fashion for Oriental things The 'Gothic taste' represents a modish interest in Gothic forms, and enjoys intermittent popularity from the middle to the end of the 18th century A classical revival is given form and fresh character by Robert and James Adam. The 18th century ends with a new classical Greek revival

19TH CENTURY (1800–1820)

PERIOD	FURNITURE	METHODS OF CONSTRUCTION
Greek Revival Regency	Everything listed in the 18th and late 17th centuries in use, varied in form, and given new or additional functions Dressing tables and toilet tables are increasingly elaborate Introduction of the ottoman	Cabinet making Turning Veneering Japanning Inlaying Spring upholstery

MATERIALS	MAKERS	STYLES AND FASHIONS
Mahogany, Rosewood, Satinwood, Oak, Elm, Beech, Ash, Yew and other native woods and fruit woods Woven canework, bamboo, basket or wickerwork Marble Glass Leather Fabrics, including woven horsehair Various metals	All those listed in the previous period	The Greek Revival, conducted under the direction of architects Revived interest in classical design, interpreted in terms of furniture design by Thomas Sheraton The so-called English Empire style is derived from this classical revival Fashionable interest in Gothic forms maintained

19th CENTURY (1820–1837)

PERIOD	FURNITURE	METHODS OF CONSTRUCTION
Pre-Victorian	Everything listed in the 18th and late 17th centuries Suites of furniture now in general use Cheap furniture made in quantity—straw chairs and 'White' Wycombes Metal bedsteads also made in large numbers in the eighteen-thirties	Cabinet making Turning Veneering Japanning Inlaying Jointed metal Cast metal members Spring upholstery

MATERIALS	MAKERS	STYLES AND FASHIONS
Mahogany, Rosewood, Walnut, Oak, Elm, Beech, Ash, and other native woods Metal, including cast-iron, wrought iron, and brass Leather and various fabrics Glass Marble Canework, basketwork, or wickerwork	In addition to the craftsmen working by hand, like cabinet makers, chair makers and turners, wood-working machinery is used by the furniture manufacturing trade, that is becoming established	The Gothic Revival begins, and acquires an emotional character Architects begin to lose their influence General decay of taste Beginning of interest in old furniture, particularly of the Elizabethan and Jacobean periods

19TH CENTURY (1837–1900)

PERIOD	FURNITURE	METHODS OF CONSTRUCTION
Victorian	All basic articles listed since the beginning of the 18th century, variously elaborated Mechanical and adjustable furniture, variations of the rocking chair Revolving adjustable chairs Fitted furniture Metal bedsteads	Cabinet making Turning Bending Veneering Japanning Jointed metal Cast metal Spring upholstery

Materials	Makers	Styles and Fashions
Mahogany, Oak, Walnut, Satinwood Every type of native and imported wood Iron, cast and wrought, and brass Glass Marble Leather and various fabrics Canework and basket or wickerwork Plywood	Furniture manufacturers using mechanical production methods, and also employing cabinet makers and upholsterers Turners Chair makers Carvers and gilders Polishers Artist-craftsmen, who are both designers and makers, like William Morris and Ernest Gimson	Fashions derived from French 18th and early 19th century models: copies of 'antique' English designs Handicraft revival started by William Morris in the eighteen-sixties Collecting 'antique' furniture becomes popular in 'seventies and 'eighties *L'Art Nouveau* appears in the 'nineties, and stimulates the 'Quaint' style Architects like Voysey and Mackintosh begin to exert an influence on furniture design at end of the century

20TH CENTURY (1900–1950)

PERIOD	FURNITURE	METHODS OF CONSTRUCTION
Edwardian and New Georgian	Everything previously listed, plus such articles as kitchen cabinets, tubular metal framed chairs and tables, and packaged furniture Great increase of fitted furniture	Mechanised adaptations of traditional methods

Materials	Makers	Styles and Fashions
All hardwoods previously used Plywood, laminated wood Plastics Sheet metal, aluminium and steel Drawn metal tubing, steel and copper Extruded metal sections Various fabrics Rubber	Manufacturers using woodworking machinery and employing factory operatives, and others employing cabinet makers and other skilled craftsmen Self-employed artist-craftsmen Metal furniture produced by manufacturers outside the furniture trade Many skilled craftsmen employed in reproducing exact copies of antique furniture	Imitations of antique styles, both by mechanical means and by hand, and variations of those styles, have been produced by the furniture trade during the first half of this century After the rationed 'utility' furniture of the second world war, this policy of imitating traditional models and varying their form and ornamentation, was resumed The architect and the industrial designer have, since the first war, exerted a great and growing influence on the design of furniture that is made by the more enlightened sections of the furniture trade or outside the trade The modern movement in architecture has stimulated the use of new materials and new methods of construction